Making Sense
OF
History

MAKING SENSE
OF
HISTORY

Society, Culture and Politics

MUSHIRUL HASAN

MANOHAR
2003

First published 2003

Hardcover: ISBN 81-7304-492-9
Paperback: ISBN 81-7304-488-0

Published by
Ajay Kumar Jain for
Manohar Publishers & Distributors
4753/23 Ansari Road, Daryaganj
New Delhi 110002

Typeset by
A J Software Publishing Co. Pvt. Ltd.
New Delhi 110005

Printed at
Lordson Publishers Pvt. Ltd.
Delhi 110007

For
Aziz Al-Azmeh

CONTENTS

3

PART II
Where are They Gone, the Glory and the Dream?

Part III
Image and Representation: Defining Muslim Identity

1

Part IV
Independence, Partition and its Aftermath

Part V
History's Many Verdicts

Part VI
India Votes: Assembly Elections

Part VII
In the Corridors of Academia

Part VIII
Know Thy Neighbour

Part IX
Remembering 11 September

Part X
Gujarat Ablaze

Part XI
From Overseas

~~~ PREFACE ~~~

The books we write have a limited readership, but the articles published in magazines and newspapers tend to be widely read. Taking the cue from my colleagues who have published their essays and newspaper articles, I have ventured to share my understanding with the readers beyond the academic world. Though the space available to a columnist is limited, I have nonetheless tried to analyse, from the vantage point of a professional historian, some of the major events and changes that have occurred in India during the past few years. I also share my impressions gathered during my stay in some of the Western countries where I had the opportunity to teach and research.

I may not have succeeded in bringing out the 'real, live stuff' that Ved Mehta referred to, in 1957, in his book *Face to Face*. Yet, I have commented on or alluded to certain contentious issues and controversies. Without trying to buttress a doctrinaire position, I reflect on the past as well as respond to the contemporary predicaments of our society. In so doing, I draw upon traditions of unity and compositeness and invoke Gandhi and Jawaharlal Nehru because they, in their own respective ways, embodied the quintessential features of the nationalist movement. I therefore disagree with those writers, both in the academia and the media, who belittle their role in the making of modern and progressive India. Suffice it to say that I believe, as did Arnold Toynbee, who wrote about Nehru in 1967, that after the vultures have finished their scavenging, he, too, will finally be acknowledge as the great man that he was—great, though very much human.

Some readers have reacted, often angrily, to some of my
pieces. They have accused me of being a Nehruphile, a 'pseudo-
secularist'; on occasions, they have rejected even my fervent
plea for, say, the return of the Kashmiri Pandits to the Valley.
'Mr. Hasan', I was told not so long ago, 'it is too late to shed your
crocodile tears. It cannot wash away blood from the hands ôf
Kashmiri Muslims.' Mr R.S. Singh Chandel is angry at my
perspective.

Don't you think that Muslims themselves are responsible for their
problems? Sikhs, Parsis are also minorities. Why are they doing so well
in India? Have you ever tried to think over it? I am sorry to say that,
but its not only in India, but everywhere in the world, Muslims
are not progressing. So that means there is something wrong with
them. . . . This is the time for introspection. Try to change yourself
with time.

So often, thus, ideologues of both specifically 'Hindu' and
'Muslim' perspectives target those—their numbers appear
steadily dwindling in recent years—who are wedded to liberal
and secular values that are so clearly delineated in the Indian
Constitution.

On balance, though, friends and acquaintances have encouraged me to continue writing in newspapers and magazines, to
continue invoking a succession of images—images that would
harmonize with the currents of change and the country's liberal
and secular ethos. They have told me time and time again that
my newspaper articles were publishable in a book form because
they round off, in accessible prose, my reading of the past and
expound in more detail some of the points only briefly indicated
elsewhere.

Some friends have taken the trouble of translating and
publishing my articles in Urdu (*Siyasat*: Hyderabad) and Hindi
(*Amarujala*: Kanpur). They must know that I write only for
men with simple common sense, a thing which is so rare today,
and that my views and reactions can only be understood from
this point of view. Let me reiterate that I speak only to those
who have not yet lost their sense of intrinsic human values. For
they alone will understand my concerns, my anguish and me.
Lin Yutang, author of *My Country and My People*, expressed
this sentiment quite a while ago.

I have been writing a fortnightly column for the *Indian Express* since June 1997. Most of the articles published therein form part of this collection. The piece on Abul Kalam Azad was written for the millennium series (100 People who shaped India) of *India Today*; Ali Mian's obituary for *Frontline*, and the essays on caste and untouchability and secularism for *One India One People* (Bombay). I contributed to the book *Khushwant Singh:An Icon of our Age*, edited by Kamna Prasad, and lectured on Sir Syed Ahmad Khan on the occasion of his centenary at the Royal Asiatic Society, London, on 2 April 1998. 'Partition: The Human Cost' and 'Partition was not Inevitable' appeared in *History Today* (London), September 1997, and the *Times of India* (13 August 1995), respectively. The two articles on the Uttar Pradesh and Bihar elections in 1996, jointly written with Saeed Naqvi, were published in *Outlook*; the two pieces on the Assembly elections in Bengal in May 2001 were written jointly with Professor Suranjan Das, Professor of History, University of Calcutta. I am most grateful to Malini Parthasarthy for letting me cover the Bengal elections for *The Hindu*. She has generally been most indulgent. 'Understanding Islam Better', 'The Image Trap' and 'Lost Causes, Faded Credo', were published in *Outlook*.

My interview with the well-known philosopher, Rada Ivekovic, appeared in the French journal *Transeuropeennes* (Paris), nos. 19/20, winter 2000-2.

If the readers discern a thematic unity in the arrangement of the articles, it is because they have been grouped in sections for their convenience. I have mentioned dates in some articles and introduced editorial and stylistic changes, interspersed with Urdu couplets, to make this book a little more accessible. I have retained the titles given to the articles. I have borrowed ideas and interpretations from scores of writers without being able to cite them. I do, however, acknowledge their debt.

I dedicate this book to my friend Aziz Al-Azmeh, a distinguished scholar of Islam. I greatly value my friendship and intellectual association with him.

M.H.

September 2002

~~~• INTRODUCTION •~~~

Constructing the past can be painful and agonizing for historians
of modern India, especially in South Asia. This is because history
writing, a highly contested terrain from the colonial days,
inflames passions and generates massive controversies. What
does one do if the government of the day expects the historian
to conform not only to its world view but invokes the past to
legitimize its activities? Acting differently could lead to exile
and damnation. This is disconcerting because peripheral issues,
some with divisive implications, are resurrected to define and
demarcate caste, linguistic and community boundaries. State-
sponsored history writing is bad news, because it undermines
the historian's sacred autonomy and destroys his personality as
a social scientist. One only has to recall what happened in
Hitler's Germany. When history is tailored to suit the ruling
élite's ideological predilections, it invariably leads to intellectual
vandalism and a distorted reading of the past.

A historian is a guardian of the past. He traverses the rough
terrain seeking unity and coherence in societal processes. He
dialogues with the past creatively, not at the behest of the State
but to unfold its benign and complex features, its high and low
markers, its richness and bewildering variety. He sensitizes
readers to the follies of the past and the imminent danger of
letting parochial and other divisive tendencies dominate
thinking. Indeed, history would be a soulless discipline if we,
having inherited the knowledge of the previous millennium,
fail to learn lessons from the ugly happenings that have taken
place in the past. Whether we like it or not, we study the past
to make our present liveable. We must select, as R.G. Collingwood

pointed out, certain aspects of experience and confine our search for progress to these.

This is what *John Company to the Republic* (2001) is all about. Like my previous book—*Legacy of a Divided Nation: India's Muslims since Independence* (2001 edn.)—it reflects the concerns, anxieties, and dilemmas of an individual born in free India. In fact, this work represents my intellectual journey, beginning with colonial rule and culminating at the banks of the Sarju river in Ayodhya. Proceeding on this long trek, I unravel the three most important themes that have shaped the history of modern India and our contemporary experiences. These are colonialism, nationalism and communalism. To encapsulate these overarching themes in a single volume and making this book accessible, I chose the dialogue form, interspersed with Urdu couplets, rather than the gravity of academic paraphernalia. The historical and the poetic are here in fierce embrace, rescuing it from the aridity of so much academic writing.

I was nervous with the format. That is because fellow-historians tend to be conservative in responding to history being presented conversationally. So what, I said to myself, remembering Toynbee. 'I have deliberately risked my neck,' he had said, after the publication of Volumes VII to X of *A Study of History*, in his broadcast debate with Professor Peter Geyl.

My protagonists are Azizuddin Husain (historian), Jagmohan Singh (engineer) and Pradip Kumar Saxena (medical doctor). They live in Lucknow, the erstwhile capital of the Awadh nawabs, but are troubled by the communal holocaust after Partition. Why, they ask, did freedom bring in its wake so much grief, hostility, and suffering? Why were the others not like them, tolerant and respectful of one another's values and traditions? Why this painful separation of families and friends? Why?

Their conversations start with the Independence Day celebration of 15 August and carry on through the establishment of the republic in 1950, amidst 'endless cups of tea and eating *kulchas* and *kebabs*'. Aziz, the quintessential liberal, dies a broken man after the destruction of the Babri Masjid on 6 December 1992. Millions, having a stake in India's secular commitment, share his trauma.

'Let's hope,' Pradip would have said, 'that the culture of the next millennium is defined by dialogue rather than combat.'

'At the very worst,' Aziz would have murmured to himself, 'we are faced with a country that is at war with its own people.'

John Company to the Republic celebrates secular nationhood and invokes the composite traditions that have served to keep intact the social fabric of our society for centuries. 'As you know,' comments Pradip, 'we are Kayasths. My father reads Persian, Urdu and Hindi, and recites the poems of Amir Khusro, Malik Mohammad Jaisi, Kabir, Rahim and Raskhan. Why don't we talk about them in our history textbooks? I've heard of Muinuddin Chishti and Nizamuddin Auliya from him. At a time when communalism is rampant, their message of love and humanity that needs to be disseminated.'

Similarly, the book enumerates the unlovely struggle between the concept of plural nationhood and the ideology of Muslim nationalism. Pradip's unmistakable preference is for the stand taken by Gandhi, Nehru, Dr. M.A. Ansari and Maulana Abul Kalam Azad: 'I don't approve of people who celebrate religious nationalism, or contest the pluralist/composite heritage in what has been one of the most multicultural societies in the world.'

John Company to the Republic introduces the more recent debates on colonialism generally and on the eighteenth century, in particular. 'For the moment,' Aziz points out, 'one can say that no single chronology or category of prosperity and decline seems likely to fit all the region.' Pradip fiddled with the pages of the notebook in front of him. 'What you're saying,' he said abruptly, 'is that any generalization about India must necessarily sound like the definition of elephants in the fable, in which five blind men describe in consonance with the portion of the creature traced by each with his finger.'

Let me conclude with Jagmohan's words of wisdom: 'Historiography is an ongoing dialogue which does not necessarily arrive at consensus but may enhance understanding of the past by illuminating it from a variety of perspectives.'

If you are still not convinced, listen to what Aziz has to say: 'I'd say that a great writer is one whose narration of events is free from anger and malice, and is firm like the word of the supreme arbiter, Saraswati.'

I am told that *John Company to the Republic* is useful to

those 'seeking to recharge their arguments in favour of the liberal values that inspired Indian nationhood'. Moreover, it is music to my ears when told that my arguments may also be a useful corrective for all those who believe that India cannot be rescued from the Manichaean divide between its privileged communities. Indeed, one is touched when Khushwant Singh tells his readers 'to read the version of a true scholar committed to the ideals of secularism and a strong united India'.

Foot Prints (New Delhi), *July 2001*

PART I

History as Dialogue

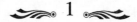

An Historian's Life in India

This spring semester (2000), Professor Mushirul Hasan, from Jamia Millia Islamia, New Delhi, is a Visiting Professor of History at the University of Virginia, Charlottesville. He is the author of five books and editor of fourteen on modern South Asia and the Islamic world. Professor Rich Barnett of the History Department interviewed Professor Hasan for the CSAS Spring Newsletter.

What was it like growing up in an academic family? Your early impressions of Bengal were probably different from those of Nirad Chaudhuri.

I left Calcutta when I was only seven, so I don't really have firm memories from there. We moved to Aligarh, where my father taught in the history department. This was a new and stimulating experience, because I was an outsider to the Urdu-speaking world (I grew up in an Anglo-Indian neighbourhood in Calcutta, close to Ripon Street). Aligarh was a big culture shock—here I was from a large, metropolitan city, going to a very small town.

What effect did your father's fame have on your life?

I was not aware of his fame, but some very famous poets and scholars came to our house. I remember A.B.M. Habibullah, Mehdi Husain, Parvez Shahidi, Munibur Rahman, Maqbul Ahmad, Nurul Hasan, Moonis Raza. Whenever my father travelled, he would bring back cheese, caviar, and a bit of duty free, so these people would gather together to have a good time.

My brother, who was tragically killed while covering the Iran-Iraq war in 1983, used to organize jam sessions in the living room. In a place like Aligarh, just imagine all these girls coming over to listen to loud music. And on Sundays, we would dress up to go to the only cinema hall that screened English films, Tasvir Mahal.

I was doing physics, chemistry and mathematics until well into high school, when I started to study Persian. Hafiz and Saadi, especially interpreted by Dr. Nabi Hadi in the Persian Department, stimulated my interest tremendously. Although I did well in maths. I really wasn't that interested, and my father did not influence me one way or the other. So I gradually drifted from subject to subject.

Then you had complete freedom to choose?

What was remarkable about my family was not only the freedom, but the complete lack of religiosity. My mother was very religious, observing Muharram with great solemnity; I would go with her to the *majlis* in Calcutta. But my father was completely indifferent, and so my four brothers never became fully involved with their religious heritage. Only my sister inherited my mother's religious commitment. I'm not being critical of religiosity, but the absence of a very strong religious ethos in the family has sharpened my understanding of several processes.

There is an abiding commitment in your career and your writings to secular and multicultural values.

For that I owe a great deal to my father, but also to the history department at Aligarh. I also had access to the world outside Aligarh: I was a debater, and even though I was young (I got my M.A. at nineteen), I took part in many competitions, met lots of people, and accessed the wider world. I was also active in student politics; I was never a Socialist or Communist, but once stood against a Jamaat-i Islami candidate, losing by only twenty-seven votes—my friends considered this a huge moral victory, and we set up our own group and invited speakers to come and address us. We had exchanges with families in Bombay. Students, both Muslim and Hindu, would come and stay with us and we would go and stay with Hindu families there. I stayed once with the famous Patwardhan family, who were very warm, although I was gently told that I couldn't use their kitchen.This was in 1968.

How did the '65 war with Pakistan affect your family?

Not at all. We didn't have any links with my uncles in Pakistan. I went there for the first time in the mid-80s, and that too by accident.The urge to go there was not strong (in 1990 I did go, but to watch a cricket match).

What led you to Cambridge?

I gradually decided to leave Aligarh. My father had gotten a professorship in Kashmir. I wanted to do modern history and so went to Delhi, where I got a job in a college—Tapan Raychaudhuri was head of the department. I taught a course called 'Ideas and Institutions in Medieval India.' I was very thrilled. I switched to modern history because I was interested in secularism, especially as it involved the tragedy of Partition.

The Aligarh experience had been very Islamic. Within that, there were diverse groups, traditions, and ideas.There was always a strong leftist presence there—Professor Maqbul Ahmad, who worked at SOAS with Miss Lambton; Dr. Munibur Rahman; and there were these wonderful sisters who were regarded as very fine poets, Zahida and Sajida Zaidi—lots of people who represented the best in our intellectual tradition, enlightened, politically correct, inspiring, rooted in their own culture but at the same time aware of Western ideas, literature, and music.

So we did lots of Western plays, such as *Oedipus Rex*. We were actually called 'The East India Company' (*laughs*). We dressed differently, we had girl friends who would visit the hostel, and go around with us in rickshaws—very non-Aligarh. We did everything that we wanted to, and this was in '68-'69, very happy and memorable days.

So you must have had some kind of abrupt change at Cambridge?

It was lonely for a while, but I was well prepared for this different world. It could be overwhelming (at Trinity people kept reciting how many Nobel laureates they had produced) but one had to buckle down and get to work. I also realized I was going back to India, so I could not waste any time and got my doctorate within three years.

What was the most terrified you have ever been?

Terrified? Terrified by the onslaught of my own students and teachers, I guess; I was forty-two and was worried about not having a job. But not at the point when I was going to be physically assaulted; then I was not terrified. I very coolly put my glasses and my watch in my pocket and thought, 'What a stupid way to die.' (My brother had died just a few years previously, covering the Iran-Iraq war.) It was a strange sensation, really. This happened as I went to my office after six months of exile, when 250 students physically attacked me, climbing up to the second floor on the outside of the building, with pipes and clubs. I was petrified before and after, but not then; I could face them. They had to swallow my spectacular entry into the University.

But you knew that you were taking a stand that was worth the risks?

Of course. I was determined. The easy way would have been to resign the office. The whole crisis lasted three to four years. I worried about support, and what would happen after. But I did get a lot of outside support, and that was most reassuring.

Was there any expression of regret on the part of your attackers?

Once I went back and performed as Vice-Chancellor for ten months, that's when the regret came, since they realized that they could have had somebody who could have transformed the University. I never wanted to leave Jamia, so I never sought to do so. Having joined as a reader, I was at the age of thirty-one the youngest full professor of history in the country. It is an interesting place, and I thought there were interesting things one could do.

My stand was that a teacher should be allowed to express his dissent. I was not commenting on any religious issue at all, beyond the issue of freedom of speech and that Muslims should not project themselves as intolerant.

Are you hopeful that this wave of intolerance has crested?

Not at all. I think that we have had a series of spineless governments, not committed to protecting the rights of any citizen or university to express views. I survived, not because of government, but because of my own inner resources, and through the support of a great many peopj: across the board, and because professionally I had very strong credentials.

Civil society is not ordered around strong, liberal, humanistic values yet. That is really the problem. There are enough dissenters. Look what happened to M.F. Hussain, the way this great painter has been treated. Look at the way films are banned and theatres attacked. The ideological storm troopers of certain political parties, in their attempt to enforce homogeneity in society, are trying to stifle liberal and democratic values.

The questions that Muslim society especially should have asked in the postwar period have not been asked. Why has the democratic experiment not worked in Muslim societies? Closely related to this question is that of reforms. The plea is for a certain kind of inner reflection on how far you can go, within the Koran and Sunna, to make your society more egalitarian, to promote emancipation and education, especially for women. The internal contradictions of Muslim societies arise from the absence of democratic movements. Reform movements first developed in a colonial context, but postcolonial Muslim societies have not produced outstanding reformers or intellectuals. India is far ahead of most, despite its poverty, colonial legacy, and heterogeneity. The Indian Constitution is a masterful document; it would be folly for any government to tamper with it. But what rules of governance there are in Islamic postcolonial societies seem to have been trimmed and tailored to suit the exigencies of the élites.

How would you compare teaching UVA students to your own students in India?

I don't think it's that different; the language of the teacher is the same. I've even taught through an interpreter in Rome. That was difficult, but it worked. I've never taught as many as forty students before, as I do here, but they don't seem to have any problems, even though they have not studied India before. Their intuitive understanding amazes me, really.

You have developed quite a following. Congratulations on naturalizing yourself so quickly.

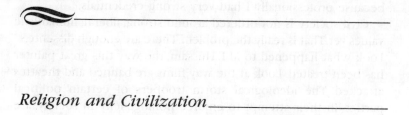

Religion and Civilization

This land of over a billion people has been the cradle of three religions—Hinduism, Buddhism and Jainism. Here people worship the mountains, the rivers, the stars, the morning sun, and the glittering stars. Millions yearn for the opportunity to dip into the many sacred rivers that flow from the Himalayas to cleanse their body and soul. When dead, they want their ashes to be immersed into these rivers.

The Ganga and the Yamuna rivers have flowed from time immemorial, but organized religion did not exist at the dawn of civilization in what is known as the Indo-Gangetic belt. The religion that developed around 2000 BC. until roughly 500 BC was embodied in a collection of hymns, ritual texts, and philosophical treatises called the Veda. The final authority of the Vedas (*Rg Veda*, the earliest of these texts, *Yajur Veda*, *Sama Veda*, and *Atharva Veda*) embody the essential truths of Hinduism.

The seventh and the fifth centuries BC witnessed the rise of various heterodox movements, notably, Buddhism. Its founder, a scion of the ruling class, repudiated the authority of the Vedas and the ascendancy of the priests, i.e. Brahmans. He underlined the 'Four Noble Truth': (a) that all life is inevitably sorrowful;

(b) that sorrow is due to craving; (c) that it can only be stopped by the stopping of craving; and (d) that this can only be done by a course of carefully disciplined and moral conduct, culminating in the life of concentration and mediation.

The simplicity of this message reached far and wide. Yet, Buddhism has practically disappeared from the land of its birth. Hinduism, with its remarkable capacity to absorb various traditions, has assimilated some of its principles. Jainism, originating at the same time and in the same region as Buddhism, survives as a separate religion, though its one time ascendancy in parts of western and southern India is lost. Unlike Buddhism, it did not spread beyond the land of its birth.

And then came the monotheistic religion of Islam from a distant land, aggressive in its posture but quick to adapt itself to the local cultural and social milieu. The early encounter in the western coastal region with the Arab traders was peaceful, but not after the Muslim settlements elsewhere and the establishment of Muslim dynasties. Tensions developed not between two religious entities—Islam and 'Hinduism'—but between a centralized Empire and the local potentates. The Turks, the first to establish their rule in north India in 1206, created not an Islamic polity but a state based on the traditions of kingship they had inherited. Like the Turks, the Mughals, descendants of Chingiz Khan and Tamerlane, also made India their home in 1526. They did not set out to create an Islamic State, though some used the Islamic rhetoric to legitimize their imperial designs. When this happened, they rocked their own boat. Indeed, the Mughal empire weakened in the seventeenth century because of the breakdown of the consensus among the ruling élites, such as the Mughals, the Rajputs and the Marathas.

From a few hundred Muslims who marched through the Khyber Pass for wealth, power and glory, Islam spread rapidly gaining converts by force as well as through persuasion. Most converts were drawn from the depressed castes, who were kept out of the Hindu caste structures. Islam's egalitarian principles offered them the hope of a better future. The Sufi orders, counterpoised to orthodox Islam, also gained converts. They incorporated many Hindu beliefs and practices, and identified closely with local values and traditions. In a sense, they spearheaded the 'Little Tradition' in a society that was relatively free from the homogenizing role of orthodox Islam and Hinduism.

It is hard to detail the dialectics of the Indo-Muslim encounter in this short note. But suffice it to say that the 'clash of civilizations' theory, or the supposed enmities dating back to the early Arab or Turkish invasions, is refuted by the process of widespread acculturation in Indian society for centuries. This process was aided by a number of factors, including the amorphous character of Hinduism, the rise of heterodox movements, with their emphasis on *bhakti*, or devotion, and spiritual cleansing rather than outward rituals, the appeal of Sufi ideas, and the inter-community alliances forged by the medieval rulers to sustain and fortify their empire.

Three additional points deserve merit. First of all, the entry of Muslims in South Asia through so many and such separate doorways, their spread by so many different routes over many centuries, and the diffusion of Islam in different forms from one area to the other, ensured its bewildering variety.

Second, Islamic dogmas and tenets were incorporated into regional and local belief structures and rituals. For this reason, Islam, past or present, was by no means a part of the 'Great Tradition'—codified, rigid and unchanging, insular and closed to external influences. If anything, the history of the Muslim presence illustrates the disjunction between the formal ideology of Islam and the actual day-to-day beliefs and practices of Muslims.

Finally, the spread and variety of Muslim religious sites and their co-existence with Hindu, Buddhist, Jain, and Christian places of worship provide living testimony to the fusion of ideas and beliefs. This is what leaders of the Indian nationalist movement, Gandhi and Jawaharlal Nehru included, described as 'composite culture'. This is what formed the bedrock of secular nationalism, the essential feature of the Indian Constitution, and the basis of the secular Republic.

Do examples of Hindu-Muslim synthesis vindicate the clash of civilization theory? Or do they reveal the survival of pluralist values in India? A society in transition—and a large country like

India will always remain in a transitory stage—is always pregnant with new possibilities.And yet history and contemporary politics, though mired in various controversies, rekindles the hope that this vast sub-continent will retain its multicultural character. The long journey—from colonial bondage to freedom on 15 August 1947—had its high and low points. From the last quarter of the nineteenth-century, the nationalist leaders endeavoured to evolve an inclusive ideology designed to embrace various castes, communities, regions, and languages. But they encountered two major difficulties. First, they had to contend with the policies of the British government that fostered the growth of religious identities, and used one community against the other to counter the rising tide of nationalist sentiments. Identities were, thus, created not around groups or class affinity but around religion. Politics was structured not around interest groups, but around religious categories. For India, this was a recipe for disaster. Immediately, the existing Hindu-Muslim differences came to fore.The ensuing result was the polarization of Indian politics around religious lines. The Partition of India was the outcome.

Second, there were sharp divisions within the nationalist ranks over their strategies in achieving their goals. It was easy to prepare a blueprint for the struggle against the British, but difficult to weld so diverse and divided a people into a coherent whole. Some public men, and these were mostly trained in British-run schools and colleges, preferred a secular ideology, divorcing religion from politics and political mobilization. Others invoked the symbols of Hinduism to bring about social change and sensitize the masses to the exploitative character of British rule. Regeneration was their common cry, but they differed over the means. Political independence was their common goal, but their method of mobilization was not the same.

These contested visions dominated the twentieth-century discourses. Indeed, they survive till this day. Independence brought some relief, but the ago-old issues have yet to be resolved in this era of globalization. A tradition-bound society, with its multi-faceted personality, is still struggling to reconcile tradition with modernity. True, India adopted a democratic and secular Constitution, but the place of religion in politics continues to be ceaselessly debated. With 120 million Muslims and other religious minorities, notably Sikhs and Christians, the outcome of this debate will in large measure determine the future contours of India's pluralist society.

It is widely argued, more so after the violent dispute over the Babri mosque (built by a Mughal governor, in 1526, at the birthplace of the Hindu god, Rama), that the secular option, exercised by the Westernized élites, hardly reflects the concerns of the people whose lives are inextricably bound with their religion and their inherited traditions. What is not made clear is how this image (Orientalist?) of a spiritualist Indian nation runs contrary to the values of a secular polity and society. The secular ideal is, indeed, rooted in the soil and nurtured in the sturdy, long-standing indigenous traditions of Hinduism. Thus the architects of the Constitution held *Sarva Dharma Sambhava* (Unity of Faith) as the solid foundation for harmonious living. They claimed their concept to be consistent with the eclectic, reformist trends in Indian society, and approximated with Mahatma Gandhi's concern to strengthen the moral edifice of the State.

The debates were conducted at various levels. These were largely the outcome of India's encounter with the Western culture and civilization in early nineteenth-century. Admittedly, the intelligentsia grudgingly accepted British rule, but the response to the new ideas flowing from the West was a mixture of acquiescence and rejection. The coming of the missionaries, their evangelical fervour and their proselytizing activities heightened religious and cultural anxieties. Thus began the search—one that continues even in this millennium—of the Hindu past, its philosophical underpinning, and its metaphysical dimensions. This was also an era when serious efforts were underway to homogenize the segmented Hindu population, and to create what the historian Romila Thapar characterizes as 'syndicated, semitized Hinduism.'

The encounter with the West led to much soul-searching, and to a reappraisal of Hindu society. Nineteenth-century thinkers discovered, much to their dismay, that all was not well with their great religion. The rigidity of the caste system had a debilitating effect on the Hindu caste structure; *Sati* (burning of widow on the funeral pyre after the death of her husband) and female infanticide were widely prevalent. The challenges were two fold: first, equip the Hindus to face the cultural and religious assault of the West by acquainting them with their great religious traditions; second, to give birth to a resurgent Hinduism that would be free of Islamic and Christian accretions.

The intellectuals ferment gave birth to not only powerful movements of religious and social reform, but also informed the nationalist ideology in the 1870s. Yet religious and social reformism did not present a unified world-view. Nor did they reach out to all sections of society. The backward castes, or Dalits, had an altogether different agenda. They were busy fighting against their subordination by the upper castes. The Muslim communities, too, were left outside the pale of the nineteenth-century reform movements. In effect, although reformers and preachers nurtured a pan-Indian vision, their caste, region or community defined their concerns.

Just as the backward castes clamoured for their rights within the caste hierarchy, so did the politically advanced sections of the Muslim community. As a political minority, they sought political safeguards in a representative government. As a religious minority, they asked for cultural autonomy, a demand raised with unfailing regularity by the immigrant communities in Western Europe. Western democracies have artfully dealt with or ignored such demands, but the Indian National Congress (founded in 1885), spearheading the liberation struggle, had no answers.

In the end, Mohammad Ali Jinnah, a London-trained barrister, asked for a separate Muslim nation on the basis of Hindus and Muslim representing two different religions, cultures, and civilizations. This was the 'two-nation' theory. The Congress resisted the idea for a while, but in the end Jinnah earned his Pakistan on 14 August 1947. The great Indian nation was irrevocably divided. And like Poland, Ireland, Palestine, and Cyprus, this division took place with the connivance and acquiescence of the colonial power.

The Partition of India was a holocaust, a brutal experience, and a cataclysmic event. Millions died, millions were displaced, and dispossessed. And yet, the political leadership in India, led by its first Prime Minister Jawaharlal Nehru, began its 'tryst with destiny' warily. The strength and vitality of their experiment rested on a model guaranteeing full citizenship with equal rights and obligations. This formula was certainly superior to the Islamic alternative being worked out in neighbouring Pakistan.

India's agony over religion is not yet over. The sacred rivers flow from their source up the Himalayas, but their water is contaminated by the bodies killed in caste and Hindu-Muslim violence. The road to the sacred sites is wide open, but fouled by casteist and communal publicists. Bells rings in the temples and the call for prayers goes out from the mosques, but the politics of hate has reached their precincts.

All said and done, the secular ground has been narrowed but it has, mercifully, not disappeared. The appeal of Hindu nationalism, once rising on the crest of a popular wave, is beginning to wane. The coalition, headed by the Hindu nationalist party at the Centre, is in disarray. The critical issue for religious minorities is whether they are adequately equipped to occupy this territory along with other democratic and secular tendencies. Their options are clear-cut: to either draw strength from the secular forces or to seek refuge in Islamist ideas. For the first option, the turf is negotiable. The later course can only increase the stranglehold of the retrogressive forces.

The Hindu, 3 and 4 November 2001

*What made Ravinder Kumar so Special?*_____

The death of a politician routinely finds space in newspapers, whereas the passing away of a distinguished academic usually goes unnoticed. Recently, the President and the Prime Minister condoled, quite rightly of course, the sad and premature death of the 38-year old IT ambassador Dewang Mehta, chairman of NASSCOM. What saddens me, however, is the silence at the death of Professor Ravinder Kumar, a man who combined intellectual distinction with a very admirable character. Is it the case that we have lapsed into a lazy scepticism? Do we value our scholars less and less? Have we discarded our age-old tradition of revering persons of intellect? Or, are we, living in an era of unbridled globalization, losing interest in keeping alive the principles for which they stood? I don't blame the President or the PM; the problem lies with the erosion of our value system.

Who was Ravinder Kumar, and why was he so special? Though most remember him as the director of the prestigious Nehru Memorial Museum & Library [NMML] and chairman of the Indian Council for Historical Research [ICHR], what at first attracted me to him was his habit of challenging assumptions that one is apt to take for granted. His intellect stood out clear-cut, robust, and confident. He was energetic and passionate in his feelings, suave, meticulous in his ways, and very seldom excited. He sought out the company of learned and clever people, regardless of where they stood in the political spectrum, and delighted in their conversation.

Some aspects of his role as the head of the NMML deserve attention. For one, he created a liberal space for different voices to be heard, and extended support to NGOs, feminists, civil libertarians, and left wing groups. He hosted Sahmat's exhibition on Ayodhya, and stood by the organizers when the exhibits caused a furore in some circles. Similarly, when moves were afoot to get rid of me from my university, he led a delegation to the then Education Minister, Arjun Singh. At a time when I felt lonely and abandoned, Ravinder boosted my morale and confidence. He valued dissent, defended academic freedom, and rallied around the victims of religious bigotry and intolerance.

His other quality was reflected in his concern for merit and talent, and his encouragement to young and upcoming scholars. Here, too, merit and not his personal preferences influenced him. The Centre for Contemporary Studies, his brainchild, offered refuge to so many brilliant researchers who were unable to make their way into the university system. Here, they had access to the excellent archival facilities, created by B.R. Nanda [the first director of the NMML] and his colleagues. And yet this institution's greatest asset was the accessibility of the director— a scholar who was restless, eager to learn, exhort, and share his insights. The researchers found him knowledgeable and wise; they found him warm and affectionate and kindly in the highest degree. Time and time again he would emerge from the confines of his office to meet his colleagues in the library's annexe or in Kutti's canteen. He would discuss, often with monotonous regularity, his idea of India as a civilization rather than a nation state. He would engage with Karan Singh on Aurobindo Ghose, with Dharma Kumar (d. 2002), Romila Thapar and Sumit Sarkar on social history, with Ramachandra Guha on cricket and environment, with Aijaz Ahmad on Marxism, with Nasir Tyabji on industry, with Geeta Kapur on cinema, and with Kumkum Sangari on gender issues. Such was the galaxy of scholars he had gathered at Teen Murti House.

Occasionally, he discussed his experiences at the Punjab University and the universities in Australia where he taught and researched. He did not ever mention his own writings produced in Australia. Many of us had read and benefited from his book *Western India in the Nineteenth Century* (1968). Focusing on the years 1818 to 1919, this work, once debunked by the radical historians at the Jawaharlal Nehru University, traced the history of rapid social and political transformation in Maharashtra. Not only did he pay particular attention to the changes, but traced their connection with the social ideals and the political objectives that inspired the British rulers, and shaped their administrative policy.

Ravinder's seminal contribution to Gandhian studies is reflected in the edited volume on the Rowlatt Satyagraha. His own essay on the nature of urban society and urban politics in Lahore was brilliantly conceived and crafted. His introduction, too, was insightful. Setting aside the traditional accounts, he examined how Gandhi, an individual without any established position of leadership, mobilized a society as complex as India. What, he asked, was the complexion of the social groups which responded to the Mahatma's initiatives? What were the local discontents that he channelized into a movement of protest? And finally, did the support for the Rowlatt Satyagraha vary from region to region and as between urban and rural society?

Ravinder's writing talents dried up during the last couple of decades, and yet he was capable of new thought and imagination. He belonged to a type which is now perhaps extinct, the type who would abandon the greener pastures of Australia to teach and research in India, the type of a quintessential liberal whose zeal and inspiration was derived from the liberal/secular values rather than from divisive ideologies. His greatest strength was that he knew where he wanted to go, and that every action of his was grounded on a good reason.

In a country where very little remains of institutions, Ravinder demonstrated how it was possible to strive for the highest academic and intellectual ideals within an institutional framework. In a country impregnated with religious intolerance, his life reveals how the finest intellectual sensibility can fashion the most open and humane outlook in private and professional life. In a country where history writing is being tailored to right-wing perspectives, Ravinder alerted us to the fact that myth making and stereotyping will reduce history to polemics. Studies dealing with the political ferment in 1919, he had observed, were polemical rather than scholarly.

Ravinder's accomplishments, both as a historian and an institution builder, deserve to be known outside the academic community. When they are recognized, we hope that there will be fresh attention to analysing the contribution of scholars like him and rescuing them from the mists of history.

18 April 2001

Myth, Metaphor and Event (I)*_____

Calcutta was once described as the city where wealth and poverty have reached their respective heights and depths. Such a description applies to Farrukhnagar too, once a prosperous town in the Gurgaon district of Haryana. For long, this was the main depot for the salt extracted from saline springs in the neighbourhood, but the industry declined in early twentieth century and became soon extinct. For a while, Farrukhnagar, on a branch of the Rajputana-Malwa Railway, emerged as a trading centre because of low railway freight. People made money and lived well, but the country's Partition disturbed the social equilibrium and disrupted the economic life of over 40,000 people.

More than five decades later, Farrukhnagar looks like a ghost town—backward, impoverished, and lacking in basic civic amenities. Though some *havelis* are maintained and attract a handful of European tourists, the streets are strewn with rubbish. The markets, once buzzing with activity, are deserted even on a working day. Most people are unhappy with the current state of affairs; no wonder, they express their disgust with the ruling party by voting for the opposition in local and state elections. *'Nagar to marne wala hai'* (the city is about to die), commented the 55-year old Prem Chand Aggarwal, owner of a textile shop in Bura Bazar.

This prophecy may not come true. Farrukhnagar, a major producer of *jowar*, has the potential of developing into a major *mandi*. Some local farmers are already beginning to do well by transporting their produce to Najafgarh where they fetch a higher price. Land prices, lower here than elsewhere, encourage rich farmers and traders to invest in Farrukhnagar. All this augurs well for the future, though local bodies will have to redouble their efforts to create the infrastructure for growth and prosperity. On balance, however, it may take quite a while for their personnel to give up their lazy habits and their lacklustre style of functioning.

Event, Metaphor, Memory: Chauri Chaura 1922-1992 (1992) is the title of Shahid Amin's fascinating study.

Farrukhnagar, only a few miles away from the famous bird sanctuary in Sultanpur, is not just a remote or inconsequential place dotted on the map of Haryana. Its chequered history dates back to the early 1730s when Faujdar Khan, a Baloch chief appointed governor by the Mughal Emperor Farrukh Siyar, founded the town. But this distant past has receded into the background in popular consciousness. Even though people live blissfully in the shadow of the sprawling Sheesh Mahal, which houses the office of the municipal committee, they are not curious to know the name of its builder. A huge fort dominates the landscape, and yet they do not care why its walls and gates are crumbling, or why the Archaeological Survey of India has so wilfully neglected the large octagonal well, built by the Bharatpur Jats who occupied Farrukhnagar from 1757 to 1764.

Yet some memories are selectively invoked: the freedom struggle in the area is a favourite theme for the elders to talk about. They recount the tales they heard from their parents—tales of how the *gora platoon* (literally, white troops) did not enter Farrukhnagar for six months during the 1857 revolt for fear of public reprisals. They tell their children how Nawab Ahmad Ali Khan offered money and ammunition to Bahadur Shah Zafar in Delhi, and how the British eventually humbled him. They narrate, in a genre that is fast disappearing in most places, how the British troops, having defeated the last Mughal emperor, marched into Farrukhnagar through the Lal Darwaza, a structure that is still intact, killing people, plundering the town, and arresting the beleaguered nawab. To create the image of a popular hero and lend substance to their anti-colonial rhetoric, they tell you how the nawab was handcuffed and made to walk to Delhi, a distance of over 60 miles. Elements of drama, pathos and tragedy constitute an integral part in their simple narrative.

The story goes on with the nawab, a victim of British (the term always used is *gora*) machinations, reaching the capital on a hot and sultry day and his execution, along with Raja Nahar Singh of Ballabhgarh and the chief of Jhajjar. The 73-year-old Daniel Masi, a Dalit Christian who has pictures of B.R. Ambedkar plastered on his wall, became teary describing the nawab's martyrdom from a Hindi text entitled, *Bhule-bisre: Shaheed Ahmad Ali Khan* (The Forgotten Martyrs: Ahmad Ali Khan).

Is Ahmad Ali Khan, then, as popular a local hero as the Rani of Jhansi in Bundelkhand, or Kunwar Singh, the 'father of Bhojpuris'? Though people refer to his courage and patriotic fervour, there are no folk songs associated with him. Oddly enough, his memory is kept alive through the various public events where local *netas* (Farrukhnagar is a segment of Pataudi Assembly constituency) dwell on the glorious past of their town and highlight its contribution to the Independence struggle. This is how the local roots of nationalism are unravelled to the students, many of whom are merely acquainted with the 1857 revolt in Delhi, Meerut and Kanpur and not elsewhere. This is how they get familiarized with their own pantheon of freedom fighters. The nawab is among them. So is Rani of Jhansi. To make his point, a young graduate recited this to me:

> How valiantly like a man fought she,
>   the Rani of Jhansi!
> On every parapet a gun she set,
> Raining fire of hell,
> How well like a man fought the Rani of Jhansi,
> How valiantly and well!

Partition memories are fresh, particularly among the surviving descendants of the 850 Punjabi migrants who settled here from faraway places like Mianwali and Dera Ghazi Khan.These families, now living in well-demarcated Punjabi *mohallas*, prospered after Independence. Quite a few moved out of Farrukhnagar in search of greener pastures. But the elders, now living in the shadow of the past, nurse bitter memories of their dispossession and displacement. Sitting under the shadow of a *pipal* tree, a 75-year-old lady from Mianwali told me, '*Dharti ne paani chor diya*'. An English translation can hardly convey the intensity of the feelings summed up in these five words. Believe me, this is perhaps the most telling comment on Partition violence I had read or heard for quite a while.

7 August 1998

*Myth, Metaphor and Event (II)*_____

Following my journey to Farrukhnagar, I travelled on the Delhi-Alwar highway to explore what meanings people attached to freedom, the golden jubilee celebrations, and the change wrought in their lives by Independence. The experience was rewarding, though the hazards of talking to strangers in an unfamiliar place became all the more apparent on this trip. Several people raised their eyebrows when I fired a question at them. Who was I? What brought me to the villages of Mewat (the districts at the junction of Alwar and Bharatpur in Rajasthan with Gurgaon in Haryana)? Perhaps a CID man deputized to conduct an enquiry or a 'foreign agent' with a mission to destroy national unity and stability?

My driving licence and the university identity card failed to impress teachers and students at the Madarsa-e Muin al-Islam in Nuh. They offered me a *charpoy* to sit under a *neem* tree but refused to talk. Nuh, with some 15,000 people, is an old salt-manufacturing town. In 1933-4, it was the focal point of the Meo nation's new political life, the storm centre of an important peasant movement led by Chowdhry Mohammad Yasin Khan, Syed Mutalabi Faridabadi and the Marxist historian K.M. Ashraf. Today, some elderly people recall their names but most are unfamiliar with Mewat's past or the region's struggle against the Maharaja of Alwar. They only have memories of Hindu-Muslim riots in Mewat, starting with the one in Hodal (the last town in Gurgaon near the UP border) in August 1947.

Fellow-academics talk of rapid socio-economic change and the social revolution in the countryside. Come to Nuh to be proven wrong. This otherwise historical town, first mentioned in written history in the time of Prithviraj Rasa, survives uneasily on the fringes of urban life. Though the quality of life has improved, most people are still poor and uneducated. The place is also a victim of civic neglect. With its broken roads, open drainage, inadequate water supply and long hours of 'load-shedding', Nuh appears to be an area of darkness in the otherwise prosperous state of Haryana.

Wherever we went, people complained of deteriorating civic amenities. The civil hospital, encircled by heaps of rubbish, exists only in name. And because medicines are in short supply, most patients are invariably referred to a doctor in Gurgaon or Delhi. Children have virtually no access to a decent school or college. Nuh has just two 'recognized' matriculation-level schools and a private degree college. Government schooling is still prized, though the state schools offered an inferior education to that available from the few private schools. Muslims in general, and Muslim girls in particular, are under-represented at all levels of the schooling system.

Compare Nuh with Sohna, a few miles beyond the fast-developing town of Gurgaon. Known to Delhiwalas for its sulphur springs, Sohna has many factories and industrial plants, including Datt Mediproducts, OK Play India, Continental Value, Titagarh Stells and Innovative Tech. Pac. It may be decades before such plants appear in Mewat, or the fruits of progress reach this backward region.

What do fifty years of Independence mean to the poor, the sick, and the uneducated in Mewat? '*Aap bare logon se poochiye. Azadi to unko mili hai*' (Ask the rich and the influential; they are the ones who have reaped the fruits of Independence). At most places the standard answer was '*Bas guzara kar rahe hain*' (barely managing to survive). In Nuh, the Punjabi refugees were decidedly hostile to the Gandhian and Nehruvian legacies. A refugee from Lyallpur said gleefully, '*Nehru ka chapter hi nahin hai*' (Nehru is inconsequential). His icon was Netaji Subhas Bose rather than Gandhi. 'Gandhi is responsible for the present mess. He was too soft towards the Muslims, allowing them to live in India.' A frail looking Meo Muslim intervened to say that the Mahatma brought peace to the region and rehabilitated the Meo Muslims.

These two and their companions in Nuh's grain market mirrored the religious cleavage that had developed after the demolition of the Babri Masjid. Yet, in an area with a long-standing history of social and cultural fusion and inter-community amity, the religious boundaries are still not so sharply demarcated. Most shopkeepers in the grain market transcend their prejudices, and their identities become negotiable. While memories of a syncretic past have faded and replaced with an exclusive historical consciousness, particularly after the Babri Masjid episode, Hindus and Muslims voice common socio-economic grievances.

But there is no room for complacency. The status quo may not last for long. Religious zealots and political fundamentalists threaten to undermine the fragile communal equilibrium. Most people, as in Malabh village, only have hazy ideas about Gandhi, Nehru and Maulana Azad, and know very little about the meaning and content of freedom, nationalism, or patriotism. '*Azadi* from what?' asked Mohammad Isa, a former *panchayat* member. 'Come to the wheat-growing village of Chandeni to discover our plight.' 'There isn't enough water to irrigate our fields', added a school-teacher. The struggle for existence, camouflaged behind smiling faces, goes on.

With little to do outside the harvest season, most people in Malabh sit around their mud houses or a dilapidated *haveli*. There are some shops but no customers. While young boys and girls roam the dusty lanes, their elders sit around listlessly around a makeshift roadside *dhaba*, inhaling fumes from passing buses and trucks. They are energized five times a day by the call for prayer. Malabh has three grand mosques, symbols of a resurgent Muslim identity, but no full-fledged school. Here, as elsewhere, the state is in full retreat.

For the women, agency and autonomy have little relevance. Influenced by the Tablighi Jamaat, a conservative Muslim organization, Muslim women cannot create their own space and challenge the dominant meanings through song, speech and action. They may not sing or watch TV. They are socially almost powerless. The issue is not empowerment but sheer survival. As the President of the Republic reflected on the state of the nation in a television interview, women in Malabh were getting ready to cope with the inglorious uncertainties that will follow the crack of dawn.

21 August 1998

Myth, Metaphor and Event (III)

A few decades ago Dalpat Khan, son of Chand Mal of Kherla village, would have been a common Muslim name in Mewat. That is when many Meos bore Hindu names or tagged on Khan to a Hindu name. Nowadays, more and more define their identity within the blueprint laid down by the Islamists. Dalpat Khan, 65, told me that his own children were called Bashir Ahmad and Abdul Subhan.

We met Daud, 73, reclining on a *charpoy* at the Khalsa *dhaba*, owned by a Sikh from Pathankot. He journeyed to Pakistan in August 1947, settled in Kaniyaka beyond Lahore, but returned, along with 100 families, to Kherla after seven months. *'Dil nahin laga; Mujhe apne ghar ki yaad aati rahi'* (I was not at home; kept thinking of my homeland). He recalled listening to Gandhi at Ghasera and was impressed by his humanity and his concern to rehabilitate the Meo Muslims in their ancestral land. But, then, what have they gained since the Mahatma's historic visit to the region? *'Azadi ki khushboo yahan nahin hai'* (The fragrance of Independence has not reached us). Why? 'Ask the politicians,' he says. *'Chara khate hain dehat me dudh dete hai shehar me'* (We provide the fodder for the cattle, but the milk goes to the city).

Large parts of Mewat are unaffected by the winds of socio-economic changes, though Kherla village, with its TV sets and refrigerators, is an island of prosperity (thanks to entrepreneurs like Din Mohammed who operates 350 trucks in Gujarat).Though the tall and bearded Daud Khan owns large tracts of land, he blames the politicians for their economic plight. 'Gone are the days of Gandhi and Nehru. Present-day *netas* are different; they don't keep their promises. Where, for example, is the river that was supposed to flow from the East Yamuna Canal in Ballabhgarh to this area?'

The same story does the rounds in Malabh, 7 km from Nuh. Here people refer to the 278 deaths in 1996 caused by the outbreak of dengue. How and why this happened is anybody's guess. Why such criminal neglect? 'Why deny us proper roads, schools and clean drinking water? Why deprive us of a small-scale industry? Is it because we are Muslims? If not, why are our sufferings not alleviated?' I had no answers. We simply felt disheartened listening to their tale of woes for the second time within a fortnight.

As we turned on the ignition key to hit the road to Nuh, people pleaded with us to convey their grievances to the authorities. I tried telling them that my intervention will not move the bureaucracy or the politicians, and that nobody pays heed to a historian harping on the familiar story of misery, deprivation, and civic neglect. Who cares, I reminded myself, whether the people of Malabh have drinking water or not. Why provide roads, electricity, schools and health centres in the rural hinterland? Surely, the essence of *swadeshism* is that the poor must learn to take care of their needs. I felt like telling Daud Khan and his friends who had looked after us during our visits to Mewat:

> God never sends a time when you too mourn—
> When you too find life-easing sleep forsworn,
> When joy has spent with you its long bright hour
> And left the cup of your existence sour;
> When, its bright mirror tarnished with hot tears,
> Your mind is filled with swarms of anxious fears,
> And thronging misery comes with gnawing tooth,
> Till only an old dream is left of youth.
>
> FAIZ AHMAD FAIZ

I expected to find angry and agitated Mewatis. Did they not express their resentment in the past, as in 1857, against their oppressors? Were they not inspired by the *Mahabharat* in verse, authored by the Mewat poet Sadullah, and by the courageous deeds described in the ballads of the battle of Panch Pahar, or the raid on Dholagarh? Today, that spirit of revolt and defiance, the hallmark of Mewat's turbulent history, has been replaced by a sense of defeat and despondency.

Increasingly, the Meo Muslims turn to the Tablighi Jamaat for spiritual solace. I was reminded of the description of *tabligh* parties, travelling on foot, with blankets thrown on their shoulders and parched grain or bread tied in a corner of the mantle, their tongues engaged in repeating the name of Allah.

The activities of Madarsa-e Islamia, housed in an attractive mosque off the national highway, reflect a conscious effort to redefine Meo identity in strictly Islamic terms. Such institutions, though small and modest in their goals (the four teachers receive a paltry salary of Rs. 2,000 per month), mirror the transformation in the consciousness of peasant/pastoral communities.

The Meos were truly different from orthodox Islam; they represented the 'little' tradition, neither speaking nor understanding the language of orthodoxy. They lived in a world of their own, untouched by the religious decrees of theologians. Converted to Islam in different periods, they retained many Hindu beliefs. In this way, Mewat emerged as a model of composite living and inter-cultural fusion. Sadly, it has now turned into a graveyard of India's syncretic traditions.

It will require a dissertation to explain why this has happened. Suffice it to say that, besides the trauma of Partition and the displacement of some 8,00,000 Meos that remains a reference point in subaltern consciousness, the Tablighi Jamaat has to a large extent transformed the social and cultural landscape. 'Saare Mussalman sudhar gaye' (All the Muslims have been reformed), announced Mohammad Isa, head of the Tablighi branch in Malabh. The region emerged from darkness into light in the new climate of faith and piety. Beards were grown freely, polytheistic marriage ceremonies were discarded and Hindu customs were abandoned. For these reasons, the Meo Muslims take pride in the Tablighi Jamaat as a body committed to religious cleansing, moral upliftment, and spiritual regeneration.

Is there a connection between the religious identity of the Meos and their underdevelopment? The withdrawal of the State from developmental projects has, indeed, created space for various organizations to promote their specific agenda. At present, the unfolding of certain events sensitized us to the contribution that religious mobilization, particularly during the dispute over the Babri Masjid, can make to people's sense of vulnerability and opportunity in all spheres of life. Local riots, as in Mewat in December 1992 and discriminatory policies, do not disappear on their own, but require sustained social and political efforts. An organized secular and radical movement is required if the material conditions of the average villager—

woman or man, Hindu, Muslim or Scheduled Castes—are to be improved in the foreseeable future.

5 September 1996

The Captain's Innings

This article is about a man who recaptured, for a time, the aristocratic strain in Indian cricket. He was a brave, vigorous and adventurist right-hand batsman, piling up 15,425 runs in first class cricket between 1957 and 1976, including 33 centuries. Having made both a fairy-tale entry and several fairy-tale comebacks to big cricket, his run tally in test matches was 2,793, with six centuries. Ramachandra Guha, the cricket-historian, tells us how two stunning performances in England and Australia earned him the title of the Nawab of Headingley and Melbourne. He led the Indian side in 40 of the 46 matches he played. He did so with amazing success. Comparisons are odious, but he was certainly India's most dynamic skipper, a cult figure for over a decade. He is no other than 'Tiger' Pataudi. I was pleased when he agreed to talk to me, and doubly happy to exchange pleasantries with his charming wife Sharmila Tagore.

I was not going to discuss cricket with Mansur Ali Khan or talk about his high-profile family that includes the Bollywood star, Saif Ali Khan. My long-term interest was to trace the social profile of his distinguished family that was connected with Pataudi and the princely state of Bhopal. The more immediate purpose was to explore how Mansur, having played his long innings on the 22-yard strip, related to the daily chores of life. The aristocrats living in Farrukhnagar were long gone. How does a surviving aristocrat of the same region respond to the decline of the nawabi order, the diminishing influence of his family, and the rise of new social classes who have no affinity with his lifestyle? What, in the present political climate, were the social and intellectual engagements of a man who had spent his early years at Winchester and Balliol?

Mansur does not bemoan the collapse of the feudal order, though he is critical of those who blame the princely families for the ills that plague our society. Yes, he takes pride in his ancestry and heritage. Why should he not? His father, a 'conscientious objector' to Jardine's Bodyline tactics, led the Indian team against England in 1946 and was an outstanding cricketer. In 1947, he did not pack his bags for Pakistan, preferring to persuade the Muslim peasants on his Pataudi estate to stay put in India. In a region where organized communal violence reached its high watermark after Partition, not many Muslims heeded his advice.

The Bhopal family, with its illustrious line of begums, has had a chequered career.* One of them, Sikandar Begum (d. 1868), introduced agricultural, economic, administrative, and legal reforms. She was bold enough to do away with purdah and appeared in public attired in military accoutrements. Sultan Jahan Begum, who succeeded Shah Jahan Begum (1868-1901), revealed incipient nationalist leanings when she declined to endorse Allied War aims. She criticized British repression and told Punjab's Political Agent that General Dyer and Michael O'Dwyer should both be stripped of their pensions. Her son, twice Chancellor of the Chamber of Princes, was actively involved in the radical politics of the 'Young Party' Muslims. This led the British government to dispute his right of succession. When, in 1930, Gandhi inaugurated civil disobedience, Nawab Hamidullah Khan (Mansur's grandfather) urged the colonial government to exercise restraint and reprimanded Lady Willingdon for her disparaging remarks about the Mahatma.

The fortunes of this family dwindled after Bhopal, on the lapse of British paramountcy in 1947, merged with the Indian

---

*Shahaharyar M. Khan, *The Begums of Bhopal: A Dynasty of Women Rules in India* (New Delhi, 2000) and Claudia Preckel, *Begums of Bhopal* (New Delhi, 2000).

Union. Like his counterparts in other former princely states, the Nawab-Chancellor was confused by the turn of events. He was pensioned off and received a privy purse of Rs. 11,00,000 of which Rs. 1,00,000 was allocated to the heir-apparent who eventually migrated to Pakistan. In 1960, Hamidullah Khan died in the Middle East in forlorn obscurity.

The abolition of privy purses was a bombshell. 'We knew that privy purses will not continue forever, but we should have been given some time to set our house in order', observed Mansur in a melancholic tone. The imposition of urban ceiling in Madhya Pradesh was the last straw. The Bhopal family, now at the mercy of politicians, lost 1,100 acres of urban property in Bhopal and over 1,000 acres of agricultural property. Now-a-days, Mansur spends much of his time knocking at the doors of lawyers to seek redress in the courts. It is a battle that many have lost.

A career in politics may have helped to consolidate the inherited assets, but that was not to be. The murky world of regional and local politics is by no means everybody's cup of tea. Though persuaded by Rajiv Gandhi and Arjun Singh to contest the election from Pataudi, the khadi-clad politician in the making found the going tough. His defeat at the hustings did not hurt, for his chances of winning were dimmed by the caste politics of Haryana. The Babri Masjid's demolition, on the other hand, was too bitter a pill to swallow. 'The thought and structure of the country', he commented, 'was demolished by the actions of a handful of fanatics.' Nowadays, Mansur stays clear of organized politics, though he lends his name to various Muslim outfits committed to the community's educational uplift.

I asked Mansur Ali Khan to define himself and his identity. He looked puzzled. He made a couple of ambivalent remarks emphasizing his cosmopolitan background and, at the same time, pointing to his parents who were both devout Muslims. But he may have noticed my unease with his unreflective response. So, he chose to write the following lines to me just before leaving for London for medical treatment:

I am a Muslim, but I identify more with people who share my edu-
cational/social background, no matter what their religion. I believe in

God, but I do not think that He expects me to rely on Him exclusively, for my health and happiness. Given the choice of having Gary Sobers or God on my side, I would choose Sobers since I do not think God is interested in taking sides in cricket matches.

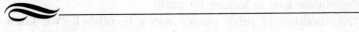

2

*Towards a Shared National Identity*_____

In one of her witty books, *The Moving Finger*, Agatha Christie introduces a girl fresh out of school and lets her ramble on about what she thinks of it. 'Such a lot of things seem to me such rot. History, for instance. Why, it's quite different out of different books!' To this, her sensible elderly confidant replies: 'That is its real interest.' This seems like a perfect point of entrée for commenting on 'The uses and abuses of history', a central theme discussed during the 19th International Congress of Historical Sciences at the University of Oslo (2000).

In the preface to his first book published in 1924, Ranke did not presume, as did most historians, to sit in judgement on the past; that he only wanted to show 'what had really happened'. Needless to say that it has been difficult for historians to establish historical truths or to defend the cult of objective historical inquiry. What the professional historian can strive to achieve is to live up to the ideals of intellectual honesty and not allow oneself to be controlled or manipulated by various agencies. At a time when knowledge is so highly politicized in the developed as well as the developing societies, one hopes that the past is not instrumentalized and distorted for political and other purposes.

We study history to attain self-knowledge. By way of illustrating his thesis, R.G. Collingwood tried to show how our knowledge that human activity is free has been attained only through our discovery of history. The point is well taken. At the same time, the knowledge of history has been used, or perhaps misused, to legitimize chauvinistic national identities, authoritarian regimes, and military dictatorship. This was so in nineteenth century Germany. As George G. Iggers pointed out at the Oslo seminar, the task of research aided the construction of a national identity and this is exactly what the historians did, in the case of the so-called Prussian school even openly. Historians went into the archives not so much to be guided by the sources as to find support for their arguments that preceded their research. Likewise, virtually all historians on both sides of the lines rallied under the flag in the First World War as citizens and not as professional historians.

In countries like Israel memories of the past, namely the Holocaust of 1941-5 and the Arab-Israel war in 1948-9, coalesced with invented myths, or official truth, to determine the collective identity of the Jewish people. Several Israeli historians, having subjected their reconstruction of the past to the interest of the State, the party and nation, hammered home the Zionistic myths. But, at least on the 1948 war, the 'new' historians introduced a discordant note: the desire for territorial expansion, they argued, was just as prominent as the desire for peace among many Israeli leaders. They pointed out that most Palestinians fled as a result of acts of war, in some cases Palestinians were deported by Israeli forces and there were also massacres. It was, commented the historian Lars Hoff, far from being David's battle against Goliath: the Israeli forces were in the majority throughout the war and, with the exception of the first few weeks, they also had superior weapons. When the historians presented their findings in the 1990s, they were fiercely attacked, as it was feared that the Israeli/Zionist identity will unravel.

British historians writing on India invoked certain aspects of medieval rule to underline that the British did more for the benefit of the people than the despotic medieval Sultans. Henry Elliot, a leading historian of that camp, referred to 'the few glimpses we have, even among this single volume, of Hindus slain for disputing with Muhammadans, of general prohibitions against processions, worship and ablution, of other intolerant measures, of idols mutilated, of temples razed, of forcible conversions and marriages'. He candidly conceded that his purpose was to make 'our native subjects more sensitive of the immense advantages' of British rule. Sadly, some major literary writers, publicists and historians appropriated these images of the Muslim presence in India. As a result, our understanding of the past derives largely from the interpretation of Indian history made in the last two hundred years.

Nobody can take exception to the rewriting of our history: historiography is, as George Iggers mentioned in his paper, an ongoing dialogue which does not necessarily arrive at consensus but may enhance understanding of the past by examining it from a variety of perspectives. Yet one should be wary of myth-making, of romanticizing the past, and selectively invoking certain incidents to lend legitimacy to a contemporary ideology. History can be misused to settle scores or used in different ways in association with nation building.

'Useful' use of history for a nation can, for example, be conciliation—or the opposite, to increase hate or antagonisms. I believe it is possible to seek the truth and achieve reconciliation. This is precisely what is taking place in South Africa under the aegis of the Reconciliation Commission. The aims of the Commission are to help the country achieve reconciliation and to engage in a corporate nationwide process of healing through contrition, confession, and forgiveness. That is why the truth is so central to the exercise. I believe we too need a Reconciliation Commission in order to build up a shared national identity by interpreting the past independently of state-sponsored ideologies. Liberal and secular-minded professional historians must dictate the ground rules for public debates and not ministers and bureaucrats who raise themselves to the position of irrefutable prophets.

Regardless of the recent outcry and the decision of the ICHR to withhold the publication of the 'Towards Freedom' volumes edited by Sumit Sarkar and K.N. Panikkar, the track record of such historians has been impeccable. Their commitment and integrity inspires hope and pride: despite the vulnerability of the historical profession, there is a stubborn resistance to state-sponsored historical writings and to the rewriting of history for short-term political gains. Our major responsibility is to defend the freedom of information and expression that is so central to our profession. As Antooon de Baets from The Netherlands stated, 'the reason for this priority is clear: without these freedoms, historians cannot discharge their first professional obligation—the pursuit of historical truth—nor their other social responsibilities towards past, present and future society.'

18 October 2000

*The Shadow of Tipu Sultan*_____

I wonder if the practitioners of history in India will agree with Ranke's memorable phrase, 'the writing of history is a matter of conscience'. True, the general level of historical scholarship in India has improved since independence, yet so many of us tend to be biased, prejudice-ridden, and prone to implausible generalizations. 'Remember your moral responsibility to our readers', admonished G.P. Gooch, a distinguished British historian. But, alas, so few heed his sane and sober advice. And for so few is the single-minded pursuit of 'truth' the goal.

Ideally, the reading of history should produce a certain temper of mind, a certain way of thinking and feeling about contemporary events, and their relation to the past and the future. In reality, the agenda of Hindu and Muslim polemicists has been to perpetuate myths, create icons to suit ideological predilections, valorize rajas and sultans in opposition to the other, and romanticize certain periods of history to construct the mythical image of a 'Golden Age'. Such an exercise, initially aided by the colonial historians but later spurred on by the rise of nationalism, has led to a distorted version of the past, reinforced social, cultural and religious boundaries, and widened existing cleavages.

I do not wish to comment on the extensive polemical

literature demonizing the Turkish or Mughal (not Muslim) rulers. Like so many liberal-left colleagues, stigmatized as 'pseudo-secularists', I do not spend sleepless nights finding an alibi for their conduct. We feel indignant only when called upon to account for the demolition of temples or conversions during the medieval period. Or, when Islam and the Muslim communities are portrayed in the light of the actions of some intolerant sultans. Please tell me how and why Abdul Ali, a weaver in Bhiwandi, can be held responsible for Mahmud of Ghazni's assault on Somnath? Why target him and others because his co-religionist, Aurangzeb, the son of Shah Jahan, was belligerent towards the Hindus in the last quarter of the seventeenth century? Why should 120 million Muslims, born and brought up in this country, be given the choice to either go to Pakistan or to *qabristan* (graveyard) just because a sixteenth-century ruler built a mosque on a disputed religious site?

Today, Karnataka is the battle ground for an acrimonious debate centred on Tipu Sultan, one of the key figures in the mythological and historiographical constructions of the subcontinent. It all started early in 1990 when the BJP [Bharatiya Janata Party] sought a court injunction to prevent the screening of a television serial entitled, *The Sword of Tipu Sultan*. The complainants argued that the series presented Tipu sympathetically as a secular ruler, rather than the fanatical Muslim persecutor of Hindus they imagined him to be. VHP [Vishwa Hindu Parishad] and Bajrang Dal activists have aired the same arguments to decry the state-sponsored celebrations to mark 200 years of Tipu's martyrdom. So the battlelines are drawn between those who insist that the 'Tiger of Mysore' was a martyr to the cause of Independence, and those deriding him as a tyrant and a Muslim bigot. My fear is that the southern states, so far untouched by the great communal debates raging in the Indo-Gangetic belt, will soon be embroiled in a protracted controversy.

Why should we hold a brief for Tipu? Our concern is to remind readers that the Mysore ruler employed a large number of Hindus in high offices, sanctioned generous grants of rent-free land to temples and mosques, patronized pilgrimage sites, including the great *Math* at Sringeri, and wrote to its Swami to pray for his success in war against 'the hostile armies that have marched against our country and are harassing our subject'.

Turn to any number of scholarly books, including one authored by my father, Mohibbul Hasan (*History of Tipu Sultan*, 1971), to discover how Tipu's patronage to construct, say the massive temple at Sibi, gives the lie to the notion that Hindus, solely because they were Hindus, suffered discrimination or persecution at his hands. Also Kate Brittlebank's insightful comment in *Tipu Sultan's Search for Legitimacy* (1997) that Tipu's assertion of his identity as an Islamic ruler took place against the background of, and in harmony with, the syncretic religious practices of the south. More generally, the historian C.A. Bayly has argued that prior to 1860 there was no identifiable 'Hindus', 'Sikh' or 'Hindu' identity that could be abstracted from the particular circumstances of individual events or specific societies, and Tipu's attitude appears to confirm this (*Indian Society and the Making of the British Empire*, 1987). Other works, notably by Susan Bayly, on the interaction between Muslim, Hindu and Christian traditions in the south have identified a borrowing of symbols and ideas, a frequently shared vocabulary, and an interweaving of motifs within a common sacred landscape. Not surprisingly, these syncretic tendencies are targeted by fundamentalists of all hues (*Saints, Goddesses and Kings: Muslims and Christians in South Indian Society 1700-1870*, 1983).

Yet, there is no reason for Tipu's admirers to elevate him to the heights of a Sufi or place him on a pedestal: he was, after all no more than an able and energetic ruler. His territorial ambitions, rather than any nationalistic sentiment, led him to forge alliances with the French against the British. His generosity towards the Hindus does not make him 'liberal' or 'secular' in an age when these expressions made little or no sense whatsoever. What is therefore required is a cool and dispassionate analysis of Tipu's actions in the context of the turbulent decades of the eighteenth century in the south and the subcontinent generally.

People often speak of 'the verdict of history' and 'the philosophy of history'. According to Gooch, there is no agreed verdict, only individual verdicts, no agreed philosophy, only a welter of conflicting ideologies. 'Are there or will there ever be final study of the human adventure? If so, they have not yet been found.'

The Lessons of History

> How could I tell my tale in this strange land?
> I speak a tongue they do not understand
>
> MIR TAQI MIR

This is not the first time that the 'history controversy' has captured newspaper headlines. This is not the first time that right-wing polemicists have directed their ire against some historians. Why target those who have raised the country's intellectual profile since Independence? Why sensationalize non-issues in the media at a time when major national questions deserve greater attention?

History is not an inventory of dead people and dead things, but a key to life in its fullness and all its aspects. This is what some of us, engaged in exploring the historical landscape, have learnt from our leading Indian historians. We have benefited from their forays into the past, their secular interpretations, and their repudiation of the colonial perspective. Starting with D.D. Kosambi's works, Indian historical writing reached its most creative phase in the 1980s. Even though Marxist historians berate the 'subaltern' historians, their engagement is delightfully refreshing. In the ever-changing intellectual climate around the world, it is best to take cognizance of new ideas on the intellectual horizon, introduce a nuanced discourse, and stay clean of the sterile debates centred on individual kings and dynasties.

Liberal and Marxist historians have sensitized us to this reality. Frankly, their political activism and social engagement is equally admirable. Read the writings of R.S. Sharma and S. Gopal on the Babri Masjid controversy. Whether we agree with them or not, there is no denying their moral courage and conviction in an otherwise cynical academic ambience. Many others, including Romila Thapar, Sumit Sarkar and K.N. Panikkar, have stood against concerted endeavours to communalize knowledge. Such persons have not made their peace with the establishment. Some may nurse a grudge against them for personal reasons, but can hardly deny the value of their scholarly interventions in civil society. No wonder, right-wing polemicists and a handful of disgruntled historians have invented issues to attack them.

The root of the current outburst lies in the first major row in 1977. A futile controversy was triggered leading to a virtual ban on some NCERT [National Council for Education, Research and Training] textbooks. True, some of them needed substantial revisions. But the critical issue then, as indeed now, is whether historical events and processes should be tailored to suit the ideological predilections of a political formation, or interpreted, as is commonly done in any academic tradition, on the strength of established norms of critical scrutiny and scholarship. The past must be read and analysed in different ways, but a version resting on biased assumptions must not be allowed to creep into our curriculum.

It is easy to understand the discomfort with radical ideas and interpretations. Indeed, an organization was formed some time ago to counter, as it were, the agenda of the Indian History Congress. But I am not aware of its scholarly output. For the moment, state resources should not be used to stifle dissent or to exclude historians from academic bodies owing to political considerations. Knowledge should not be controlled or censored in a democracy. In other words, a change of government or the ruling élites must not lead to a book being withdrawn from a school or college. Students must have access to different viewpoints and decide whom they want to read.

A word on the recent controversy centred on the ICHR. The problem is not with the personnel or the ideological proclivities of its governing council. The council, an advisory body, meets occasionally to approve various academic and administrative decisions. Scholarship flourishes outside and not within the precincts of 35 Ferozeshah Road (where the ICHR is housed), while scholars earn their reputation with or without the ICHR's monetary support. It is unfortunate if some people have cornered or misused scarce resources, though the key issue is ICHR's overall performance and its credibility as a viable body for facilitating research. These aspects require a public review and a healthy debate. It is undeniable that the ICHR is plagued with internal dissension, and that it has led a lazy existence for years. Nonetheless, an individual or a group cannot be held responsible for its failings. Today, somebody has to revitalize the ICHR, make it accountable to the scholarly community, and ensure that funds are dispersed on academic grounds.

Finally, let me turn to the ICHR-sponsored 'Towards Freedom' project (Arun Shourie, now Minister in the Cabinet, wrote a series of articles accusing the editor's of misappropriating funds, a charge we, the editors, hotly denied in the press). True, the scheme was ill conceived and lazily implemented. Equally, much public money has been squandered over the decades. But please remember that we joined the project in January 1989 and not earlier. Remember, too, that not one of us received an honorarium or travelled overseas in connection with the project. How and why the ICHR spent Rs. 165 crore must be investigated. What an editor receives after the completion of his volume is hardly an adequate reward for the effort that goes into the making of a big book.

Nobody defends the delay in publishing the planned volumes, though the responsibility rests elsewhere and not with my colleagues. For this reason, it may be worth monitoring the progress after we started guiding the 'Towards Freedom' ship through the rough currents of the ICHR. Our performance may not, however, impress those who have little idea of the scale and magnitude of the enterprise.

So, what explains the vilification campaign against the liberal-left historians? Whatever the motives, the rhetoric of a few must not sway our intelligentsia. The country's climate is already vitiated; let it not be vitiated any further.

As a nation we derive strength from the variety and multiplicity of ideas, though the delicate and sensitive task of constructing the past cannot be assigned to publicists and the carriers of a divisive 'nationalist' agenda. It is legitimate to critique the liberal, Marxist and the post-modernist interpretations, but I doubt if one needs an orchestrated campaign to conduct such an exercise. As for the liberal-left historians, their writings bear testimony to their scholarship and their commitment to preserving India's pluralist character.

Endangered Liberal-Left Historian

I filled the bloodstained pages with the story of my love
And went on writing, even though my hands were smitten off.

GHALIB

The Indian History Congress is a premier body of historians. It has repeatedly affirmed its commitment to a 'scientific' and secular reading of the past and taken the lead in producing a certain temper of mind, a certain way of thinking and feeling about contemporary events and their relation to the past and the future. Moreover, scores of historians, who assemble every year in the month of December, have taken unequivocal positions against the Emergency (1975), the vandalism at Ayodhya on 6 December 1992, and the recent attack on the Christians. So often in the past they have offered refuge to their persecuted colleagues, and accommodated the liberal-left streams of thought.

Founded a decade ago in memory of Safdar Hashmi, Sahmat has acted as a bulwark against a certain variant of cultural nationalism, and kept alive the secular values of our cultural and intellectual life. Whenever authoritarian structures and religious orthodoxies have stifled dissent, Sahmat has offered its platform to them to express their anxieties. It has defended not only the universalistic values of tolerance, freedom and dissent, but also provided an effective forum for the marginal and suppressed voices of women, Dalits and the minorities, whose past is yet to be recovered in the pages of history.

The artist and the scholar operating outside party structures and the political establishment can at best sensitize the intelligentsia to the values that are dear to them and lay down the parameters of a healthy and creative debate. They cannot be expected to strictly define the thought-processes of the young and impressionable minds.

History seeks to discover causal laws connecting different facts, in the way physical sciences discover interconnections among facts. It is a question of an enhanced understanding of the past, 'ever devouring the transient offspring of the present' (Bertrand Russell), and not just a record of individual men, however great. It relates the present to the past, and thereby the future to the present. Indeed, history has been a desirable part of everybody's mental furniture, because it makes visible and living the growth and greatness of nations, enabling us to extend our hopes beyond the span of our lives. In all these ways, adds Russell, knowledge of history is capable of imparting to statesmanship, and to our daily thoughts, a breadth and scope unattainable by those whose view is limited to the present.

The study of history is often recommended on the ground of its utility in regard to the problems of present-day politics. Yet it is necessary to limit and define, more so in the Indian subcontinent with its mixed legacy of colonialism, Hindu majoritarianism and Muslim nationalism, the kind of guidance to be expected from it.

I do not wish to dwell on the story of the colonial construction of our past and the use of colonial knowledge in conjuring up images of peoples and countries for fortifying the ideological edifice of the Empire. What needs to be underlined is the independent and autonomous discourse among Indian social reformers, religious preachers and publicists on certain themes. At the same time, the reference point for several major debates has been provided by the knowledge produced during the colonial era by the colonialists themselves. Among the leading Indian thinkers, Vivekananda, Aurobindo and Gandhi were acutely sensitive to this reality.

The nationalist discourse on the Muslims and on inter-community relations illustrates my point. We learn, for example, how the British homogenized Muslims like 'castes' and 'tribes' and accommodated them within political and bureaucratic schemes as a separate and distinct community. We know that it suited the Muslim leaders to represent an 'objectively' defined community and contend with others for patronage, employment, and political assignments. What is, perhaps, not too familiar is the ambiguity and fuzziness in nationalist thinking about the corporate identity of Muslims.

Most scholars and politicians readily endorsed the colonial view that the Muslims were historically separate and distinct from the other communities and, for that reason, required special concessions. So that the political language within which the Congress sought accommodation with Muslim political activists rested largely on British perceptions and political calculations. The energy derived from recognizing Muslims as a distinct religious and political unity implied that the basic terms of reference precluded any lasting solution of the communal tangle.

Today, a professional historian must set the record straight by challenging many of the colonial and 'nationalist' assumptions, and popularize historians as creative performers echoing the collective experiences of our people. The liberal-left historians, in particular, need to change their role, more so when history is being made more accessible and immediate by political and religious orthodoxies whose principal project is to colonize the minds of the people. They can no longer wait and watch and allow the initiative to be wrested by the protagonists of conservative nationalism.

16 January 1999

It's Story-time Folks_____

Drums beat announcing the dawn of a new era—the era of knowledge and Indian awakening. The raving and ranting against Dr. M.M. Joshi must cease, for he is the sole custodian of our ancient values and heritage. While some of his Cabinet colleagues grapple with global issues, including the escalation of terrorism and its ramifications on our region, he marshals his resources to face the intellectual terrorism unleashed by left-wing historians. Today, the high priest of Shastri Bhawan is busy chanting a new mantra that might change the country's intellectual landscape. The signs—from Kashmir to Kanyakumari—are that the great Indian renaissance has ushered in under the aegis of a physicist-turned politician.

Fortunately, the Shastri Bhawan-controlled bodies and their handpicked men have fallen in line. Their collective wisdom, for which they deserve accolades, has already yielded tangible results. As the proud inheritors of the vast corpus of knowledge from Vedic times, we are now adequately equipped to share it with the rest of the world. Some hotheaded Marxists may contest the view, but the widespread acceptance of astrology and Vedic Mathematics has amply vindicated Dr. Joshi's stand. His magic formula has worked, raising the prospect of a resurgent India drawing strength and sustenance from its ancient pool of knowledge and wisdom.

His detractors unfairly tarnish Dr. Joshi's image. Turn to his predecessors in the Education Ministry. Maulana Azad, free India's first Education Minister, vaguely talked of liberal education reflecting India's pluralist and multi-religious ethos. His successors, notably M.C. Chagla and Syed Nurul Hasan, were hotheaded secularists lacking in vision and perspective. Dr. Joshi's blueprint is, on the other hand, characteristically new and different. Imbued with a mission firmly anchored in Hindutva, he repudiates old-fashioned notions of liberal humanism, intellectual dissent and tolerance. He consults nobody, except the RSS stalwarts. In his pursuit of truth he invokes their world view rather than the relevant provisions of the Constitution. So, please do not be surprised if he decides to include M.S. Golwalkar's *Bunch of Thoughts* in our college curriculum, a book, so argue its avid readers, that is far more patriotic in its content than the texts produced by Gandhiji or Jawaharlal Nehru. Reading habits must change in order to reflect the political climate in the country.

Consider, from Dr. Joshi's vantagepoint, the enormous damage caused by the reading of Marxist historians in India. Claiming to be 'objective' and 'scientific', they question our understanding of the wonder that was India. Why does Romila Thapar, whose books are unfortunately widely read, question the theory of Aryan race? Why does R.S. Sharma, whose scholarship on social and economic history is (regrettably?) widely acclaimed, question conventional wisdom about the status of women and the Shudras in ancient Indian society? Besides reducing our heroes to regional or local potentates vying with each other to seize power and authority, such historians introduce elements of caste and class strife in our land of honey and sugar. They even refer to Jain temples and Buddhist stupas and maths being destroyed, and to Buddhism being banished from the land of its birth. In this way, they keep tarnishing India's fair name the world over.

Why did Irfan Habib write the Mughal's agrarian history when all that was required was to catalogue the atrocities perpetrated by the Muslim rulers? And this fellow, Bipan Chandra, goes on and on about colonialism, economic nationalism, the popular character of the nationalist movement, and the divisive aspects of communalism. Finally, what's all this blasphemous talk of subaltern history, people's history, dalit history, and gendered narratives?

With their blatant misuse of history, for which they have received worldwide recognition from our enemies, Dr. Joshi's assault on left-wing writers seems justified. One may not be able to revive the Jacobin methods of dealing with adversaries, but a case can certainly be made out for placing the Marxist historians under detention, for they are, so says the NCERT director, a threat to the stability of the nation. Suddenly a few superannuated historians, having written their textbooks more than two decades ago, endanger the nation's well being. So what if other societies value their historians? Dr. Joshi is nurturing a new breed of historians whose identity will be revealed to the world after the UP elections.

Besides redoubling efforts to construct the real or imagined glory of the ancient Indian history past, the consensus is to concentrate less and less on the medieval period—from the thirteenth to the mid-eighteenth century. Already, the NCERT curriculum has decided to reduce the history content. So, the easy way out is to detail the heroic deeds of Prithviraj, Rana Pratap, Shivaji, and Ranjit Singh (to mollify the Sikhs), and forget the rest of the story. It should be easy to drop, with the help of an obliging NCERT director, references to Amir Khusro, Malik Mohammad Jaisi, Akbar, and Dara Shikoh. Demolishing the Taj Mahal may not be such a great idea, for it may well be construed by George W. Bush as an act of terrorism, but one can at least try convincing our kids that the Taj had been built on a temple site.

Indian history is read all over the world, and social scientists have access to facts to interpret our history and draw their conclusions. Still, the NCERT is justified in deleting certain objectionable passages. What's wrong in claiming that Jainism existed before Mahavira? In fact, Buddhists could be encouraged to make a similar demand. Religions predating the birth of their founders or prophets can add to the collective weight of our ancient civilization. In short, on the strength of the ancient beginnings of our history we can quite easily solve all our present-day problems of poverty, hunger, illiteracy, caste oppression, and gender inequality. Dr. Joshi, heir to the great Brahmanical tradition, knows it better than any one of us.

The Jats and the Maratha ransacked Delhi, the Sikhs sided with the British during the 1857 revolt, and the RSS/Hindu Mahasabha stayed aloof from the anti-colonial struggle and avoided going to prison. These are documented facts, and yet they must not be brought to light. Indeed, if I lived in the land of Nathuram Godse's birth, I may have insisted that he should not be mentioned as Mahatma Gandhi's assassin. This is what respecting popular sentiments is all about.

Several medieval rulers, including Mahmud of Ghazni and Aurangzeb, destroyed and desecrated temples, and forcibly converted to Islam scores of Hindu groups and families. These are irrefutable facts. What, if Muslims feel offended by such references? Rest assured, Dr. Joshi will consider their sentiments whenever the process of deletion starts afresh.

26 December 2001

The Deafening Clash of Myth and Fact

In the second half of the nineteenth century, textbook transmission formed but one facet of the wider significance of print culture. We know, for example, how contestations over history reveal the part played by school textbooks as ideological tools in the Raj's projection of itself through critical representations of pre-colonial past.

We also know how the British government carefully monitored, with the aid of an extensive bureaucratic network, what was to be included in, or left out from, the school or college curriculum. Thus, an elementary treatise on the art of writing the Persian character was recommended by the Director of Public Instruction as 'original and scholarly, and will be of use in schools'. In another case, Munshi Zakaullah, headmaster of a school in Delhi, was rewarded 'for the industry displayed in the preparation of this excellent series of scientific works, and for his public spirit in publishing them'.

Indian historians during the colonial period were sensitive to the importance of writing textbooks in order to contest the colonial version of the past. Thus the Allahabad-based historian, Iswari Prasad, produced a *History of Medieval India* 'to correct the common errors of history and to make the presentation of the subject as attractive as possible'. He made clear, in 1925, that a historian was not a party politician or a political propagandist, and that his function was to state and interpret the facts without allowing his own prejudices to influence the discussion of his theme or warp his judgement.

The moral of the story is this: our historians possessed the skills and expertise to write textbooks and that, after independence, this task should have been left to individual writers and not undertaken by the government. Officially sponsored works run the risk of being withdrawn, as illustrated by the experience in 1977 and now, with a change in regime. Besides, writing textbooks at the behest of a government can turn messy in a society where the reading of the past is contested with unfailing regularity. Even where contestations are not so sharp, the norm is to encourage wide learning and not to prescribe a set of books produced by an official body.

Alas, we have paid little attention to the curriculum and the method of teaching in our schools. Krishna Kumar's recent book—*Prejudice and Pride: School histories of the Freedom Struggle in India and Pakistan*—points to the poor quality of history teaching in schools and its indifference to the child's intellectual development and interest in the past. History teaching, according to him, does not translate itself into a concern for the children who are at the receiving end.

In addition, history teaching serves as a means of ideological indoctrination. So that history's role in arousing an interest in the past and respect for it gets totally sidelined. Both in India and Pakistan, history is pressed into service to promote the project of nation building. Consequently, the rival ideologies of nationalism are underlined not to heighten the critical faculties of our students but to create a sense of pride in their Indian or Pakistani citizenship. This being the case, the selective marshalling of intellectual resources reinforces not only stereotypes and prejudices, but also widens the existing rift between the people of India and Pakistan.

Doubtless, India and Pakistan are separate geographical entities. But, then, is it fair to deny to their school and college students their shared past and collective memories? The painful reality is that the project of history writing in Pakistan, more than in India, has been tailored to suit the ideologies of the ruling élites. As a result, our shared past is bruised and fragmented. *Indian* histories are being written, often untidily, by *Indian* historians; Pakistani historians are, at the same time, busy writing the history of Pakistan with little or no sense of the unities in their past. In this melee the *historian of the subcontinent*, without being rooted in his fatherland or motherland, turns into a comic figure. Asked to analyse an artificially contrived and divided past, his attempts to discern elements of unity, continuity and coherence invite rebuke and repudiation.

The State in Pakistan has invested a great deal to rationalize the two-nation theory. In India, on the other hand, the eclecticism of the first generation of liberal and left wing historians has given way to chauvinistic versions of the past. Instead of harnessing the creative energies of our students, their staple diet consists of an odd mixture of myths, mythologies, legends and modern-day fantasies. The arduous journey of a historian is, thus, wasted.

Authors of the *History of the Freedom Movement in Pakistan* and *Struggle for Freedom* (Vol. 11 of the Bharatiya Vidya Bhavan Series) had a common project—to undermine what was, in essence, the composite perspective on, and the pluralist interpretation of, Indian history. This convergence is not accidental, for Hindu and Muslim nationalists formulate their theories on the strength of separate religious communities plotting their destiny in a sharply defined Muslim or a Hindu universe. Their world-view on various other matters, nowadays projected in deciphering the past, has been largely shaped by much the same assumptions. Hence, the secular spokesman becomes their common enemy, and designated as the intellectual terrorist.

Today, our students our exposed to another intellectual threat, i.e. attempts to design region, ethnicity, or community-based curricula. If this trend continues in the form of pandering to Sikh or Jat sentiments for electoral reasons, we may soon find ourselves reading just the Jat, Sikh and Maratha histories. What will happen to *Indian* history is anybody's guess.

History, stated R.C. Majumdar, co-author of a major textbook published in 1946, did not respect persons or communities; second, that its aim is to find out the truth by following the canons commonly accepted as sound; finally, to express the findings irrespective of political considerations. If so, let us avoid playing politics with students, and let us also scrupulously refrain from invoking symbols of discord in order to legitimize our contemporary political concerns. Education has a vital role to play in helping India and Pakistan overcome the chronically unsettling effects of their interlocked frames of perception. Inculcating a respect for the past and the curiosity to make sense of it is a major educational challenge for societies where denial of the past and the urge to change it has enjoyed popular validity (Krishna Kumar).

Hopefully, Kathmandu has shown the way. An India-Pakistan History Congress in Delhi or Lahore may well be the next step towards healing the wounds of the past. If not cricket, let the teaching of history be an instrument of peace in the sub-continent.

10 January 2002

Historical Disarray:
The Re-writing of Textbooks

Rewriting history textbooks is a desirable exercise. And yet the recent enterprise lacks transparency; hence, the criticism, levelled by two former directors of the NCERT, that 'never before in its history was NCERT viewed with mistrust by a large section of the academic opinion'. They concede that the history textbooks, written by some of the country's outstanding historians, added significantly to the NCERT's prestige.

Lack of transparency breeds suspicion. One suspects, therefore, that the rewriting involves no more than an imaginary construction of the past, i.e. the claim that the *Rig Veda* is 7,000 years old; the Aryans had spread from India and colonized the world and that they had all the possible knowledge and sciences; Buddhism and Jainism were just trends within

Hinduism; consequently, Ashoka, having renounced Hinduism, bears the brunt of their criticism. Historical imagination has its place, but then it is imperative to define the strict limits within which that imagination is bound. The exercise that is being undertaken now does not force historians to rethink the categories and assumptions with which they work, or to justify the manner in which they practise their discipline.

This being the case, the agenda of rewriting history textbooks necessarily jeopardizes historical study as normally understood. Just as the arrival of post-modernist theory in the 1980s led to 'an extended epistemological crisis' in the West, India's current intellectual climate and the ensuing historical controversies have thrown the historical profession into disarray. Such is the power and influence of the BJP polemicists that a growing number of people, drawn mainly from the urban élites, are abandoning the quest for an objective approach to the past. No wonder so many historians are worried about the future of their discipline.

In 1977, the past became a casualty in the ideological battle of the present. However, the storm blew over owing to the fragile nature of the Janata coalition. With the establishment of the BJP-led government in February 1999, the BJP-RSS combination began its veritable cultural counter-revolution, its subversion of the academia through its time-tested method of infiltration and rewriting of textbooks and 'fine-tuning' of curricula.

The Janata government's intervention was feeble; the present one however represents a strong body of opinion in the country that subscribes to the view that the 'Hindus' have been 'wronged', and that their histories have been distorted at the hands of 'secular fundamentalists'. Exponents of this view say in effect: 'You have invaded and pillaged our past. You, the inheritors of the Nehruvian legacy, have robbed us of our present. And you have endangered and perhaps compromised our future.' This kind of criticism is often accompanied by very harsh, even coarse, language, and has given rise to a new term of abuse, the word 'intellectual terrorists'. Earlier, the common expression 'pseudosecularists' was coined to denote the liberal and Marxist writers. Now, the same term has been salvaged and reconditioned and turned to a new purpose.

The critical assault comes principally from political activists, polemicists, propagandists, some journalists and, in recent years, from the unwarranted intrusion of expatriates. Right-wing historians, too, mostly echo the rhetoric of Hindu extremist politics, tracing the misfortunes of Bharat to centuries of tyrannical Muslim rule with the aid of partial, selective, and narrow sources. Instead of studying and interpreting other cultures by the same standards and criteria as their own, without prejudice or condescension, their scholarship is designed or even trimmed to serve some non-scholarly purpose, whether religious or regional or ideological or other.

What they are saying is that the critical approach is forbidden to us, and that we should accept what is selected, prepared, processed, and presented for our instruction. So that even to mention—let alone to discuss or explore—beef eating in ancient India, the destruction of Buddhist stupas and Jain temples by the Hindu kingdoms, or the role of a venerable Sikh guru—is denounced as evidence of unpatriotism and of Christian-Muslim designs. The same applies to other delicate topics as the fate of the Indus Valley civilization, the antecedents of the Aryans, the mythical Saraswati river, and the caste system. The range of taboos is very wide.

What has changed from the previous decades is that, under the present dispensation, the historian is not expected to raise embarrassing questions, confront orthodoxy and dogma, and represent all those people and issues that are routinely forgotten or swept under the rug. Today, the issue is between prejudice and propaganda on the one hand, and rational arguments and scholarship on the other. What we have, in other words, is dialogue of the deaf, with no genuine debate.

India is a multi-cultural and multi-religious society, and yet a single definition of Indian culture and society is projected through educational channels. Notice, for example, the changes announced by the NCERT in the school curricula in January 2002. The relative importance of 'our' history and 'their' history can be seen in the apportionment of space and attention to ancient and medieval India. In addition, one unit of the social science syllabus that looks at the features, spread and basic values of 'major religions' leaves out Islam. The motivation is clearly political and ideological. Sometimes there are other variants. Although the 'Advent of Islam' is included in the social science syllabus for the next class, it is put in a unit alongside West Asia. That's because, says the HRD Minister, Islam 'grew out of that area—its history is linked with the history of the Arab civilization, its spread and emergence'.

Why should we study 'their' history? The NCERT seems to be saying that it is not 'our' business or that it is not relevant— a word with new and sometimes menacing implications—to 'our' needs or concerns or purposes. Islam is, after all, alien to the Indian environment, even though almost simultaneously with political conquests in the seventh century Islam began to find lodgements on India's western coast. Muslims and Christians, wrote Guru Golwalkar, 'are born in this land, no doubt. But are they true to its salt. Are they grateful towards this land which has brought them up? Do they feel that they are the children of this land, its traditions and to serve it as their great good fortune? No.'

Soon after Independence, a nation-wide consensus emerged on promoting rationality and preserving the composite values of this society. We need to revive that consensus and pay heed to Jawaharlal Nehru's advice to students in 1950: 'Keep your windows and doors of your mind always open. Let all winds from the four corners of the earth blow in to refresh your mind, to give you ideas, to strengthen you.'

6 February 2002

Revisiting Anti-Nazi India

The feverish Nazi activities in India during Second World War, including a conference in Bombay on 17-22 July 1939, under the pretext of celebrating the anniversary of 'The Deutscher

Club', is not part of popular history. The *Bombay Sentinel*, a paper leading the anti-Nazi crusade, listed major and the 'little Fuehrers' in the country. Discussion took place on how the people's anti-British temper provided the basis for Nazi propaganda, and why the Nazis, the Fascists and the Japanese militarists, the three anti-Comintern Powers, were interested in India.

In 1939, Jawaharlal Nehru expressed concern that the German Consuls, the German firms, the India representatives of German firms and some Indian students in Berlin were engaged in promoting the Nazi agenda. There was much scope for their activities, according to him, because the Muslim League and the Hindu Mahasabha spoke the same 'totalitarian language'. Nehru was right. The otherwise irreconcilable Hindu and Muslim fundamentalists were attracted by totalitarian doctrines, though they approached them from two opposite directions. Militant Hindus like V.D. Savarkar interpreted the Nazi's glorification of the so-called Aryan race as a vindication of his or her own doctrine of race and caste. The Palestine issue, on the other hand, misled the Muslim communalists, a trump card the Nazis used to sedulously foster anti-Jewish sentiments.

Nehru hinted at the pro-Nazi proclivities of some professors at the Aligarh Muslim University. One of them was Dr. M.B. Mirza, who studied in Germany and had attended the Nazi Congress in 1938. Addressing a Muslim League meeting, the zoology professor endorsed Hitler's political creed. 'You are being taught the creed of passive resistance. I ask you not to believe in this creed. It is meant for the cowards only. As the necklace decorates the neck of women, guns should decorate the shoulders of men.'

Indeed, there was a time when Hitler and Mussolini were honoured by some youthful Indian patriots in colleges, along with those of Mazzini, Garibaldi, Dan Breen and other such Italian, French and Irish revolutionaries. To them, they represented a dynamic force in world politics, knight-errants sallying forth to strike at the demon of British imperialism. But all this changed when the Nazi-Fascist combination stood exposed in all its hideousness, shorn of its ideological trappings.

Last week I came across a poster at the Statsbibliothek in

Berlin. It was issued by the Anti-Nazi League in 1939 and printed by the *Times of India* Press. The first line—'Post this in all Public Places'—is printed in bold letters. The second states: 'Wanted Dead or Alive! Wanted! Reward Rs. 50,000. ADOLF HITLER FOR MURDER.' Hitler's habits, according to the poster, were: loves parades, goose-stepping, brawls like a donkey while giving lectures, plotting, murder, arson, loot and kidnapping. And his antecedents: claims to be German, which he speaks badly, but is really Austrian. Formerly a wall-painter and bricklayer. The final warning in the poster was to avoid any mention of democracy, pacifism and truth in his presence.

This poster caused consternation in official circles. It was carefully analysed at various bureaucratic levels. And the conclusion was that, besides violating Section 2 (10) of the Indian Press (Emergency Powers) Act, its contents grossly insulted the German nation and its leaders. Bombay's Police Commissioner conveyed this to T.K. Menon, Secretary of the Anti-Nazi League. *The Times of India* management apologized for printing the poster.

T.K. Menon headed the Anti-Nazi League. He called for the boycott of German goods, for which he invited sharp criticism in the columns of *Princely India* (Bombay), edited by P. Gopal Pillai, and *Karnatak Bandhu* (district: Dharwar). Menon claimed that he had received the matter used in the poster or news-sheet from the Empire Unity League in High Holborn, London, and that the *Daily Mail* printed such posters that were distributed in England.

As a nation striving against foreign rule, the Congress, along with the Socialists and Communists, expressed solidarity with other oppressed people—be they Italian Socialists, Jews, Ethiopians, Chinese or the Spanish loyalists. Gandhi, for one, did so with his usual sensitivity. However, the credit for the anti-Nazi propaganda must go to Nehru. He repeatedly dwelt on the danger of fascism and showed why the Indian nationalists should not let their movement take a turn for totalitarianism. He called for countrywide demonstrations to sympathize with the people of China. He travelled to Spain to convey to the loyalists the country's sympathy and solidarity for them.

In recent years, India has repudiated the Gandhian and Nehruvian legacy. We kept mum when the Serbs and the Croats massacred the Muslims in erstwhile Yugoslavia. We did not protest against the US belligerence towards Iran and the unjustified sanctions imposed on Iraq. Above all, we have ceased to espouse the Palestine cause with the same degree of enthusiasm. For such reasons, our international credibility has suffered in recent years.

The only way to recover the moral ground we occupied during the Nehruvian era is to take principled positions on various international issues, especially those relating to human rights and national sovereignty.

28 November 2000

Kashmiri Pandits must Come Home

Khuda hi ki ibadat jin ko ho maqsood ae
Akbar ko kyon baham lade go farq ho tarz-i ibadat me.

Why should men fight, whose aim is to worship God?
What matter if they worship him in different forms?

'Kashmir', wrote Jahangir, 'is a garden of eternal spring, or an iron fort to a palace of kings—a delightful flowerbed, and a heart-expanding heritage for dervishes.' By far the most important observation of the Mughal emperor was on the long tradition of religious tolerance and pluralism in Kashmir, starting with Syed Ali Hamdani and Sheikh Nuruddin in the fourteenth century. In one tale, it is said that when a baby, Nuruddin refused to take his mother's milk and would drink only from Lalla Deb, the Kashmiri mystic.

A century later, Sultan Zainul Abidin exemplified a more civilized adherence to harmonious communal relation. According to Kalhana's *Rajatarangini*, he participated in Hindu religious festivals, visited Hindu shrines, and had the Sanskrit texts read to him. English observers of the late nineteenth and early twentieth century in Kashmir found shared popular religious traditions especially in the countryside. Thus W. Lawrence referred to the 'delightful tolerance' between the followers of Islam and Hinduism.

By invoking such fragments from Kashmir's history, I underline that Islam did not come to the subcontinent in a single time-span; consequently, its diffusion took place in a variety of forms from class to class and from one area to another. In its local and regional specificity, therefore, Islam cannot be portrayed as a social entity whose 'essential' core is immune to change by historical influences. Thus in Kashmir, as indeed in the south of the Vindhyas, Islam evolved a tradition of worship marked by a striking capacity to accommodate itself to indigenous patterns of faith and worship. It gained a foothold because of its capacity to forge links with the religions and peoples of the wider society, and to offer a form of access to the divine which could be grasped and built upon through means already present within these societies. This intermixing was neither 'degenerate' nor a product of superficial accretions from Hinduism. The sharing of beliefs and practices was built up into a dynamic and expansive religious system (Susan Bayly).

The nationalist movement drew upon these syncretic or multireligious tendencies to create a 'national sentiment', an expression that has recently acquired special significance. But the major differences in its usage, then and now, must not be lost sight of. For one, most of the nationalist leaders—from Gopal Krishna Gokhale to Nehru—realized that a national sentiment can be created, particularly in a colonial context, by drawing upon the shared experiences and memories of the country as a whole and not a segment thereof. Hence they used symbols reflecting India's composite and pluralist ethos. That would explain why the historical memories associated with Ayodhya, Kashi and Muthura were not invoked. Indeed their aim, which the Muslim League leadership in the 1940s failed to grasp, was to forge a joint anti-colonial front and to unite the people rather than divide them along religious lines. One can fault their judgement and lack of foresight in dealing with minority fears and aspirations, but it will be hard to place them in the dock for mixing up the misguided religious fanaticism of a majority segment with the 'sentiments' of the nation as a whole.

By all means one should dutifully talk of national duty and sentiment when armed infiltrators and their patrons threaten the nation's security. But not otherwise. A cursory glance at the political landscape in the 1930s and 1940s, particularly in Punjab and Bengal, reveals systematic attempts to strengthen the region, as opposed to the amorphous Indian nation, as a powerful and cohesive entity. This was the logical consequence of the political arithmetic worked out in the Act of 1919. After Independence, the spurt in provincialism, often rooted in ethnic and linguistic assertions, found expression in the clamour for linguistic states. Increasingly, the identity of the nation as such (which is, at any rate, a construction), meant little to, say the Jats in Haryana, who discovered that the pickings lay in their territorial strong-hold and not in the bruised nation state commanded by the politicians and bureaucrats sitting in Lutyen's Delhi. In the subsequent political arrangements, the nation, as visualized by the its protagonists in the 1920s and thereafter, stood fragmented.

The Kashmiris, having long suffered the indifference of their rulers, tried conveying much the same message to Delhi. They did so not as Muslims *per se* but as citizens of a region that had acquired its own distinct identity over the centuries. Before acceding to the Union, they had acted in unison to struggle for their rights and found a leader in Sheikh Mohammad Abdullah to guide their destiny. Incidentally, the Sheikh nurtured the vision of a Kashmiri identity within the Indian nation. His was, indeed, a singularly secular and forward-looking movement for the Kashmiris and not only for the predominantly Muslim population in the valley. Sadly, the self-righteous statesman in Delhi lost the import of his message. He was ignored, rebuffed and incarcerated by Nehru and the wise men, some from the valley itself, around him.

Today, the valley is not how Jahangir or Lawrence had found

it. Sheikh Abdullah's secular dream lies in tatters. Devotees who once thronged the lofty temples—Jahangir described them in his *Memoirs*—are apprehensive. The Dal Lake, surrounded by armed garrisons, weeps for the dead and wounded. The flowers at Chashm-e Shahi and the Nishat Bagh have yet to blossom as the journey of their lovers—from Punjab to Kanyakumari—has yet to begun. Moreover, the streets of Srinagar, as indeed the glorious saffron fields that Jahangir described so vividly, seem desolate without the Kashmiri Pandits who embody all that was beautiful in Indo-Islamicite society and culture. They seem to be saying to each and every passer-by: Kashmir will have no peace without their presence. They have been and will remain an integral part of our being.

Militancy and terrorism forced the Kashmiri Pandits to abandon their home. At this juncture, it is important for the disparate Kashmiri Muslims to make strenuous efforts to invite the Pandits to return to their homeland. In fact the moral legitimacy of their movement will depend on their capacity to respect the identity of the Pandits and accommodate their interests. It is outrageous to displace, as the Palestinian and Kosovo experiences illustrate, people from their land of birth just because they profess a different religion. This is what Syed Ali Hamdani and Sheikh Nuruddin, great Kashmiri mystics, would have said way back in the fourteenth century.

19 January 2001

3

Relics of a Monstrous Past:
*The Guilt of a Nation*_____

The Nazi regime showed itself capable of mass murder against virtually any group of people. But no other group of victims occupied the role in Hitler's mind, as did the Jews. No other victims were threatened so totally and pursued so relentlessly. And no other victims died so helpless and abandoned. When the Nazi regime finally collapsed in defeat, some 6 million Jews (approximately one-third of world Jewry) had perished.

One is reminded of the Holocaust wherever you travel in Deutschland. Take Berlin, the future capital of Germany. If you board a train at the Wittenberg S-bahn (surface railway system), you will not miss the plaque listing the concentration camps in Europe. Chelmno, Belzec, Auschwitz, Sobibor, Treblinka, and Maidanek echo the pain, anguish and sufferings of millions of, among others, the Jewish people. Turn just a few blocks from Kurfurstenddamm, with its many shops, and you will notice the Jewish Museum, a magnificent specimen of modern architecture. The architect is Daniel Liebeskind, whose family in Berlin was virtually wiped out during the Holocaust. He returned to the city in 1989 to capture the trauma of the Jewish community in Germany.

The Museum, financed by the City of Berlin, may well turn out to be a major symbol of the collective guilt of the German nation. It will remain, for all time to come, a sad and grim reminder of how the Jews were deprived of civic equality and barred from various professions (1933), how marriage and sexual intercourse between Jews and Aryans was forbidden (1935), and how another wave of legislation in 1938 impoverished the Jews by stripping them of their property. The same year, on 9 and 10 November, Joseph Goebbels incited the Kristallacht riots (The Night of the Broken Glass). People watched passively while 20 synagogues were set on fire and Jewish businesses vandalized. Appropriately enough, Liebeskind's pillars outside the precincts of the Jewish Museum symbolize exile and emigration.

Berlin was once the centre of Jewish life in Germany. In 1933, the year Hitler became Chancellor, 1,60,564 Jews lived in Berlin. Their numbers dwindled to 75,334 in 1939. That is when Hitler's vision to clear Germany of Jews through emigration was translated into practice by Himmler's SS. Five years later, only 5,100 Jews remained in Berlin. Today, there are 10,000 registered with the Jewish Community Centre. They are mostly immigrants from Eastern Europe who started coming into the city after the collapse of communism in 1990.

If you have strong nerves, visit the Sachsenhausen Concentration Camp in Oranien-burg, near the Reich capital of Berlin. Built in 1936, this camp imprisoned 2,00,000 people from various nations between 1936 and 1945. Tens of thousands died of hunger, disease, forced labour, maltreatment or by organized murder operations of 33,190 people. As many as 41,830 prisoners died while they were transferred to other concentration camps. The Jews at Sachsenhausen were removed in October 1942 to Auschwitz, following Himmler's decision to 'free' all the concentration camps in the Old Reich of Jewish prisoners.

You see the relics and traces of a monstrous regime in the Commandant's area, the SS Casino, the roll call area, the site of the gallows, the barracks, the prisons, the crematorium and extermination site Station Z, execution trenches with bullet catch and automatic gallows, and a pathology laboratory with a cellar of corpses. You see much more and realize the enormity of the tragedy, the deep psychological obsessions of Hitler and his men who saw the Jew not only as the cause of present ills, manifested above all in the rising Bolshevik threat, but also as the very metaphysical source of evil.

At the same time, one is comforted to learn about the heroic struggle waged against the Nazis. Photographs of many brave men and women, particularly Communists, tortured and killed in this camp and elsewhere, reinforces your faith in humanity. Some died without capitulating before the forces of tyranny. Appropriately enough, Soviet and Polish units of the Red Army liberated the camp on 22-3 April 1945.

The Holocaust casts its shadow over many aspects of Jewish life. But in responding to its catastrophic consequences, many Jewish groups have failed to draw lessons from their own history. In Israel, in particular, they have turned a blind eye to their obligations towards the beleaguered Arabs and disregarded the legitimate claims of the Palestinians. In their search for their 'Promised Land', aggressive Zionists have displaced and dis-possessed millions of Palestinians from their homeland. The state of Israel will vindicate its *raison d'être* only by recognizing the demand for an independent Palestinian state with Jerusalem as its epicentre. The historic injustice done in 1948 and thereafter must be set right.

We, in India, must learn from the Holocaust. The burning of the synagogues was a ghastly and chilling event, a prelude to the spread of fascism in Europe. We must not let those scenes be re-enacted, for such brazen acts of vandalism destroy the moral and social fabric of any society. Places of worship must not be vandalized. In a multi-religious country like ours their presence symbolize the fulfilment of a secular dream. India will cease to be the envy of the rest of the world if some hotheaded fanatics take away our dreams. The same applies to symbols connected with the Buddhists, Turks, Mughals, and the British. We may not like them, but can we deny that they form part of an Indian heritage?

Turning to more recent times, it may be worth setting up an archive on India's Partition. We need a Spielberg to unfold the horrors perpetrated, in 1946-7, in the name of religion. True, taking testimony on video involves many issues, including the time factor, the public act of witness, and a pedagogically effective medium. It is also true that the video testimony is a new genre, with its own realism and sociology, a genre with implications we do not, as yet, completely understand. Still, the initiative may be worthwhile for recording a tragic and traumatic phase of our twentieth century history.

27 June 1998

Going beyond Apologies

'Air-India announces the departure of its flight (131) to Rome.' We were thrilled to hear that our national carrier, with its repu- tation sullied over the years, was departing on time. There were more surprises after being air-borne. Treated gently by an indulgent crew, we realized that a handful of conscientious people can infuse dynamism into many an institution. When I returned to Delhi a few days later, my experience with the Air- India flight was equally pleasant.

Our pilot, A.A. Gadgil, was amiable and quite refreshing in detailing the route of his aircraft. Unlike the dull and routine description of his counterparts, which nobody listens to, I found my co-passengers paying serious attention to whatever he said to us throughout the eight-hour journey. He spoke eloquently in English, Italian and Hindi. What a relief! As our plane flew over Pakistan, he talked of the historic links between India and that country, the Partition of the subcontinent, and its bloody aftermath. He informed us of the great cultural, religious and intellectual centres in Iran and the clash between the Perso- Hellinistic civilizations. He referred to the Bosphorus and the dividing line, so to speak, between the Occident and the Orient. As we approached Rome, he told us about the Renaissance and the great artists of that period. Well done, Mr. Gadgil.

So dear readers, do not always run down the national carrier. Fly Air-India when you travel to Rome next. Pay attention to

what Mr. Gadgil has to say and enjoy the warm hospitality of
his colleagues.

My conversation with fellow-passengers, mostly Italians,
centred on the controversy generated by Queen Elizabeth's visit.
They wanted to know about the massacre at the Jallianwala
Bagh and my personal reactions to the persistent demand in
certain quarters that the Queen should tender an apology for
the happenings in Amritsar. It was a tall order. But having declared
myself as a historian of modern India, I was constrained to
offer an explanation.

There is no denying that the massacre of innocent and
unarmed people at the Jallianwala Bagh unfolded certain unpleasant aspects of colonial rule in India. Equally, the government's brutal repression and its reactions thereafter created
space for the anti-colonial movement to gather momentum.
Mohammad Ali Jinnah remarked in 1920: 'the death trap in the
Jallianwala Bagh . . . would move even the stones. That horrible
butchery was committed in the name of law and order. I have
tried to find out one single word . . . cowardice. No, butchery.'
And the great Urdu poet Mohammad Iqbal wrote:

> The dust of the garden says to every bird in the orchard
> Don't yet remain indifferent to the ways of Heaven
> Its seed has been watered with the blood of martyrs
> Don't ye grudge to shed tears for this building.

The Mahatma, having returned from South Africa in 1915
was able to channelize the popular discontent against Pax
Britannica in an extraordinary manner. He thought that, from
about 1919, onwards, the character of British rule began to
change for the worse. It betrayed its ideas, subjected Indians to
the most humiliating indignities, and showed contempt for
public opinion. Gandhi turned 'disloyal' and declared himself
an implacable foe of the Raj. For him, as for millions of Indians,
the Rowlatt Act and the Jallianwala Bagh massacre marked the
turning point.

Doubtless, the violence unleashed by General Dyer led to a
colossal human tragedy in Amritsar, and that we need to remind
ourselves of many other stories of British repression. At a time

when the usage of words like 'colonialism' and 'imperialism' is no longer in fashion in some academic circles, it is all the more necessary to reveal the exploitative character of British rule and its debilitating effect on the economy. For a nation troubled by the bitter legacy of Partition, it is important to understand how the British created communitarian solidarity among some Muslim groups, and how they legitimized their identity through formal constitutional arrangements. Finally, we need to analyse the implications of the divide and rule policy, which was essentially designed to undermine the pluralist character of our society.

These aspects need to be examined afresh from the several different perspectives that are available to us. But there is no justification for invoking historical memories for short-term political gains. There should, indeed, be no place for crude versions of nationalism. Why, for instance, should anybody insist that the Queen, who was not even the ruler in 1919, apologize for General Dyer's crime? So what if the Japanese apologized for the atrocities committed in Korea. The head of every nation can't repeat this. Are we going to ask Bill Clinton to tender an apology for the crimes committed by the Americans in Vietnam? Or have we forgotten the harrowing experiences of the Vietnamese? Is it not enough that the Queen visited Amritsar and described the Jallianwala Bagh massacre as a distressing episode? Moreover, we should be comforted by the thought that General Dyer is deservedly consigned to the dustbin of history.

We should endeavour to strengthen rather than weaken our ties with the United Kingdom. The issue of Kashmir, which seems to have triggered a controversy owing to Robin Cook's indiscreet remarks, should not stand in the way of enduring trade and business relationship. Are we prepared to be isolated in the international arena just because somebody has a different point of view on Kashmir? I think not. As a mature democracy, let us be patient, tolerant and accommodating. Let us coolly define our national priorities and defend our interests without presenting the false image of occupying a high moral ground.

It is immaterial whether Britain is a 'third-rate' power or not.

The important point is that it continues to be an important trading and commercial centre with a fairly well developed service sector. It still occupies, despite its dwindling fortunes in the post-War decades, an important position in the comity of nations. We may think that we are the best, though in reality there is much to learn from the working of several British institutions, including its educational system. Let us therefore not raise issues that may estrange India-British relations.

18 October 1997

Truth with Reconciliation

I was not pushed out of a train. I was not prevented from entering Cafe Fish at the yacht mole or the Famous Fish Company at the entrance to Durban's harbour. I was not made to sit at the back of an aircraft bound for East London. I noticed no designated places for 'whites', 'blacks' and 'coloured' people. This is South Africa for you, four years after the collapse of the racist white regime.

While the world was largely insensitive to the horrors perpetrated by the Afrikaners, the unthinkable happened in 1994. A nation was born under a new sun, cleared of a horrible past, matured from a tentative beginning and reaching out to the future with confidence. Yet the brutal murder of an 11-year-old child a fortnight ago by a white farmer is a reminder of the ugly remnants of apartheid.

Wherever you go, one is reminded of the misery foisted upon African people through a web of heinous legislation, such as the pass laws, influx control, and the beer system. The story is too grim and tragic to be told, and yet it is hard to ignore the 'white man's burden' in the form of rape, abduction, murder

and assassinations. The Kwa Muhle Museum in Durban provides
a vital link with the city's apartheid past. Its founding credo
reads: 'this is a museum about power and powerlessness and
the struggle for human dignity by ordinary people. Let this
never be forgotten. Let us be mindful of the abuses of the past
and the human capacity, in all its diversity and richness, to
overcome'.

Otherwise, life goes on as usual in the bustling cities of
Johannesburg, Durban and Cape Town. Violence is not rampant
as was predicted by the prophets of doom. Nelson Mandela, the
presiding genius over South Africa's destiny, is still striving for
a rainbow coalition. Economists debate what ails the economy,
social scientists discuss the constitution approved on 10 December 1996 at Sharpeville, scene of an infamous massacre that was
in itself a defining moment in South Africa's struggle for political
freedom and human justice, and the media focuses on 'Truth
and Reconciliation' hearings whenever the drama unfolds on
television.

Yet, all that glitters is not gold. Tension is brewing as Nelson
Mandela comes to terms with the problems of governance. The
35 million blacks are angry and dissatisfied with the slow pace
of reforms. Public rhetoric, as in neighbouring Zimbabwe where
Robert Mugabe's inept and corrupt regime is collapsing, is not
matched by action. Squatter campuses and shanty towns haven't
disappeared. Unemployment among the blacks is still very high,
while massive cuts in public expenditure dim the prospects of
securing jobs.

In Cape Town, the health authorities would wield the battle-
axe rather than the scalpel to cut 3,816 jobs and close five
hospitals by July this year. The real problem is the absence of a
strong middle class in South Africa. There are just not enough
qualified black applicants for skilled jobs. They hold only 8 per
cent of the nation's top jobs. Part of the reason is their limited
access to education during and after the apartheid years. In
1996, the number of black students at universities in, say, Pretoria
was 4,788 as against 19,425 whites. The number of black teachers
in Cape Town was 141, as against 1,395 whites. Though
affirmative action has made some difference—the number of

blacks in public service rose 13 per cent between June 1995 and June 1996—the overall progress in most sectors of the economy is abysmally poor.

Tension is mounting, moreover, on account of the unassailable dominance of the 5.3 million white inhabitants. They constitute 10 per cent of the population but control trade, commerce, industry, banking, agriculture and education. Mandela himself denounced white privilege and called for a distribution of wealth to poor black. Though Thabo Mbeki, his soft-spoken successor, exudes optimism in his pronouncements, South Africa has a long way to go towards achieving its goal of improving the lives of its impoverished black citizens.

The average income of the whites is $17,060, that of blacks is $3,005. In rural areas, the conservative Afrikaners, with their penchant for brutalizing black tenant labourers and farm workers, retain their extensive farmlands. Having perpetrated crimes against humanity for 47 years, they have now organized themselves into vigilante groups for 'protection'. Why? Because they view themselves as victims of reverse discrimination. Protection against what? Just because a handful of white farmers have been killed? Such paranoia, some might say, comes naturally to the white descendants of exiles, refugees and mercenaries who, having flouted all norms of decent and human behaviour in the past, continue to enjoy the good life and reap the rewards of their oppression. Most people I spoke to were disappointed that only 30,000 whites emigrated between 1994 and 1996. They would like many more to leave.

So what happens to Mandela's rainbow coalition? Some say that granting amnesty to killers is to mock the truth, and that they will have no truck with reconciliation. 'If the Nazis were tried at Nuremberg', an angry youth told me at Cato Manor in Durban, 'why allow the Afrikaners to go scot-free?'

The anger and indignation is understandable, but the more striking and commendable aspect of South African society today is the humanity of its black people, their sense of pride and dignity, and their remarkable spirit of tolerance and understanding. Though haunted by the painful memories of an agonizing past, most people seem convinced, in the words of the poet-writer Manda Langa, 'that the past in which we live so vividly cannot be repeated'. The golden pledge, hallmark of the constitution, is: 'never, never again shall the laws of our land rend our people apart, or legalise their oppression or repression. Together we shall march, hand in hand, to a brighter future.'

We seem to have a 'message' for every other country, but can we not learn a few lessons from South Africa? When remembering our freedom fighters, we must not forget those countless men and women in South Africa who laid down their lives for freedom, social justice and human dignity. This is the essence of what Gandhiji taught us.

2 May 1998

Muslim Diversity in India and Iran: Many Worlds, One Universe

At a time when some in the West talk of a green menace and others are prepared to go along with Samuel Huntington's vision of the future in terms of a clash of civilization, participants from Iran and India happily discovered a convergence of interests and aspirations and their long-standing cultural contacts. Though the harsh realities of living in a unipolar world and a globalized economic order was taken note of, they were nonetheless able to identify the spaces for an open-ended cultural dialogue based on a nuanced understanding of our respective societies.

How, then, to sustain an India-Iranian dialogue? Surely, it is not good enough to invoke the poetry of Amir Khusro or the magisterial historical works of Abul Fazl [the sixteenth-century historian in the court of the Mughal Emperor, Akbar]. For us in India, the task ahead is to acquaint people living in Iran with the strength and vitality of our democratic and secular experiment. A democratic empowerment of the lower castes, the chief catalyst for what has been described as the second democratic upsurge, has made India's democracy more inclusive and participatory. Indeed, the Indian political regime is one of the most democratic in the world by most conventional measures of political participation, electoral and party competition, and persistence of parliamentary institutions.

Equally, the people of Iran should know a great deal more about the loose and widely divergent tendencies amongst India's 120 million Muslims. As in Iran where Islam incorporated a variety of outlooks and orientations and has been capable of multiple levels of discourse and interpretations, in its local and regional specificity, the 'essential' core of Islam in India has not been immune to changes by historical influences. Ordinary Muslims are not, as one is often led to believe, members of a monolithic community sitting sullenly apart, but were active participants in regional cultures whose perspectives they shared. Those holding the reins of leadership locate problems and find answers to contemporary dilemmas within the democratic and secular paradigms and seek adjustments not as members of a larger religious collectivity. They accept state laws without insisting on the application of the Islamic law, except in the case of marriage, divorce and inheritance. In sum, beneath the so-called unity of the Muslim community, it is necessary to uncover a variety of religious and political outlooks and competing agendas. This may well unravel the 'mysteriously known essence' (Edward Said) of Islam in India and Iran, and challenge the world-wide perception of a monolithic 'Islamic threat'.

This is not all. Whether for exploring our heritage or for the noble cause of forging closer cultural ties, we need to incorporate rather than discard the colonial factor in our discourses. Furthermore, we need to be mutually sensitive to Western mis-representation, stereotyping, and the colonial construction of a hostile politico-ideological structure, a different civilization, and an alien economic region. These representations have, after all, lent depth and legitimacy, even after decades of Independence, to 'primordial' loyalties and identities in India and Iran. To resolve these problems, some of which are threatening to tear apart the fabric of our neighbours, we need to question the colonial assumptions about our societies and develop our own theories of State and society.

Sadly, the Indian academia has neglected the study of our neighbours. For the recent initiative to get off the ground, we need to contextualize Iran's history and contemporary politics and not be influenced by the images, myths, and the categories invented by some Western scholars. Contrary to popular perceptions, Iran is not the bastion of Islamic fundamentalism threatening to overrun its neighbours, but a society trying to come to terms with its past and its contemporary dilemmas.

Let's respect Iran's search for its own identity. After all, religion and the State have been intertwined ever since the establishment of the Safavid dynasty, and that it is impossible to delegitimize the role of Islam or the *ulama* in popular mobilization. Notice, for example, that on two more occasions—the Tobacco Protest (1891-92) and the Constitutional Revolution (1905-11)—Islam and the Muslim divines played an important opposition role in the emergence of modern Iranian nationalism. Today, Islam continues to be a source of government legitimacy in Iran. Successive governments will continue to appeal to Islam to enhance their authority, buttress nationalism, legitimize policies and programmes, and increase popular support.

My second proposition centres on the role of Shia emotionalism, which assumed special significance and provided the inspirational model for the Revolution. Indeed, evocative Shia symbols contribute to the making and crystallization of Iranian self-consciousness, and lend a special and distinct character to Iranian nationalism. Historically, Shia Islam has exercised a far-reaching influence on Shia political culture than Sufi tendencies have in Sunni societies. Among other aspects, it has influenced the nature and character of Iranian nationalism. The symbolic component of politics in Iran, especially after the inglorious regime of the Shah, is especially significant because it could have been used as an instrument of persuasion as well as coercion. Yet bargaining models of politics suggest that, persuasion rather than force, is increasingly considered to be the basis of politics in Tehran.

My final point is that politics in Iran is sufficiently complex. As a result, attempts to reduce it to a single formula leads to mystification; rather than being monolithic, Muslim politics, while aspiring to *umma*-wide universals, derives its force and significance from the specific contexts, times, and localities in which it takes place. 'Islam' cannot thus be a threat, any more than the 'West' can be for Muslims. Muslim politics have a transnational dimension, as is illustrated by the responses to Israel's illegal occupation of Palestine, but this does not imply that one Muslim cultural unit has coalesced or that a transnational Islamic space has acquired dominance.

Foreign policy makers in India and proponents of a civilization dialogue have to come to terms with an Iranian personality and an Iranian ethos that is different from Arab/Turkish nationalism. They need to recognize this reality in order to negotiate with Tehran on a familiar terrain. Let me conclude with Tagore's sentiment, who visited Persia in 1935:

> The night has ended.
> Put out the light of the lamp
> Of thine own narrow dark corner
> Smudged with smoke,
>> the great Morning which is for all
>> appears in the East.
> Let its light reveal us to each other
> who walk on the same path
> of pilgrimage.

29 November 2000

*The Stormtroopers at Bamiyan*_____

The images of the Buddha exude love and compassion, the quintessential features of his teachings. Whether perched on a hilltop or in the serenity of a cave, they bring to humanity the message of peace and brotherhood. In a geographical dictionary written in the thirteenth century, the author Yaqut refers to the images of the Buddha at Bamiyan. 'Nowhere else', he wrote, 'is there anything to equal these.' Abul Fazl, historian at Akbar's court, noted the sculptured 'colossal images', one said to be 80 'yards' high, the other 50 'yards'. They are (were) actually 53 and 38 metres high.

At the beginning of this new millennium, the Taliban regime has very different ideas. In a brazen exhibition of religious fanaticism, its stormtroopers have let loose their religious fury on sites and symbols of veneration, if not actual worship. They have established beyond doubt that Talibanization represents nothing but regression, and the aggressive and evil propensities of man. 'It is immaterial', underlines the Indian History Congress resolution, 'if the Taliban claim that they are doing it to fulfil what are alleged to be the prescriptions of Islam. No religion is entitled to sanction the destruction of the works of another faith.'

Round one of this unequal contest between the booming guns and the smiling Buddha may belong to the *mullahs* in Afghanistan, but the Taliban regime has forsaken the right to be heard by the international community. For decades to come, the devotees of the sage from Kapilvastu, as well as those millions who treasure works of art, will be haunted by the images of a decapitated Buddha, his arms and limbs smashed by modern weaponry.

This act of vandalism vindicates the position of all those, both in India and elsewhere, who oppose the reassertion of religion in public life and politics. Moreover, it is a stern reminder to the Western governments, who have nurtured the Taliban with the avowed goal of containing communism in the region. Now that the monster is out in the open, it is devouring its own people and destroying its own rich cultural inheritance.

The public outcry in the West is a case of too little, too late. Long ago, Cicero asserted that there was a true law 'namely' right reason, which applied to all persons and was unchangeable and eternal. But the Taliban, impervious to reason and rationality, couldn't care less. Imposing their own codes on an impoverished and deeply fractured tribal society, they have disregarded the legitimate aspirations of their own people for political participation, social justice, and human rights. Now, in this brazen act of vandalism, they have alerted the world to the dangers of religious extremism and the urgent need to counter it forcefully and effectively. 'The happenings in Afghanistan', maintains a Sahmat statement, 'are a clear demonstration of the threat that fundamentalism of all hues pose to the creativity, culture and civilisation of the world.'

Not so long ago, the Prophet of Islam conceived of the Muslim community as 'a single hand, like a compact world whose bricks support each other'. Mind you, Afghanistan is no *dar al-Islam* (land of Islam) or *dar al-aman* (land of peace). Nor are its leaders seeking to emulate and realize an Islamic religio-political vision. At best, this country is at war with itself. The enemy lies within its own borders. The Taliban use Islam as a weapon to suppress dissent, invoke the Islamic law to legitimize oppression against women, and employ the rhetoric of holy war to consolidate their authoritarian structures.

At the same time, it is worth remembering that religious extremism is not restricted to or inherent in any one religion. What happened in Bosnia-Herzegovina is fresh in everybody's mind. Similarly, what is happening in Israel is naked aggression on the rights of the Palestinian people.

Negotiating with the hotheaded zealots can most definitely be a nightmarish experience. What, then, is the way out? External intervention is ruled out, for it will harden attitudes and aid, as the Iranian experience illustrates, the cause of Islamic fundamentalism. The only hope lies in the willingness of the people in Afghanistan to overthrow the Taliban regime and organize its burial in the Central Bamiyan province itself, 125 km west of Kabul. For their own survival and the preservation of their own cultural heritage, they should perform the final rites. I realize this is easier said than done. Yet the world, which is on their side at this juncture, awaits their verdict against their rulers.

The challenge today is not to stereotype or project a monolithic threat but to distinguish between the life-patterns of the majority and a minority who justify their activities in the name of religion, caste, ethnicity or political ideology. It is therefore not surprising that the Muslim countries, including Pakistan and Muslim organizations all over the world, have condemned this act of barbarism perpetrated by the Taliban. Muslim scholars and politicians in India, too, have unequivocally expressed their anger and indignation. They realize the seriousness of the Taliban menace and how it endangers their own position in an otherwise pluralist society.

For these reasons, it is not fair to compare the destruction of the Babri Masjid with the ugly happenings in Afghanistan. Doubtless, what happened on the banks of the Sarju river in broad daylight was a heinous act. It was a brutal assault on India's *sanskriti*, its multi-cultural and multi-religious ethos that is best exemplified by Ustad Bismillah playing the *shehnai* at the Vishwanath Temple in Varanasi or the visitations of thousands of Hindus at the shrine of Khwaja Muinuddin Chishti. Yet, the vast majority of people in this society, then and now, are not wedded to the *Hindutva* agenda. Let's not forget that they rejected the *Sangh Parivar* in UP, the storm centre of the Hindu mobilization campaigns. Let us not forget that they are wedded to the preservation of our composite legacy. This is indeed what makes India different. This is surely what makes living in this country worthwhile.

I raise my voice against Hindu and Muslim extremism without the fear of being guillotined. This cannot happen in the Afghanistan of today. I invoke Gandhi and Nehru with unfailing regularity without the fear of reprisals from the BJP government. It is, indeed, the legacy of these outstanding men that fortifies our confidence in the survival of our democratic and secular republic.

7 March 2001

In Black and White

Do we know about the bedroom escapades of our past and present leaders? No, we don't. But here (in the United States) they do, as Kennedy's family and Bill Clinton discovered the hard way. Let me remind you of a 200-year-old controversy triggered by the newspaper editor, James T. Callender. Let me tell you, furthermore, that it continues to create a media firestorm. Scores of books and articles, as indeed a Merchant-Ivory film (Jefferson in Paris), take the reader from Montichello, an ideal plantation of the Old South at the end of the nineteenth century, to the court of France in the waning days of the reign of Louis XVI.

At the heart of the controversy are Sally Hemings (1773-1835), who was born a slave and died one, and her liaison with Thomas Jefferson, the third President of the United States. She serves, to the Afro-American intelligentsia at least, as a symbol of a society that oppressed women, ethnic minorities and the poor. She would have remained in obscurity, except for certain revelations that were confirmed in November 1998 when *Nature* magazine reported the DNA tests that strongly suggested Hemings giving birth to at least one child fathered by Jefferson at age 65, and possibly as many as six. As a result, for the first time in May last year, her 35-odd descendants were invited to a meeting of Jefferson's descendants at the Montichello estate in Charlottesville [Virginia]. As if this was not enough, a month ago more evidence was discovered, this time casting doubt on the claims of the descendants of Tom Woodson, who assert that Woodson was the product of the Hemings-Jefferson affair.

Charlottesville, the site of the DNA tests, stole the limelight once again. It had been the locus of yet another famous historical debate about identity: the mystery of Tsar Nicholas's supposedly long-lost daughter, Anastasia. DNA testing firmly established that Tsar Nicholas did not have a long-lost daughter. Or if he did, she was not Anna Anderson, the woman who lived in Charlottesville until the end of her life and who claimed that she was the child of Nicholas and Alexandra who had escaped the massacre of the Romanov family.

Thomas Jefferson was no ordinary mortal. He is a symbol of American Independence, the architect of the celebrated Declaration of Independence, the first of the three achievements memorialized on his tombstone. No wonder, despite the efforts of the Federalists and others opposed to him to keep the story of Jefferson and his slave mistress alive during the early nineteenth century, traditional Jefferson scholars assured readers that the reappearance of the 'ugly tales' was the result of politics. If Sally told the 'pathetic' and 'twisted' story, it was because she wanted to increase her own, her children's, and her family's self-esteem. In this way, they paid heed to their mentor's last request to a friend 'take care of me when dead'.

Not all agree. Their intransigence stems from a potent combination of adherence to white supremacy, class bias, and hero worship. Besides, they are simply ill equipped to see the humanity of blacks as equal to that of Jefferson and his white family. To them the honour of Jefferson is so important that they were to be given the benefit of every doubt no matter how unreasonable. The honour and dignity of Hemings and her family are, on the other hand, of little consequence. False heritages, as a scholar reminds us, are precisely what many people in society want and perhaps need. Didn't Jefferson himself proclaim: 'Falsehood will travel a thousand miles while Truth is putting on her boots.'

While the Hemings-Jefferson story is indeed the raw material of which scandals are made, there is more to this acrimonious debate. The mere possibility of such a relationship seems to stand in complete opposition to everything that Jefferson wrote, said and stood for. It is this evasion of truth and apparent breach in his character that has led to a serious reappraisal of Jefferson's character and personality.

A contributor to the *Journal of Negro History* underlined that the President preached against miscegenation but practised it. He condemned slavery but owned one of the largest slave populations in Virginia. Known to the world at large as the man who had once written all men are created equal, he wrote about racial difference, in literally, black and white terms, almost always to the detriment of black people. He considered the blacks to be inferior, not only to the whites, but also to the

American Indians. In his 'Notes on the State of Virginia', he denies the African's capacity to learn or love. Such writings contradict the liberating tone of his more publicised documents.

What about James T. Callender, the man who published the Hemings story, revealed a love affair of Alexander Hamilton, called George Washington a scandalous hypocrite, and labelled John Adams a hoary-headed incendiary? He is not in the dock anymore, but is not forgiven for attacking Jefferson, an American icon. He is not exonerated for accusing the Great Jefferson of having sexual relations with a black, the ultimate taboo in a land where social acceptability and racial purity go hand in hand. Moreover, the declaration of 'new truths' has created problems in the world of academia.

The fundamental problem is how to accommodate the new knowledge into Jefferson's biography and to recognize the difficulty some white Americans have in dealing with their own racial heritage, which may or may not include a dark-skinned ancestor. Many Afro-American writers, on the other hand, refuse to traverse the straight, wide, white road of American history.

All said and done, the DNA evidence is one of those tiny details, in itself conclusive of almost nothing. But when put together with the other evidence at hand, and when its implications are confronted, we can begin to see a new world, to craft new interpretations, to engage the past in new ways, and to ask the old questions anew.

In this way, adds the editors of a recently published book, 'all of us are the heirs of the world Sally and Jefferson created, engaged in the individual and collective enterprise of trying to make sense out of the world that they have bequeathed us'.

An inscription I read every morning outside the Cabel Hall in the University of Virginia, founded by Jefferson, reads: 'For here we are not afraid to follow the truth wherever it might lead, nor to tolerate any error so long as reason is left to combat it.' Will the HRD Ministry in Shastri Bhawan consider using this for their entrance?

5 April 2000

Victimhood of Vietnamese

'We are wallowing in mud, guts and blood over here and who cares?' one soldier wrote home during the height of the American involvement in Vietnam. He did not live long enough to witness the last day of the Republic of Vietnam, the end of a massive American evacuation operation, and the final chapter of an American tragedy. A journalist from aboard the *USS Mobile* reported in April 1975: 'Vietnam now will know a kind of peace. Whether the nation will tear itself apart in assessing guilt or adjust with compassion and develop a new sense of purpose— is another matter.'

This was 25 years ago. 'Nothing we did over there did any good', observed Darrell White, 25, who lost both his legs in a Viet Cong raid in 1969. Robert S. McNamara, former Secretary of Defence, endorses this view, though his belated admission is cold comfort to the families who lost their near and dear ones. Today, the images of that brutal war, including the My Lai (Songmy) massacre in November 1969, are blurred. Yes, the Americans are busy digging a crash site in a remote corner of Laos along the old Ho Chi Minh Trail. That is where the A-6 A went down on 29 September 1969. Families mourn their dead; their names etched, chronologically, in white on the polished granite of the Vietnam Veterans Memorial dominating Washington's Mall. But the rest are preoccupied with their chores, enjoying the fruits of a surging economy. America's real GDP grew up by an annual 6.3 per cent in the second half of 1999, unemployment is barely over 4 per cent, and consumer spending is booming.

In retrospect, the fall of Saigon, stated one commentator on the Public Television last week, appears to be a debacle but not a disaster. How many people have the time or inclination to reflect on a protracted, bloody and futile war in Vietnam? How many wish to know about the Promethean clash of colonialism, nationalism, communism and Americanism? Some people still count their dead or missing persons and mourn those promising lives snuffed out through ignorance, hatred and fear. But, as I walked past the Vietnam Veterans War Memorial, I wondered how many gave a thought to the 9,25,000 or more North Vietnamese and Viet Cong who laid down their lives to defend their freedom and sovereignty. There is no memorial for them in Washington or anywhere else in the US, though for their families the pain of disillusion and lost hopes, of tortured loyalties and shattered families, of guilt and grief, will burn for years.

What drove American leaders—from Harry Truman to Gerald Ford—was a domestic paranoia centred on a right-wing McCarthyite reaction, and, in his time, a bureaucratic monster that wanted to prove and improve itself and do the job of stopping communism. The Defence Department's 'Pocket Guide to Vietnam' stated that US troops were in Vietnam 'for the deeply serious business of helping a brave nation repel Communist invasion'. This may have satisfied the gullible, but the more thoughtful and more fully informed were not impressed. No country can build a political state for any other. In the end the war, based on misplaced assumptions, turned out to be all about death and destruction in the wake of aggression.

In June 1966, an overwhelming majority of Central Virginians polled by the newspaper, *Daily Progress*, favoured crushing North Vietnam to its knees even if it meant using more troops and bigger bombs. Soon thereafter, all hell broke loose when turmoil and convulsion erupted across the campuses. Violence escalated from coast to coast in the spring of 1968, with Columbia University being the focal point. Rioting was intensified in the spring of 1969, when Harvard and Cornell universities became centres of agitation, and disorders of the year before erupted again at Columbia. Students and youths wearing buttons and armbands, joined by a minority of their elders, took part in marches, rallies, religious services, vigils and readings of the names of Americans killed in Vietnam.

Here, in this seemingly benign University of Virginia, tempers were frayed as students joined the anti-war demonstrators. Two busloads of students went to Washington in the fall of 1967 and joined in the march to the Pentagon by some 75,000 others from throughout the nation. Stopping the 'war-machine' and disrupting the activity of the Pentagon were the aims of the demonstrations.

The bombing of Cambodia by President Nixon and the death

of four students at Kent State University aroused outrage and intensified unrest at Virginia and many other colleges and universities. A student leader in his comment reflected the mood, 'We must now resist to the hilt. These fists have to be clenched, and they have to be in the air. When they're opened we hope it's in friendship, not around the trigger guard of a rifle. But if we're not listened to, or if the issue is forced, they may well open triggerguards.' But the session of 1970-1 in Charlottesville witnessed a cooling of the revolutionary fires at Virginia.

In the spring of 1972, the Student Council at the University of Virginia protested against the stepped up bombing of Vietnam, but this was far milder than the riots at Harvard, the University of Maryland, and elsewhere. 'That about sums it up', states an official publication of the university. 'The university had survived the crisis of 1969-70, and Jeffersonian principles of academic freedom and freedom of speech had been kept inviolate.'

True, many institutions survived those tumultuous years. Yet the war, besides being highly controversial, had a profound impact on American polity and society. For one, the credibility of the system, especially the Presidency, was greatly eroded. 'We were the suckers, the pawns', said a soldier who won a Bronze Star and two purple hearts in Vietnam. Second, the massive demonstrations against the war radicalized campus life, bringing important issues of popular participation and democratic functioning to the fore.

Finally, it led to the slow but steady empowerment of Afro-Americans and women. Though grudgingly, many conservatives decided to throw open their establishment to the less privileged sections of society. Even as staunch defenders of the *status quo*, they knew that the policy of exclusion was not going to work in the post-Vietnam era. The other day, I met a couple of students close to Jefferson's magnificent Rotunda. One of them told me: 'It's always the old who lead us to the wars, it's always the young who fall, but I ain't gonna march anymore.' Then, he ambled off with a group of tourists on a tour of the grounds.

19 April 2000

PART II

*Where are They Gone,
the Glory and the Dream?*

Fables of Faith_____

> *Kha-pi ke ghar main baithye aur gaiye bhajan*
> *Kashi se jal, Pryag se amrood leejiye.*
>
> Relax and refresh yourself by singing bhajans,
> And by getting water from Banaras and guavas from Allahabad.

I bet you have not heard of Abdur Rahman of Bijnor, a graduate of the M.A.O. College at Aligarh, and his comment that, besides the *Divan-e Ghalib* (Collection of Ghalib's' poetry), the *Rig Veda* was India's revealed book. For some critics, this was blasphemy, pure and simple.

Thanks to Jagjit and Chitra Singh, most of you have heard of Ghalib. But do you know what he wrote about Kashi or Banaras? This is not all. Long before Bijnori and Ghalib, a great Sufi by the name of Syed Abdur Razzaq (1724-1836) lived in a tiny village called Bansa, in Awadh. Symbolizing the ecumenical traditions in the self-contained world of the Sufis, he took part in Diwali celebrations and watched *bakhtiyas* perform the life of Krishna. He had visions of Ram and Lakshman; and sometimes Krishna too would send his *salam*.

We know little about them, because they are remote from us in time. Let's, therefore, begin with the more familiar figure of Ghalib. In October 1827, he set out for Kolkata. Part of the way he travelled by river; and the final stage, from Banaras to Kolkata, he did on horseback. He reached Kolkata on 20 February 1828— almost a full year after he had set out from Delhi. Banaras particularly enchanted him; hence the long lyrical Persian poem of 108 couplets in its praise. It is entitled *Chiragh-e dair* ('The Lamp of the Temple'). The beauties of Banaras have 'their coquetry in a rose garden intoxicated and brim-full of blandishment; their graceful walking embraces the hundred turmoils of Judgement Day!' By contrast, Allahabad (Prayag) was a ghost city, dull and uninspiring, its people unfriendly and inhospitable. Such was his revulsion that he decided not to touch Allahabad on his journey back home.

Our poet, having rented a *haveli* at Sarai Naurangabad, spent a month in the city of Shiva. From its alleged founding in the sixth century BC, it had grown to be one of northern India's largest in early nineteenth century. The region, moreover, was one of the most densely populated on the subcontinent, more than twice as dense as any European country. Ghalib noticed the daily arrival of pilgrims seeking salvation, or taking part in seasonal fairs and eclipses. He enjoyed, as he sat down to write to friends, the paradise-like environment of natural beauty, the temple bells ringing, and the devotees walking hurriedly towards the Ganga. He felt invigorated by the salubrious climate, the forests along the river, the streams and waterways all through the city. His poetic description of the Ganga reveals, more than any other dimension, his patriotic revaluation of the country's common cultural and religious heritage.

In another long Persian poem Ghalib argues that the special customs of a country must not be destroyed. Rejecting infidelity (*rasm-e kufr*) was all very well, but rejecting the Divine Bounty made little sense. 'Negation without affirmation is nothing but error'; indeed, one cannot affirm God and deny His signs. Kashi was, thus, a 'sign' of God. Besides its all-India prominence as a centre for pilgrimage and worship, it was a microcosm of Indian life, customs and popular belief. It was indeed, so wrote Ghalib, the Kaaba of India. In his vie, 'If Ganga hadn't rubbed its forehead at the feet of Banaras, it wouldn't be pure. And if the sun hadn't sailed through its nooks and corners, it wouldn't be so bright.'

More than thirty years later Ghalib still remembered his stay with pleasure: 'What praise is too high for Banaras? Where else is there a city to equal it? The days of my youth were almost over when I went there. Had I been young in those days I would have settled down there and never come back this way.'

Finally, it is instructive to turn to Shah Abdul Razzaq of Bansa, a site of piety and devotion, and to observe the triumph with which he brought back, from his forays into the neighbouring districts, the 'Little Traditions' into his world view. He visited the Magh *mela* at Allahabad, interacted with the *jogis* and *bairagis*, joined the theatrical performances featuring popular stories about Krishna and the *gopis*, and often went into a state of ecstasy listening to Kabir's verses. In this dimension, the Hindu gods were also his friends and thereby the well wishers of all the disciples and followers amongst the Muslims as well. Two of his well-known disciples were Champat, the leaders of the *bairagis* from Awadh, Chaitram and Parasram.

A disciple of Champat, in fact, experienced a vision of Krishna after Shah Abdur Razzaq recited some Hindi *mantras*. On another occasion, his miracle made it possible for Parasram to feed his guests at a feast he had organized. The final story is located somewhere in the Deccan. Here, walking through a dense forest, Shah Abdul Razzaq met Ram and Lakshman near a pool (without knowing their identity). They treated him as their guest, offered him sweets, and left behind a lion and a bear under his protection. The next morning the two, leading a herd of cows and buffaloes, showed up and directed the Shah to the village. Later, when he returned to discover their identity, he found that they had disappeared. Their disappearance confirmed his belief that they were, in fact, the great Ram and Lakshman. Indeed, the Shah believed that the two had fully realized their essential oneness with the Divine Being in whose likeness they were made.

The historian's task is not to speculate on what might have been. His duty is to show what happened and why. I have tried to do so. Some of the other key question, i.e. the causes for the erosion of composite values and the rise of religious-based identities, can barely be answered in this essay. Yet, I share these stories with you, hoping that you will be sensitized to our plural heritage, and not be misled by the rhetoric of Hindu and Muslim fundamentalists. There is plenty for you to do. Please remember what Akbar Allahabadi (1846-1921) had to say:

> I say the same to Hindus and the Muslims.
> Be good, each, as your faith would have you be.
> The world's a rod? Then you become as water.
> Clash like the waves, but still remain one sea.

26 June 2001

Composite Heritage of the Qasbahs_____

Qasbah has no English equivalent. The generally accepted picture is of a place with a distinct urban status that possessed a mosque, a public bath and a judicial officer (*qazi*). As such, it was more than 'a geographical expression'. Moreover, as a product of economic and political dynamics and in its ethos and cultural manifestation, the *qasbah* as an entity did not exist outside Awadh.

The historian C.A. Bayly traces the evolution and significance of *qasbahs*, and sensitizes us to the entrenched position of the 'Islamic gentry' in the smaller *qasbah* and their role in transmitting Islamic learning. Put simply, in these units, gentry families—soldiers, administrators, scholars, theologians and Sufis—lived not as socially unified communities, but as aggregates of sub-communities. Just as Christianity played a fundamental part in developing the associational make-up of city life in Europe, so did Islam in the *qasbah* life in Awadh without, of course, disturbing its social equilibrium.

What needs to be underlined is the composite heritage of the *qasbahs*, to delineate how they formed an important background to, and produced a favourable environment for, the steady emergence of liberal and secular convictions. I also wish to suggest that the *qasbahs* predisposed *ashraf*, or gentry families, to the rational and ethical dimensions of Islam. Some of them thus became typical carriers of moral and ethical piety in urban areas. In their devotion and selfless service, they mirrored the values associated with *qasbati* living. Sliding into a world of new issues and diverted to new preoccupations, they commented on social issues—on women's education and the abolition of the *purdah* system, for example.

The point to stress is that such men lived, contrary to popular supposition, in *qasbahs* and not just in the sprawling urban centres, and that their world view was shaped by their local rather than a regional or a more cosmopolitan pan-Indian experience. Thus, Syed Mohammad Baqar, a *rais* of Ahrauli but married into a Rudauli-based Syed family, supported girl's education, called upon the Congress to focus on such pressing issues, and appealed to its leaders to desist from frittering away its energy pursuing anti-government polices. The Lucknow-based journalist-essayist, Abdul Halim Sharar, wrote strongly against Muslim women observing *purdah*. Later, Mohammad Ali, a *taluqdar* of considerable stature from Rudauli, joined the ranks of such enthusiasts. His example as one of the influential men in Bara Banki district did, it was thought, sway the attitude of his more conservative fellow-*taluqdars* towards girl's education and *purdah*.

This is not all. Proponents of socialist and communist ideas from the 1930s onward were often drawn from *qasbah*-based families. Whether the *sharif* upbringing of the *qasbah* families, with its emphasis on acquiring knowledge and observing a degree of austerity, did actually engrain in the 'Muslim socialists' universal humanist values or not is hard to ascertain. What is clear is the enunciation of socialist ideas by, say, Mushir Hosain Kidwai, the *taluqdar* of Gadia in Bara Banki. The Urdu poet, Syed Fazlul Hasan (Hasrat) of Mohan in Unnao district, emphasized that no struggle against exploitation and oppression can overlook the contribution of Marx and the Marxists, and the values brought to the forefront by communism in a form that has not been surpassed.

Quite a few liberal-radicals also belonged to Shia families. While the Shia claims implying an automatic progression from Shiism to liberalism or socialism is dubious for the simple reason that among their 'inherent' beliefs were those derived from a variety of sources and not just from their own 'basic' cultural norms. Yet, this fortification of the Shia tradition itself merits a proper explanation. It is doubtless true that Imam Husain's martyrdom at the bank of the Euphrates in Karbala, in AD 680, has become a powerful, enduring, and evocative symbol of resistance to tyranny. 'I opened my eyes', recalled the Balrampur-born Urdu poet, Ali Sardar Jafri, 'in the shadows of knowledge and *tazia*. The first sound I heard was that of lamentation and mourning of the martyrdom of Husain. When I came of age, I found the whole world was a house of mourning.'

Behind the façade of a benign existence, deep-seated tensions afflicted *qasbah* society. The *ashraf* groups themselves did not act in concert as a unified community, divided as they were by hierarchy, status, and family feuds. They had complex, parallel, and interlocking interests that were expressed via different social networks. Besides, they were plagued by mental laziness, an extravagant lifestyle, internecine family disputes over property leading to endless litigation, and loss of land caused by huge debts.

Taking Mohammad Baqar as an example, we can see the difficulties experienced by *ashraf* families threatened by pauperization. His ancestor, a petty landowner in Ahrauli, headed for Gorakhpur to take up a judicial appointment in the British court. But the fortunes of his family changed owing to disputes over property. Basharat Ali resigned from his government job in 1885 and returned to Ahrauli. The court case dragged on for years, and was ultimately decided against him. The biter experiences of the family may well have led Baqar to comment, with a touch of irony and sarcasm, on the *qasbah* life, its value system, and the degenerative lifestyle of the local elites.

Max Weber stressed that honourable persons are expected to be above the claims of power, based on mere wealth. In order for economically powerful persons to become honourable, they have to display an honorific style of life. Baqar defines, at the beginning of the twentieth century, the content of piety and appropriate styles of life in a *qasbati* social milieu. He may well have established, unwittingly of course, the important connections between status groups, styles of religiosity, everyday status activities and the *qasbah*.

Today, terms like *qasbah* or a *qasbati* culture do not convey the same meaning. *Qasbah* as a social and cultural entity is, in fact, not only a lost idea but has also vanished without leaving any substantial legacy behind it. Yet the *qasbah* has to be reinstated in our discourse to understand the confluence of ideas and movements, and to capture the continuum of high and low points in its histories. Hence, it is important to explore at least one principal facet of *qasbati* living—the ideology of pluralism, and its strength in uniting different sections of society.

Our students should be told how landed groups and service families built a partnership in the late nineteenth and early twentieth centuries to manage their lives, and how they invested into strategies of collective action where mutual commitments overshadowed distinctive identities, outlooks, and communitarian pursuits.

30 May 2001

Syed Ahmad Khan's Unfinished Agenda

> A thousand hues mingle as the wine cup goes round
> A thousand attires come and go as the ages unfold
> But that smoke-cloud of sandal and flower
> A handful of spring in the bower
> (Now) remains unfettered
> The meadows of paradise;
> The life-arrow shot from eternity's womb
> A prisoner, from the direction enclosed
> Has slipped far, far away, and
> Become a quest.

In the 1860s, Syed Ahmad Khan (1817-98) made a tryst with his co-religionists to change their image in the eyes of the colonial government, and sensitize them to the importance of Western education.

The Syed was a leading educationist and reformer. His scholarly works, for which he received recognition from the Royal Asiatic Society of Great Britain and Ireland in 1864, were equally impressive. For a man born into a feudal family that had experienced the trauma of the declining Mughal empire, he was highly pragmatic and realistic in his orientation and attitudes. For a man tutored in Islamic learning, he was remarkably broad-minded and forward-looking. A visible symbol of Muslim re-generation and a catalyst of social and educational reforms, he possessed the intellectual resources to reconcile matters of faith with the more immediate task of rescuing Muslims from their downward spiral. He laid emphasis on interpretation and not conformity, on innovation rather than on blind acceptance of the Islamic Law. Like some of his counterparts in Egypt and Turkey, he set high value on the social morality of Islam and justified the adoption of Western ideas and institutions in Islamic terms as being not the introduction of something new but to return to the spirit of Islam. The practical implications, which the new ideas from the West justified, were more closely related to Indian circumstances. They were not to live as the British themselves lived, but to carve out a place for themselves within the establishment. It was necessary not to imitate the West but to accept only some of its values as at least a second-best substitute for the vanished Muslim glories.

With his sharp analytical mind and his acute sense of the working of historical forces, the Syed recognized change and movement in history. He knew his Islamic history well, but he knew his Islam even better. He could thus comprehend the scale and depth of reform ideas and currents, identify elements of change and continuity, and discover a sound theoretical basis for a constructive dialogue with the West. The conclusion he drew and the message he communicated were directed against the theologian's ill-founded assumptions about the West and ill-informed criticism of his own project. He describes in a letter to a friend how, after 1857, he became concerned for the reform and education of his community in the modern sciences and in the English language. Despairing of existing commentaries and their preoccupation with trivia, he 'deliberated on the Quran itself and tried to understand from it the principles on which its composition is based'. He found, just as his contemporary Mohammad Abduh did in Egypt, that if Koranic principles were adopted there will remain no incompatibility between modern sciences and Islam. He tried to resolve the difficulties inherent in the four traditional sources of Muslim law by a dialectical, rationalist exegesis of the Koran. He scrutinized the classical data of the *Hadith* (Traditions of the Prophet), and placed emphasis on *ijtehad* as the inalienable right of every individual Muslim. Finally, he rejected the principal of *ijma* (consensus) in the classical sense that confined it to the Muslim theologians.

Syed Ahmad did not waver in his belief in the eternal truth of Islam and the capacity of the Muslims to rise to the pinnacle of human greatness. All that he wanted was to build a bridge that would connect his faith with this new science. In a speech at Lahore in 1884, he argued: 'Today we are, as before, in need of a modern *ilm-al-kalam*, by which we should either refute the doctrines of the modern sciences or undermine their foundations, or show that they are in conformity with the articles of Islamic faith.' The axiom of his theology was: 'The Work of God (Nature and its fixed laws) is identical with the Word of God (Koran).' So that the aim of his college, stated Mohamed Ali, a distinguished product of the Aligarh College, was 'to create for young Musalmans a centre with the true Islamic atmosphere, so that its alumni would not merely be educated and cultured men, but educated and cultured Musalmans'.

The ideal that Syed Ahmad placed before himself, when framing the scheme of the Muslim University, is best expressed in his own words. 'Science', he said, 'shall be in our right hand and philosophy in our left; and on our head shall be the crown of "There is no God but Allah and Mohammad is his Apostle".' To him, every word of the Koran is, both word and meaning, the Word of Allah revealed to the Prophet of Islam. Such was his conviction that he even denied the intermediation of Gabriel. He stated, 'I desire not a Koran as a message from the Trusty Gabriel. The Koran that I possess is altogether the discourse of the Beloved.'

And yet several Muslim theologians denounced him as a heretic, apostate, or atheist. He was abused as a *Nechari* (Urduized form of Naturist), and fiercely attacked for demythologizing the Koran. One of his aunts refused to see him 'on account of his taking too kindly to the culture of the foreigner and the infidel'. One of his prominent detractors travelled to Mecca to secure religious decrees condemning both Syed Ahmad's religious views and anyone who would aid such a heretic in starting a college. But, in the long run, the Aligarh reformer's efforts paid off. A new generation of Muslims who, having been alienated by the formalism of the traditional theologians, became convinced that pursuing modern education would vindicate rather than undermine the message of Islam. In fact, Syed Ahmad's formulation of the doctrine in modern instead of medieval terms inspired the newly-emergent Muslim bourgeoisie to emulate his example and found educational centres modelled on the Aligarh College. Thus a Madarasatul-Islam in Sind and the Dacca College were set up; the latter, like Aligarh, gained university status after the First World War. The Muhammadan Educational Conference, which the Syed founded in 1887, held annual meetings in different cities and afforded opportunities for exchange of though and propagation of reforming ideas. Following its conference at Madras in 1901, the Muslim Educational Association of South India was established.

Mohamed Ali noted in 1923 that 'when the dust of controversy is laid a little more, Islam in India would recognise the worth of Syed Ahmad Khan. . . . His militant rationalism, even if it gave rise to violent controversy, roused the Muslims out of their stagnant complacency'. His prophecy was fulfilled. Sections of the Muslim intelligentsia broke loose from the shackles of orthodoxy and continued the cause of reforms and reinterpretation of orthodox doctrines. Thus the historian Ameer Ali followed the Aligarh reformer in advancing modern concepts for reorienting the structure of Islamic social and religious thought, and in drawing a distinction between the moral precepts and the specifically legal Koranic provisions. In a moving tribute to his intellectual mentor, Altaf Husain Hali, poet and biographer of Syed Ahmad, wrote:

The world has seen how one man has aroused a whole land, one man saved a caravan from destruction.... True it is that there is a dearth of men in our nation, and if the fragments of broken vessels are piled high, yet among them lie fragments of jewels concealed. Hidden among the gravel there are pearls to be found; and mingled in the sand are particles of gold.

In his 'Preparatory Years', Syed Ahmad unveiled to the young Abul Kalam Azad the true spirit of the Koran. Comparing him with the Bengali reformer Raja Rammohun Roy, Azad emphasized that by challenging traditional values and outmoded beliefs the Syed represented the forces of change. 'The battle was fought here in Aligarh and Aligarh is the visible embodiment of the victory of the forces of progress', he declared. And in his own endeavour to cement the bonds of Hindu-Muslim unity, the Maulana was inspired by Syed Ahmad's example who used the metaphor that Hindus and Muslims were the two eye's in Mother India's face. Mohammad Iqbal, too, described him as 'the first modern Muslim to catch a glimpse of the positive character of the age that was coming'. He was 'the first Indian Muslim who felt the need for a fresh orientation of Islam and worked for it'.

The Aligarh College was, in reality, the visible embodiment of the victory of the forces of progress. New schools of research, interpretation and reconstruction of Muslim thought developed in what was then a sleepy town, 80 miles from Delhi on the Grand Trunk Road. Never before in South Asian Islam did so many poets, writers and scholars congregate at one place and in one generation. The college was the site where the creative genius of several Muslim scholars flowered. It was here that movements of reform were consummated. A typical Aligarh version of reform, based on nineteenth-century liberalism and humanism, grew up in opposition to the orthodox stream represented by the theological seminary at Deoband. Zakir Husain, a long-serving Vice-Chancellor of the Aligarh University, claimed in 1955: 'The way Aligarh works, the way Aligarh thinks, the contribution Aligarh makes to Indian life . . . will largely determine the place Mussalmans will occupy in the pattern of Indian life.' Such a claim will not stand the test of historical scrutiny, though it does indicate the importance attached to the university in the intellectual resurgence of the Muslim communities in the subcontinent.

I have briefly outlined Syed Ahmad's reformist concerns for three principal reasons. First of all, I wish to underline the significance of placing the intellectual history of Indian Islam on the curriculum of academic institutions in the West. If we are concerned to understand the historical evolution of Islamic societies, we need to explore areas outside the Arabian Peninsula. If we are concerned to change the stereotypical images of Islam and its followers, perpetuated by scholars like Samuel Huntington in recent years, we must come to terms with the histories of the Muslim communities in the subcontinent. Finally, if Western countries have a stake in liberal and secular ideas, they must try to unmask the liberal face of Islam, pay heed to the liberal voices, and explore the complex interplay of modernist ideas with traditionalist thought in Muslim societies. By the same token, liberal and democratic regimes and not feudal and authoritarian governments need the backing of the West.

Research on Muslims is still mired within traditional frameworks and dominated by widely accepted stereotypes. The existing categories have been questioned but not changed; consequently, ideas and movements associated with Muslims are classified as revivalist rather than reformist, communal rather than secular, separatist rather than nationalist and, finally, reactionary rather than progressive. In this scheme, Syed Ahmad Khan and his associates are dismissed as 'separatist', a pejorative expression used for those not conforming to majoritarian nationalism. The stereotypical figure of Syed Ahmad as the architect of Muslim separatism, mesmerized by the British, remains unaffected by his contribution to the making of a Muslim renaissance in the last quarter of the nineteenth century. Thus the political scientist, Partha Chatterjee, devotes just a few lines to Syed Ahmad and his associates in his oft-quoted book *Nationalist Thought and the Colonial World*. Similarly, with the notable exception of Gail Minault, the American historian, the pioneering role of some of his notable contemporaries in reforming Muslim women finds little mention in conventional or unconventional histories and critiques of nationalism.

The Muslim intelligentsia must share the blame for neglecting a rich and vibrant legacy. The intellectual energy released by Syed Ahmad and the 'first generation' of Aligarh students lost its momentum once the Muslim elites, jockeying for positions in the colonial state, became more and more concerned with creating an organizational base for staking their claims in the newly-emerging power structures. The ambition of an average student, drawn from the landed classes and the upper bourgeoisie, was to join the 'heaven-born'. His pride was soothed, thanks to early pan-Islamic stirrings, by being reminded that he was a unit in the great democracy of Islam, and in witness of this brotherhood he jauntily wore the Turkish fez on his head. The traditional curricula at the college, with emphasis on fidelity to the raj and the social origins of its students, bred a sectarian milieu. Hence, while the Hindu bourgeoisie in Bengal and Maharashtra took to liberal ideas, the Muslim communities in general took comfort from time-honoured aristocratic values. Thus, despite the apparent similarities in curricula, not only was education much less broad-based for the Muslims but it did not always favour the growth of liberal ideas. Aligarh produced, for the most part, cautious pedagogues instead of a few thinkers of surpassing boldness. There appeared a cloud, to borrow Clifford Geertz's expression, of not very distinguished and usually rather unoriginal academics.

The few who possessed the skills to address issues of reform were unable to correct colonial stereotypes or stir a discussion comparable in depth and vigour to the debates outlined in Albert Hourani's incisive book *Arabic Thought in the Liberal Age*. Part of the reason was their self-image as part of a community—a monolithic *umma*—that remained, or was normatively expected to remain, the same across divisions in space and time. This theme was often powerfully expressed across a number of elite scholastic factions, especially of Sunni Islam, for whom Sufi and syncretic practices and Shia beliefs in general, were just so many deviations from the norm. Time and again the theme of eternal and unmitigated Hindu-Muslim hostility was echoed. So also the view that internal differences among groups of Hindus and/or Muslims were secondary and irrelevant to the more fundamental religious cleavage.

Muslim intellectuals—from Lahore to Dacca—did not examine such convictions in the light of their normal way of living. Had they done so, they would have discovered simple evidence of great internal political, moral and social tensions and their disruptive effects. In this way, they would have understood themselves better and made their conduct and behaviour intelligible to others. By the time Syed Ahmad came of age, they were either busy bemoaning the departed glory of Islam or lamenting the eclipse of the Mughal empire. Some decided to wage a futile holy war against the British; others were engaged in deciding whether India was a land of war or peace. Inspired by the successors of Shah Waliullah, such debates, conducted in the framework of medieval scholasticism, were sterile and inconsequential, more so at a time when the Mughal empire had collapsed beyond redemption and the imperial edifice was already firmly in place in many critical regions. Arguably, the debates were inconsequential because the Muslim elites and their interlocutors were left with no choices. They had to come to terms with the raj not as privileged but as colonized citizens. In other words, they had to negotiate with its representatives, regardless of their hostility and prejudices, and accept the reality of the hegemonic presence of an imperial power. Whatever the Muslim apologists might say, the reality is that the Muslim intelligentsia before Syed Ahmad and the 'Aligarh movement' were intellectually ill-equipped to read the writings on the wall.

Historical works produced during the last quarter of the nineteenth century were mostly of uneven quality, and limited in scope and conception. Most writers and publicists, including the scholar Shibli Nomani, a professor at the Aligarh College, dwelt on the history of Islam in the Arab world and not on the richness and bewildering variety of Islam in India, and its composite and pluralist features. Some others were preoccupied with the purity of their racial pedigree to the exclusion of other issues, including the impoverishment, indebtedness and socio-economic backwardness of their community. Most were insensitive to Muslims being converted to Islam at different times and for different reasons. They failed to comprehend their commonality of interests with the non-Muslims, and erred in foisting Islamist ideas on, say, the Meos of Mewat, the Jats in south-east Punjab or the Moplahs on the Malabar coast. Indeed, most were hopelessly out of tune with the ground realities when they whipped up religious passions, in much the same way as the Hindu nationalists did over the Babri Masjid nearly five decades later, around the Khilafat symbol. An average Muslim was misled into believing that the future of Islam rested on the protection of a corrupt, decadent and ineffectual institution. Eventually, the leadership itself was put to shame when the Turks abolished the Khilafat and sent the Khalifa packing to a distant land where he died in anonymity. *Chaak kar di Turk-i-Nadaan ne Khilafat ki Qaba*, is all that Iqbal could say to express his solidarity with his aggrieved community.

Incidentally, Syed Ahmad was the only prominent Muslim to dispute the claims of Sultan Abdul Hamid II, the Khalifa of Turkey. Though condemned by Jamaluddin Afghani for being candid in rejecting pan-Islamism, Syed Ahmad was the first to recognize that the pan-Islamic stir, though in its embryonic form in the 1890s, threatened to wreck his effort to prop up the Anglo-Muslim alliance in India. He wanted to cut the silver chord which tied Muslims to the so-called international fraternity, spoke against the Turcophilia among Muslims, and argued that they were legally bound to obey the writ not of an external Khalifa but of the British Indian government. The logic of his argument was simple enough: India's Muslims had to carve out a destiny within the Indian environment and not turn to an alien power and authority for their moral or religious sustenance.

All said and done, there were important lessons to be learnt from the Syed's warnings against the pan-Islamic tendencies, and from the imminent collapse of the Khilafat movement in 1922. But the Khilafatists, caught up in their own dilemmas and predicaments and misled by the romantic vision of a unified Muslim community from North Africa to Indonesia, threw to the winds all the caution they had learnt at the feet of their mentor. Some realized their mistakes belatedly, but the damage had already been done. A false sense of community identity was heightened which came in handy two decades later when Jinnah, taking advantage of the political landscape during the Second World War and the complacency and hot-headedness of the Congress leaders, changed his political trajectory to demand a separate Muslim nation. The Khilafat movement, which was simply out of tune with Syed Ahmad's agenda, had led to Hindu-Muslim antipathies. The Pakistan movement, despite what historians ranging from I.H. Qureshi to Akbar Ahmad might say, polarized Indian society along religious lines for the first time in its history and destroyed, once and for all, the unity and continuity of a rich and vibrant Indo-Muslim civilization.

Finally, let me turn to the tendency—more pronounced in the subcontinent than elsewhere—to establish that Syed Ahmad was the progenitor of a 'Muslim nation'. Though his appropriation by the ideologues of the two-nation theory and the historians of Pakistan carries no conviction to me, let us briefly consider his political concerns.

It is, at first, hard to make sense of Syed Ahmad's fiery denunciation of the Congress. Hindu-Muslim unity was, after all, close to his heart and a constant refrain in his public utterances. In 1873, he declared that he did not care for religion to be regarded as the badge of nationhood. Common territory, he argued, imposed upon Indians the obligation of mutual co-operation in order to ensure the common good. He advocated separation between matters religious and political. Spiritual and religious matters, he asserted, cannot have any connection with worldly affairs. A true religion only stated cardinal principles comprising ethical values and only incidentally dealt with worldly problems. In 1884, he made clear that by the word '*qaum*' (nation/community), he meant both Hindus and Muslims. In his opinion, 'it matters not whatever be their religious belief, because we cannot see anything of it; but what we see is that all of us, whether Hindus or Muslims, live on one soil, are governed by one and the same ruler, have the same sources of benefits, and equally share the hardships of a famine'.

The Aligarh reformer was no religious bigot or Hindu baiter. He was more tolerant and broad-minded than many of the early Congress leaders. Having worked closely with Hindus in the Scientific Society, the Aligarh British Indian Association and the United Patriotic Association, communal concerns did not figure in his favourite college project. If anything, his scheme was, in the words of Mohamed Ali, 'open to all religions, communities and denominations and absolutely free from the taint of religious or racial tastes'. He sought and secured generous support from Hindu rajas and zamindars and made sure that leading Hindus were well represented in the managing committee and among the teachers. Hindu students even outnumbered Muslims in some of the early years of the college; cow-slaughter was banned as a concession to their religious susceptibilities.

Syed Ahmad's political concerns were no less secular; in fact, there was very little in his early attitudes to suggest that he wanted separate and favoured treatment for the Muslims. He was the first to argue that the 1857 upsurge had been caused by the monumental indifference of the East India Company to the economic plight of the masses, and the failure to grant Indians some form of advisory representation in the council. He supported local self-government and the right of Indian judges to try English defendants. He wrote, moreover, in defence of Indians entering the Indian covenanted civil service and revived the British Indian Association at Aligarh to join the campaign to restore the age of entrance for the civil service examination from nineteen to twenty-one.

If so, how does one explain the Syed's outburst against the Congress in 1887 and thereafter? Many explanations already exist. My own understanding is that the Syed's arguments against the Congress were not his own, and that he was in large part influenced by Theodore Beck, the 'pretty young man with pink cheeks and blue eyes', who joined the Aligarh College as its Principal in 1884.

Beck, a radical of sorts as an undergraduate at Trinity College, Cambridge, matured to become a hard-headed Tory in India. He was averse to Gladstonian Liberalism, suspicious of the Congress intentions and hostile to those British politicians and civil servants that were soft towards Indian aspirations. W.S. Blunt, William Digby, Samuel Smith and John Slagg were 'cranks who united on India'; Richard Temple, W.C. Plowden, Richard Grath and Charles Turner were 'men of danger' and 'the dupes of every impudent journalistic liar'; W.W. Hunter was 'a notorious humbug'.

Beck's mission was to stamp out 'sedition' in order to bolster imperial rule. For this, he assiduously cultivated Muslims to create a 'strong conservative school of thought' and complete a breach between them and the Bengali-dominated Congress. He kept his students on a tight leash, herded the scattered elements of opposition to the Congress into the United Patriotic Association, prompted some students to congregate at Delhi's Jama Masjid to collect signatures for an anti-Congress petition to Parliament, and kept on feeding the *Pioneer* and the government with anti-Congress reports. He thus foresaw the emergence of a gigantic Muslim organization in upper India with a distinct political creed. This would naturally suit the government, 'which will have some people to defend it. . . . We shall have a body of men bent on rooting out the fallacies of the [Congress] argument.'

The college was peripheral to Beck's concerns, because political affairs 'swallowed up' much of his time. Ignoring accusations of dereliction of duty, he took pride in having 'a finger in every pie'. He could, therefore, boast that there were 'very few Englishmen in the country so well up as myself in the Congress business'. 'I am more excited about this blessed Congress', he wrote to his mother in April 1888, 'than about anything else. . . . It seems likely this Congress will create a great stir in this part of India, and I shouldn't be surprised if some jolly good rows occur. The opposition has got well on its legs.'

Beck goaded Syed Ahmad into taking anti-Congress postures. After the Syed's now famous Meerut speech, he gleefully recorded: 'We have played off our 81 ton gun against the Congress again.' The ageing Syed, in turn, could hardly match the young Principal's boundless energy and passion, and lived up to his expectations of playing the anti-Congress drum loud and clear. In addition to being disturbed by the rising tide of Hindu nationalism, manifested in the activities of the Arya Samaj, the Hindi Pracharini Sabhas and the anti-cow slaughter bodies, he dependend on government's support for keeping the college flag flying.

Yet, Aligarh's first generation students, brought up under Syed Ahmad's influence and tutored incessantly on the virtues of loyalty to the raj, were not all cut out of the same cloth. Soon after his death, some moved into the political arena with a fresh ideological disposition, a distinct style of politics and a new ideological orientation. They repudiated the political legacy of the sage from Aligarh, though some pointed out that their radical temper was consistent with the intentions of their mentor. Mohamed Ali, for example, announced in an Urdu verse:

> It is you who had taught the community all this 'mischief'
> If we are its culmination, you are its commencement.

In a career spawning more than three decades, Syed Ahmad made concessions to his own detractors and, more importantly, capitulated far too readily before his British patrons. He became an uncritical admirer of Western culture and civilization, especially after his visit to England in 1869-70, and was insensitive to the disruptive role of British colonialism. He would have surely known what was being said and written by the early nationalists on the British exploitation of the people and the country's wealth, but he chose not to comment or reflect on such matters.

At the same time, the hallmark of his public role was the exemplary courage, which so few Muslims in the nineteenth century displayed in their public conduct, in pursuing his educational mission. He could have settled for a cosy but lazy life in one of the *havelis* of Delhi, revelled in the glory of a bygone Mughal past, and felt at ease in Delhi's vibrant cultural life in the company of poets like Ghalib. Instead, he chose the rough terrain, the dusty road to Aligarh, to leave his imprint on the city, the State and the nation. Imbued with a vision and sense of idealism, he raised hopes among his compatriots who had decided to stew in its own juice following the suppression of the 1857 revolt. He fortified their confidence at a time when the favourite pastime of some of Syed Ahmad's close friends, depressed and frustrated by their loss of power and privileges, was to bemoan the ebb and flow of Islam. He moved with the times, responded to the winds of change, and urged his community to seize the opportunities, howsoever limited, grudgingly offered by British rule.

It is tempting to judge Syed Ahmad by our standards and to

enumerate his limitations and inadequacies. Such a temptation
needs to be resisted if we wish to locate the history of ideas in
their proper context. After all, the Aligarh reformer was neither
a revolutionary nor did he live in revolutionary times. Therefore,
he should be remembered for what he accomplished under
difficult circumstances and what he set out to do. Doubtless,
his agenda relating to social reforms, education and gender
empowerment was limited, but, then, he was confronted with
the combined opposition of the theologians and the Muslim
elites. The Muslim bourgeoisie was too small in numbers to be
pressed into service to organize or lead a reform movement. It
was, furthermore, distrustful of the British, apprehensive of the
Congress designs, and firmly committed to an Islamist framework.
These factors would have imposed severe constraints on Syed
Ahmad's mission to plot a bold, reformist trajectory. For this and
other reasons, he could not have operated, even if he desired
to, from the vantage point occupied by social reformers like
Raja Rammohun Roy or Iswar Chandra Vidyasagar.

Syed Ahmad's legacy lives on after Independence. The Aligarh
Muslim University he founded ran into rough weather for a
decade after Partition, but it has expanded vastly thereafter. Its
graduates, once tempted to seek employment in neighbouring
Pakistan, are now comfortably placed in business, industry and
the professions in India and in other parts of the globe. Go to a
district town in UP and you see the familiar sight of BA (Alig.).
Travel to Birmingham or Cleveland and you are sure to find the
Aligarh Old Boys' Association listed in the telephone directory.
Here and elsewhere, far removed from the humdrum of campus
life, the 'Aligarians' regard themselves as a close-knit community.
Whether in Sydney or in Toronto, they congregate each year
on 17 October to celebrate 'Sir Syed Day'. They fraternize with
each other, and revive memories and associations of the years
spent in Sir Syed, Viqarul Mulk or the Mohsinul Mulk Hall. In
short, there is great pride in being part of Aligarh's old boys
network.

Aligarh has negotiated with its past and succeeded in creating
a niche for itself in the country's academic structures. But, as
its alumni celebrate the centenary year of their founder this

year, they face the uphill task of preparing the fraternity of teachers and students to meet the challenges of the next millennium. They need to complete Syed Ahmad's unfinished agenda of fostering liberal and modernist ideas and take the lead, once and for all, in debating issues of education, social reforms and gender justice. They need to interpret Islam afresh in the light of worldwide intellectual currents, come to terms with the winds of change, guide the 120 million Muslims within the framework provided by India's democratic and secular Constitution, and equip them to cope with the harsh realities of life. This is what the great visionary Syed Ahmad would have expected them to do.

With the Jamia Millia Islamia, its closest counterpart, unable to rise to the occasion during its lazy existence since Independence, they can no longer settle for a cosy life. Marshall Hodgson observed over two decades ago, 'the problem of the Muslims of India is the problem of the Muslims in the world'.

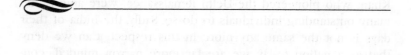

Ghalib and his More Tolerant Times

Unlike the Hindu and Christian traditions, sensual pleasure in this world is commended in Islam when it occurs within the bounds of legitimate union. The pursuit of pleasure within the defined limits is indeed enjoined by Koranic verses and by the statements of the Prophet. A number of holy texts repeat the contention that sexual pleasure in this world is merely a foretaste of pleasure to come in heaven. All in all, paradise is the realm of pleasure so accentuated as to be perpetual and consummate, so much so that it is said that the blessed do not sleep, for fear slumber may divert them from their pleasurable occupations.

Tired by the coverage of America's sabre-rattling and arrogance over Iraq [this refers to the Gulf war] and weary of the murky happenings back home, I turned to the Muslim Paradise narratives in the Arab world. I scratched my head to recall what the Urdu poet Mirza Ghalib had to say on the subject. My reading sensitized me to our appalling ignorance of the variety of views and interpretations of Islamic tenets. Those of you who are sometimes swayed by the Islamists or the Hindu polemicists are probably not even aware of the disjunction between the formal ideology of Islam and the day-to-day beliefs and practices of Muslims. Many do not recognize the simple fact that large segments of the Muslim population have been integrated with other communities and that their views and responses are far more complex and diverse than the statements found within the corpus of received opinions on the subject.

Second, lessons are to be learnt from the ease with which some sections of the Muslim intelligentsia in the second half of the nineteenth century questioned and challenged inherited knowledge and conventional wisdom. Ghalib and Syed Ahmad Khan, who pioneered the Delhi Renaissance, were among the many outstanding individuals to do so. Sadly, the India of their days is not the same any more in this respect. Can we deny that as a nation today we are far more narrow-minded, conservative and intolerant than ever before?

This is not the occasion to lament or bemoan the decline in our intellectual values, but I certainly want to ask in passing why a sixteenth century mosque was destroyed in broad daylight? Why did the weight of Muslim orthodoxy stifle the liberal viewpoint on the Shah Bano issue [the controversy generated by the grant of maintenance to a divorced woman]? Why was a professor [this refers to the agitation against me for my remarks on the banning of Salman Rushdie's *Satanic Verses*] banished from his university for over four years?

To illustrate Ghalib's notion of Paradise, I quote just the three verses; I leave the rest to your imagination.

Hum ko maaloom hai jannat ki haqiqat lekin,
Dil ko khush rakhne ko Ghalib ye khayal achchha hai

I know the truth, but, be that what it will,
The thought of Paradise beguiles me still.

Sunte hain jo behisht ki taariph sab durust
Lekin, khuda kare wo tera jalwa-gaah ho

All that they say of paradise is true, and yet
God grant it be illumined by your radiance.

And, on a lively note, notice the following:

Wo cheez, jis ke liye hum ko ho behisht aziz
Sewaye baada-i gulfaam-i mushkboo kya hai?

For what else should I value Paradise
If not the rose-red wine, fragrant with musk?

Nobody knows whether Ghalib is enjoying his red wine or
not, but we are certainly regaled by his exquisite poetry, his
distinctive style, his universalism and humanism, his defiance of
authority, his repudiation of established traditions and conventions, and his irrepressible and unabashed sense of humour.

Born exactly two centuries ago in Agra but settled in Delhi
at the age of 15, Ghalib did not write for a Muslim audience or
an Urdu-speaking readership. These distinctions did not matter
to him. He took pride in not being shackled by religious dogmas
or traditionalism, and paid scant regard to the outward observances of Islam. His broad and tolerant attitude is shown in his
letter to Munshi Hargopal Tufta: 'I hold all mankind to be my
kin, and look upon all men—Muslim, Hindu and Christian—as
my brothers, no matter what others may think.' He wore no
sectarian badge, no sectarian colour. In fact, at his death there
was some confusion as to whether his funeral rites should
follow Sunni or Shia rituals.

The poet revelled in being eclectic and independent in his
outlook and unorthodox and unconventional in his views. He
could thus demand from God treatment consistent with his
self-respect and question why, in the Islamic tradition, the written
testimony of the angels and not the witnesses' defence will be
accepted on the Day of Judgement.

The angels write, and we are seized. Where is the justice there?
We too had someone present when they wrote their record down.

The implied criticism of, and the lack of reverence for God, was the hallmark of Ghalib's prose and poetry. Once he was looking at the sky and was struck by the apparent chaos in the distribution of the stars. He said: 'there is no rhyme or reason in anything the self-willed do. Just look at the stars scattered in complete disorder. No proportion, no system, no sense, and no pattern. But their King has absolute power, and no one can breathe a word against Him'. Yet nobody among his contemporaries issued a *fatwa* against him. Nobody condemned him for his scepticism. When he died on 15 February 1869, large numbers of people, Hindus, Muslims, Shias and Sunnis, took part in the funeral procession.

The poet who 'brought the love of poetry with him from eternity' hoped that his poetry would win the world's acclaim when he was gone. His confidence has proved to be well founded, though he has not earned the same degree of recognition which his achievements merit. Perhaps, his bicentenary would have been celebrated with greater fanfare if he had been born in Calcutta, Bombay or Pune. Perhaps, he would have been better known if he had not written in Urdu, a language that languishes in the lanes and bylanes of Muslim localities.

Ideally, a nation in search of composite symbols and eclectic traditions should have appropriated a poet of Ghalib's stature. Instead, he has been conveniently passed on to, and his fate sealed by, heads of various Urdu academies.

7 March 1998

The Politics of Laughter

Historians explain the past, and with that our duty is finished. 'The dead are dead', stated A.J.P. Taylor in his essay on the 1945 famine in Ireland. 'They have become so many figures in a

notebook.' Yet their histories need to be told, their values understood and interpreted to unravel the past in all its complexities.

This essay is more in the nature of constructing, in the
words of the Fernand Braudel, a history of brief, rapid, nervous
fluctuations in the life of a family tucked away in Masauli
village in the Bara Banki district of UP. It is about a humorist
whose writings in English are much imbued with the spirit of
the age in which they were written—an active, self-confident
spirit infused by the rising tide of Indian nationalism. The fact
that they are so eminently representative of the period enhance
their appeal and ensure to them an enduring quality of historic
interest.

Wilayat Ali 'Bambooq' (1884-1918), a member of the Kidwai
gentry, was educated at the M.A.O. College, Aligarh, the nursery
of outstanding young Muslims who were to be heard of a great
deal in politics, literature or journalism of the following decades.
He experienced the intellectual and political ferment during
the first two decades of the twentieth-century, and witnessed
the tremendous upsurge of anti-British feelings amongst Muslims
that paved the way for the Khilafat and Non-Cooperation
campaigns (1919-22). He belonged to a movement with serious
intents, but while his contemporaries and friends held forth
from public platforms, he laughed at British rule and made fun
of it in his skits and sketches.

His political pursuits were highly serious but their expression
was humorous and satirical. He made roaring fun of that mongrel
culture which had evolved in India under British rule. Thus, in
his gallery of caricatures, are the 'England Returned Barrister'
desperately aping the Sahibs in manners and speech and
pretending to have forgotten his native tongue during his brief
sojourn in England. There are, in addition, specimens of the
Babu culture in India from the *patwari* to the deputy collector
and the honorary magistrate, comic both in their servility to
their white superiors and their arrogance towards the common
people.

Bambooq's home in Bara Banki was the centre of lively group
of radical intellectuals, and simple lovers of good food and
intelligent conversation. On many weekends his friends would

travel to this dusty town armed with resolutions or memoranda for forthcoming Congress or Muslim League meetings, and spend the evening pulling leisurely at long hubble-bubble, filling the air with the smoke of scented tobacco, bandying Urdu or Persian *ghazals*, reciting their compositions in verse or prose, or shouting at each other in violent, political argument. Sons of feudal families, whose earlier generation had never earned their own living, they were no lean and hungry carcass with dire intents against the colonial government. The nationalist agitation was still the affair of the educated middle class; freedom's battle was still fought with words. It was the kind of political setting in which the writer and the speaker rapidly came to the forefront. Bambooq, for one, made his mark quickly as a writer.

And yet Bambooq had only one foot in Lucknow's political and literary élite; the other foot was firmly planted in the family past. He tried preserving the values he had inherited from his family—hospitality, filial devotion and constancy in friendship. His house was packed with guests and poor relations. It was a free hostel for any boy from the village who had to study in the local high school. It was a gratuitous inn for country bumpkins whom litigations or business with the magistracy brought to the district town. It was the den of local nationalist agitators, the rendezvous of politicians and journalists. In this house, rustic coarseness and urban refinement lived cheek by jowl and country yokels and sophisticated gentleman sat down to eat at the same table.

Bambooq accepted every tie of kinship or friendship he had inherited. He was not the least embarrassed if his rustic past intruded on his urbane present. As he sat among friends, a country bumpkin with his *dhoti* tucked up to his knees and bedding swung on his long staff would barge in. Invariably, he would announce to the company that he was his uncle or cousin by some twist or turn of the Kidwai blood stream. Bambooq's generosity was clandestine and only limited by his income and the debts he could raise. When he would drag one of his ragged and shabby looking visitors into a corner to whisper to him, the household suspected that some money was being passed on. His acts of generosity came to light after his premature death at the age of 33 in July 1918.

Bambooq's values and way of life would have perished with him but for the fact that Rafi Ahmed Kidwai, his nephew, was growing up in the same house. His uncle's example sank deep into the recesses of Rafi's being. From his uncle, Rafi learnt to take no heed of morrow, and to cast his bread on the waters, to conceal the bounty of his heart like a private vice. Joking and laughing, he made events and things look easy. When Rafi moved to ministerial mansions in free India, he recreated in them the setting and atmosphere of the home in which he had grown up as a boy. At 6 Edward Road (now Maulana Azad Road) in New Delhi, the past and the present lived side by side.

Rafi largely relived Bambooq's political style. Like his uncle, he transacted business amidst roaring fun, and banter and gossip. He did not run around the world looking for a hero because he had found one in Jawaharlal Nehru. He took after his uncle's terror of the public platform and his preference for the back-rooms of politics. 'When he talked', recalled the civil servant Y.D. Gundevia, 'he blinked and blinked and blinked, and some-times looked at you with his eyes almost shut.' As it turned out, his commitment and his staying power were greater than that of almost anybody else who was thundering from the plat-form of the district.

As an essayist Bambooq could hardly be expected to create a large following. What he could do was to stimulate the imagin-ation of his readers, and this he did not only in special cases, where minds similarly attuned used his articles creatively, but also in the widest circle of his readers. Credited with literary excellence, his sketches claim to survival rests on being part of the social history of the time.

4 October 2000

*Lucknow on my Mind*_____

With its broad expanse of palaces, groves and gardens, courts and squares, and its many mosques and *imambaras*, Lucknow was a prime city until the British annexed Awadh in 1856. The Rumi Darwaza and the adjacent mosque, the great Imambara, whose central hall is one of the largest vaulted rooms in the world, forms the apotheosis of Asaf ad-Daula, the fourth Nawab of Awadh. W.H. Russell, the *London Times* correspondent, commented in 1858-9: 'Not Rome, not Athens, not Constantinople, not any city I have seen appears to me so striking and beautiful as Lucknow.'

Lucknow was the centre of learning, the home of leading Urdu poets and writers who left their indelible mark on the city's literary life. This is where many of the ideas and innovations helped shape the modern face of north India's classical music tradition. This is where cultivation of delicacy and refinement took place. This is where young sons of the nobility spent time at the best known salons for instructions in etiquette, the art of conversation and appreciation of Urdu literature. As regards learning, says Abdul Halim Sharar, the noted contemporary Urdu writer, 'Lucknow was the Baghdad and Cordoba of India and Nishapur and Bokhara of the East.'

What have we done to this city after Independence? The Jama Masjid, the handsome Chattar Manzil, the glittering Shah Najaf mausoleum or the La Martiniere, a Christian landmark symbolizing the zeal of the French soldier, General Claudie Martin, may still charm you. But all that glitters is not gold. The Mahmudabad House in Qaiser Bagh, venue of the famous Congress-Muslim League meetings in 1916, is a mute witness to Lucknow's steady decline. The nearby Baradari, once the focal point of Awadh's cultural renaissance, is a grim reminder of Lucknow's bygone era. You are sure to hear loud bands playing Hindi music, but there is no Jigar, Josh or Majaz to regale the audiences with their poetry.

Turn to Latush Road, adjoining the busy Aminabad bazaar, or the areas in Chowk and Nakhas. Notice the filth, the squalor, the crumbling houses and chaotic bazars. So what if the authorities have abdicated their civic responsibilities? So what if those occupying the seat of power have no time for the beleaguered residents of such localities? So what if the state is not visible in Lucknow? Is it not the same everywhere, in Agra, Kanpur and Banaras? True, a city has to adjust to the processes of change, but at what cost? Other cities around the world have, surely, responded to the pressures of modernization without giving up their character.

The noteworthy feature is that the old city, except for some pockets of affluence, is largely inhabited by the poor or the salaried classes that are unable to cope with the harsh realities of living in a sprawling urban site. This is especially true of those traditional families who, having given up their leisurely lifestyle in the neighbouring towns (*qasbahs*), find it increasingly difficult to compete with the more enterprising migrants who poured into Lucknow after Partition. The city's wealth, which is largely generated by its being a key centre of the country's railway system, is controlled by a new class—dynamic and spirited—but somewhat rustic and entrepreneurial in temper and outlook. The old values, which characterized Lucknow's society for well over a century, have been sadly forsaken.

As for Lucknow's erstwhile position as the Baghdad and Cordoba of India, the news is none too good. The Firangi Mahal, once the prime centre of learning in north India, languishes in the Chowk. The Shia College, founded by the Raja of Mahmuda-bad in 1917, is in disarray. The Nadwat-al ulama, started by Shibli Nomani in 1894 to act as an interlocutor between the traditional and Western systems of education, is no longer regarded as the leading centre of Islamic studies in India. The Lucknow University, established in 1921, has surely seen better days. Ram Advani, who runs a bookshop in Hazratgunj against heavy odds, bemoans that Lucknow's cultural and intellectual life has come to a virtual standstill.

The political landscape has, likewise, changed beyond recognition. Having enjoyed the distinction of being in the forefront of the nationalist movement, Lucknow is these days the principal area where caste-based politics is conducted without any qualms whatsoever. Each political combination is busy forging opportunistic alliances. Almost every politician is pitted against the other in order to gain positions of authority. The new crop of politicians is unconcerned, unlike their illustrious predecessors in the 1950s and 1960s, with the dwindling fortunes of the city. No wonder, India's most populous state remains abysmally poor and backward.

The responsibility must rest, equally, with successive Prime Ministers, most of whom belonged to UP but did little to promote literacy, boost agricultural production or build the infrastructure for industrial expansion. Except for the western districts, which benefited from the 'green revolution', most parts of the state have not been cared for. Since the mid-1980s, the mandir-masjid imbroglio sidetracked the more immediate socio-economic issues and polarized sentiments along religious lines.

If the past is a guide to the present, it is never too late to learn from Lucknow's past, its enviable record of harmonious inter-community relations, and its composite and syncretic cultural traditions. It is still possible to invoke these values by placing Lucknow on modern India's cultural and intellectual map. One should draw comfort from the fact that the Lakhnavis, having lived through the trauma of the 1857 revolt and Partition, were able to get their act together after Independence and surge ahead in their quest for a better life. There is no reason why they cannot do so now.

Surely, a city's growth and prosperity largely depends on the government. Yet, the people of Lucknow will need to make strenuous efforts to restore and preserve some of the beauty and splendour of their city. Their friends in India and overseas will await the outcome of their initiatives. In case you are not convinced, please turn to a book, edited by a distinguished French scholar, Violette Graff. *Lucknow: Memories of a City* (New Delhi, 1997) is a testimony to the author's love for the city and its people. Lakhnavis must not let her down through their neglect, and indifference.

15 November 1997

Death of a Seminary

The Mughal Emperor Aurangzeb granted the property of a European merchant to a learned family in Lucknow. This was named Firangi Mahal, and this was the name by which the family is known. Any student of modern Indian history would know how some of the learned men of Firangi Mahal made Lucknow the centre for the study of medicine, religious jurisprudence, Islamic philosophy, logic, social and physical sciences, and theology. Any student will be equally familiar with its role during the Khilafat protest and the non-cooperation movements in the early 1920s. That was when Gandhi visited this institution to conduct his parleys with its spiritual head, Maulana Abdul Bari. 'At no time', wrote the essayist-novelist, Abdul Halim Sharar, in *Lucknow: The Last Phase of an Oriental Culture*, 'can one find a centre of learning in Delhi like the Farangi Mahal'.

Longing to see the place and talk to its inmates, I reached Lucknow's historic locality, Nakhas, in the very heart of the city's wild disorder. 'Where is Firangi Mahal?' I asked a gentleman conspicuous in a red beard that fanned out to his shoulders. 'What? How am I supposed to know?' he answered curtly. Pacing up and down the crowded street, I stopped at the Shia College gate where the *chowkidar*, with enormous black moustaches, mumbled for a while before directing me to a poorly-lit lane. 'It is somewhere there', he said hurriedly. What surprised me were their disquieting, impenetrable naivete, their ignorance, and their total lack of awareness of their immediate surroundings.

Making my way through the alleys with considerable difficulty, I reached my destination. Just then, I saw the urine of the sacred cows spread slowly in great puddles. A man stood not far away praying, moving his lips. Gripped, as soon as I entered, by the shadows and the silence, I tried to fix in my memory as many as possible of the things I saw around me in the brief instant I stayed there. What I saw and experienced repulsed me. Believe me, there was nothing much to write home about.

Today, the Nadwat al-ulama, also in Lucknow, flourishes.

Firangi Mahal, on the other hand, languishes in the Chowk *mohalla*. To cut a long story short, this institution is a living testimony to the decline of traditional centres of learning. The Firangi Mahal family itself disintegrated after Partition, some opting to go to Pakistan while others stayed put in India. Muslim politicians in UP talk big, but they pay little attention to the revival of those institutions that can still play a role in the community's intellectual and cultural life.

The moral of the story is that Firangi Mahal, despite its glorious past, is not a site that inspired me to pay a second visit. If I do wish to know its history, my best bet, I discovered after returning to Delhi, was to read a book published last month. A British scholar, who has written perceptively on Islam in South Asia, is its author. Anyone who has, like myself, benefited by Dr. Francis Robinson's earlier work on Muslim separatism in the United Provinces (now Uttar Pradesh) is bound to treat anything that he writes with special attention. In this work, he uncovers the world of the pious and learned men of Firangi Mahal, plots their trajectory through two centuries, and explains their complex relationships with the society outside the boundaries of the seminary. 'The learned and holy men of the Firangi Mahal family', writes Francis Robinson in his lively style, 'are a remarkable body of people in the history of South Asia; indeed they would be remarkable in that of any society.'

Why? Many of them were scholars and teachers for nearly three centuries, drawing students and disciples not only from all parts of India but also from places as far away as Arabia and China. Second, many of them were perceived as men of piety by their followers, who followed their advice on religious/ theological matters. Third, at a time when Western ideas and institutions were beginning to threaten inherited traditional values, the role of the *ulama* of Firangi Mahal was to defend Islam and the Muslim communities. In so doing, they acted as guardians, interpreters and transmitters of Islamic knowledge. They made available and interpreted to each generation the central messages of Islam, i.e. knowledge of God's word and how to know it in one's heart.

Several members of the family turned to other callings, joining government service, journalism, or the medical profession (*unani*). But many more survived as teachers transmitting the word of God and the skills required to understand it. Indeed, they were quite often the ones who exemplified the family code of right conduct. 'Watch me', stated Maulana Abd al-Razaq, 'so long as I follow our pious predecessors, follow me; and if I do not follow our pious predecessors, do not follow me. Our predecessors were better than we are, because they lived closer to the time of the Holy Prophet.'

Besides these fascinating details, Dr. Robinson provides a useful supplement to the conventional outlines of the historians of South Asian Islam. The chapter on scholarship and mysticism in Awadh is sound and instructive. What it does is to place the *ulama* of Firangi Mahal in the context of an Islamic world system based on shared systems of formal and spiritual knowledge. There is a lot more for the specialist to read, especially the last two chapters of the book.

The value of this lies in Dr. Robinson's own contribution and in the synthesis, which it offers, of the work of a generation and more on the impact of colonialism on traditional societies. This is a central theme—if not the central theme—of nineteenth century Islam in South Asia, and in dealing with some of its critical aspects, the author provides, and deserves our thanks for providing, a useful starting point for further advance.

This is a stimulating book, factually informative, clearly arranged, and well provided with footnotes that direct the reader to the relevant authorities. But like most writers with a thesis, Dr. Robinson tends at times to exaggerate. He sees the Firangi Mahal influence everywhere and is inclined to prove too much. He writes with feeling, if sometimes repetitively, on how good and great was the *ulama* of Firangi Mahal. All said and done, however, *The Ulama of Farangi Mahall; and Islamic Culture in South Asia* is certainly a readable and authoritative account. It is a record of a bold and heroic attempt to repair the ruins of a crumbling edifice. I hope it will make its appeal to an even wider public.

13 June 2001

The Sociology of Muharram_____

It began exactly nine days ago when the Muharram moon was sighted in the distant horizon in Lucknow. Immediately, the women, including the newly wed, removed their jewellery, their bangles and flashy clothes. For the next nine days, they will set aside comfort, luxury and convenience. Politicians will turn pious for a change; musicians will put away their musical instruments, and poets, accustomed to regaling audiences with *ghazals*, will switch to writing elegies and dirges. Whether in Lucknow, Kolkata, Mumbai or Chennai, notice the long procession of *taziyas* (replicas of Husain's tomb) and flags along the streets with a vast crowd of mourners, who scream out their lamentations and beat their breasts. At night, you may well notice the glow of a million lamps from the illuminated *imambaras* (where the mourners congregate), with their domed tombs, shining, gleaming, and reflecting the light of many crystal lamps.

Today is the ninth day of Muharram, a day of mourning marked with utmost solemnity. Clad mostly in black clothes, millions around the globe will set aside their daily chores to grief for the grandson of Prophet Muhammad, Husain, and his seventy-two companions who were brutally killed on the banks of the river Euphrates in Karbala (Iraq) in AD 680. They will march, as they do year after year, through the lanes and by-lanes in fervent lamentation chanting 'Ya-Husain, Ya-Husain', rhythmically beating their chests, self-flagellating, carrying *taziyas*, his coffin, his standards and insignia, and his horse.

Tonight, groups of women, largely Hindus, will move about the villages wailing and reciting *dohas*, mostly improvised lyrics, on the epic tragedy. They will offer flowers and sweets at local *karbalas* (sites where the replicas are consecrated), and seek Husain's intercession to cure the diseased, avert calamities, procure children for the childless, or improve the circumstances of the dead. For the rural communities Husain's trials and tribulations inspire faith in a universal nemesis ensuring justice for oppressed souls.

It is not unusual for the Hindus to participate in Muharram observances. W.H. Sleeman found, in 1849, Hindu princes in central and southern India commemorating Muharram with illuminations and processions. In Gwalior and Baroda, both Hindu states, Muharram was observed with splendid solemnity. In Lucknow, thousands of Hindus chanted *dohas* along with the Shias and Sunnis. Muharram had passed off peacefully in Banaras, a Hindi newspaper reported in July 1895. 'When it is Hindus who mostly celebrate [*sic*] this festival [*sic*], what fear can there be.'

Husain is everybody's hero, the embodiment of virtues of piety, courage and self-sacrifice. He did not seek power or office. He represented the authentic voice of Islam, and, for that reason, boldly challenged the un-Islamic practices of the Umayyad ruler, Yezid. He laid down his life but did not compromise with a bloody-minded tyrant. He is the leader of the lovers, the free cypress from the Garden of the Prophet, the meaning of the great offering mentioned in one of the Koranic verses, the building of the confession of faith. He is, like his father Ali and his grandfather, a model of the Perfect Man who becomes a martyr in his strife for God's unity against the rulers of this world.

Every age brings forth a new Yezid, but resistance to tyranny, as is illustrated by Husain's legendary example, is incumbent upon every man of faith. No wonder, his followers rally round him year after year to share his family's pain, anguish and trauma. Employing the paradigms of Husain and Karbala, Mohammad Iqbal had sent forth the following message:

Nikal kar khanqahon se ada kar rasm-i Shabbiri

Emerge from the confines of the *khanqahs* and,
re-enact the example set by Husain.

Husain's martyrdom has served, to the Shias (as opposed to the Sunnis) of all times and in all places, as an everlasting exhortation to guard their separate identity and to brave their numerical inferiority in the face of firmly established and some-times oppressive majorities. It makes sense in terms of a soteriology not dissimilar to the one invoked in the case of Christ's crucifixion—just as Christ sacrificed himself at the altar of the cross to redeem humanity, so did Husain on the plains of Karbala to purify the Muslim community of sins. The reasons for the popular appeal of Muharram ceremonies becomes apparent when one adds to all this the cathartic effect of weeping as a means of releasing pent-up grief over the agonies of Husain's family.

The ritual recreation of Karbala creates an environment that, in Clifford Geertz's terms, establish powerful, pervasive, and long-lasting moods and motivations in men and women by formulating conceptions of a general order of existence. Clothing those conceptions with such an aura of factuality make the moods and motivations uniquely realistic.

Sadly, Muharram has ceased to be a common symbol of veneration in the subcontinent. It leads to Hindu-Muslim fracas, especially when Muharram observances coincide with Dussehra. It triggers Shia-Sunni riots in Lucknow, the site of all sorts of polemical controversies. Shias and Sunnis have separate grave-yards, separate mosques, separate schools, and separate religious and charitable endowments. These institutions define the boundaries within which they are required to stay apart. One cannot but bemoan the fact that they live as separate entities in a world fashioned by the religious and political leadership.

In Pakistan, the lines of cleavages are sharply demarcated following the rise of Shia militancy and the spurt in Sunni fundamentalism in the wake of the Taliban incursion. Whatever the reasons, the fact is that a nation created for Muslims in the name of Islam stands deeply divided along sectarian lines. Women wail in agony and young men speak angrily of revenge as sectarian violence takes its toll in different parts of the country. The results are there for everybody to see. Muharram practices, which have always been rejected by Sunni purists as un-Islamic (as corrupting as Hindu beliefs and customs), are now being targeted with greater intensity. Consequently, Muharram has become an exclusively Shia concern in its format as well as in the composition of the participants. A powerful symbol of unity has, thus, been transformed into a potent vehicle for sectarian mobilization.

Ten days of mourning will culminate tomorrow, the final mournful tribute to the Lord of the Martyrs. Cries of *Wa Mohammda, kushta shud Husain* (Oh Muhammad, Husain has been martyred!) will rend the air. In the stillness of the night, hear the following heart-rending lament:

> When the caravan of Medina, having lost all
> Arrived in captivity in the vicinity of Sham
> Foremost came the head of Husain, born aloft on a spear
> And in its wake, a band of women, with heads bared.

4 April 2001

The Heart-in-Pieces Generation

Two outstanding novelists who dominated the literary scene for nearly two decades after Independence have been largely forgotten. Today's novelists may not replicate Ahmed Ali and Attia Hosain's genre of writing, but their powerful and creative representation of change, decay and uncertainties in a given historical context should inspire upcoming novelists. Their characters were real, for they mirrored the anxieties of a generation faced with stark choices before and after Independence. The author's personal dilemmas and predicament were reflected in the portrayal of individuals and families who debated the contemporary situation, discussed their preferences, and plotted their trajectory in accordance with their ideological predilections. In the end, they did not just produce a novel or two but insightful social histories as well.

Ahmed Ali, born a year after the transfer of capital from

Calcutta to Delhi, published his novel *Twilight in Delhi* in 1940. It is a delicate and highly sensitive summation of the histories of a city that had changed its mood, character and personality for centuries. It depicts, moreover, 'the decay of a whole culture, a particular mode of thought and living, now dead and gone already right before our eyes'. Didn't Mirza Ghalib say: *Shama har rang me jalti hai sehar hone tak.*

Yet the city ravaged by the Marathas, the Jats and the British during and after the 1857 revolt was the city of Ahmed Ali's dream. Here 'dwelt the chosen spirits of the age', wrote Mir Taqi Mir. It was, in Ahmed Ali's words, 'the embodiment of a whole culture, free of the creedal ghosts and apparitions that haunt some of modern India's critics and bibliographers chased by the dead souls of biased historians of yesteryears'. Ahmed Ali would have preferred to live and die in the city of Mir and Ghalib. But that was not to be. He could not return to Delhi from Nanking where he was on a deputation from the government of undivided India. He fretted and fumed at the Delhi airport but was not allowed to disembark. In just a few moments, his Indian identity was snatched away from him and he was forced to languish in Karachi, a place that was alien, remote and distant for a *Dehalvi* like him.

Attia Hosain, who died at the age of 84, was a consummate stylist with the sensitivity to encompass wide-ranging human emotions in a sentence or two. Her novel and collection of stories, commented Anita Desai, 'are delicate and tender, like new grass, and they stir with life and the play of sunlight and rain. To read them is as if one had parted a curtain, or opened a door, and strayed into the past.' *Sunlight on a Broken Column*, the only novel she wrote, was published in 1961. As a classic of sorts, it brilliantly illuminates aspects of a feudal society trying to come to terms with the changes ushered in by the nationalist movement. There is tension in the air as uncle Hamid and his son Saleem discuss their conflicting ideas: 'No one seemed to talk anymore, everyone argued. . . . It was as if someone had sneaked in live ammunition among the fireworks. In the thrust and parry there was a desire to inflict wounds. Even visitors argued. A new type of person now frequented the house. Fanatic, bearded men and young zealots would come to see Saleem; rough, country-dwelling landlords and their courtiers would visit my uncle.'

Her prose is exquisite, delicate, and charming. It is, in the words of Anita Desai, the literary equivalent of the miniature school of painting in India, introduced by the Mughals. Equally, Attia Hosain's novel and short stories reveal a rare sensitivity to the changes taking place in Awadh society, to the imminent decline of the feudal order, and the confusion and insecurities of those trying to come to terms with the rapidly-changing world around them.

Hundreds of thousands of families were faced with the necessity of changing habits of mind and living conditioned by centuries, hundreds and thousands of landowners and the hangers-on who had lived on the largesse, their weakness and their follies. Faced by prospects of poverty, by the actual loss of privilege, there were many that lost their balance of mind when their world cracked apart. Others retired to anonymity in their villages. This was the end my uncle had prophesied. This was the end our theories and enthusiasm had supported. Like death and all dissolution it was an end easier to accept with the mind than as a fact.

Attia Hosain knew her social and cultural milieu better than most. She came from a taluqdari family of Awadh and was privileged to study at La Martiniere School for Girls and the Isabela Thoburn College in Lucknow. She was the first woman graduate from any taluqdari family. And yet, her feudal background did not deter her from taking part in left-wing activities and attending the first Progressive Writers' Conference and the All India Women's Conference in Calcutta in 1933. She moved to London in 1947.

Events during and after Partition are to this day very painful to me. And now, in my old age, the strength of my roots is very strong; it also causes pain, because it makes one a 'stranger' everywhere in the deeper areas of one's mind and spirit except where one was born and brought up.

Ahmed Ali and Attia Hosain were brought up differently and in completely diferent environments, and yet they had so much in common. Both were attached to liberal, composite and eclectic traditions, the hallmark of Delhi and Lucknow's social and cultural life. Both were wedded to a humanistic world-view that was free of bigotry, intolerance, and sectarianism. Both were uneasy with and anguished by the Partition of the country; indeed, they belonged to a generation that has lived with its heart shattered. And both died in a country that was not theirs. If they had exchanged letters, they may have written the following to each other:

> *Rahi nagufta mere dil me daastan meri*
> *na is dayar me samjha koi zabaan meri*
>
> MIR TAQI MIR
>
> How could I tell my tale in this strange land?
> I speak a tongue they do not understand.

21 February 1998

Imagining India: The Story of Salvation

'Here Saadat Hasan Manto lies buried—and buried in his breast are all the secrets of the art of story writing. Even now, lying under tons of earth he is wondering whether he or God is the greatest short story writer.' This is how Manto (1912-55), the *enfant terrible* of Urdu literature, wrote his own epitaph a year before his death.

Ismat Chughtai (1915-91) wrote short stories, sketches, essays, plays, novellas, and novels. Drawing themes from the lives of the Urdu-speaking women for her best stories, she wrote with an authenticity that no male writer could have matched. She brought into the ambit of Urdu fiction the hitherto forbidden terrain of female sexuality and 'led her female contemporaries on a remarkable journey of self-awareness and undaunted creative expression'. In more ways than one, she changed the complexion of Urdu fiction.

Krishan Chandar, Rajindar Singh Bedi and Manto were her contemporaries. So were scores of brilliant poets associated with the Progressive Writers' Movement. Ismat Chughtai was a fellow traveller in their creative journey. Tahira Naqvi, in her recent book *My Friend, My Enemy: Essays, Reminiscences, Portraits,* has put together Ismat's essays, reminiscences and portraits. The effort is commendable. True, Ismat Chughtai's pungent and nuanced style is missing in this English translation, and yet the collection bears the imprint of her strong personality. We hear her loud and clear. We see her in various moods—angry, bitter and disillusioned at times. At the same time, she was boisterous, full of optimism and buoyancy. She was unsparing in her criticism of sub-standard works, but appreciated good literature with her characteristic generosity. She was certainly much less pretentious than several of her contemporary Urdu writers. Refined and sophisticated like Quratullain Hyder, wit and humour reached new heights in Ismat Chughtai's writings.

This collection illustrates the evolution of Urdu language and literature from 1930 onwards. For a historian like me, its value is enhanced by the fact that the essays mirror the joy and expectancy of an era, and capture the mood of India's painful transition from the colonial era to Independence and Partition. Ideas flow from Ismat Chughtai's pen without being convoluted in their presentation. As the leading light in the Progressive Writers' Movement, her engagement is serious and reflective without being imbued with a proselytizing zeal. She is critical of some people around her, but there is hardly any malice, rancour or bitterness in her writings. Disgusted with the happenings around her, including the bloody and brutal Partition of the country, she appears poised, controlled and almost magisterial in voicing her anger and discontent. Notice the following lines in the essay 'Communal Violence and Literature': 'Communal violence and freedom became so muddled that it was difficult to distinguish between the two. After that, anyone who obtained a measure of freedom discovered violence came alongside.'

Notice, too, the humane portrayal of Majaz, the anguished poet of the 1930s and 1940s and her candid assessment of his

contribution to Urdu poetry. 'The old Majaz was a passionate
rebellious youth, now he is a tired, spent man. He was a
turbulent, gushing windfall, now he is a river that has been
dammed. Let's see what happens when this dam bursts.'

Not all the pieces are reflective. But, then, one is adequately
compensated by the inclusion of an excerpt from 'Lihaaf (Quilt),
a brilliant short story for which Ismat Chughtai was tried in
Lahore on a charge of obscenity. Equally moving is the pen-
portrait of her brother who died of tuberculosis, and the long
essay on Manto. She was needlessly harsh in dismissing Manto's
Siyah Hashiye (Black Margins) as rhetoric rather than reality.
But she was deeply pained by his premature death. 'The world
that let him die', she cried out, 'is my world as well. Today it let
him die, and tomorrow I, too, will be allowed to die in the same
way. And then people will mourn. . . . Meetings will be held,
donations will be collected, and because of a dearth of leisure
time no one will be able to attend these meetings. Time will
pass, the heaviness on the chest will slowly diminish, and people
will forget everything.'

We hope not. Ismat was too great a writer to be lost in the
mist of history. Urdu is dead or dying in India. Long live Ismat
and Manto, Faiz and Firaq!

Writers like Ismat and Manto were not different or 'unique'
just because they used Urdu, the language of the other, to
express their creative energies. Like many of their contemporary
Hindi and Bengali writers, they illuminate aspects of our
collective existence that are often left untouched by political
and economic practices. They offer multiple versions of 'truth'
and thus contribute to a richer understanding of social and
historical contexts.

A more basic point needs reiteration. Generally speaking,
Indian literature has played a crucial role in shaping the cultural
and political struggles and contemporary consciousness.
Moreover, it has long played a crucial part in giving marginal
groups a voice in the great ferment and tumult of the subcontinent. Some of the most interesting new writing has
emerged in the context of the radical protest movements of
the disadvantaged groups, such as the Dalits and women. Not

surprisingly, Indian storytelling has proved to be an instrument of resistance to tyranny, as well as a site of reconciliation and reversal of the orthodoxies of hatred that pervade the subcontinent's politics.

Munshi Premchand, the master storyteller, explained: 'literature . . . shows us the path, he arouses our humanness, infuses in us noble feelings, broadens our view. . . .' He believed in the social function of art. The writer, for him, was a missionary who had to gear his writing to the deliberate portrayal of reality—in particular its decadent features, with the intention of reforming it. 'Our social and political circumstances', he wrote to a friend, 'force us to educate the people whenever we get the chance. The more intensely we feel, the more didactic we become.'

Of all the forms of literature in modern times, fiction is a privileged site because in fiction, perhaps better than anywhere else, one can see the working of ideology in the lived experience of society. I refer to short stories because of its pivotal position among various forms of literature, holding as it were 'eternity in a grain of sand'. In the words of Amitav Ghosh, 'nothing that India has given the world outside is more important than its stories. Indeed, so pervasive is the influence of the Indian story that one particular collection, *The Panchatantra* (The Five Chapters) is reckoned by some to be second only to the Bible in the extent of its global diffusion.' The short story, both in its epic form and in its modern version, has been vital to the creation of the traditions of narrative and the diffusion of a civilization, 'the chosen instrument of the subcontinent in the springtime of nationhood'.

Scores of writers, Manto and Ismat included, capture the trauma of Partition, the woes of divided families, the agony and trauma of abducted women, the plight of migrants, and the harrowing experiences of countless people who boarded the train that took them to the realization of their dream, but of whom not a man, woman or child survived the journey. These experiences are portrayed through characters like Zahid in Attia Hosain's *Sunlight on a Broken Column* or a Saddan in Rahi Masoom Reza *Adha-Gaon* (Half-a-Village). Literature truly evokes the sufferings of the innocent, whose pain is more universal and, ultimately, a vehicle of more honest reconciliation than political discourse.

Board Krishan Chander's *Peshawar Express* or Khushwant Singh's *Train to Pakistan* to grasp the implications of what happened before and after the midnight hour. Explore Rahi's Gangauli village to uncover the intricate and almost imperceptible way in which the politics of Partition worked its way into people's consciousness, and read through the pages of *Sunlight on a Broken Column* to discover how the Pakistan movement split families on ideological lines and heightened their anxieties.

Manto, for one, was accused of cynicism and sensationalizing a tragedy. A critic even went so far as to say that Manto had desecrated the dead and robbed them of their possession to build a collection. The fact is that Manto and other creative writers expose not only the inadequacy of numerous narratives on Independence and Partition, but provide a foundation for developing an alternative discourse to current expositions of a general theory on inter-community relations. They portray a grim and sordid contemporary reality without drawing religion or a particular community as the principal reference point. In the words of Krishna Sobti, whose best-known Hindi writings on Partition are *Sikka Badal Gaya* and *Zindaginama*, fiction writers about Partition preserve the 'essential human values'.

We, on the threshold of the next millennium, are in a different position than the men and women of August 1947. Our choices are not limited to exile, death, or resignation.

10 April 1999

Raging against the Dying of the Light: Through Jafri's Eyes

> We the dwellers in the ruins of love
> Sowed the trees of our dreams in the sand of yesterday;
> There being no shade, we sleep under the desire for shade.
>
> N.M. RASHID: 1912-76

His attire may not have changed for decades. Maybe, he wore in the mid-1930s the same loose-fitted Lakhnavi pyjama as a student at the M.A.O. College in Aligarh. Maybe, he always ran his hands through his hair as he spoke or recited his poems in *mushairas*. Certainly, his soft but firm voice had not changed over time. He spoke poignantly and elegantly on his favourite themes. His eloquence was legendary, reminding his admirers of the best traditions, now forgotten, of *marsiya* (elegy) recitation. His numerous books and essays portray vividly and with great artistic skill the social realities of living under colonial rule and post-colonial governments. Outside the public spaces, he was a very vivacious and amusing talker with a strong sense of wit and humour that seems to come naturally to men of culture and refinement among the Urdu-speakers.

During his lifetime, Ali Sardar Jafri had more than his share of detractors. His poetic sensibilities were called into question not by serious scholars but by anti-Communist polemicists. 'As soon as the poet in him hands over the pen to the propagandist', wrote one of them, 'the beauty somehow vanishes. . . . He is angry, but there is no nobility in his anger.' He was chided for hobnobbing with and seeking favours from the ruling establishment from the days of Indira Gandhi. To some critics, Bertrand Russell's description of Bernard Shaw—as an iconoclast he was admirable, but as an icon rather less—may well be applied to Jafri as well.

My reasons for writing on Jafri may not make sense in this day and age. The word 'composite culture', the cornerstone of his philosophy, will sound hollow to those who have driven the Kashmiri Pandits out of their homes or the militants who have killed innocent pilgrims on their spiritual journey to Amarnath. This is, surely, not the Islam that Sultan Zainul Abidin or the great Sufi saints of Kashmir professed and practised. Give peace a chance, Jafri would have said, in the wounded valley.

Jafri's political credo rested on a strong commitment to rationalist thought; hence his fascination for Mir and Iqbal. Sadly, however, his rationalism will not appeal to the persons responsible for jettisoning the 'Towards Freedom' project of the ICHR. [It decided not to publish the two volumes compiled by Professor Sumit Sarkar and K.N. Panikkar, two leading Marxist historians.] As a champion of diversity, he would have said that if individuals are to retain that measure of initiative and flexibility which they ought to have, they must not be all forced into one rigid old; or, to change the metaphor, all drilled into one army. In the words of Faiz, 'Let colour fill the flowers, let the breeze of early spring blow.'

Yet, let us not allow the voices of the Jafris and the Kaifi Azmis to be stifled by the weight of religious or political orthodoxies. Political parties will come and go, but India is too precious a civilizational entity to be used as a pawn on the chessboard of opportunistic politics. I am not interested in exploring the 'Idea of India'; my idea of India is anchored in the vast array of knowledge and wisdom derived from saints, sages, poets, writers and musicians, and my interest lies in my country's survival as a civilizational entity. That is what the Progressive Writers' Association, pioneered by men like Premchand, Sajjad Zaheer and Mulk Raj Anand, stood for. Socialism, the historian V.G. Kiernan wrote in *Poems of Faiz*, was the new revelation that young idealists could invoke to exorcize communal rancours, by uniting the majority from all communities in a struggle against their common poverty, and to make independence a blessing to the poor as well as to the elite.

The men and women who were a part of this struggle embodied a vision that has not ceased to be relevant even after the demise of socialism. Even though history has taken a different turn, an apt tribute to them will be to preserve some of the values they represented.

An apt tribute to Jafri, the symbol of our cultural renaissance, will be not to strangulate the language that he wrote in. So often he would say that the unfair and harsh treatment meted out to Urdu, the language of Mir, Ghalib, Iqbal and Raghupati Sahay 'Firaq', underlines the secular foundations of our society. Perhaps, he was asking for the moon.

In some ways, Jafri was a victim of the criminal neglect of our society; sadly, there wasn't enough in the family kitty to pay for his medical expenses. His wife Sultana had to depend on the goodwill of loyal friends. But, in many other ways, her late husband was a lucky man. Unlike Ghalib, he received recognition during his lifetime: a prestigious national award came in handy for the dwindling family fortunes.

All said and done, Jafri was fortunate enough to be a witness to, and an active participant in, some of the tumultuous events of this century. He observed and commented on the rise and fall of colonialism. He shared the agony and pain of living under the British and protested strongly, along with Faiz and scores of other Hindi, Bengali and Urdu writers, against colonial rule. He shared the joy of freedom, but bemoaned the vivisection of India. He envisioned a socialist world but saw its painful demise in the land of Lenin and Stalin. He spoke for the poor and the hungry and constructed pictures of a society that encouraged the young to envisage possibilities which otherwise they would not have dreamt of. He saw his country embroiled in wars with China and Pakistan but refused to acquiesce in the hypocritical high moral tone of the government. Here, as Russell wrote of Joseph Conrad, 'his intense and passionate nobility shines in my memory like a star seen from the bottom of a well. I wish I could make this light shine for others as it shone for me.'

Allow me conclude with the following lines:

Neither Chengiz lives any longer, nor Timur,
What have survived are the people.
The youthful waves of the ocean of Time
Gush and flow from eternity to eternity.
Ours is a story of the millennia;

For we are invincible, eternal.
We are the designs and patterns of civilisations;
We are the aspirations of the hearts;
We have been ever engaged in struggles;
We are the sharp swords of history.

This general optimism is much more likely to lead to good results than the somewhat lazy cynicism that is becoming all too common. This is not the moment, Jafri would have said in his inimitable style, to deride secularism and mock at multi-culturalism.

9 August 2000

A Dying Strain of Music: V.G. Kiernan

> *Rat yun dil men teri khoi hui yad ai*
> *Jaise virane men chupke-se bahar a-jae,*
> *Jaise sahraon men haule-se chale bad-e-nasim,*
> *Jaise bimar ko be-vajh qarar a-jae.*

Last night your faded memory filled my heart
Like spring's calm and advent in the wilderness,
Like the soft desert footfalls of the breeze,
Like peace somehow coming to one in sickness.

Let me take you out on a journey to the idyllic surroundings of 20 Lauder Road, in the tiny village of Stow in Scotland. If you don't know Stow, the easiest way is to go along the A7—it is 27 miles from Edinburgh—and continue through this long, thin township to near its southern end. Here lives Professor V.G. Kiernan, the man who translated into English the above lines of Faiz. His house is near a crossroad with a War Memorial and a café to the right, and a church 100 yards ahead to the left.

Kiernan, born in 1913, is physically in sound health, and mentally quite alert. In case you don't know him, let me tell you that he is one of Europe's leading Marxist intellectuals of the post-War decades. Along with the two other eminent historians, Christopher Hill and Eric Hobsbawm, he was an active member of the Communist Party of Great Britain until the Russian tanks stormed into Hungary in 1956.

He is widely known in literary circles of the subcontinent for translating Iqbal and Faiz. What is probably not so well known is that Kiernan lived in India from 1938 to 1946, teaching, writing and broadcasting. He taught at the Sikh National College and the Aitchison College in Lahore, north India's leading cultural, literary and educational centre. Lahore was then the home of several renowned Urdu poets and writers, many of whom were swayed by socialist ideas. Prominent amongst them was Mian Iftikharuddin, Mohammad Taseer, and Faiz. Kiernan, having studied at Manchester Grammar School and Trinity College, Cambridge, joined them to create a 'Bloomsbury' group in Lahore. He returned to England where he taught in the history department of Edinburgh University for nearly thirty years before retiring as Emeritus Professor.

The Professor has not recorded his experiences, but he vividly remembers the political turbulence and uncertainties following the outbreak of Second World War. He found Punjab to be a politically benign province, though the rest of the country was astir. There was excitement across the country when the Congress ministries resigned in 1939 and, more importantly, when Gandhi launched the Quit India movement in 1942. 'The patriotic fervour that gripped the nation', he added, 'was truly impressive. I was happy to be a witness to the unfolding of great events.' He expressed strong reservations about Gandhi and his use of Hindu symbols, but acknowledged his greatness. Charming and charismatic, the Mahatma understood the workings of the imperial system.

Kiernan met Nehru a few times, admired his courage, his idealism, and his commitment to the building of a modern India. Greatly moved when he heard Nehru's 'tryst with destiny' speech in England, he said to me: 'India had the good fortune to have Nehru as its first Prime Minister. Compare him with

Soekarno in Indonesia and you'll know what I mean.'

Mohammad Ali Jinnah was 'vain' and 'conceited', 'some kind of a fundamentalist, a hothead without the vision of a modern nation. I didn't approve of him. There isn't much to write home about his political legacy.' India's democracy, on the other hand, is firmly rooted. Though Hindu fundamentalists tarnished the country's fair image during the Babri Masjid affair, the secular forces are strong enough to withstand their onslaught. 'India must not be allowed to degenerate into a Hindu polity.'

'Yes, the Partition was a colossal blunder. No, no, it shouldn't have happened. The Hindus and Muslims were not separate 'nations'. Certainly not in Punjab where the cross-communal networks were strong. Believe me, I didn't notice much difference between my Hindu, Sikh or Muslim friends. Nobody did. Lahore was such a cosmopolitan city. It isn't so any longer. I found it pretty dull visiting the place some years ago.' As he wrote in his introduction to *Poems by Faiz:* 'The Panjab was still in many ways a Sleepy Hollow where life moved at the pace of the feeble cab-horses drawing their two-wheeled *tongas*; where young men could indulge in old carefree idle ways, with long hours of debate in coffee houses and moonlight picnics by the river Ravi.'

'My comrades in the Communist Party had no idea what the Partition movement was all about. They erred in their judgement then and later, though some amongst them realized their mistakes later on. P.C. Joshi was more open to criticism; B.T. Randive was dogmatic. Yes, yes, a Stalinist. But then most communists I worked with were selflessly devoted to their cause. They were men of steel. I am proud of my long association with them.'

Inka dam-saz apne siwa kaun hai?
Shahr-e janan men ab ba-safa kaun hai,
Dast-e-qatil ke shayan raha kaun hai?
Rakht-e-dil bandh lo, dil-fagaro chalo;
Phir hamin qatl ho-aen yaro, chalo.

Who is their intimate, besides us?
In the city of the beloved who now is pure,
Who is left worthy of the executioner's hand?
Let us once again go to be murdered—friends, come.

When asked to comment on the collapse of socialism and the disintegration of the Soviet Union, Professor Keirnan looked visibly upset. He quietly moved from his chair and offered to make some tea for his guests. When he returned from the kitchen with tea and cakes, he looked troubled. I decided not to press the issue. The discussion was over.

As the sun began to set in the distant Scottish hills, we took leave and were on our way to Edinburgh.

I was saddened to drive past 'Woodcroft', the name of the house inscribed on the gate. I had met the Professor twice before, but this was surely going to be my last meeting with a friend of India and a leading scholar and intellectual. I was reminded of Faiz, whom he had translated with such skill:

Bam-o-dar khamushi ke bojh se chur,
Asmanon se ju-e-dard rawan,
Chand ka dukh-bhara fasana-e-nur
Shahrahon ki khak men ghaltan,
Khwabgahon men nim tariki,
Muzmahil lai rabab-e-hasti ki
Halke halke suron men nauha-kunan!

On gate and roof a crushing load of silence—
From heaven a flowing tide of desolation—
The moon's pale beams, whispered regrets, lying
In pools ebbing away on dusty highroads—
In the abodes of sleep a half formed darkness—
From Nature's harp a dying strain of music
On muted strings faintly, faintly lamenting.

30 May 1998

*The Importance of being Khushwant Singh*_____

I do not claim friendship or association with Khushwant Singh. I first met him just a couple of years earlier at a conference in Rome. Our last encounter was towards the end of the last century at the office of the *Outlook* magazine where we put our heads together to select twenty outstanding figures of the twentieth-century. Doubtless, he had his own preferences. At the same time, he paid attention to what the other panellist had to say. My surprise and disappointment came when he dismissed Azad summarily as a virtually inconsequential leader.

I said that my acquaintance with Khushwant Singh is just a couple of years old. Yet I seem to have known him well enough through his writings. While writing my doctoral dissertation at Cambridge, I read his *A History of the Sikhs*. It was a nicely crafted work of scholarship that introduced me to the fascinating history of Sikhism and the region of Punjab. Whatever present-day specialists might say, the two volume *History of the Sikhs* established Khushwant Singh's scholarly reputation. Yet, he wasn't one to settle for a professorial chair in Delhi, Amritsar or Patiala. He was the kind who was looking for spaces to express his creative energies. Eager and restless, he surged ahead in quest of his intellectual journey. In the words of Ghalib: 'So this is our position: here we stand / And here we shall continue in our stand.'

Editing *The Illustrated Weekly of India* was the highpoint in Khushwant Singh's journalistic career. Though castigated by some for changing the character of the magazine that had hitherto catered to middle-class sensibilities, his readers loved the Sardarji for being innovative, unorthodox and provocative. Sadly, his subsequent journalistic enterprises turned sour. The magazine *New Delhi*, though innovative in some ways, did not inspire confidence in his readers. He had to swallow the bitter bill of closing down *New Delhi*. Some of his colleagues felt uncomfortable with his style of functioning and his proximity to the ruling establishment.

Similarly, Khushwant Singh's parliamentary career as a Rajya

Sabha member was grounded well before it could take off. Though a Congress nominee, he was fiercely independent-minded to be anybody's yes man. Besides, the rough and tumble of politics was not his cup of tea. Drinking his *chota* peg in his Sujan Singh Park house and encircled by his women friends, he would have probably echoed the following lines from his favourite poet, Iqbal:

> Anon, he carries on with the Church,
> At other times he is in league with temple-dwellers.
> His creed and his code is but bargaining
> An Antara in the role of Haydar.
> Outwardly he displays concern for the faith
> Yet inside he carries the thread of the infidels.
> Smiling with all, he is friend of none
> Forsooth snake is a snake when laughing.

Sure enough, Khushwant Singh made his peace with the establishment on occasions. But, all said and done, he has kept intact his image of an iconoclast and a non-conformist. He is somebody who questions conventional wisdom, flouts established norms, and disregards time-honoured conventions He is neither pretentious nor self-righteous like Nirad Chaudhuri. A broadminded Sardarji, he is able to laugh at himself and at others. He is tolerant, secular, and strongly wedded to multi-culturalism. Had he been trained in mathematics or delved deep into philosophy, I would have probably compared him with Bertrand Russell for his commitment to peace, liberalism and humanism.

Khushwant Singh is not a creative genius, but his extensive writings have given most of us immense pleasure. Some years ago, I read *Train to Pakistan* (1956), one of many novels on the Partition theme. This widely read novel (the paperback edition sold 1,00,000 copies) won the Grove Press Award of $1000. In a style that is moving but not necessarily innovative, it depicts the brutal destruction of the traditional harmony that had prevailed in the Punjab village of Mani Majra, where Sikhs and Muslims had lived amicably. 'By the summer of 1947, when the creation of the new state of Pakistan was formally announced, ten million people—Muslims, Hindus and Sikhs—were in flight.

By the time the monsoon broke, almost a million of them were dead, and all of northern India was in arms, in terror, or in hiding. The only remaining oases of peace were a scatter of little villages lost in the remote reaches of the frontier. One of these villages was Mani Majra.'

Reading this passage from *Train to Pakistan* I was reminded of the observation by Malcolm Darling, a civil servant of Punjab. During his tour in 1946-7 he found, in the tract between the Beas and Sutlej rivers, much similarity between Hindus and Muslims. He asked how Pakistan was to be fitted into these conditions. Khushwant Singh may tell you that this question has not lost its relevance even today.

Urdu, a victim of Hindi chauvinism, has lost its place in free India. Yet Khushwant Singh, unmoved by the linguistic claptrap, has introduced the richness and bewildering variety of Urdu to English-speaking readers. He translated (along with M.A. Husaini) Mirza Mohammad Ruswa's nineteenth century novel, *Umrao Jan Ada*. Ram Babu Saxena, the historian of Urdu literature, had this to say about the novel: 'It is extremely readable, is written in flowing picturesque style, with a systematic plot and with characters brought out in relief. It is harmonious and consistent throughout and is exceedingly entertaining. Nowhere could be found a greater air of verisimilitude or a more fruitful copy from life.' These considerations may have inspired Khushwant Singh to undertake the translation.

Khushwant Singh translated Iqbal's *Shikwa* and *Jawab-i Shikwa*. The translation is marred by errors and does not compare in quality with that of A.J. Arberry's *Complaint and Answer* (Lahore, 1953). Yet the credit for making these moving poems, written in 1909 and 1912 respectively, accessible to so many readers goes to Khushwant Singh.

Incidentally, the *Shikwa* and *Jawab-i-Shikwa* swayed a generation of young Muslims, many of whom were closely tied with Indian nationalism. Salim Ali, the celebrated ornithologist, recalled how Shuaib Qureshi entertained him with 'the moving, patriotic and pro-Islamic verses' of Iqbal. 'One of the recitations, the beauty and sonorousness of which still rings in my ears, is the touching *Shikwa* of the vicissitudes of the island of Sicily, once an important Muslim stronghold in Europe.' Choudhry Khaliquzzaman, Shuaib Qureshi's contemporary, recalled: 'when we were not talking the Brothers (Mohamed and Shaukat Ali) generally sang poems of Iqbal from *Shikwa, Shama aur Shair, Sicily, Fatima*, etc. These were of course the poems which had made Iqbal the idol of the Muslim youth.'

For the uninitiated, let me quote a few verses from these two powerful poems that form part of *Bang-i Dara*:

> In the temples of idolatry, the idols say, 'The Muslims are gone!'
> They rejoice that the guardians of the Kaaba have withdrawn.
> From the world's caravanserais singing camel-drivers have vanished;
> The Koran tucked under their arms they have departed.
> Those infidels smirk and snigger at us, are You aware?
> For the message of Your oneness, do You anymore care?

> Our complaint is not that they are rich, that their coffers overflow,
> They who have no manners and polite speech nothing know.
> What injustice! Here and now are houris and palaces to infidels given:
> While the poor Muslim is promised houris after he goes to heaven.
> Neither favour nor kindness is shown towards us anymore;
> Where is the affection You showed us in the days of yore?

In the twilight of his long and distinguished career some people may find fault with Khushwant Singh or decry him for this or that, but they cannot deny that this man has enriched our cultural and intellectual life for well over three decades. As an outsider to this city, it is hard for me to think of Delhi without him. The British historian Percival Spear once wrote on Ghalib's Delhi. Some day, I may venture to write on Khushwant Singh's Delhi.

> The seven skies are revolving night and day.
> Something is bound to happen, why worry then?

When the grand old man is gone, many of us will miss him, including those like me who have not known him personally. I can hear him say to us:

Happy that day when I set out
to leave this barren wilderness.

26 January 2000

Halide Edib: Woman who Looked
Tomorrow in the Face

With debates on colonialism and nationalism receding into the
background and being replaced by an odd, unwieldy and often
unintelligible combination of esoteric themes, it is no wonder
that several important texts are consigned to the dustbin of
history. I therefore venture to introduce a remarkable text and
its equally remarkable author from Turkey. The author is Halide
Edib (1884-1964) and her book, published in 1937, is entitled
Inside India. There is food for thought for those who are curious
about the minutiae of India's political history in the 1930s,
as well as those interested in the great themes—nationalism,
colonialism and communalism. There is this imposing figure,
imposing through its burning passion and that amazing power
over the language that grips the attention and is so intimately
connected with the writer's personality.

A bewildering variety of Western images and representations
of India exist, and yet one can both learn a great deal more
from *Inside India* and enjoy the sparkling of its author's intellect.
One is struck by the empathy and understanding displayed by a
person whose entrance into the Indian world was in itself an
event in her life. She was not concerned to imagine, inscribe or
invent India, but to come to terms with its multifaceted personality. Her idea of India was firmly anchored in the historical
and sociological insights she gained during her stay in India in
early 1935.

Halide lived through some dizzying changes in her generation. As a woman with a revolutionary mentality, she was a part of a momentous transformation in Turkey, traumatic but epoch-making and irreversible. She shared her countrymen's hatred for colonial occupation. On one occasion, she addressed the crowd with the words, 'When the night is darkest and seems eternal, the light of dawn is nearest.' Again, she asked the people to take the sacred oath that they would not bow down to brute force on any condition. 'We swear,' answered thousands of voices. She wore a nurse's uniform. She even wore the army uniform to thwart the Greek assault. When forced into exile, she disguised her husband and herself to cross the dark restive waters of the Bosphorus. She did all this because of her unflinching faith in the stubborn perseverance of the Turkish people to prepare for their liberation.

Halide Edib and Jawaharlal Nehru knew each other well. They would have found each other congenial, because they possessed the quality, greatly valued by each of them, of being entirely free from dogma. Their intellect stands out clear-cut, robust, and confident against the background of their times. With all its ambiguities, the past served as a reference point to unify the nation and its fragments. Though Nehru's judgement was clouded by the country's Partition, he knew that a modern and secular Republic was the only answer to India's chronic problems. Halide, too, believed that nationhood could not be built on religion. Religion was a reality for the people, but it was purely a relation between God and the individual. It, therefore, had no relation with the State.

Halide mind is, like that of Nehru, vibrant and eclectic. Sharing Nehru's antipathy towards organized religions, she was dissatisfied with orthodox Islam and the intolerance of Christianity but 'charmed and soothed' by her reading of Buddha. Nehru recalled that she had told him about Swami Vivekananda visiting her school in Constantinople when she was a little girl. She remembered how impressed she had been by his presence. As was the case with Nehru, she had an infinite longing for the infinite, in religious thought as in every other thought activity.

Halide was the first Muslim Turkish graduate from the

American College for Girls at Uskudar (Scutari) in 1901, and one of the first Turkish feminists to establish the Society for the Development of Women. She played a major role in the Turk Ojak ('Turkish Hearth') clubs, designed to raise Turkish educational standards and encourage social and economic progress. This programme included public lectures attended by men and women together, a great social innovation. In her twenty novels, essays and memoirs, she borrowed extensively from Ziya Gokalp's (d. 1924) thesis on the status of women in pre-Ottoman Turks, a thesis that served as a basis in formulating the official history of the Turkish republic during the 1930s. Indeed, her name is constantly invoked for and intertwined with the emancipation of Turkish women.

Dominating the literary scene as 'the only canonical female writer' until the 1960s, Halide denied being a feminist. She did not believe in one sex in any country rising and struggling for its rights. Emancipation was a joint venture of man and woman. Consequently, it was through sharing her responsibility and bearing her own burden with man that a woman could win her freedom. Going by current feminist's trends, she was not a feminist. Yet for decades, she was not only an authoritative spokesman of women's rights fighting for their empowerment, but also set an example by refusing to accept polygamy. Commented the historian Arnold Toynbee, one of his ardent admirers:

In parting from her first husband, she had been fighting a battle for a vital human right in the teeth of the law that was then in force, and she had not been fighting simply for her own hand. It had been a battle for all the women in Turkey and, indirectly, for all the women of the rest of the Islamic World as well.

Halide shared her experiences in the eight lectures she delivered at Delhi's Jamia Millia Islamia. When Mahatma Gandhi listened to her on 19 January, he drew many a parallel between the story of India and Turkey, and found, owing to their common suffering, an indissoluble tie binding India to Turkey. Moreover, Turkey's large Muslim population had so much in common with India's Muslims, 'who are flesh of our flesh and blood of our blood and bone of our bone.' 'May Begum Saheba's coming in our midst result in binding Hindus and Muslims in an indissoluble bond.'

On 19 November 1962, Toynbee met Halide in Istanbul. She lived in the quarter between the Conqueror's Mosque and the shore of the Marmara in which she and her husband had settled after returning home from exile. But Adnan Adivar had died in 1955. Now, when he was no more, the old impetuosity had given way to tenderness. Adnan's widow lived in her love for him. She died on 9 January 1964. As a writer, as a patriot, as a woman, and, above all, as a human being who had loved and been loved, Halide had lived to the full.

22 August 2001

Kaifi Azmi's Idea of India

The poet who nurtured the vision of a united India should have died at the time of the Partition. But he did not. He lived in a world, fashioned by Nehru, that was becoming more tolerant, more secular, and more socialistic; in short, a better place to live in. Besides, he was too strong a character to be swamped by the communal tide. Nurtured in the Marxian revolutionary tradition and imbued with revolutionary idealism, he soldiered on sharing Faiz Ahmad Faiz's hope: 'The hour of the deliverance of eye and heart has not arrived/Come, come on, for that goal has still not arrived.'

He should have died on 6 December 1992; instead, he magisterially invoked Rama to appeal for communal peace and inter-religious understanding. The truth is that Kaifi Azmi, having been a witness to the communalization of Indian politics and society in the 1940s, dreaded the resurgence of hotheaded fanatics, Hindus and Muslim alike, in free India. He, therefore, invoked the historical and mythical symbols of the past to ward off an imaginary attack. Time and time again, he acted as the nation's conscience, alerting his readers and audiences to poverty and hunger afflicting our society, and to the threat of war, violence and intolerance. But his ideological adversaries were not listening. The Shah Bano affair, followed by the demolition of the Babri Masjid, signified the defeat of Kaifi's idea of India. For once, religious fundamentalists were able to rein in his otherwise irrepressible spirit.

The pogrom in Ahmedabad was the last straw. *Aj Shabbir pe kya alam-e tanhai hai* [What a world of lonelines lies upon Shabbir (Imam Husain: grandson of Prophet Muhammad was martyred at Karbala) this day!]. Kaifi may well have echoed this line from the legendary poet Mir Anis.

Kaifi passed away just a couple of days before Muslim families in a Gujarat village were forced to sign a bond defining the terms and conditions of their return to their own homes. *Kul-i Nafsun Zaiqatul Maut* (each person has to taste death), says the Koran. Surely not at the hands of religious fanatics, Kaifi would have added.

Kaifi abandoned a Shia theological seminary in Lucknow to plunge into the world of revolutionary nationalism. Many young Muslims, fired by a socialist vision for their country, did likewise. Indeed, Kaifi's political and creative journey began with the Progressive Writers' Movement in the mid-1930s, and in the company of gifted Urdu and Hindi writers and poets. Prominent amongst them were: Sajjad Zaheer, Firaq Gorakhpuri, Faiz, Ali Sardar Jafri, Krishan Chandar, Rajinder Singh Bedi, Jan Nisar Akhtar, Rashid Jahan, Ahmed Ali, Anand Narain Mulla, Majaz, and Ismat Chughtai. All had one thing in common—the readiness to put their convictions above their personal ambitions.

Even after the Progressive Writers' Movement disintegrated following the Partition, Kaifi continued to produce poetry of quality. His earlier collections, *Jhankar* (1944) and *Akhir-e Shab* (1947), had already earned him critical acclaim. *Awarah Sajde*, famed for its *Masnavi Khanah*, enhanced his reputation as a front-rank poet. That is because he did not care for outworn causes or post-modernist discourses; instead, writing in a simple and uncomplicated way he exposed pretences, weighed everything anew, and voiced human sufferings and aspirations. In politics, A.J.P. Taylor had written long ago, there can only be one of two answers—'Yes or No, For or Against'. Kaifi never doubted what had happened or which side was in the right. His characters were all drawn in black and white, the good very good, the bad very bad.

Kaifi was a quintessential communist, and not just a liberal humanist. As such, he never wavered in his principles and never deserted them. Indeed, the socialist ideals were at the core of his literary development as well. Yet, he was one of those poets who put loyalty to his country above loyalty to all else, and his example has been admired, though not always followed.

Defiance, dissent, and protest have been the hallmark of Urdu poetry. Yet, some of the progressive writers made peace with the establishment: most of them were too willing to accept awards and gifts from the government. This marked Kaifi off from his colleagues. He was not dependent on connections or on party; he was self-made. All his life, he wrote as though he would change the life of the wretched of the earth, the poor and the deprived. All his life he condemned imperialism and colonial aggression, and voiced the agony of the freedom-loving people in Vietnam and Palestine. He hated tyranny and oppression wherever they occurred. With his head held high and his voice commanding respect and attention, he doggedly fought for victory and found many worthy causes for which to fight. The effect sometimes ponderous, was always sincere, like the strokes of a great hammer.

Kaifi was an individual with a strong personality—resolute, self-confident and with great powers of physical endurance. He was, above all, a visionary, an iconoclast and a revolutionary. Though there have been greater Urdu poets, there has been none more charismatic and, for that matter, none so popular. Again, to paraphrase A.J.P. Taylor's comment, the steady men of solid principle and minds are the ones who achieve effective success.

Kaifi's eloquence and his splendid declamatory style,

punctuated with the pause, embellished by a flourish of his hand, exemplified his self-confidence and verve. This was bequeathed to him by his Shia upbringing. The tragedy at Karbala was an existential reality, a powerful, enduring, and evocative symbol of resistance to tyranny. What happened at the bank of the Euphrates in Karbala (AD 680), recalled Kaifi's friend and contemporary, Ali Sardar Jafri, symbolized not only martyrdom, but also social justice. Both Kaifi and Jafri opened their eyes in the shadows of knowledge and *tazia* (replica's of Husain's tomb). The first sound they heard was that of lamentation and mourning for Husain's martyrdom. When, for example, Jafri came of age, he found the whole world a house of mourning. 'The seventy-two martyrs in the battle of Karbala,' he wrote, 'are symbols of the highest sacrifice for truth and liberty of the human conscience.' Jafri wrote his epic poem *Karbala* along with a number of other poems with the same symbols. Kaifi, too, wrote *marsiyas* (elegies) in his early days.

Not so long ago, I spent a couple of days with Kaifi Azmi in Pune. Majrooh Sultanpuri had just died, and Kaifi, remembering him fondly, reminded me of his following lines: 'I had started all alone towards the goal but/People kept pouring in and swelled into a caravan.' Sadly, Majrooh, Jafri and Kaifi are not around to lead the Indian caravan on its perilous journey.

15 May 2002

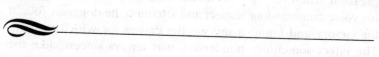

❧ PART III ☙
———•••❧•••———

Image and Representation: Defining Muslim Identity

≈ 1 ≈

*Understanding Islam Better*_____

Notwithstanding Edward Said's powerful critique, Islam has been well served by 'Orientalist' researches over the last century. Scores of German, French and British writers translated and edited Islamic texts, analysed different aspects of Islamic beliefs, and explored facets of Muslim societies. Some created and helped to perpetuate the colonial 'myth' and stereotypes about Islam and its followers; many others, on the other hand, attempted to understand, appreciate and place in perspective the depth, richness and variety of the Islamic civilizations.

You can tell the difference by comparing the volume and quality of such writings with the scholarly literature produced in India. Consider the history of medieval rule from 1206 to 1757 (officially 1857), the large Muslim population in the sub-continent and their presence, so to speak, as a major component in the evolution of India's society, polity and economy. Consider, too, the chequered history of inter-community relations leading to the Partition of the subcontinent on 15 August 1947, and the destruction of the Babri Masjid.

Yet the literature on these and other related historical themes is either inadequate or sketchy or marred by a majoritarian perspective. The upper castes, convinced of their own superiority in the realm of ideas and thought, considered Islam as a rather crude approach to the problems of philosophy and metaphysics (Nehru). There were, consequently, no serious interpreters of Indian Islam, no counterparts of Al-Beruni, Amir Khusro, Abul Fazl, Abdur Rahim and Dara Shikoh. The Muslim intrusion was treated as a break in the continuity of brahmanical traditions; Indian culture was equated with Vedic culture, Indian philosophy with Vedanta, Puranas and the Upanishads, and Indian religions with Hinduism.

Islam had no Max Mueller to detail how its dogmas and tenets were gradually incorporated into regional and local belief structures and rituals; how Muslims, most of whom converted to Islam at different points of time and for different reasons, were integrated with the rest of the population. In the few works that exist, Islam is mistakenly viewed as part of the Great Tradition—codified, rigid and unchanging, insular and closed to external influences. Its followers, whether converted or not, are cast in a specifically Muslim/Islamic mould. Their identity is understood, defined and described, regardless of economic status, caste, language and region, in strictly textual terms.

Quite a few scholars in the West have repudiated the essential notions of Islam. Annemarie Schimmel, Professor at Harvard University for over 25 years, is one of them. I listened to and benefited from her lectures, especially at the Jamia Millia Islamia in Delhi. I have gained insight from reading *Gabriel's Wing: A Study into the Religious Ideas of Sir Muhammad Iqbal, and Islam in the Indian Subcontinent*. Her pioneering study on Iqbal, published in 1973, is by far the most authoritative work in English. Her writings on Sufi Islam are meticulously researched. They have raised the standard of debate on a theme that is neglected in our educational institutions.

Most of Schimmel's monographs reflect her depth and range of scholarship and her engagement with a cultural and intellectual history that so few of us in the subcontinent have either understood or come to terms with. She has uncovered the variety and diversity of the Muslim/Islamic traditions, and shed light on its interaction with other cultural values and streams of thought.

For the 73-year-old scholar of such standing, it must be disconcerting to be drawn into a recent controversy. Over 200 German scholars, including the celebrated Gunter Grass, have not taken kindly to the award of Germany's highest peace prize to Schimmel (*Times of India*, 5 November 1995). Why? Because she is a 'welcome guest in totalitarian Islamic states who ignored human rights violation'. Second, that she was not as harsh as other German intellectuals in criticizing Iran's *fatwa* against Salman Rushdie.

On close reflection, the critique of her approach, methodology and interpretation is legitimate. But why grudge the award? As a historian of ideas, she has earned it through her consistent long-standing scholarly contributions. Her linkages with Iran or the other 'unpopular regimes' are not widely known in this country, but one must recognize the hazards and constraints of researching in 'hostile' countries. It is easy, for example, to organize goodwill missions to, say, Pakistan or India. But it is a nightmare for a solitary researcher, with no institutional or media backing to obtain a visa for research. So, you either abandon your area of specialization or wait endlessly for the denial of an entry permit.

The Rushdie affair has to be treated on a different footing. We do not yet know what Schimmel said or wrote. As a keen observer of Muslim societies, both past and present, she would have appreciated the sense of anger and outrage. If she distanced herself from the controversy over the *Satanic Verses* and its author, it was probably because she was convinced that Rushdie tried to malign, denigrate and caricature Islam, its Prophet and other holy men. In a way, she echoed the hurt feelings of those Muslim communities who have been the subject of her researches.

The standards set by Gunter Grass & Co will embarrass many sections of our liberal and left intelligentsia. Our governments ban books periodically. Yet, this does not cause a flutter in the media or in academic circles. A professor in Jamia has been vilified and denied entry into the campus for three years. Who cares?

Consider, too, how the Rajya Sabha and the West Bengal Assembly condemned Khushwant Singh, a high-profile journalist-author for his comments on Tagore. Yet the champions of free speech and intellectual freedom swallowed the bitter pill. There were many hue and cries over the banning of *Satanic Verses*. But there is total silence over the banning of Rushdie's most

recent novel, *The Moor's Last Sigh*. Why? In a nutshell, the issue
is not Rushdie or Tagore or the merit of their creative writings,
but to uphold, defend and preserve democratic and secular
values at the risk of being 'indiscreet'. So many individuals and
groups learnt this simple lesson the hard way during India's
liberation struggle.

Schimmel is in the news for wrong reasons. But the storm
will blow over. Her work will survive and inspire scholars of
'Indo-Muslim' society, religion and culture. She has many friends
and admirers in this country who wish her well. She could
well be reciting a verse of Ghalib, one of her favourite poets:

*Ham kahan ke dana the kis hunar me ekta the
Besabad hua Ghalib dushman Aasmaan apna.*

27 December 1995

The Image Trap

The expression—Muslim Identity—is widely in vogue. It was
not just the central plank of Jinnah's polemical two-nation theory,
but is constantly pressed into service to devise communitarian
strategies, advance religio-political claims, and nurture the vision
of a unified Muslim community. The postcolonial Indian State
has lent credence to notions of Muslim identity without examining its implications and consequences.

The conventional notion is that Islam as such provides a
complete identity, explanation and moral code for Muslims,
and the mere fact of people being Islamic in some general
sense is conflated with that of their adherence to beliefs and
policies that are strictly described as 'Islamist' or 'fundamentalist'.
In the terms of a typical Orientalist cliché, Islam was not just a
religion but a complete way of life.

This approach is untenable. A Muslim, like his counterpart in any other religious group, has many acts to perform and roles to play. He identifies in varying degrees with different individuals and groups based on ethnicity, language, region, profession and so on. In other words, at no time is one boundary the sole definer of his identity, although at any one time and for any one issue one boundary may become more prominent and define the us-them divide.

This is not all. A Muslim, like a Hindu or a Sikh, has multiple identities. Should we then harp on his Muslim/Islamic identity and ignore everything else, including the 'secular' terms in which he relates to more immediate and pressing socio-economic needs and his wide-ranging interactions with his class and not just his Muslim brethren? Some dispute the depth and nature of this interaction, but that does not justify a discussion in terms of an absolute Muslim/Islamic consciousness.

If, as we are told by scores of writers, centuries of common living and shared experiences could not create composite solidarities, how could a specifically Muslim identity emerge out of their multiple and diverse experiences? First of all, it is important to avoid Islam's reification in the realm of political ideas; instead, we need to consider what political ideas any particular group of Muslims holds, and the relations between these and their social conditions and practice. Within this framework, ordinary Muslims from Kashmir to Kanyakumari will emerge not as members of a monolithic community sullenly apart, but as active participants in regional cultures and traditions whose perspective they share.

Turn to scores of local and regional studies which clearly reveal that Indian Muslims are better integrated with fellow-countrymen of other religious beliefs, and that their views and responses are more diverse and complex than the statements found within the corpus of received opinions on the subject. They illustrate the disjunction between the formal ideology of Islam and the actual day-to-day beliefs and practices of Muslims. Above all, they identify those regional local traditions and cultural features of Indian Islam that were components of, and contributions to, what the liberal and secular nationalists meant by the concept of a composite culture.

Consider another point. One wonders why the debates on such themes are almost exclusively based on writers and publicists who are known to stress elements of discord and separation. If one is interested in a balanced, objective and rounded view, it is necessary to consider other explanations as well, especially those constructed around secular and pluralist conceptions and counterpoised to an essentialist view of Indian Islam.

To begin with, try exploring the largely unfamiliar world of those Muslim scholars, artists and creative writers who contested the definition of Muslim identity in purely religious terms and refuted the popular belief that Islamic values and symbols provide a key to understanding the 'Muslim world-view'.

We may well discover that they, more than anybody else, unfolded our past to discover elements of unity, cohesion and integration, sensed the awful consequences of political solidarity being built on religious ties, and questioned the conviction (or myth) in certain Muslim circles that Hindu nationalism endangered the future of Islam in India. Their notable contribution in providing historical legitimization for multiculturalism and religious plurality should not go unnoticed. And their sane and sober voices must not be stifled by the weight of Muslim orthodoxy or Hindu revivalism.

The intelligentsia creates mirrors through which we see ourselves and windows through which we perceive reality. It is these mirrors and windows that define the boundaries of ideas and institutions. The intelligentsia's role—both as creators of a cultural outlook and the product of the milieu—is central to this writer's view of what happened in India generally and among certain Muslim groups in particular.

So, what does one make of Muslim identity in contemporary India? It is doubtless true that economic discontent, coupled with communal violence, lends weight to notions of identity and acts as a catalyst to communitarian strategies. Yet Muslim scholars and activists often take recourse to a definition that rests uneasily on the Islamic concept of a unified *millat*, and which will always be problematic. So too its projection in the political arena. It is indeed hard to sustain and locate unified communitarian interests in a mixed and diverse population. Hence the importance of drawing a sharp distinction between political polemics and actual ground realities.

If so, what does one make of the self-image of a minority, religious or otherwise? In a nutshell, the language and vocabulary of community-based politics need decoding because the dominant priest-politician combination has, for its own reasons, projected a certain image of itself and the community it purports to represent. As if this was not enough, the state has legitimized their status without questioning their credentials as the spokesmen of their community. Rajiv Gandhi should have posed this question to Syed Shahabuddin, Imam Bukhari and Salman Khursheed during the Shah Bano controversy when they mobilized the Muslims against the Supreme Court judgement and defended a retrograde piece of legislation. He did not do so.

Let us therefore settle the issue in this fiftieth year of our Independence through a nationwide referendum. Let us, once and for all, decide who represents whom. Otherwise, Muslim politicians, many of whom have been repeatedly humbled by the electorate, will continue to act as the self-proclaimed conscience of Muslim interests. All those who have a genuine stake in the future of our secular polity should call their bluff.

Bana hai sheh ka musahib phire hai itrata
Wagar na shehr me Ghalib ki aabroo kya hai.

Struts about so brashly because he is the Sheikh's flunky,
Otherwise, what is his worth in this city, who cares for him?

28 June 1997

*An Adjective to the Muslim*_____

Nationalist Muslims! This expression has been dinned into us for years and is still being bandied about in scholarly and popular writings. Much to my discomfiture, some of us are frequently described as a 'Muslim intellectual' with a pronounced 'Nationalist Muslim' perspective. What, I might ask, is this supposed to mean? Like most of my colleagues, we have no desire to flaunt our identity, which is, at any rate, defined by our vocation in life and not by our religion. Many of us write as a historian for the community of social scientists and not for a religious entity, Hindu or Muslim, while our interpretations, based on empirical research and our understanding of historical processes, are shared or rejected by scores of people across the board. So why single out and label us as 'Nationalist Muslim?'

Some writers have used it innocently for those Muslims who were actively involved in the liberation struggle. They did so to define their role vis-à-vis the colonial State and their stand on the communal issue. In the 1940s, the activism of the 'Nationalist Muslims' vindicated the Congress stand of representing the Indian nation rather than a segment of it. How could the Congress, then, forsake them for the illusory prospect of an accord with Jinnah and the Muslim League? How could leaders like Gandhi and Nehru sacrifice personal friends and political comrades at the behest of Jinnah or at the altar of political expediency? No wonder, their presence in various high-level confabulations became a bone of contention between the Congress and the Muslim League. On the eve of the crucial meeting between the Viceroy and Jinnah on 1 October 1939, the 'Nationalist Muslims' seemed like the 'wrecking horse'.

In much of historical and polemical literature, however, the usage of 'Nationalist Muslims' as an exclusive category reflects a mindset. The unstated assumption is that the 'majority' community is the sole, nay 'natural', custodian of nationalism and patriotism: in fact the term 'Hindu Nationalist' was coined for those who collaborated with the raj, flaunted their Hinduness and inflamed religious passions. In the case of the Muslim communities, it was generally presumed that nationalism as a concept was alien to them and inconsistent with the teachings of Islam. Islam in India was, according to a liberal writer like K.M. Panikkar, 'frankly communal, and its outlook was governed by the single fact of ensuring to the Islamic nation in India its independence and authority'. True, the Muslim communities had their share of obscurantists and communalists, but this did not justify the polemic against an entire community on the basis of a standardized and canonical view of Islam.

The simple argument is that a community's identity, past or present, cannot be understood, defined and categorized in strictly doctrinaire terms. Where do the 'Nationalist Muslims' fit in the scenario of a community that was supposedly resistant to nationalistic ideas? Quiet simply, they are singled out as out of the ordinary in their devotion to nationalistic causes. After all, most of their co-religionists were, as the creation of Pakistan illustrates, not only out of tune with their ideology and politics but were invariably on the wrong side of the binary divide. This line of reasoning is widely accepted because Muslims continue to be treated, quite wrongly of course, as a special category in historical analysis.

For the moment, let us accept 'Nationalist Muslims' as an explanatory category. If so, one must surely, by the same logic, designate Gandhi and Nehru as 'Nationalist Hindus'. Mercifully, this is not done, though not for the reasons that will appeal to some of us. So far so good. But, then, how best to describe a *kisan* or a trade union leader? Was Muzaffar Ahmad, a Communist, a 'Nationalist Muslim' and his comrade P.C. Joshi a 'Nationalist Hindu'? Surely not. In other words, though religion and religious symbols have played a part in moulding popular consciousness, most individuals and groups do not act as members of a religious collectivity.

Let me cite two examples. Ansari, Congress president in 1927, stated: 'I consider the brotherhood of man as the only tie, and partition based on race and religion are, to my mind, artificial and arbitrary, leading to divisions and factious fights.' Similarly, Maulana Azad affirmed some years later: 'I am proud of being an Indian. I am part of the indivisible unity that is Indian nationality.

I am indispensable to this noble edifice and without me this splendid structure of India is incomplete. I am an essential element, which has gone to build India. I can never surrender this claim.' Now, where does one locate such discourses, and their protagonists? How is this language different from that of Gandhi, Nehru or Bose? What is specifically *Muslim* about it?

In a nutshell, identities, religious or otherwise, are created through a dialectical process. Often, they are superimposed to lend credence to a stereotyped image of a community. In consequence, the actions of the 'Nationalist Muslims' that should ideally be part of the nation's collective memory, are intertwined with the Muslims alone. In such a scenario, Rammohun Roy belongs to 'us'; Syed Ahmad Khan belongs to 'them'; Tagore is 'ours'; Iqbal, author of the most secular national anthem ever to be written, in South Asia, is 'theirs'. In this way the nation's heritage is partitioned with remarkable ease.

We need to situate prominent men in public life in a perspective that will enlarge our appreciation of their role and prevent their appropriation by a denominational group. It may be fruitful to treat the Muslim presence in, say, the Congress, or in other political groupings, as part of and not independent of the process of nationalist mobilization. This is surely how the role of individuals like Azad can be best understood. This is surely how a country, desperately in search of unifying symbols, can pay tribute to its freedom fighters.

21 November 1998

*Salvation is Secular*_____

The representation of a privileged Muslim community has been woven around a palpably false theory of Muslim appeasement. The reality, one that is still not adequately recognized in government and bureaucratic circles, is that India's 120 million Muslims lag far behind other communities in literacy, government and private employment, business and industry. They have low levels of income in urban areas, especially when measured in per capita terms. More than half the population lives below the poverty line: fewer urban Muslims work for a regular wage or salary than members of other religious groups do. Widespread illiteracy and a higher dropout rate at the elementary stage are additional problems. That is why the average literacy rate among Muslims is much less than the national average. Most Muslim women, in particular, do not receive school education, let alone higher education. Their empowerment is both a challenge and an urgent necessity.

Regional variations exist, especially where the Muslims, along with Christians, enjoy benefits in the shape of liberal admission to institutions and scholarships, or in UP, Bihar and Delhi where job opportunities have steadily increased after Urdu earned its rightful status. Signs of progress and prosperity are visible in some parts of Rajasthan, Gujarat, Maharashtra, Andhra Pradesh, Tamil Nadu and Kerala. Yet the overall picture is disconcerting. The worrying aspect is that the Muslims will remain, unless remedial measures are taken, outside the area of state employment and in the unorganized sector either as workers or as self-employed petty bourgeoisie.

This was the principal theme of several conferences held at Delhi's India International Centre (IIC) in recent weeks. Much anguish was expressed, over generous helpings of *qorma, biryani* and *nan,* over the community's woeful under-representation in many sectors of the economy and polity. Most participants bemoaned, as their predecessors have done over and over again, that opportunities for economic advance are specially blocked for Muslims because of official neglect and discrimination. This, they insisted, has contributed to Muslims being 'the hewers of wood and drawers of waters'.

Around the same time some other individuals and groups, far removed from the plush IIC surroundings, floated the idea of launching not one but several Muslim political parties. Such moves are afoot in Bangalore, Hyderabad and Delhi. Who knows, the bubble may burst sooner than later. If not, this may turn out to be an ominous trend. My fears are based in part on past experiences and, in part, on present-day social and political realities. I recount the fate of the Majlis-e-Mushawarat (in the 1960s) in UP and the imminent collapse of similar outfits surfacing thereafter. For one, democratic institutions though easy to work with, do not always lend themselves to being effectively used or manipulated by religious collectivities. Second, the Muslim share of the votes is, all said and done, small in most constituencies, though they tilt the balance in some. So that, as the sole spokesmen of their co-religionists, Muslim political activists, regardless of their tall claims, have not carried much influence in decision-making processes. Nor have they acquired the profile of backward caste leaders in UP or Bihar. Here the caste configuration has altered the political landscape, and ensured that Muslims play second fiddle to the more dominant caste alignments. Although politicians of all hues will continue to court Muslim for electoral gains the steady decline of the Congress has, in reality, gradually diminished the value of the 'Muslim vote'.

Muslim leaders, unless tied with progressive political formations, will remain minor players in any electoral or political arrangement in New Delhi as well as in Lucknow and Patna. What they can do best, more so after the collapse of the Congress hegemony, is to make their choices from a large number of secular options available in the political marketplace and hitch their fortunes with secular combinations.

After all, this strategy has paid off in recent decades, though perhaps not to everybody's satisfaction. To give you an instance, Urdu has earned its rightful place in certain districts of UP and Bihar, despite the lukewarm approach of the Congress and the stout opposition of the BJP, owing to the intervention of leaders like Mulayam Singh Yadav and Laloo Prasad Yadav. An Urdu university was set up in Hyderabad by the United Front government. Similarly, non-Congress governments in several southern states have initiated various compensatory programmes, including reservation in certain sectors, and supported various community initiatives in education.

The broad-based alliances with secular parties in Bengal, Tamil Nadu and Andhra Pradesh, though periodically strained, have paid rich dividends. The moral of the story is that the Muslim communities, whether for tactical or other tangible reasons, must work out, as they have so often done after Independence, cross-community linkages, not community-based ones. In other words, the secular and democratic regime must provide the overarching framework to build new political networks. Taking refuge in or drawing sustenance from fundamentalist organizations, some unwittingly perpetuating the community's backwardness through their ill-conceived Islamist agenda, is a recipe for disaster.

Nobody can take exception to the pursuit of one's faith. Nobody can object to Muslims starting schools and colleges, including *madaris*, reforming charitable endowment (*auqaf*), improving the status of Muslim women, generating employment, and energizing the defunct Muslim institutions. After all, the Al-Ameen Educational Society in Bangalore, the Islamic Foundation in Chennai and the Muslim Education Society in Kerala have undertaken such activities. Perhaps, many more groups will surface elsewhere and learn a lesson or two from the constructive engagements of Christian missions, the Arya Samaj and the Ramakrishna Mission. Why, then, is it necessary to create an exclusive Muslim political front? I think it is patently foolish and a counterproductive move. Issues of poverty, education and social emancipation afflicting the Muslim communities cannot be resolved by flexing one's muscles.

5 June 1999

Muslims in Free Fall:
*Myths of Appeasement*_____

The Central Government allocated Rs. 9,568.68 crore in the
ninth five year plan (1997-2002) for the 'empowerment' of
the 145.31 million Muslims, Christians, Sikhs, Buddhists and
Zoroastrians. In addition, the Ministries of Human Resources
Development and Social Justice and Empowerment administer
a number of welfare schemes for them. The Maulana Azad
Foundation, with a corpus of Rs. 30.01 crore, is in the business
of promoting Muslim education; the National Minorities
Development and Finance Corporation (NMDFC) provides
concessional finance for setting up self-employment ventures.

If you are prepared to introduce sciences and mathematics
in your curriculum, apply for government funds for modernizing
your *maktab* and *madrasa*. If you live in one of the 41 minority-
concentrated districts, take advantage of the community poly-
technics and the Industrial Training Institutes. If you require
pre-examination coaching, look out for the 380 NGOs that will
train you to compete for various jobs. The good news is that
27,770 candidates have already benefited from this scheme. The
other good news is that 54 Computer Centres function in various
parts of the country.

So, go out into the wide world for the pickings and grab the
opportunities. But this is easier said than done. For one, whereas
funds are available in plentiful, there is inadequate data on the
beneficiaries of various schemes. The NMDFC, for example,
claims to have disbursed micro credit worth Rs. 114.70 lakh,
but nobody knows whether the funding has been extended
fairly and judiciously. It will appear that government agencies
dole out monies without monitoring their impact on the
minorities.

It is true that state governments are guilty of routinely furnish-
ing insufficient information; one awaits the outcome of the
multi-sectoral development plan launched in 1995-6. Equally,
the reports of the National Commission for Minorities, a statutory
body, are hardly ever tabled in Parliament. Surely, this is not

good enough if we are earnest about 'affirmative action', i.e. reducing the existing imbalances or inequities in the distribution of the nation's resources.

Surely, a government seeking to empower the minorities as the agents of socio-economic change and development must not abdicate its responsibility of undertaking surveys and preparing status reports. Indeed, now that the tenth five year plan is being discussed, my plea to the government is to initiate, with the help of academic institutions and NGOs, extensive surveys and field reports on the social and economic profile of the minorities. The Vice-Chairman of the Planning Commission needs to be reminded that such an exercise was last undertaken in 1983 by Gopal Singh at the behest of the Home Ministry. That is when the Prime Minister, Indira Gandhi, had stated: 'The India of our dreams can survive only if Muslims and other minorities can live in absolute safety and confidence.'

The results are for everybody to see. Let me remind you that Gopal Singh found a large majority of Muslims living in rural areas. They were mostly landless labourers, small and marginal farmers, artisans, craftsmen and shopkeepers. More than half of the Muslim urban population, approximately 35 million out of nearly 76 million, lived below the poverty line. The rest were self-employed. Fewer urban Muslims worked for a regular wage or salary than members of other religious groups did. The *Report* pointedly referred to a rather alarming percentage of the poorer sections among the Muslims in UP and Bihar.

The *Report* furnished information on widespread illiteracy and a higher dropout rate at the elementary stage of education. The average literacy rate among Muslims was 47 per cent, less than half the national average of 52.11 per cent. Muslim women—more than half the total Muslim population—did not receive even school education, let alone higher education. The *Report* underlined the limited Muslim access to government-sponsored welfare projects and their small share in private public employment.

My engagement is not with the causes of Muslim backwardness, for which the explanations range from the general to the specific. The fundamental issue is to ask if the picture is any different now. It may not be appropriate to describe the Muslim communities as 'the hewers of wood and drawers of water', but the harsh reality is that there is not much to write home about their progress since 1983.

It is true that regional variations exist. In general, however, widespread illiteracy, low incomes, irregular unemployment and high incidence of poverty point to a low level of human development. The literacy level is on an average 10 per cent less than the national level: in states like Bihar it is as high as 98.1 per cent in rural areas compared with 21.8 per cent in Kerala. In Jammu & Kashmir, the percentage of illiteracy among Muslims in rural and urban areas are 86.9 per cent and 43.2 per cent respectively. The Ninth Five Year Plan Document itself concedes that the Muslims, women and girls included, remain educationally backward and their traditional institutions like *madaris* are yet to adopt the modern syllabus and be integrated into the mainstream education. Most continue to depend upon the low-income traditional artisanship and other similar occupations.

In 1983, the Muslims were grossly under-represented in public services, and predominant in the 'self-employed' category. The report of the subgroup on minorities (1996) constituted by the Planning Commission illustrates that there are no signs of any significant improvement. Whether it is the police or the railways, the state or the all-India services, Muslim representation is appallingly low. Relatively fewer urban Muslims work for a regular wage or salary, and their representation in the 'casual labour' category' is higher than that of other communities. Abusaleh Shariff's seminal study reveals that, in urban India, 53.4 per cent of Muslims are self-employed as against the figure of 36 per cent amongst Hindus. In rural areas, the annual household income for Muslims as a social group is below the all-India average, as well as below that of the Christians.

We will continue to debate why this is so.The more important challenge is to review existing approaches and strategies, identify those areas for minority uplift that require immediate attention, and devise mechanisms to implement government schemes. For the time being, one can draw comfort from an

official document that refers to 'a more pro-active state intervention for empowering the minorities'.

7 *February 2001*

Nipping Thought in the Bud

Not so long ago, we took pride in some of our theological
seminaries for their role in the anti-colonial struggle. Today,
they are portrayed as nurseries of 'sedition'. Schools at Deoband
and Lucknow were once showcased as vibrant symbols of
secular India. Come 11 September 2001 and, suddenly, they
were regarded as the source of all evil. *Madaris* and *makatib*
are vigorously assailed for fostering 'fundamentalist' ideas. Sadly,
the current debate is more influenced by the Taliban upsurge
and is, for that reason, based on misplaced suppositions and
imaginary fears.

The Turks established the earliest known *madaris* in north
India in the thirteenth century. During Mohammad bin Tughlaq's
reign (1325-51), Delhi alone had a thousand *madaris*. A sixteenth
century British traveller visiting Thata—now a picturesque ruin
near Karachi—reported 400 large and small *madaris*. In the
eighteenth century, the *Dars-i Nizami* (devised by Mulla
Nizamuddin) became the standard syllabus. The curriculum
was confined to the purely religious sciences. The Holy Koran
was at the heart of the curriculum, and its memorization the
highest scholastic attainment. The Dar al-ulum in Deoband
(founded soon after the 1857 revolt) and the Nadwat al-ulama at
Lucknow (founded in 1894) adhere to the *Dars-i Nizami*. They
maintain uniformity in belief and practice by determining what
is true or desirable in accordance with the Koran and the
Traditions of the Prophet.

So far so good. The real problem—one that afflicts the traditional system of learning—lies with their managers who brook no intrusion in their special field of instruction. A majority of them shut themselves off from the contemporary world in their mosques and *madaris* denouncing each other and dubbing everyone else as ignorant, irreligious and atheistic. Only exceptional men, such as Syed Ahmad Khan, the founder of the Aligarh Muslim University, Shibli Nomani, founder of the Nadwat al-ulama in Lucknow, and Maulana Azad, attempted to reconcile tradition and modernity by building bridges between the two. But such men were too few and the results of their labours too limited.

If you don't already know it, let me tell you that the other major problem, for which the *madaris* invite criticism, has been the unchanging character of the curriculum. Aurangzeb, the last of the great Mughal emperors, reprimanded his former teacher for having taught him Arabic, grammar and philosophy rather than subjects more practical for a future ruler of a vast empire. Syed Ahmad Khan echoed the same view, pointing to their syllabus being 'unsuited to the present age and to the spirit of the time'. Others, too, have criticized the curriculum for encouraging memorizing rather than real understanding. The scholar Fazlur Rahman commented: 'By organically relating all forms of knowledge and gearing these to dogmatic theology the very sources of intellectual fecundity were blighted and the possibility of original thinking stifled.'

Today, the Islamist orientation of the *madaris* afflicts Pakistan but most certainly not India. The crux of the matter here, and one that commands immediate attention, is the narrowing down of the general field of learning, and the consequent decline and stagnation of Muslim scholarship in our country. I object not to the imparting of religious education but to the abysmal failure of the *madrasa* system to equip students to compete in the wider world. India's Muslims must have their share of men with turbans and flowing gowns, but they must also produce, in equal measure, front-rank professionals.

For this to happen, the secular and religious leadership has to alter both the tone and the tenor of the curriculum in order to make it responsive to the requirements of this millennium. During the course of its history, Islam has developed the capacity to meet challenges creatively. The basic problem now, however, is what are the elements in its history it should emphasize and recombine for its effective self-statement in the present scenario; what it should modify and what it ought to reject (Fazlur Rahman). There is, I believe, much less ambiguity in the realm of education. The principles of intellectual integrity necessitate a fundamental reconstruction of educational thought.

In the second half of the nineteenth century, the traditional system of education was reorganized to prevent the influx of subversive ideas from the religiously alien and 'morally inferior' British, and to put a premium on unorthodox thought and learning. Today, the Muslim communities are faced with a different challenge, i.e. to define their agenda in response to the currents of change and progress. A standard curriculum that excludes rational sciences is simply not good enough; instead, there is a serious need for a constructive and bold humanism that would restate and reinterpret Islamic educational ideas in the contemporary social and cultural environment.

At the same time, the current mindset towards our traditional centres of learning needs to be changed. Just as all the 'Hindu' or Arya Samajist schools do not spew venom against Islam and Christianity, so also the *makatib* and *madaris* do not necessarily nurture fundamentalist ideas. Mostly dependent on public donations and drawing students from poor families, they survive on the margins of India's educational paraphernalia. How can they breed terrorists? In the past, the same *makatib* and *madaris* produced leading theologians, political activists (thousands went to jail in response to the Gandhian movements) and liberal reformers. They can still be the source of (for example, the Deoband school) and the inspiration behind rationalist thought and reformist initiatives.

The real problem is the prevalence of widespread illiteracy and a high drop-out rate at the elementary stage. It is not clear whether Muslim children are not sent to schools because of economic constraints, or the sting of the prevailing bias against Urdu, or because parents in larger arts and crafts centres hardly consider it worthwhile to give their children higher education. But one thing is for sure. Part of the reason why *makatib* and *madaris* flourish is because the State has not done enough to promote 'secular' education in *mofussil* towns and the rural hinterland. Hence, children of poor Muslim families flock to religious schools. For decades now, these schools have performed a useful and legitimate role (as do the *Gurukuls* or the Christian schools). Let us not treat them with suspicion and disdain, but urge the government to creatively intervene in secularizing (not crass secularism) their curriculum and methods of instruction.

Islam is all about the 'surrender to the Will of the God', i.e. the determination to implement the command of Allah. Given the place assigned to knowledge in the Koran, one hopes that the managers of *madaris* will discover a fuller meaning of their role in Muslim society. The degree and effectiveness of their vision may affect not only their own future but also much of the world around them.

20 March 2002

Don't Teach me Patriotism

This war [the Kargil war], hopefully the last, was thrust upon us. It was aggression, pure and simple. We have responded well though belatedly to the challenge. The army has, as always, risen to the occasion. The government muddled its way through after initial blunders, but on balance exercised restraint in dealing with a potentially explosive situation. The international support was a coup of sorts, an asset in conducting military operations in a hazardous terrain. Never before in post-Independence history has India's stand been so powerfully vindicated. This factor alone has contributed to Pakistan's isolation even in the so-called Muslim world, forcing its government to retreat. Nawaz Sharif's military exploits have not gone down well in his own country. Clearly, his calculated gamble has not paid off.

Often, a limited or full-fledged military operation can lead to short-term gain. But, in the long run, these so-called gains run into rough weather. One's hope is that Pakistan has learnt its lesson and will desist from aggression. Kashmir's future, hanging in the balance for over fifty-long years, should be discussed bilaterally. At the same time, Pakistan's Prime Minister must know from past experience that the Valley cannot be handed over on a platter just because some armed marauders, or *mujahidin* violate the Indian borders. As a leader with a popular mandate, he has no reason to be swayed by the rhetoric of the Islamists or the military establishment.

Peace and diplomacy must be given a chance at our end. The Shimla Accord [between Indira Gandhi and Z.A. Bhutto] and the Lahore Declaration can still be invoked, for reviving the peace process, in our stable and mature democracy. When a nation sits down to do its sums, the rhetoric of war, the sound and fury of the guns, and the politics of revenge and reprisals, will seem utterly futile. This is what one must learn from post-war Europe. Militarism, now on everybody's lips, is an easy answer to aggression, but not a solution to our long-standing disputes with Pakistan. Those who created a war-like climate, and this includes most notably the English-language press and the Star News network, must exercise caution and self-restraint. Militant nationalism, though a saleable commodity in the market-place in a crisis, must not be allowed to run amok. Flaunting patriotism at the heights of the barren Kargil mountains is hardly a substitute for mature judgement and a balanced appraisal of national priorities.

Once the booming guns are silenced and the euphoria is dissipated by the harsh realities of daily existence, the deep-seated fissures in our polity and society are bound to surface. Yes, the country will be dotted with war memorials, but we will soon forget our war widows and have our injured soldiers at the mercy of their relatives. The eyes that shed tears in middle class homes for the dead and wounded soldiers will dry up. The focus this summer—from the World Cup to Kargil— will shift to yet another battle, this time of the ballot. Somebody will then write a book on the 'Forgotten Martyrs', to be released at 7 Race Course Road.

The news of the war being over would have reached even the tiny hamlets in Kanyakumari. But the war mongering continues relentlessly. Such is the rhetoric that one has the creepy feeling that the enemy is perched not on a hill top in Kargil but within our own society. No cricket matches with Pakistan, declares Kapil Dev. Forever, say Bal Thackeray and Vir Sanghvi editor of the *Hindustan Times* in unison. Outside the cricket arena, the 77 year old Dilip Kumar, once a national icon, is targeted. The man, who reached the commanding heights of Indian cinema as an actor, is harassed by a bunch of goons. Why? Because his real name is Yusuf Khan. Because he chose to live in Bombay and not Peshawar. Shabana Azmi and Javed Akhtar [poet and script-writer], whose progressive ancestry is nobody's concern, belong to the 'Green Brigade' because Bal Thackeray says so. You can achieve stardom, but must do something different, something extra, to be an 'Indian'. For this, please turn to Thackeray for advice.

From now on, the likes of Thackeray will decide who is a patriot and who is not. People who have not even walked through the corridors of a college building will remind us of our heroes and heritage. And we, the professional historians, will be made to take lessons in history writing from second-grade polemicists and propagandists. Such is the cheerless prospect, the imminent danger, if those who preach and practice violence define nationalism and patriotism.

Dilip Kumar's only consolation is that self-styled patriots have also vilified a venerable scholar of a prestigious seminary in Lucknow [Nadwat al-ulama] because of certain statements attributed to him, which he has repeatedly denied. I do not agree with Ali Miyan's stand on certain issues, but his extensive writings bear testimony to his commitment to our democratic and secular polity. This is what he wrote in 1960. 'The Muslims are not only citizens of an equal status with anybody in India; they are also among its chief builders and architects, and hold position second to none among the peoples of the world for selfless service to the motherland.'

Even if he had not made these observations, there is no reason for him or anybody else to declare their allegiance to India from their housetops. That is why I was distressed to note that 'Muslim intellectuals' found it necessary to express solidarity with the soldiers. By all means do so, but why as 'Muslims'? Were any of the 'Sikh', 'Hindu' or 'Christian' intellectuals obliged to act likewise? Did they congregate as a religious entity? The predicament of the organizers of the Muslim intellectual meet apart, their anxiety to establish their nationalist credentials does not carry much conviction. Born and brought up in this country, the 120 million Muslims belong not to two circles but the one and only Indian circle, I repeat the *Indian circle*.

I return to the first point. Once the anger and excitement subsides, we may find that the interests in which India and Pakistan conflict are immeasurably less important than those in which they are at one. Survival is the first and most important of their common interests. This has become a common interest owing to the nature of nuclear weapons. The essential points, which both sides must realize, are that the continuation of con-flict is disastrous to both, and that the gain to be derived from peace is one of quite immeasurable magnitude. Brinkmanship and surrender are by no means the only alternatives.

17 July 1999

2

Hatred of a Humanist:
*Nirad C. Chaudhuri*_____

Nirad C. Chaudhuri, the pukka sahib nurtured in the Victorian traditions, believed in the benevolence of the British intentions and lamented, in no uncertain terms, the eclipse of the empire. The British empire in India was and 'remains one of the central facts of universal history and the concrete evidence that the British people have discharged one of their primary roles in history. They could not disinterest themselves in it without abrogating their historical mission and eliminating themselves from one of the primary strands of human evolution.'

Autobiography of an Unknown Indian, published in 1951, was a milestone in the career of this Kishoreganj-born Bengali intellectual. It set him free from the enclosure that his country and society had become for him, and the freedom was as much social as vocational. At the same time his relentless critique of everything Indian invited the wrath of our intelligentsia and caused embarrassment to the Bengali *bhadralok* in Calcutta who could not, despite their innate desire, add his name to their list of icons, which had stopped at Bose. He acquired the reputation of being a Katharine Mayo, anti-Indian, anti-Hindu, and anti what have-you.

The irrepressible author was not bothered by what his countrymen felt so long as the BBC feted him in London and Winston Churchill read his book. Adverse publicity, at any rate, helped, rather than hindered, the sale of his book. As for his Bengali compatriots, he had nothing much to add except that the post-Tagore generations in his home state were scarcely equipped to comprehend the meaning and depth of his ideas and intellectual explorations.

I cannot bring to light the many interesting facets of Nirad Babu's scholarship but I do wish to underline an aspect that has not been touched upon in the numerous newspaper obituaries. This relates to his harsh and polemical criticism of Islam and its followers in India.

He became conscious, as he tells us in his autobiography, of a new kind of hatred for the Muslims during the Swadeshi movement (1906). A cold dislike for them settled down in his heart. He rejoiced at Italy's attack on Tripoli in 1911, and when Turkey joined the German side at the end of 1914 'so that the Muslims will be taught a lesson'. Strongly anti-Muslim in 1920 (in his own words) owing to the pan-Islamic upsurge, he was uneasy with the 'menacing assertiveness' of the Bengali Muslims. He was repelled by the cheerless prospect of living in a province where Muslims would be a dominant social and cultural entity.

Why? The answer comes from Nirad Babu himself. 'Nothing was more natural for us,' he observed, 'than to feel about the Muslims in the way we did.' He and his friends were told, even before they could read, that the Muslims had ruled and oppressed the Hindus, spread their religion with the Koran in one hand and the sword in the other, abducted Hindu women, destroyed temples, and polluted sacred places. 'As we grew older we read about the wars of the Rajputs, the Marathas, and the Sikhs against the Muslims, and of the intolerance and oppression of Aurangzeb.'

So, what was the verdict? Muslims constituted a society of their own with a distinctive culture. They could not be absorbed into a unified nation. For this reason the arguments trotted out by Gandhi and Nehru to contest their demands were 'false' and 'foolish'. In his days the gigantic catastrophe of Hindu-Muslim discord did not surprise him a bit, because this conflict was implicit in the very unfolding of Indian history. Nehru, in particular, failed to comprehend this reality owing to his social and cultural affiliations—'more a Muslim than a Hindu, so far as he is anything Indian at all'.

Whenever he saw a *burqa*-clad person, he apostrophized her mentally: 'Sister! You are the symbol of your community in India.' The entire body of the Muslims, according to him, was under a black veil. And his advice to them was to immigrate to Pakistan. 'There is something unnatural in the continued presence of the Muslims in India and of the Hindus in Pakistan, as if both went

against a natural cultural ecology.' Food for thought for Bal
Thackeray!

What explains the hostility of this self-proclaimed liberal
humanist towards the Muslims? Nirad Babu's own explanation,
one that holds true for scores of Bengali intellectuals in the
past and present, is illuminating. Bengali thinkers and reformers,
in his view, based their life work on the formula of a synthesis
of Hindu and European currents. Islamic trends and Muslim
sensitivities did not touch the arc of their consciousness. They
stood outside as an external proletariat. In fact, the Bengali
culture of the nineteenth century built a perimeter of its own
and specifically put Muslim influences and aspirations beyond
the pale.

Nirad Babu lived long enough and yet he had earned for
himself the right to enter the next millennium. If *Yamdoot* had
not taken him away from his home in Oxford, he would probably
have written yet another book reflecting on the previous millennium. He would have surely retained his intellectual flair, his
intellectual energy, and his eagerness to critique anybody and
everybody.

All said and done, we need a Nirad Babu in our country
where mediocrity and intellectual mendicancy have acquired
full and wholesome legitimacy in academic, bureaucratic and
governmental circles. We need an iconoclast like him who can
blast the political establishment for its monumental failure to
fulfil the basic material needs of our teeming millions. We need
a fiery thinker like him who can raise his voice against the
inertia and listlessness that has beset our academic institutions.
We need somebody who can strengthen multiculturalism and
pluralism, somebody who would recognize the role and place
of the minorities, Muslims included, in a democratic and secular
polity.

Given his ideological predilections and his deep-seated
prejudices towards the Muslims, Nirad Babu was perhaps not
cut out to play this role either as a historian of ideas or as a
citizen of the world.

7 August 1999

An India for Sir Vidia:
A Million Mutilations_____

Intellectually, wrote Nirad Chaudhuri in the mid-1960s, the European mind was outraged by the Hindus precisely in those three principles which were fundamental to its approach to life, and which it has been applying with ever greater strictness since the Renaissance: that of reason, that of order, and that of measure. Discussing E.M. Forster's *A Passage to India*, his main criticism was that the major Indian character, Aziz, and most of the supporting Indians were Muslims. Nirad Babu believed that Forster did this because he shared the liking the British in India had for the Muslims, and the corresponding dislike for the Hindus. So that Dr. Godbole, the chief Hindu character in the novel, was not an exponent of Hinduism but a clown. Doubtless, this criticism was unjustified. But the noteworthy point is that Nirad Chaudhuri did not comment on why, with some notable exceptions, Muslim characters did not figure creatively in Bengali literary writings (outside the circle of Muslim writers) for well over a century. Equally it is not clear why he, the self-styled defender of Victorian (rather than Indian) values, was flustered by the presence of an Aziz in *A Passage to India*. One will have to turn to his other writings to explain his own antipathy towards Islam and the Muslims.

Yet another writer of Indian origin fulminates against Islam and the Indian Muslims. He is none other than Sir Vidiadhar Naipaul, whose ancestors left India in the early-1880s as indentured labourers for the sugar estates of Guyana and Trinidad. Having explored an area of darkness and chronicled the histories of a wounded civilization and a million little mutinies in India, he decided to fire his shots at the world of Islam. This was the beginning of a long-term laboured project. Long before Samuel Huntington earned his reputation for expounding the clash of civilizations theory, the Trinidad-born writer alerted his Western readers to the growing Islamic menace. *Among the Believers*, his Islamic journey to Iran, Pakistan, Malaysia and Indonesia, led him to represent Islam as a hostile and aggressive force, and caricature Muslims societies as rigid, authoritarian and uncreative.

'Islam sanctified rage, rage about the faith, political rage: one could be like the other. And more than once, on this journey I had met sensitive men who were ready to contemplate greater convulsions.' *India: A Million Mutinies*, published in 1990, conjured up the same images, though he was much more restrained in his overall reflections on the country as a whole. He referred to the 1857 revolt as the last flare-up of Muslim energy in India until the agitation, 80 years or so later, for a separate Muslim homeland. He found bazars in Lucknow expressing the faith of the book and the mosque. Everything in the bazar, he felt, served the faith. (For all these years, I have searched in vain for such a bazar in a city that I know better than Naipaul). Two years after this book was published, he came out in virtual defence of the destruction of the Babri Masjid. Naipaul may have derived satisfaction from his compatriot in Oxford, Nirad Chaudhuri, being on the same wavelength.

Today, Naipaul's worldview remains unchanged. Hindu militancy, he says in a recent interview to the *Outlook* magazine, is a necessary corrective to the past, a creative force. To say that India has a secular character, he adds, is being historically unsound. This makes Naipaul a worthy chairman for the committee that is being readied for a major political rehearsal— the review of the Indian Constitution. He rejects the possibility of Islam working out reconciliation with other religions on the subcontinent. Islam is a religion of fixed laws. This, he points out, goes contrary to everything in modern India. This is, in just a few crispy sentences, the clash of civilization theory applicable to the subcontinent.

There is a great deal of talk nowadays of rewriting our history. Naipaul has quite a few brilliant ideas for the newly appointed chairman of the Indian Council of Historical Research. One of them is to give voice to the 'defeated people'. Mind you, not the poor or the downtrodden but the *Hindus* living in *Hindu India*. To add poignancy to our historical narratives, Naipaul suggests that we concentrate on a more tragic and more illuminating theme. That theme is the 'grinding down of Hindu India'. So, revive memories of temples being destroyed, Hindus being forcibly converted to Islam, and Sikh gurus being mercilessly executed by the Mughal emperors.

If one has to build a modern India by invoking the brutal past, the prescription is to rubbish the forces of assimilation and integration in Indian society. Finally, if the ICHR chairperson heeds Naipaul's advice, he will drop Gandhi from the history syllabus. That is because Naipaul regards the Mahatma as uneducated, and not a thinker. He has no message today, even though Indians have used the very idea of Gandhi to turn dirt and backwardness into much-loved deities. The *Hind Swaraj* is so nonsensical that it would curl the hair of even the most devoted admirer. Mercifully, Nehru is spared for being a democrat and a humane person who did not abuse his power.

Naipaul's exposition is clumsy, naïve and gibberish. He is as much ill informed about India as Samuel Huntington is about the world outside the Western Hemisphere. He talks of India's fractured past solely in terms of the Muslim invasions and the grinding down of the Hindu-Buddhist culture of the past. He must know that celebrating the coming of the Turks or the vandalism of the Islamic zealots is nobody's favourite pastime. The historian's job is to come to terms with Turkish, Afghan and Mughal rule, study their polities objectively, and examine the consequences of their policies dispassionately. Fuming and fretting, which is what Naipaul does in this interview, takes you nowhere. Anger, remorse and bitterness are not a substitute for serious study and analysis.

We have both inherited and self-created problems and difficulties. But we must have time and our own spaces to sort them out. Most of us will therefore prefer not to be told, by people living in Mayfair Gardens or Manhattan, how to move into the next millennium with our heads held high. Believe me, some friends living overseas can be our worst enemies.

27 November 1999

Sir Vidia's outburst against Forster_____

Lord Curzon, governor-general of India, drew up a list of princes with homosexual tastes. He attributed it largely to early marriage, to a boy getting tired of his wife, or of women, at an early age, and desiring the stimulus of some more novel or exiting sensation. When he heard that a young prince had shown homosexual tendencies, he sent him to the Imperial Cadet Corps to learn self-discipline. The Secretary of State for India was not surprised that this particular prince had taken to 'the special Oriental vice.' His own experience of schools, seminaries and colleges for boys led him to believe that these institutions were 'infected with some immorality or other.'

In much of official discourses, homosexuality was despised not only as unmanly, but also dreaded as a threat to military discipline. Hence, Indian prostitutes were seen as necessary to the satisfaction of the soldiers' physical needs. If those needs were not satisfied, dire consequences were envisaged. The soldiers' masculinity would be at risk—the prospect of homosexuality was raised whenever there was talk of excluding prostitutes from cantonments. Various steps were therefore taken to register prostitutes, inspect them, and detain them in hospital if they caught venereal diseases (Kenneth Ballhatchet).

This may serve as a background to Sir V.H. Naipaul's recent outburst (*Indian Express*, 3 Aug.) against E.M. Forster (1879-1970), the celebrated author of *A Passage to India* (1924), and the Cambridge economist, John Maynard Keynes. When people run out of new ideas, they take recourse to such raving and ranting to capture media attention. Forster and Keynes were homosexuals all right, but it is grossly unfair to describe them as 'exploiters'. It is ludicrous to suggest, moreover, that Forster visited India in 1912 to solely satisfy his desire for 'garden boys'.

The British philosopher Bertrand Russell had known Keynes, ten years his junior, and had a healthy respect for what he later called the sharpest and clearest intellectual he had ever known. 'When I argued with him I felt that I took my life in my hands,' he wrote; and, asked by somebody what he had thought of

Keynes, he replied, 'Obviously a nice man, but I did not enjoy his company. He made me feel a fool.' I bet Sir Vidia would have felt the same way had he met Keynes, hard at work in King's College on his *Treatise of Probability*. In the early 1920s, though, Russell found Keynes busy with politics and moneymaking and doubted if he ever thought about probability.

Forster read Kalidas's *Sakuntala* and the *Bhagavad Gita* and learnt all about the Ajanta frescoes before his journey to India. His host was Dr. M.A. Ansari, later the Congress president (1927). He sat in the verandah of the house—*Behisht* (Paradise)—by the old city's wall in Delhi's Mori Gate listening to the doves and green parrots making conversation in the garden. The *Behisht* was thronged by unexplained visitors— sitting cross-legged on the beds or on the luggage. There seemed to be no set meal times, but whenever Forster crossed the threshold, tea and poached eggs were served and Ansari's wife, who observed *purdah*, would send cigarettes, betel nut and *itr* (perfume). 'I am in the middle of a very queer life,' he told a friend, 'whether typically Oriental I have no means of knowing, but it isn't English.'

Altogether he was charmed with India. It was quite different from anything he had heard. He describes an evening at a nautch party with dancing girls. Arranged by Ansari, it was attended by Mohamed Ali, editor of the Delhi paper, *Comrade*, who contemplated suicide as the message reached him that the Bulgarians were only 25 miles from Contantinople. Mohamed Ali was indiscreet to share his experience at the nautch with a fellow-journalist, and not long afterwards, there appeared in *The Times* a report of how a leading Muslim, on the eve of Turkey's defeat in the Balkan war, had spent his evening at an 'orgy'.

Forster interests his readers not because he was a pucca gay, but because he wrote *The Passage of India*, deservedly the best known of his novels. One is also fascinated by his intimate relationship with Ross Masood (1889-1937), son of Syed Mahmood, a judge reputed to be an alcoholic, and grandson of Syed Ahmad Khan, the founder of the Aligarh Muslim University. For one, their's is—the only one that I know of in twentieth century India—a brilliantly documented affair. Second, their fondness for each other was reciprocal and based on trust and understanding. Masood, Forster was to say later, woke him up out of his suburban and academic life and showed him new horizons and a new civilisation.

The depth of their relationship, though never fulfilled physically, belies the charge levelled by Sir Vidia against Forster. Studying at New College in Oxford, Masood yearned for Forster's company and expressed his romantic affection in no uncertain terms. Once he suggested, 'let us get away from the conventional world [?] & let us wander aimlessly if we can, like two pieces of wood on the ocean & perhaps we will understand life better.' On another occasion he wrote: 'Centuries may pass, years may turn into 2000 centuries and you never hear from me & you are not to think that the great affection, the real love & the sincerest admiration that I feel for you has in any way diminished.'

Masood was a striking and exuberant figure, well over six feet tall, with a sonorous and beautiful voice. He learnt Latin, played tennis, and recited Ghalib. He handled the British splendidly. If they patronised him, he let them have it back, very politely. There was the occasion, for instance, when some undergraduates broke into his room, saying they objected to his 'unmanly' use of scent. 'We'll see who's unmanly', was his reply, and he challenged one of them to a wrestling-match and wiped the floor with him. Masood returned to India reluctantly in 1912, worked for a few years in a legal practice, joined the Nizam's service, and played a part in the founding of Osmania University. He became vice-chancellor of the Aligarh Muslim University but resigned in 1934, a year after he received knighthood.

All these years Forster felt lonely and desolate, but that is not a story I am going to tell. My plea to Sir Vidia is not to demonise gay men but to accord to them the respect they deserve. Keynes and Forster, in particular, were men of distinction and surely not champions of an 'aggressively plebeian culture,' a charge he recently levelled against Tony Blair's government.

8 August 2001

Kalyan Singh's Mandir Agenda

Qayamat tak wo sardari ke qabil ho nahin sakte.

Doomsday will come before they are fit to rule.

AKBAR ALLAHABADI

Uma Bharti and I appeared in a talk show. Her body language was not the same any more. Finding her restrained and conciliatory, I concluded that she was trying to represent BJP's moderate face. It was not before long that I discovered my optimism to be misplaced. I felt cheated when the Chief Minister of UP, Kalyan Singh, declared his commitment to the rebuilding of the Ram temple at Ayodhya. Was the Chief Minister speaking out of turn, or did he have the BJP's mandate to announce his plan? If so, was Uma Bharti aware of the happenings in her own party?

Whatever his political compulsions, Kalyan Singh should not be allowed to disturb the *status quo* in Ayodhya. Somebody should remind him of the people's verdict in November 1993. That was when the BJP, fresh from its 'victory' in Ayodhya, suffered major electoral reverses not only in his home state but also in Himachal Pradesh and Madhya Pradesh. He had stated that if his party got even one seat less than the 221 it held in UP, it will be tantamount to a rejection of the *mandir* movement. In the event, the party lost 44 seats.

Consider your priorities, Mr. Singh. Turn to your own state and address yourself to those millions of poverty-stricken people who have yet to receive a fair deal and whose basic needs still are *roti, kapra, aur makan.* Your state, which has been ill served by politicians of all hues since Independence, lags far behind other regions. You will find a place in history not by building a temple but by setting up industries, creating job opportunities, and building the infrastructure for future growth and prosperity. You need not spend sleepless nights over the *mandir.* Surely there are enough Ram *mandirs* in our villages to offer spiritual solace to their *bhakts* (devotees).

You preside over the destiny of a state that was once the symbol of composite and syncretic living. Although its political landscape changed with the rise of Muslim nationalism and Hindu militancy, different communities continue to live in amity and share the values of pluralism and multiculturalism. Why then introduce a discordant note with the *mandir* issue? Why rake up divisive issues that lay dormant for decades? Why create a cleavage amongst your own people? Is it not possible to cite historical precedents to unite people around symbols of unity and mutual cooperation? Instead of reminding your audience of what Babar or Aurangzeb did, why not talk of Amir Khusro, Jaisi, Rahim, Raskhan and Dara Shikoh? Why not remind your people of what the Urdu poet Akbar Allahabadi wrote in the first-half of this century:

> His radiance fills the Kaaba. He lies hidden in the temple.
> It is to Him we cry, whether as Allah or as Ram.

As the head of the most populous state, you are accountable to the nation at large. Without commenting on the conduct of our leaders or the legitimacy of this government, I wish to underline the visible signs of social change and economic progress. Life will not be the same if the Babri Masjid issue is politicized for short-term electoral gains. By raising the communal temperature, you will be acting against the larger interests of the people.

Today, the redeeming feature is that socio-economic matters figure more prominently on everybody's agenda, while the country is not polarized along religious lines, as was the case during the dispute over the Babri Masjid. Whether in UP or in Bihar, caste rather than community is the focal point of mobilization. The liberal and secular voices among Muslims are being heard loud and clear, while both Hindu and Muslim communalists stand isolated. This explains why these states have been free of Hindu-Muslim strife.

In other words, Chief Minister, it is possible to avoid the communal claptrap and forge a joint front to promote a specifically socio-economic agenda. Muslims of UP, who are quite numerous and influential in several areas, should be made a part of, and not isolated from, such a front. If you want them to feel safe and secure in their own state, please do not repeat the monumental folly you and your government committed on 6 December 1992. If you want your public image to be restored, please do not be swayed by the *Hindutva* rhetoric.

As a general rule, we must not destroy or vandalize places of worship. India has been the home of many religions. The country has been partitioned once before owing to the nefarious role of the British administrators and the miscalculation of our political leaders. So please don't become a crusader and start targeting mosques, gurudwaras, churches and synagogues. Enough is enough. What we need today is a *Naya Shivala* (new temple), the dream of poet Iqbal. Please pay heed to his following advice:

Let us reconcile those that have turned away from each other
Remove all signs of division
Desolation has reigned for long in the habitation of my heart.
Come, let us build a new temple in our land.
Let our holy places be higher than any on the earth,
Let us raise its pinnacle till it touches the level of the sky;
Let us awake every morning to sing the sweetest songs;
And give all worshippers the wine of love to drink.
There is power, there is peace in the songs of the devotees–
The salvation of all dwellers on the earth is love.

We must reject the proposal for a referendum on the Babri Masjid, aired in certain quarters and welcomed by some BJP leaders. Such an emotive issue, which has been so highly politicized by the Hindu and Muslim firebrands, cannot be resolved through a popular vote. Second, there is no precedence of a referendum in India. One wonders why the Congress did not press for a referendum on the Pakistan issue? Had they done so, the Muslims may well have voted against Partition. Who knows?

The Constitution, too, makes no provision for a referendum. An amendment at this stage will be counterproductive. Moreover, a referendum makes sense in countries with a literate and relatively homogeneous population, but not in a country of our size and diversity. Finally, has anybody considered that a referendum on the Babri Masjid is fraught with serious consequences? What, if the BJP demands one on a uniform civil code? Will the self-styled Muslim leaders agree to it?

4 October 1997

The Danger of Communal Stereotyping

The hijacking of the Indian Airlines aircraft has evoked different responses. The latest is from Rajendra Singh, the RSS chief. Obviously, he is upset over the government's decision to let off the terrorists in exchange for the hijacked passengers. I have no quarrel with him on that score. What I wish to contest is his contention that the release of the terrorists exposed the 'cowardice of Hindus'. For one, neither the decision-making bodies nor their personnel were acting as Hindus *per se*. The Prime Minister and his colleagues may have erred in their judgement, but we have no reason to doubt that they acted in the interest of the nation. They wanted to save the lives of innocent passengers and not to establish the macho image of the so-called Hindu nation. Likewise, Rajju Bhaiyya's plea, in the same interview, to make the Hindu society 'courageous' carries seeds of accentuating religious dissension in our society.

At a time like this we should be talking in terms of a concerted nationwide effort to counter terrorism. Instead, he has raised the cry of some form of *sangathan* (consolidation) of a particular community. The keywords in Rajju Bhaiyya's interview are 'Hindu cowardice' and *sangathan*. These lie at the heart of the Hindu revitalization movements for well over a century. To begin with, it was the Arya Samaj that constructed a specifically Hindu identity through a reinterpretation of Hinduism and its sacred literature, cow-protection, and *shuddhi*. From the mid-1880s, it sponsored and gradually came to perform ceremonies of readmission—*shuddhi*—to Hinduism. Although individual reconversions had little impact on Hindus in relation to other communities, they possessed great symbolic value for the internal regeneration of Hindus society. They offered hope and signified a New World in which Hindus could fight to maintain themselves and their religion.

The Arya Samaj reacted powerfully to colonial subservience and to the Muslim majority in Punjab. It, therefore, underlined the moral and spiritual degeneration of the Hindus, their weakness to withstand the Christian-Muslim assaults, and their inability to defend their hearth and home, their temples, or the honour of their women. Such an evaluation of 'Hindu character' was neither supported by contemporary events nor by some of the protagonists of Hindu revivalism, such as Madan Mohan Malaviya, who maintained that Hindus were not weak, and that in all conflicts with the Muslims, 'when they were equally matched they were never vanquished'. Yet the Arya Samaj set out to provide a vision of and pride in the Hindu nation, and make Hinduism a new living force, both defensive and even militant if necessary. Lala Lajpat Rai, one of its leading figures, stated that the tiny barge of the Arya Samaj was at that time to him the barge of Hindu nationality.

The theme of 'Hindu cowardice', now echoed by the RSS supremo in a different context, has a long career with unfailing regularity. Starting with the writings of Dayanand Saraswati, it gradually formed a major ideological component of the dominant Hindu communitarian discourses. Not only that. The myth of Hindu cowardice, always counterpoised to the militancy and aggression of Islam and its followers, gained salience in order to provide a *raison d'être* to political outfits like the Hindu Mahasabha.

Thus B.S. Moonje, the Nagpur-based eye surgeon and a leading light in the Hindu Mahasabha, argued that the real danger to Hindu-Muslim disunity lay in Hindu docility and its incapacity for self-protection on equal terms. He frequently lamented over the disunity among his co-religionists; a sense of impending doom ran through his assessment of their state. The Hindus were weak and divided, while a Muslim was a bully, savagely aggressive, and inspired by feelings of common brotherhood of religion. He, therefore, believed that the fight for swaraj was against the British as well as the Muslims—a continuation of the struggle initiated by Prithviraj Chauhan when the Mughals first assailed the Hindu Raj, culture and religion. *Sangathan* was the panacea for the ills of the Hindus.

In other words, the Hindu Mahasabha's grand project was to revive Hindu martial traditions, restore the physical virility of

Hindus, and organize them into a united and organic nation for warding off Muslim aggression. Yet *sangathan* was not good enough. Moonje laid stress on infusing a spirit of aggression in the Hindus. In his diary that I read some years ago at Calcutta's National Library, he observed (in July 1926) that Gandhi's philosophy of love and *ahimsa* caused irreparable damage to the Hindus. He added: 'I consider my mission in life now to do everything possible so that the teaching of love and *ahimsa*, of which we have been saturated since the Buddha's and Jaina's times, may not take root in Maharashtra. . . . I believe (Gandhi's) philosophy will lead to the destruction and extermination of the Hindus from the face of the world.' Oddly enough, the Mahatma, a fervent protagonist of Hindu-Muslim unity, accepted the stereotypical images of the Muslim as a bully and the Hindu as a coward. He wrote this in *Young India*: 'Bullies are always to be found when there are cowards. Hindus must understand that no one can afford protection if they go on hugging fear.'

Again, he observed on 19 June 1924: 'The Mussulman being generally in a minority has as a class developed into a bully. . . . The Hindu has an age-old civilisation. He is essentially non-violent. . . . The Hindu as a body is, therefore, not equipped for fighting. . . . They have become docile to the point of cowardice.' Gandhi appealed to Muslims to forbear because, being bullies, they could fight and fight well and could protect themselves from the attacks of Hindus. In an uncharacteristic advice, he advised Hindus to fight back because 'quarrels must break out so long as the Hindus continue to be seized with fear'.

We know that Gandhi was fervently committed to inter-community reconciliation. We know that Hindu-Muslim unity was his lifelong passion. We know that he lived and died for the cause. Why, then, did he arrive at these conclusions, and, in the process, legitimize a discourse that rested on unfounded assumptions?

A serious explanation is called for, but for the moment it is important to be alerted to the danger of stereotyping one or the other community. The massive nation-building exercise entails the strengthening of a composite and multicultural society designed to serve the interests of all sections of society. The *sangathan* of one against the other can only impede our growth and progress.

12 January 2000

Limits of Laxman's Rekha

> Before they murder us they chloroform us.
> We ought to render thanks that they are kind.
>
> AKBAR ALLAHABADI

The Bharatiya Jana Sangh was founded in 1951. Its enterprise was to convert politics from disputes about party programmes into a great battle for the cultural heart of the nation, a battle in which those who believed in the corporate integrity of the Hindu community will be aligned against the forces of Islam. Thus secularism was regarded as a euphemism for the policy of Muslim appeasement. The Muslim menace has increased a hundredfold, wrote M.S. Golwalkar after the creation of Pakistan. 'Even today', he continued, 'Muslims, whether in high positions of the government or outside, participate in rabidly anti-national conferences.'

At the beginning of this millennium, this rhetoric appears to have run its full course. First, Bangaru Laxman, BJP's newly elected president, avoids alluding to the grand themes of Hindu nationalist rhetoric at Nagpur, the citadel of the RSS. Then, the RSS headquarters are taken by surprise by his overtures to India's 120 million Muslims. And now the Prime Minister, following his 15 August address to the nation, reiterates that the RSS has its own identity 'which is entirely separate from that of the BJP.' He wants his government not to be seen or judged through the prism of any other organization.

Maybe, such overtures to Muslims are calculated to win over the liberal Hindus and not so much the minorities. Still, at the heart of the current debate is whether the Prime Minister and the BJP president have, in actual fact, distanced themselves from the doctrinal inheritance—the commanding heights of cultural survival and myths—of the erstwhile Bharatiya Jana Sangh. It brings no comfort to learn from Laxman himself that the core *Hindutva* agenda had not been given up, only shelved for the time being. Besides, it is by no means clear if his perceptions are shared by some of the BJP-RSS stalwarts, notably, Murali Manohar Joshi, and L.K. Advani, who is assiduously cultivating his liberal image.

At the same time, cynical commentators cannot brush aside the pronouncements of Vajpayee and Laxman, the first of their kind since the Jana Sangh came into being in 1951. They merit serious consideration, more so in a polity that is in a state of perpetual flux. Who can deny that the two leaders have triggered a debate that will have serious implications on future political alignments and the BJP's own trajectory in the years to come? Its immediate consequences are threefold. First, this initiative will bolster the Prime Minister's image at home and overseas as a liberal statesman. Second, it will strengthen the existing coalition at the Centre, and legitimize the non-BJP partners in continuing their support to a BJP-led government. Finally, it may take the sting out of Shiv Sena's communal campaigns in Maharashtra.

The Congress leaders, on the other hand, must be rubbing their eyes in sheer disbelief. Haunted by the spectre of losing Muslim votes in some of the closely contested constituencies, they will have to devise a new strategy to counter the BJP's latest move to court Muslim support.

Muslim leaders tend to stew in their own juice. But they, too, have been caught unawares by the turn of events since 15 August when the Prime Minister spoke from the ramparts of the Red Fort on cultural pluralism. It is doubtful if their views— either in support of, or in opposition to, the BJP—would influence electoral choices in the forthcoming Assembly elections. Conventional wisdom apart, the 'Muslim vote' is rarely swayed by the rhetoric at Delhi's Red Fort or the Jama Masjid. If any-thing, it is tied to local and regional interests and aspirations. The voting patterns in UP and Bihar illustrate this. At any rate, it will take quite a while for the Vajpayee-Laxman message to sink in, and more than an election to heal the wounds caused by the demolition of the Babri Masjid. Moreover, I imagine that the Vajpayee-Laxman combine will find it extremely difficult to dispel the impression that the BJP, even in its present incarnation, is committed to the RSS agenda.

Viewed from Delhi's vantagepoint, all is well except for the 'sell out' being negotiated with a celebrated bandit [Veerapan] by elected governments. But the ground realities, i.e. the fears and apprehensions of the minorities at the deeper levels of society, are hardly reflected in newspaper reports or TV news capsule. Move from the centre to the periphery to discover how the BJP and its allies flex their muscles. Realistically speak-ing, the chief arenas of cultural contest and religious disputation lie well beyond the manicured lawns and gardens of state capitals.

Even at the head of a coalition government, the BJP continues to pursue its *Hindutva* agenda. Christians continue to face the wrath of the VHP and Bajrang Dal enthusiasts, while the Ayodhya issue is kept alive by their strident clamouring. Liberal institut-ions are undermined and replaced with self-styled votaries of *Hindutva*. Voices of protest and dissent are stifled by political and religious orthodoxies. This is bad news, as the painter Surendran Nair discovered the hard way when his painting was withdrawn from the National Gallery of Modern Art [in Delhi] last week. Likewise, while the ICHR withdraws authoritative works of leading historians, history textbooks are being rewritten. But, unlike the 26 artists who pulled out of the exhibition in protest, the community of historians has shown little inclination to exert pressure on the ICHR to review its ill-advised decision.

These trends run contrary to the Prime Minister's vision outlined at the Red Fort. Moreover, they will not instil confidence in the new *Laxman Rekha* that is being drawn for the nation. In fact, confusion reigns supreme; the BJP leaders fail to either speak or act in unison. Yet the Prime Minister's initiative, cynically conceived or not, must be given a chance to run its full course. It should not be rejected on the basis of his political record in yesteryears, or the doctrinal inheritance of the BJP.

All said and done, the signs are that the nation is weary of the Hindu nationalist rhetoric, and that it cannot surge ahead without a national consensus that would draw on the cultural and intellectual resources of different segments of society. The BJP may or may not have arrived at this conclusion, but its leaders may well have discovered that cultural nationalism is no substitute for good governance. They may have reached the inescapable conclusion that the idea of India rests not on M.S. Golwalkar's *Bunch of Thoughts,* but on the vision nurtured by the founding fathers of the Indian constitution.

Agar mazhab khalal andaaz hai mulki maqasid me
To shaikh-o-brahman pinhaan rahen dair-o-masajid me.

If their religion hinders us in working for our country's good
Shut up the shaikhs and Brahmans in their temples and mosques.

5 September 2000

Bangaru Laxman's Pipedream

Swapan Dasgupta (*India Today*, 18 September 2000) admonishes India's Muslims not to retreat 'into fundamental ghettos sustained by foreign funding'. Assuming that the criterion for nationhood is determined by loyalty to the BJP, he expects them 'to forge an expedient working relationship' with that party. Without referring to the historical roots of their estrangement, he warns them of 'the grim consequences of a contrived alienation'. Besides the Muslims, this stern warning must alert millions of others who may have decided not to vote for the BJP in the forthcoming

Assembly elections. I fear the next step will be putting the Christians on the firing line.

In his customary acerbic tone, the columnist proceeds to target the *mullahs* as well as the 'modernists'—people like you and me who pursue our vocation in life unobtrusively, raise our voice against intolerance and religio-political bigotry, and nurture the vision of a strong and united India. Why? The answer is that you and I share 'a deep-rooted . . . aversion to the BJP', and that we do not recognize its leaders as the new *avatars* guiding our nation. The vehemence of his vituperation reaches its crescendo when the Bakhts and Naqvis are compared with Azad, Abdul Ghaffar Khan and Rafi Ahmed Kidwai. This is adding insult to injury.

This is not all. Swapan Dasgupta, the columnist, is indignant because the certified 'engineers of secularism' and 'secular fundamentalists' have dismissed as a sham Bangaru Laxman's overtures. Although cynicism and bitterness is so palpably re- flected in the usage of such expressions, the noteworthy point is that Bangaru Laxman has struck a favourable chord among some Muslim spokesmen. If others have not joined the band- wagon, it is because their local and regional interests, coupled with their ideology, are not served by tying up with the BJP. Neither the first nor the second set of people act as Muslims *per se.*

Sure enough, the self-appointed Muslim leaders (not the Bakhts or the Naqvis) will decide whether Bangaru Laxman's gesture merits a degree of reciprocity or not, though the decision will ultimately rest with the Muslim peasant in Bara Banki, the coal mine worker in Dhanbad, and the fishermen in coastal Andhra. For the moment, though, the BJP president will have to come to terms with the widespread aversion to his party—an aversion, I hasten to add, shared by many castes, communities and political groupings. If he has a special fondness for the Muslims and desires their 'expedient relationship' with his party, he will have to devise ways and means of redressing their grievances. If he wants them to soften their opposition, he will have to airlift the Hindutva ideologues to the Staten Island [in the US] for rest and recuperation. In short, he will have to accept the primacy of the Constitution as the reference point for nurturing a national perspective.

This brings me to the Congress-led Muslim 'mass contact' campaign of 1937. Flaunting my knowledge of history is not my style, and yet one has to refute ill-informed views and interpretations. First of all, Nehru, the architect of the idea, was impressed by the favourable Muslim response to the 1937 election campaign. The ensuing drive reflected a change from the corporate conception and strategy of direct appeals to Muslims to a policy of more self-conscious, secular appeals, and direct strategy of developing support. Contrary to what Swapan Dasgupta thinks, the strategy paid off. By mid-1938, a hundred thousand Muslims were enrolled as primary members of the Congress outside UP, Bengal, and the NWFP. Of these, 25,000 were from Bihar, 15,000 from Madras, and 13,995 from Punjab.

The campaign petered out not because of Muslim opposition, but because it was devoid of any social and economic content and that it offered too little, too late. The secularist, radical rhetoric alarmed vested interests. The Muslim Leaguers perceived a threat to their very existence and felt that, unless they woo the poor Muslims in urban and rural areas, they might find the Congress walking away with their flock. Although Congress and the League had existed as separate organizations, never before was there such a rivalry between them for association with the Muslim masses.

Second, the Congress effort was in large part confined to urban areas with little activity expended in the villages or among the underprivileged groups, thus averting Nehru's interest in disassociating Muslim peasants from Muslim landlords. Nisar Ahmad, an advocate from Bahawalpur, complained that Congress had not reached the Muslim masses—'the backbone of the community'. The pattern of mobilization was thus similar to that of 1930 to 1932, when Congress leaders minimized civil disobedience propaganda in areas with high proportion of Muslims in order to avoid igniting communal passions.

Finally, the strategy fell prey as well to a divided Congress and to opposition from Hindu nationalists that feared the influx of Muslim activists having a critical and unacceptable influence on party policy. People like G.B. Pant, J.B. Kripalani and Morarji Desai girded themselves to resist the campaign that threatened their political dominance and raised the chances of Nehru's Muslim and Communist allies dominating the Congress. Part of their strategy was to starve mass contact committees of funds, to fill them with rank communalists, and to ensure that Muslims were eased out of Congress committees. Thus senior Congress office-bearers in Gorakhpur led a Holi procession with spears, swords, and sticks on display. Khushi Lal, chairman of the Dehradun municipal board, lamented that Congressmen tried imposing a social boycott of 'the Muslims for the sins, imaginary or real, of one or two'.

Important lessons must be learnt from the 'failure' of the 'mass contact'. One of them is that national unity, grounded in the principles of democracy, secularism, social justice and equity, must be the cardinal political assumption in the nation-building enterprise. The other is not to stigmatize a community, Hindu, Muslim, Sikh or Christian, but to help build bridges of fraternity and understanding. It will be comforting if religious and political fundamentalists can be converted to this idea sooner than later.

19 September 2000

Forgotten Dreams of Forgotten Men

A national daily reported last week that there was no reference to Delhi in the textbooks prescribed for the primary schools. One is not surprised. I wondered if there was any reference to some of the historic figures of Delhi. Hence the urge to write this column.

Two individuals in public life, who need to be rescued from the mists of history, were not men wrapped in the folds of the banner of religion, tradition and traditional morality. They were neither guardians of the Islamic way of life nor did they claim to lead their lives in accordance with Islamic teachings. They maintained that religion played a part in shaping man's conduct and ideas, and yet they desired the political ideal to conform to the spirit and not to the letter of Islam. They neither sought to revive their heritage as a base for their own self-identity nor did they try to eliminate the Hindu influences interwoven into their life. They were Hakim Ajmal Khan and Dr. Mukhtar Ahmad Ansari.

Both created an organic synthesis between traditional religious values and the humanist values that were not specific to Islam. They were exponents of a liberal-humanitarian ideology without restricting and twisting its application for the benefit of any single community. At the heart of their conception was the idea of virtuous citizens, respectful, and trustful towards one another, even if they differed on political and religious issues. The Indian community they had in mind was not likely to be blandly conflict free, but tolerant of their opponents. By invoking such valid precepts of political and social morality, Ajmal and Ansari created a model of a public figure that was worth emulating.

Ajmal Khan personified gentlemanly manners, both as a noted practitioner of *unani* medicine and as a public figure. He was a link between the old order and the new, and yet he was much more than that. Living through the decaying Mughal culture and nurtured in Pax Britannia, he satisfied the standards of two radically different cultures, the aristocratic and the democratic. He was not a synthesizer of ideas, but of diverse movements experienced during his lifetime. Without offering any *grandes illusions*, he championed a number of causes, preferring the austere appeal to the style of the rhetoricians. He recognized—which so few contemporary Muslims did—the need to enhance the status of women in society. He established women's section in his Yunani and Ayurvedic College in 1909. Towards the end of his life he drew attention to the physical deterioration of Muslim women owing to the *purdah* system.

With his aristocratic background and his professional interests tied to the British and the nawabs, he nonetheless noticed the ferment around him—the Home Rule movement, the Rowlatt satyagraha, and the Jallianwala Bagh massacre—and responded to the aspirations of his people. He could have stayed away from stormy meetings and noisy demonstrations and yet retain the goodwill of the people around him. But he chose to be drawn, without any personal motive, into the political arena. Without wielding political power, his moral authority was unassailable. He enunciated no great principles, but laid bare, through his personal, professional and family life, the outlines of a future multicultural society.

Working against heavy odds, Ansari did his best to preserve and promote Ajmal Khan's legacy. The medical doctor was, indeed, a worthy successor to the Hakim, for he fits into any of the multiple meanings one attaches to the concept of '*adab*', or right personal or political conduct. Like Ajmal, he had multiple identities that shaped his personality and informed his worldview. And like his senior comrade, his diverse concerns found expression in the variety of roles he played—from playing Macbeth at the University of Edinburgh to presiding over the destiny of Delhi's Jamia Millia.

What endeared Ansari to his contemporaries were his sobriety, and his sense of duty and dedication. He acted as the bridge between the old school of medicine and Western science and, as an arbitrator between the contesting claims of Hindu and Muslim ideologues. He brought something new and something different in the prevailing political milieu. For one, he saw clearly the incompatibility of nationalism or narrow religion with the sort of democracy he dreamed for his country. Writing to a friend just before his death, he stated: 'I consider the brotherhood of man as the only real tie, and partitions based on race or religion are, to my mind, artificial and arbitrary, leading to divisions and factious fights.'

Secondly, he firmly opposed the movement to organize a politically separate Muslim community. Hence his resignation from the Khilafat Committee in 1925, and his estrangement from the Ali brothers who had joined hands with the conservative establishment. He often repeated, what had long been Azad's political axiom as well, that future India must be a field of cooperation between men of different faiths. They could live according to the tenets of their faith, but introducing theological subtleties into modern political forms could be dangerous. Indian Muslims, according to him, have all along erred in identifying their manners and customs with the prescription of their faith. Religion and social life were no doubt inseparable, but it was necessary to distinguish between conservatism and stagnation.

Ansari was often criticized for his consistency, consistency in his loyalty to political comrades, consistency in providing succour to the poor and sick, consistency in upholding political morality, and consistency in championing the cause of communal harmony and national unity. Yet, consistency is not a feature attributed to a successful politician. But, then, his mission in life was not that of a successful politician, it was that of a pioneer.

This *tour de force* provides a perspective for understanding an era when some of our public figures sublimated their more immediate political interests to the public good. It is true that some persons traded convictions for wealth or power, weakened the foundation of our monumental national edifice, and disrupted a national consensus by raising strident sectarian demands. Yet, there were those who resolved the disparity between beliefs and deeds, made sacrifices as a sort of sublimation or compensation for high ideals, and nursed the vision of a harmonious society. Indeed, they were not the gold-diggers of modern India, but young and old idealists whose conception of society rested on equality and cooperation among Indians. With Ajmal Khan's death in 1927, wrote C.F. Andrews, 'passed away . . . one of the last links of this Old Delhi'. 'We are not likely to see the like of Dr Ansari again,' concluded Mahadev Desai in his tribute.

2 May 2001

On Maulana Abul Kalam Azad

The maker of phrases survives the maker of things in history. There is nothing so swiftly forgotten, says Gore Vidal, as the public's memory of a good action. This is why great men insist on putting up monuments to themselves with their deeds carefully recorded since those they served will not honour them in life or in death. Heroes must see to their own fame. No one else will.

It is not at all surprising why history books in Pakistan make no mention of Azad, except to echo the Quaid-i Azam's view that he was a Muslim 'show-boy' Congress president. What is surprising is how a man of Azad's stature has been submerged beneath the rationalization of the victors—the founders of Pakistan—in our own country. This is the man whom Nehru called 'a very brave and gallant gentleman, a finished product of the culture that, in these days, pertains to few'.

Azad was the *Mir-i-Karawan* (the caravan leader), said Nehru. That he wasn't. Though not detached from the humdrum of political life, he was not cut out to be an efficient political manager. He was comfortable being a biographer rather than a leader of a movement. He was not somebody who traversed the dusty political terrain to stir the masses into activism. That is why he settled for Gandhi's leadership, acted as one of his lieutenants during the Civil Disobedience movement in 1930-2, and steered the Congress ship through the high tide of the inter-War years. He spent years in jail. Some of his prison colleagues thought of him as an 'extraordinarily interesting companion', with 'an astonishing memory' and encyclopaedic information. More importantly, the Maulana embodied in his position and person perhaps the most important symbol of the Congress aspiration to be a nationalist party. His status was thus the focal point of Gandhi's clash with Jinnahs' insistence that politically no one but a Muslim Leaguer could represent Muslim interests.

Sardar Patel, the hero of the Bardoli Satyagraha and the Home Minister who carried the princely states to the burning *ghat* of oblivion, spoke and acted from the lofty heights of majoritarianism. Azad, caught up in the crossfire of Hindu and Muslim communalists, did not occupy the same vantagepoint. He had to play his innings on a sticky turf in rough weather. On occasions, his own party colleagues thwarted his initiatives and turned him into just a titular Congress head. The strident Muslim Leaguers, on the other hand, decried him as a 'renegade'.

Yet this elder statesman, sitting silently and impassively at Congress meetings with his pointed beard, remained, until the end, consistent in his loyalty to a unified Indian nation. Time and time again, he repudiated Jinnah's two-nation theory. He reaffirmed: 'It is one of the greatest frauds on the people to suggest that religious affinity can unite areas which are geographically, economically, linguistically and culturally different.' With an insight rare for those from his background, he pointed out that the real problems of the country were economic, not communal. The differences related to classes, not to communities.

Essentially a thinker and the chief exponent of *Wahdat-e deen* or the essential oneness of all religions, Azad played around with a variety of ideas on religion, State and civil society. Thoughtful and reflective, he had a mind like a razor, which cut through a fog of ideas (Nehru). Lesser men during his days found conflict in the rich variety of Indian life. But he was big enough to see the essential unity behind all that diversity, and realize that only in unity was there hope for India as a whole.

He was a man on the move, his eyes set on India's future which was to be fashioned on the basis of existing cross-community networks. His unfinished *Tarjuman-al Quran* was easily the most profound statement on multiculturalism and inter-faith understanding. His political testament, delivered at the Congress session in 1940, was a neat and powerful summation of the ideology of secular nationalism:

I am proud of being an Indian. I am part of the indivisible unity that is Indian nationality. I am indispensable to this noble edifice and without me this splendid structure is incomplete. I am an essential element, which has gone to build India. I can never surrender this claim.

To a region that has experienced the trauma of Partition the life of Azad shows how during the freedom struggle there were Muslims who worked for the highest secular ideals. To a region beset by religious intolerance the life of Azad reveals how the finest religious sensibility can fashion the most open and humane outlook in private and public life. This is what Francis Robinson, a British historian, observed some years ago:

The relative neglect of the tombs of Azad and Ansari suggests that many Indian Muslims may have lost interest in keeping their memories alive. It also suggests that Indian society as a whole may no longer value as before, and perhaps may not even know, the principles for which they stood. . . . To a region increasingly beset by communalism, the life of Ansari shows how during the freedom movement there were Muslims who worked for the highest secular ideals. To a region increasingly beset by religious intolerance, the life of Azad reveals how the finest religious sensibility can fashion the most open and humane outlook in private and public life. These are lives which deserve to be known and studied outside the purely academic community. When they are, we hope that there will be fresh attention to their memorials in India.

Chalo aao tum ko dikhain hum jo bacha hai maqtal-e-shehr mein
Yeh mazar ahl-e safa ke hain yeh hain ahl-e sidq ki turbatein.

Come along, I will show you what remains in the city's death row;
These are the shrines of the pious, and the graves of men of honesty and conviction.

Passions of a Liberal:
Happy Birthday A.A. Engineer _____

Asghar Ali Engineer has built his reputation as a scholar, journalist, social reformer and public activist. When the world sleeps, he is wide awake writing columns, drafting memoranda on civil rights, or planning his next move against the spiritual head of the Bohras. Anybody stranded in a riot-torn city would have spotted him listening to the woes of affected families, talking to the police, recording the testimony of political and social activists, and detailing his experiences in Bombay's *Economic and Political Weekly*. So many cities figure in his coverage of communal riots in free India.

Starting as a crusader for reforms among the Bohras in the late 1970s, he has maintained his hectic pace of life. He lives in a small and sparsely-furnished two-room apartment. Here, in Santa Cruz, he pursues his scholarly engagements, organizes his reform initiatives for which he has been persecuted and physically assaulted, and conducts public campaigns against communalism. Many of his goals remain unfulfilled: his reform agenda has yet to get off the ground, though he has time and again reminded us of the excesses committed by the Bohra high priest. The Nathwani Commission recommendations, which would have struck a favourable chord in any civilized society, have been consigned to the dustbin of history. Why should anybody take on the spiritual head of an influential religious minority in Western India? The Muslim intelligentsia, too, has been lukewarm in responding to his mission.

And yet Asghar Ali traverses the rough terrain as a lone crusader, firm in his resolve to fight obscurantism, religious bigotry and intolerance. For nearly two decades, he has been on the move. The good news is that he will turn 60 next week, and that scores of scholars, including some from the Western Hemisphere, will gather in Delhi to celebrate his birthday.

Asghar Ali's activities, for which he has been ostracized, disturb the status quo. At the same time he has not been a threat, except for a while when he flirted with Marxist ideas, to the Muslim establishment, religious or political. Ideally speaking, he should have been appropriated by the sober elements in Muslim society, many of whom feel repressed by the stranglehold of the theologians. His background should work in his favour, for he has studied the language of the Koran at the feet of his father, a traditional *maulvi*. Whatever his detractors may say, Asghar Ali firmly believes in the egalitarian principles of Islam and, for this reason, invokes the scriptures to plead for reforms among Muslims.

Why, then, does somebody like him not carry weight with his co-religionists? This important question needs to be situated in the context of the Muslim reform movements triggered by Syed Ahmad Khan. The more fundamental issue is why our political establishment has repeatedly paid heed to the clamouring of religious fundamentalists and turned a deaf ear to people like Asghar Ali? We know how, during the 1930s and 1940s, the 'Nationalist Muslims' were sidelined to buy peace with rank communalists. We know how the liberal perspective on the Shah Bano affair was wilfully ignored. So that when Poonam Saxena, an English teacher, tells me that liberal Muslims wield no influence in their community, I turn around and ask if anybody has ever shown any willingness to hear them and take cognizance of their viewpoint.

It takes me a while to convince her and others that the main problem has been our obsessive engagement with the strident self-styled spokesmen of the Muslims and our blissful ignorance of what the liberal-minded Muslims have stood for. We cannot test the strength of liberal opinion through conventional yardsticks. Hindu and Muslim reformers had the backing of the colonial government through legislative enactments, but their luck ran out after Independence.

Today, the future of social reformers largely depends on the extent to which a democratic regime is willing to extend its fulsome support to their initiatives. For the moment, I wish one amongst them Mr. A.A. Engineer—a long life and a happy birthday.

20 March 1999

Scholarship and Activism:
Ali Mian, 1914-1999

Lucknow was once upon a time the home of many leading educational institutions. In the early eighteenth century Firangi Mahal, which nowadays languishes in a faceless alley of Chowk, was probably one of the largest centres of learning in India. It attracted scholars not only from all parts of India, but from places as far away as Arabia, Central Asia and China. Yet Firangi Mahal lost its pivotal position in Lucknow for a variety of reasons. One of them was the establishment of the Nadwat al-ulama in the same city in 1894. The University of Nadwat al-ulama had been established, wrote Abul Halim Sharar in the early 1920s, to pay special attention to those subjects that had so far been neglected. But as the decades rolled on, the Nadwa developed conservative contours of its own, and its product became generally indistinguishable from those of the Deoband seminary in terms of theological and intellectual outlook. Both adhered to the curriculum (*Dars-e Nizamiya*) drawn up in the eighteenth century. Today, the Nadwa has over 2,000 students, with a large number of affiliated schools in India, Pakistan and Nepal. But its students, according to a Government of India report (1983), are 'totally devoid of modern secular education, which is essential to help them face the realities outside'.

Maulana Abul Hasan Ali Nadwi nursed and headed such an institution for well over three decades. Ali Mian, as he was popularly known, is no more. But this spiritual and intellectual mentor of the north Indian Muslims will be remembered for his piety, his profound scholarship and erudition. A prolific writer with over 50 publications to his credit, he wrote in Arabic and Urdu. Most of his works, available in English translations, are widely read in India, Pakistan, Bangladesh, Egypt, Syria and Lebanon. His death has created a void in the world of Islamic scholarship in the subcontinent. It is hard to see anybody replacing him in the near future. His death has saddened many of his followers and admirers, notably in UP and Bihar, who followed his religious decrees (*fatwas*) and respected his authority.

The fundamental malaise of modern Islam, remarked W.C. Smith, is a sense that something has gone wrong with Islamic history. The fundamental problem of modern Muslims is how to rehabilitate that history. This feeling, reflected in Ali Mian's book, *Islam and the World*, dominated his religious and political thinking. His studies led him to conclude that Muslims did not merely attain political and intellectual supremacy, but surpassed at one time all the others in knowledge and intellectual endeavour. In contemporary times, however, the world of Islam was in the throes of a crisis of confidence. While the way out was to take advantage of the intellectual resources of the West, Ali Main called upon his co-religionists to take pride in and adhere to the legacy bequeathed by the Prophet of Islam. 'This happy co-ordination between the ends and means . . . can alter the destiny of the world. . . . [And] this laudable task can be accomplished by no other people than the Muslims who are the successors of the last of the Apostles and the inheritors of his Message.'

These are fairly well worn out ideas. His other writings make him appear socially conservative, opposed to change, innovation and reform. For example, he said that if the forces of 'moral degradation' (including the abolition of *purdah*) were free to work themselves out, the 'rising generations in the Muslim countries would have drifted so far away from their spiritual moorings that no urge would be left in them to strive against the mounting pressures of modernism and westernise'. This is what led the venerable Maulana to decry doggedly the Supreme Court judgement on Shah Bano's plea for maintenance. This is what prompted him to defend Zia-ul-Haq's *coup d'etat*. Oddly enough, he called the death of the Pakistani strongman a martyrdom (*shahadat*), a setback to the Islamic community.

Yet within the framework of traditional Islamic scholarship, Ali Mian was perhaps the most outstanding Muslim scholar in post-1947 India. He travelled far and wide in his quest for knowledge, pursued his intellectual probing in the company of Jamaat-i Islami and Tablighi Jamaat activists, and eventually prepared his own blueprint for a safe and secure future for his co-religionists. 'The clouds will disperse', he wrote with pontifical authority in 1960, 'and there will be sunshine again. The Muslims will regain the position in the country that is justly theirs. All the schemes for national reconstruction will remain incomplete if they are left to rot and decay.'

It is this optimism that may have led Ali Mian to combine his scholarly preoccupation with activism. Shibli Numani, founder of the Nadwa, had insisted that a very large part of the national life was in the *ulama* right of ownership (*haq-i malkiat*) and they alone had or could have absolute sway (*mutlaq-al anaan*) over it. Ali Mian was wedded to this principal shibboleth in Sunni Islam. He was a founder member of the Islamic World League, based in Saudi Arabia, and the All-India Muslim Personal Law Board.

At the time when the Shah Bano issue divided the Muslim intelligentsia into two camps, Muslims turned to him for guidance. At the time when the Babri Masjid-Ramjanmabhumi controversy inflamed religious passions, they sought his mediation. He did not disappoint on either count. Playing the role of a priest-politician perfectly, he operated effectively from his home in Rae Bareli to influence the course of events from the mid-1980s. It is said that he frequented the corridors of power to advice Rajiv Gandhi to introduce the Muslim Women's Bill, and that P.V. Narasimha Rao sought his advice on the Babri Masjid impasse. No wonder, political parties of all hues, having dumped the Imam of Delhi's Jama Masjid, courted him to secure legitimacy among Muslims and gauge the 'Muslim mind'. He was sedulously cultivated as the wise, sagacious and influential Muslim statesman. Wise and sagacious he was, but I very much doubt if he carried much weight outside the Urdu-speaking belt in northern India.

Ali Mian would not have expected me to write his obituary, but I have done so as a tribute to his scholarship. He has left behind a rich intellectual legacy, although it must be carried forth in the eclectic spirit that had guided the founders of Nadwa. In the final analysis, the initiative for a real reformation of Islam in India, the *raison d'être* of Syed Ahmad Khan's activities, has to come from such institutions, and has to be thought out and translated into practice by Muslims. Perhaps the starting point is the Koranic injunction:

God changes not what is in a people, until they change what is in
themselves. . . .

Say Talaq to Triple Talaq

It is often claimed that the *Shariat* (Islamic law) permeates
almost every branch of Islamic literature, that it is the epitome
of the true Islamic spirit, the most divisive expression of Islamic
thought, the essential kernel of Islam. Consequently, it has been
argued that any legislative change in the Muslim personal law
will violate the Fundamental Rights guaranteed in the Indian
Constitution. The argument is contested, but the All-India Personal
Law Board (AIPLB) failed to take an explicit stand at their
recent meeting in Bangalore. It is no longer possible to keep
deferring an issue that affects not only Muslim women, but is
so central to their future welfare and security.

Already, demands for judicial activism are mounting from
some Muslim women organizations to amend the laws relating
to 'triple *talaq*'. Precedents from other Muslim countries,
including Pakistan, are cited to clamour for some measure of
reform in the Muslim personal law. Members of the AIPBL will
do well to pay heed to the imperious call of changing pattern
of modern life, and the necessity of attempting a larger synthesis
after the manner of the various forward-looking movements of
Islam; this is a process which is not the dead and immobile one
that superficial observers of Islamic history have usually taken
it to be.

Islam persists not through rigid negation of the forces of
changing environments and new epochs or fresh historical and
social impacts or fresh historical and social impacts but through

the adaptation to these conditions. And the fact that Islam has survived the endless vicissitudes of history conclusively proves that it adapted itself from age to age and epoch to epoch to the changing outer conditions. 'Do not put to me too many unnecessary questions', the Prophet is reported to have said. 'Whoever does it is an enemy of the Muslims because the answers given will become binding on them and thereby the liberty of action would be curtailed.' Maybe, this is what inspired the poet-philosopher Iqbal to state, in 1934, that the claim of his generation to reinterpret the fundamental legal principles, in the light of their own experience and the altered conditions of modern life, was perfectly justified.

Today, the contentious issue is not the preservation of 'Muslim identity', expressed through mosques, religious institutions, the traditional system of education, and charitable institutions. There is an overall consensus, despite the spurt in majoritarian stridency, on guarding minority rights provided by the Constitution. Nor is the sanctity of the *Shariat* in question, though the fourteenth century historian Ziauddin Barani, representing Muslim orthodoxy, had conceded that the Sultan was empowered to enact state laws (*zawabit*) even if in extreme cases they had to override the *Shariat*. Likewise, Ferishta observed two centuries later that it was not possible to rule Hindustan in accordance with the *Shariat*.

At the heart of the present debate, so argued the Deoband-educated Maulana Said Ahmad Akbarabadi in the 1960s, is the distinction between those Koranic injunctions that were specific to the Arab customary law of the time and those applicable to Muslim societies in other times. This distinction has been made in the past, and that alone enabled Islam to pass through many stages of reorientation and readjustments. The scholar of Islamic jurisprudence, A.A.A. Fyzee, positioned himself against the traditional belief that law and religion are coterminous in Islam. He argued that law is a product of social evolution and must change with time and circumstances.

In the past, the AIMPLB has not been impressed with these arguments; I doubt if they think differently now or are sensitive to the powerful and successful reformist initiatives in Muslim societies. They may settle, in response to certain court judge-ments, for a few cosmetic changes without satisfying the growing and persistent demands for gender justice for Muslim women. Perhaps, the way out is to ask for a referendum or bring about some form of consensus (*ijma*, the most important legal notion in Islam) on substantial reforms in the provisions on 'triple *talaq*' and maintenance for Muslim widows.

This is a limited agenda, and yet the urge for reforms must come from the community itself. One hopes that patience, persistence and education will lead to a reappraisal of existing attitudes, and that more and more educated Muslims will take recourse to *ijtehad* (exercise of independent judgement), defined by Iqbal as 'the principle of movement' in Islam. Who knows, some day a version of the Mutazalites (in Baghdad) may strike a favourable chord? In the ninth century, they championed reason as judge in matters of belief. According to them, the inner meaning of scriptures could be ascertained only by reason.

In its historical sequence, the existing debates, though clouded by fresh controversies after the Shah Bano judgement, owe their origin to the discussions in the Constituent Assembly and Nehru's subsequent ambivalence in deciding whether or not to provide equality before the law for all Indian women. He may have been right in thinking that the time was not ripe for bringing Muslims within the perview of a uniform civil code, but the initiative on such matters should have rested with Parliament and not the religious traditionalists and the defenders of the *status quo*.

Not many people know that Nehru's Cabinet received suggestions, in 1961, for reviewing and reforming the Muslim Personal Law. Nehru was himself enthusiastic, pointedly mentioning the changes in Tunisia, Egypt and Pakistan. Lengthy discussions followed, and the Law Ministry was asked to make appropriate recommendations. But the mere hint of an inquiry in the ministry's report led to a public outcry. A gathering of Muslim ministers and members of Parliament, chaired by Zakir Husain, the Vice-President of the Republic, echoed their senti-ments without any serious deliberation.

No government after Nehru could contemplate reforms to

ensure the equal status of Muslim women. Electorally, the risk was too great. In consequence, state intervention in the Shah Bano case came about with an eye on the 'Muslim vote' and to defend a traditionalist interpretation of the *Shariat*. This is because the political regime, acting in unison with the Muslim orthodoxy, had legitimized the AIMPLB members as the *Shariat's* sole custodians, interpreters and transmitters.

Nonetheless, let's hope that the eclectic spirit of the Prophet's message is not throttled, its theology not gagged by history and its vitality not sapped by totalitarianism. In the words of Fyzee, there is a strong case for releasing the spirit of compassion, fraternity, tolerance and reasonableness.

15 November 2000

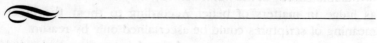

PART IV

Independence, Partition and its Aftermath

India: Darning a Patchwork Dream

Irish Portal, a British civil servant, observed in the early 1940s, 'you must never take land away from people. People's land has a mystique. You can go and possibly order them about for a bit and introduce some new ideas and possibly dragoon an alien race into attitudes that are not quite familiar to them.' But, he added, 'you must go away and die in Cheltenham'. That is exactly what the British did on 15 August 1947.

On that auspicious day began India's tryst with destiny and the quest for a new political and social order. Doubtless, it was a tall order for a postcolonial society to meet the challenges of governance and nation building. Yet the silver lining was the nationalist legacy that was still alive and kicking in a country bruised and fragmented by colonialism and the horrors of Partition. I will not venture to dwell on its contested meanings or labour to draw a distinction between nationalism and patriotism. What is noteworthy is that nationalism in India and China generated powerful anti-colonial sentiments, and provided a blueprint (give it any name you like) for welding an otherwise divided and disparate country into a nation state. So that some of its leading protagonists understood the word 'nationalism' to be an umbrella term under which were subsumed the related phenomena of national identity and consciousness, and collectivities based on them—nations; occasionally, it was employed to refer to the articulate ideology on which national identity and consciousness rested (Liah Greenfield).

All said and done the chequered career of Indian nationalism, though marred by the estrangement of many Muslims, had its triumphant moments. Though the degree to which the élites and the subaltern groups contributed to its making and development is debatable, the nationalist ideology, howsoever fuzzy, shifting and ambiguous, fired popular imagination at several defining moments in twentieth century history. In 1920, for example, when the Mahatma's spectacular mass mobilization strategies paid off. Again, when the same frail man, at the age of sixty, marched from his Sabarmati Ashram with seventy-eight followers to the shores of Dandi, a small village on the coast of Gujarat. This was nationalism, pure and simple, on the move.

The influence that emanated from Gandhi's personality, wrote Tagore, was ineffable, like music, like beauty. Its claim upon others was great because of its revelations of a spontaneous self-giving. Not only were the villages awakened to a sense of their power, but the novel conception of motion shot across the changeless horizon.

The ambiguities of Indian nationalism were its greatest strength. Whether you invoke Gandhi, Nehru, Patel or Azad, nationalism lent itself to several different meanings. This is not something to frown upon, because their discourses were, after all, located and expounded within the anti-colonial paradigm. The evolution of institutional pluralism, democracy and political stability was not contingent upon a unified or monolithic inter-pretation of nationalism. It is a lesson that we will do well to remember.

In free India, the finest hour in the tortuous career of national-ism was perhaps the drafting of a democratic and secular consti-tution, with a pronounced egalitarian thrust in its provisions. True, the notion that loyalty to the people came before loyalty to the party or government did not find favour in India, in the nineteenth century European sense where nationalism was associated with popular sovereignty. Yet the urge to clear the debris of the raj and to rebuild a new and dynamic nation state was central to the postcolonial project. These urges and the initial moves towards their fulfilment captured the spirit and essence of nationalism.

Nehru underlined in 1951 that India had infinite variety and there was absolutely no reason why anybody should regiment it after a single pattern. This is what secular nationalism is all about. As its chief proponent after Independence, the country's first Prime Minister pursued not a typically Nehruvian goal, but a goal set by the Mahatma, by Congress' secular wing, and by the left formations. A secular state as a political solution for modern India was based on the contention that it afforded the optimum freedom for the citizens to develop into fully integrated beings. This was a modern goal, rational and scientific, and, in addition, a specifically Indian goal. These values should have been apparent to all, and it was because of this that they were for Nehru and his colleagues the final legitimization for the secular state.

From the late-1950s onward, however, secularism was assailed in different quarters both as an idea and as a state policy. The historical experience of resistance against colonialism faded in popular memory, whereas the ideological edifice of nationalism was undermined by the aspirations of 'new' groups trying to assert their regional, linguistic and ethnic identities, and by the persistent failure of the state machinery to reduce social and economic inequities. Nationalism, along with secularism, became a contested term and grew out of its anti-colonial ranks into ethnic and untutored religious consciousness. Hence the discovery of new heroes, the invention of new histories, and the resurgence of sub-nationalisms in Kashmir, Assam and Punjab.

These trends are seen to be incompatible with democracy and institutional pluralism, but that is not the terrain that I will enter. My real concern is that ethnic collective consciousness in India, as indeed in South Asia generally, manifested itself politically and expressed itself in violent forms. This is signified by the assassinations of Indira Gandhi and Rajiv Gandhi. My other concern is that ethnic nationalism, though objectified by perceptions of relative economic deprivation, so easily coalesced with religious fundamentalism. This is exemplified by the murky career of Jarnail Singh Bhindranwala and the ill-advised policies of several militant outfits in Kashmir, including the brutal expulsion of large numbers of Kashmiri Pandits from their own homeland. So that much as one bemoans the absence of nationalism—in terms of a countrywide vision anchored in conceptions of social justice, minority rights and gender equality—one is wary of the division of our society into diverse ethnic communities ultimately constituting a complicating factor in 'nation-building'.

If the politics of ethnicity gained salience in the 1980s, so did majoritarionism in the garb of Hindu nationalism. For decades, its protagonists had waited on the margins of political life to establish the *illegitimacy* of the Congress-led movements against colonialism. Their other favourite pastime, for which they could draw on the writings of Savarkar and Golwalkar, was to rewrite the nationalist text in order to impose a singular, monolithic Hindu identity and to establish an unbroken *Hindu*, as opposed to a heterogeneous nationalist, tradition. The demolition of the Babri Masjid, which was no doubt hastened by the Shah Bano affair and by the outcry against Mandalization, was central to the fruition of the *Hindutva* project.

More than the mosque's physical destruction, the masjid-mandir controversy and the ensuing religious mobilization conducted by the *Sangh Parivar*, signalled a two-pronged attack on the nationalist legacy. It was directed, in the first place, against Gandhi's simple but somewhat esoteric Ram-Rahim approach to the resolution of Hindu-Muslim disputes, and against Nehru's stubborn insistence on democratic socialism and secularism. Second, *Hindutva* as the new mantra of civil society aimed at wrecking the national consensus envisaged by that mastertext called the Constitution.

The historian E.J. Hobsbawm talked of the 'Age of Nationalism'. Edward Said wrote nostalgically about nationalism in Ireland, India and Egypt being rooted in the long-standing struggle for native rights and independence by nationalist parties like the Sinn Fein, Congress and Wafd. He referred to the pantheon of Bandung flourishing, in all its suffering and greatness, because of the *nationalist dynamic* which was culturally embodied in the inspirational autobiographies, instructional manuals, and philosophical mediations of great leaders like Nehru and Naseer.

This nationalist dynamic has dissipated in the countries listed by Edward Said. In India, the demise of inclusive nationalism has been hastened by, among other factors, the *Hindutva* bandwagon. This has been replaced by state-sponsored nationalism/patriotism that is exclusive, insular, and narrow in conception. The *Hindutva* version of nationalism is exclusive because it clearly bears the imprint of an ideology that seeks to homogenize only a small segment of society around invented but divisive religious symbols and historical memories. It is narrow in outlook because the impulse for homogenization itself, arising out of the tendency to stereotype or stigmatize other religious minorities, rests on misplaced assumptions about the histories of inter-community relations.

State-sponsored nationalism, orchestrated by the print and television media, comes into play only when a nuclear explosion takes places, or when the country is at war with Pakistan. Otherwise, our *nationalism* remains dormant. In actual fact, what is flaunted as nationalism or patriotism on such occasions is nothing but militarism. Yet, it is state-sponsored militarism and not nationalism that is a saleable commodity in the political marketplace. That is why it is allowed to run amok by political managers and propagandists.

But once the booming guns are silenced and the war euphoria is dissipated by the harsh realities of daily existence, it does not take long for the deep-seated fissures in our polity and society to surface. It does not take long for us to forget our war widows and leave our injured soldiers at the mercy of their relatives. And the eyes that shed tears in middle-class homes for the dead and wounded soldiers dry up.

The stories of demolition, war, floods, cyclones and disease are over, the Hindi writer Rahi Masoom Reza would have said, the stories of life have begun, because the stories of life never end.

The hollowness of the new brand of middle class nationalism is illustrated by our lazy and lackadaisical response to atrocities on women, Dalits, tribals, minorities, and other weaker sections of society. We care for the soldiers in Kargil, but not for those killed in Sri Lanka. We build war memorials for our heroes but take very little notice of the plight of those millions who have barely managed to survive in the cyclone-hit towns and villages in coastal Orissa. We rose to the occasion when Pakistan invaded Kargil, but have not responded well to the cry for help from Cuttack and other cyclone-affected areas. Yet our pride is not hurt; our self-esteem not damaged. We accept loans and grants from the IMF and World Bank but refuse humanitarian aid from international agencies in the name of national pride. The sufferings of the cyclone victims are prolonged as politicians debate the politics of aid in devastated areas.

How do we travel into the next millennium with this light

ideological baggage? The ride is bumpy, the journey hazardous. Yet this country of nearly one billion people will need to move into the open spaces equipped with an ideology that draws upon the intellectual resources of the nationalist movement, and, at the same time, take cognizance of the worldwide currents of change. Tagore had said long ago:

Let us announce to the world that the light of the morning has come, not for entrenching ourselves behind barriers, but for meeting in mutual understanding and trust on the common field of cooperation, never for nourishing a spirit of rejection, but for that glad acceptance which constantly carries in itself the giving out of the best that we have.

27 December 1999

The Partition Debate

It is hard to comprehend how and why Mohandas Karamchand Gandhi, having dominated the political scene for three decades, could do so little to influence the Congress to take effective steps to contain Partition violence. Even if this illustrates Gandhi's diminishing political influence, we can still ask why he became 'a spent bullet', and what turned him into 'a back number'. What led him to conclude that he could not influence, much less lead, India on the eve of Independence? Was it because he had found no way of tackling the communal problem, and that he himself was groping in the dark?

It may well be that the otherwise well-tested Gandhian methods became out of place in the new political culture fashioned by the Congress. Or, do we see the balance of power tilting against him from the time he suggested the dissolution of the Congress? He had stated at the Congress Working

Committee meeting, which finally approved the Partition plan, that he would have declared rebellion single-handedly against the CWC if he had felt stronger or an alternative was available. That he did not feel strong enough to carry out his threat is a powerful indictment of the Congress party and its tall poppies.

Doubtless, Gandhi did not have a readymade answer to allay Jinnah's anxieties or curb the stridency of Hindu militants. Yet, he still commanded the allegiance of millions across the sub-continent to reconcile competing political aspirations. His charisma still worked, as in Bihar, where his presence did much to reassure local Muslims. Doubtless, he lacked the political resources to prevent Partition, and yet the transfer of power may not have taken such an ugly and violent turn had his Congress colleagues allowed him to wield his moral stick. Violence had engulfed the country, and yet he hoped that the people's goodness would assert itself against the mischievous influence.

Gandhi did not expect to convert Jinnah to his creed. Still, he counted on his party comrades to pay heed to his warnings. The fact is that they did not. Gandhi was deeply hurt, complaining to friends about his estrangement from those very Congress leaders whose careers he had nursed assiduously. Sometimes he would ask himself, 'had India free no longer any need of him as it had when it was in bondage'.

In Noakhali, a weary Mahatma, leaning against his *lathi* that had stood him in good stead in his political journey's, had to prove to the world that personal courage, moral fervour, and commitment, more than formalistic ideologies, could soothe violent tempers. In Noakhali, he would have said to his restless audience basking in the morning sunshine that violence breeds more violence. Hatred, he would have reiterated in his low and soft voice, betrayed weakness rather than strength, generated fear, heightened anxieties, and created insecurities. Never before had a political leader taken so bold an initiative to provide the healing touch not just to the people in Noakhali but to the warring groups across the vast subcontinent. And yet, never before did so earnest an effort achieve so little.

After Noakhali, Gandhi was caught up in the whirlpool of

hatred, anger and violence. Jinnah, on the other hand, streered his ship through the rough currents seeking a secure anchorage. Riding on the crest of a popular wave, he seemed oblivious to the human sufferings caused by his cry for a Muslim homeland. The Lincoln's Inn-educated barrister told Gandhi during talks in early September 1944, 'we are a nation'. Gandhi did not agree.

Was there even the slightest possibility of mediating their differences within or, outside the party structures? Were they politically equipped to push through a negotiated settlement against the wishes of their following? Frankly, the pressures from below, as indeed the exertions of senior leaders, were too strong for reversing attitudes and strategies. A groundswell of rural Punjabi support for the League was in evidence. In Bengal, the League captured, in the 1946 elections, 104 out of 111 seats in the rural areas. The Great Calcutta Killing of August 1946 completed the convergence between élite and popular communalism. Jinnah could ill-afford to backtrack. For him, achieving 'Pakistan' became a matter of life and death.

Similarly, Gandhi could not single-handedly negotiate an agreement without incurring the hostility of his own Congress colleagues. The Hindu Mahasabha and the RSS, too, emerged out of the dark corridors to ensure that Gandhi and the Congress did not yield to Jinnah's demands.

At the crossroads of communal polarization, India became a fertile ground for the idea of a divided India to nurture. Most found, willy-nilly, and that included powerful Congress leaders who had until now paid lip service to the conception of a united India, Partition the way out of the impasse. The options, if any, were foreclosed. The Congress agreed to Partition because, as Nehru stated at the All-India Congress Committee meeting on 9 August 1947, there was no other alternative. This was not an admission of failure but a recognition of the ground realities that had moved towards the polarization of the Hindu, Muslim and Sikh communities.

For Jinnah, the real and ultimate challenge was to translate his otherwise nebulous idea of a Muslim state into a territorial acquisition that he could sell to his partners in Punjab, Bengal and United Provinces. When the Lahore Resolution was adopted in March 1940, Jinnah hesitated placing his cards out in the open because he could not predict the reactions of his own allies in these provinces. But once the edifice of resistance crumbled, especially in Punjab after the deaths of Sikander Hayat Khan and the Jat leader Chhotu Ram (both had kept the Punjab Unionist Party intact), and popular support for the Pakistan idea gathered momentum, Jinnah had no qualms in defining his future Pakistan.

At every critical moment, Jinnah's great asset was the colonial government's readiness to negotiate with him as an ally rather than as an adversary. This had not been the case earlier, though Nehru had pointed out that the third party could always bid higher and, what is more, give substance to its words. The Quit India movement (August 1942) turned out to be yet another milestone. From that time onwards the League bandwagon rolled on, and Jinnah developed the habit of reminding senior British officials of their obligations towards the Muslims. Whenever he found them dithering or tilting slightly towards the Congress, he conjuring up the self-image of a wounded soul, and raised the spectre of a civil war.

Words were translated into deeds on Direct Action Day on 16 August 1946. This ill-advised call did not exactly heal the communal wounds, but proved to be, as was the undeclared intention, Jinnah's trump card. The Qaid, says Ayesha Jalal, was forced by the Muslim League Council to go for Direct Action; otherwise he would have been swept aside himself. What remains unexplained is how this decision, besides leading to the Great Calcutta Killing, sounded the death-knell of a united India. If the resignation of the Congress ministries allowed Jinnah to jump the queue and gain proximity to the colonial government, direct action confirmed his capacity to call the shots and create, with the aid of his allies in Bengal particularly, the conditions for civil strife on a continental scale.

Meanwhile, the colonial government—the 'third party'—nursed its wounds. Bruised and battered by the impact of World War II, it had little or no interest in curbing violence. As the sun finally set on the empire, the imperial dream was over. 'Your day is done,' Gandhi had written. The British, having read the writing on the wall, had no desire or motivation to affect a peaceful transfer of power. Having bandied round the view that Hindu-Muslim violence resulted from a civilizational conflict between Islam and Hinduism, they now put forward the thesis that it could not be contained once Pakistan became inevitable.

II

In the histories of imperial rule, the retreat of the British administration was an act of abject surrender to the forces of violence. 'We have lost,' wrote the British Viceroy, Wavell, 'nearly all power to control events; we are simply running on the momentum of our previous prestige.' When the dead count was taken, the people paid the price—and that too a heavy one—for the breakdown of the law and order machinery. For the most part, the small boundary force in Punjab stayed in the barracks, while train-loads of refugees were being butchered.

No one knows how many were killed during the Partition violence. No one knows how many were displaced and dis-possessed. What we know is that, between 1946 and 1951, nearly 9 million Hindus and Sikhs came to India, and about 6 million Muslims went to Pakistan. Of the said 9 million, 5 million came from what became West Pakistan, and 4 million from East Pakistan. In only three months, between August and October 1947, Punjab was engulfed in a civil war. Estimates of deaths vary between 200,000 and 3 million. An anguished Amrita Pritam appealed to Waris Shah 'to speak from the grave' and turn the page of the book of love.

Public men, social scientists, especially historians, writers, poets, and journalists shared this concern, in equal measure, and represented violence, pain and struggle in such a way as to reflect the present-day language of historical discourse. Implicit in their concern is a sense of moral outrage, an unmistakable revulsion towards violence, the fear of its recurrence, and, at the same time, the hope of its being prevented in free India and Pakistan.

Another noteworthy point is that violence is not celebrated (as was done by the Serbs and Croats in Bosnia-Herzegovina) but decried in the narratives I have accessed. Violence is, in fact, not only condemned but is so often attributed—often as a means to disguise the collective guilt of a community—to anti-social elements, unscrupulous politicians, and religious fanatics. It is worth reiterating that the 'heroes' in the Partition story are not the rapists, the abductors, the arsonists, the murderers and the perpetrators of violence, but the men and women—living and dead—who provide the healing touch.

Even at the risk of oversimplification, I wish to argue that the general tenor of the literary and political narratives, both in India and Pakistan, is to emphasize that Partition violence sounded the death-knell of those high moral values that were essential components of Hinduism, Islam and the Sikh faith. Naturally, the definition of such values, rooted in diverse trad-itions, varied. But the consensus, though unstructured, is to invoke diverse religious, intellectual, and humanist traditions to serve the crying need of the hour—restoration of peace and inter-community goodwill. Thus Nanak Singh, the Punjabi writer, invokes Guru Gobind Singh to lend weight to his moralistic plea for communal amity (he had ordained: every one of the humankind is same to me); Amrita Pritam, the Punjabi poet, vividly recalls the dark nights on the train and the images of death and destruction which Haji Waris Shah had seen in Punjab at the end of the 18th century, with the butchery and rape that accompanied Partition. For scores of writers, social activists and publicists, secularism, in the sense of anti-communalism, was a deeply held faith, an integral face of nationalism, a value to be upheld even during the difficult days of August 1947 and thereafter.

Possibly, one can take this as an entry point to vindicate the importance of a liberal and secular polity. At the same time, setting out an agenda for the future historian of Partition is not easy. The literature that has appeared during the last decade or so points to the possibilities of charting new territories, and breaking free from the boundaries defined by Partition historio-graphy. Using fiction to portray the other face of freedom, and introducing poignant and powerful gender narratives has, likewise, triggered lively discussions that go far beyond the limited terrain explored during the last few decades. When artfully undertaken, invoking popular memories too shifts the burden of the argument outside the familiar realm of élite manoeuvres and high politics to local specificities and personal and family traumas.

Realistically speaking, however, gender narratives and personal and collective memories can at best enrich Partition debates and not constitute an alternative discourse to the existing ones. Oral interviews can only go that far; they cannot be a substitute for archival research, especially because they are conducted over space and time by writers who have a agenda of their own. Historians, too, have their agenda, but their script can be read and interpreted differently. The same cannot be said of gender narratives and other accounts, often contrived, of pain and suffering. Although intellectually rewarding, our pre-occupation with pain and sorrow that resulted from Partition has limited our understanding of many other crucial areas, including the political and civic fault-lines revealed then—fault-lines of religion, gender, caste and class that still run through our lives.

All said and done, it may not be easy displacing the dominant intellectual discourses. Whether this can or should be done is not the issue at hand. The reality, is that South Asian readers everywhere still earnestly desire to know a lot more about the triangular narrative, with the British, the Congress and the League occupying centre stage, and pay no heed to the historian's plea to eschew preoccupation with national leaders and national parties.

Though sensitised to alternative discourses, most people in the subcontinent discuss not so much the enormity of the tragedy in 1947, but the factors leading to the country's division. They want to know about the intractable stubbornness of one or the other leader, and make sense of the ill-fated talks in Delhi and Shimla. In short, they wish to unfold the great drama being enacted, with the spotlight on their 'heroes' and the 'villains'. Consequently, they follow the moves and countermoves of the 'major' actors performing on the grand Indian stage to satisfy both plain and simple curiosity, or to reinforce ideas inherited from family and friends, and school and college textbooks.

In the aftermath of the 11 September and 13 December attacks, there is talk of Partition's 'unfinished agenda'. The pot is kept boiling, as illustrated by the speeches delivered by the RSS stalwarts. Today, the unending turmoil over Kashmir, the worsening Indo-Pakistan relations, and the resurgence of Islamist ideas and trends are conveniently attributed to Partition's un-finished agenda.

For the historians located in South Asia there is no escape route: they have to whet the appetite of their readers. Though it may take a long time for the scars to be healed, it is important to sensitise them to Partition as the defining moment in South Asian history, and, in the words of Intizar Husain, 'the great human event which changed the history of India'. The Lahore-based Urdu writer goes a step further. The agony of India's Partition, he suggests, could be lessened, perhaps, by exploiting the event's potential creativity: 'To salvage whatever of that (pre-Partition) culture, if only by enacting it in literature. To preserve a memory, however fugitive, of that culture before time and history have placed it beyond reach.'

Partition's impact on the individual and the collective psyche of the two nations is too deep-seated to be wished away. As a metaphor, an event and memory, it has to be interpreted and explained afresh in order to·remove widely-held misconceptions. As I read the recent outburst of the RSS chief, I know that this is easier said than done. The only hope lies in what Mirza Asadullah Khan Ghalib wrote long ago: 'My creed is oneness, my belief abandonment of rituals; Let all communities dissolve and constitute a single faith'.

The Hindu, *2-3 January 2002*

*Partition was not Inevitable*_____

Think back to 1949, when a Muslim saint was asked by Pakistani soldiers at Khori Gali, a mountain pass over the Thanedar range of Naushera, near the Line of Actual Control, to cross over to their side. He refused. India, he said, was his ancestral land where he and his ancestors lived in perfect amity with the Hindus.

Think back to Kemal in Attia Hosain's novel [*Sunlight on a Broken Column*] saying, 'I was born here, and generations of my ancestors before me. I am content to die here and be buried with them.'

Think of Kammo, Haji Ghafoor Ansari and Phunnan Miyan in Gangauli village, the setting for Rahi Masoom Reza's novel *Aadha Gaon*. Phunnan Miyan told the Aligarh boys who had descended on his village to spread the Muslim League gospel, 'Is there true Islam anywhere that you can have an Islamic government? *Eh bhai*, our forefathers' graves are here. I am not an idiot to be taken in by your "Long Live Pakistan".'

There were many Gangaulis in India, where sectarian nationalism did not conform to the day-to-day experiences of people living amicably side by side. Indeed, there were many Gangaulis where the Muslim League's message failed to strike a responsive chord.

The Khori Babas, the Kemals and the Phunnan Miyans expose the myth of 'Muslim Unity', as much as they illustrate how the Pakistan movement conveyed very different meanings to different Muslim groups.

We have lived with India's Partition for well over four decades, but continue to be confronted with and troubled by its bitter legacy, its unresolved issues. Not least of these is the assumption that Jinnah articulated the two-nation theory so forcefully that it galvanized large numbers of Muslims into joining the crusade for a separate homeland. But was this really the case? No.

Was there intrinsic merit in religious/Islamic appeals? Does one search for clues in UP, the citadel of Muslim orthodoxy? In the British policy of 'Divide and Rule' and the government's categorization of Muslims as a separate political and religious entity? In a community's perception of being different from 'others', and its élite's fears of being eased out of post-Independence power structures?

How did the nebulous concepts of an Islamic State or a Muslim government, floated by diverse groups for mixed reasons, get so quickly and effectively transformed into a powerful movement for separation?

Partition was not inevitable. As a matter of fact, the ultimate success of the League's Pakistan project was due not so much to its appeal at the level of ideas but rather the performance and subsequent resignation of Congress ministries (1939), the fluid political climate on the eve of and during the War, the Congress decision to launch the Quit India movement (1942), and the colonial government's readiness to modify its political strategy vis-à-vis the League.

In other words, the two-nation theory itself, though talked about mutely, was formally mooted only when tangible material 'considerations, especially those relating to power sharing, figured prominently on the political agenda. Both the swiftness with which the idea was actualized and the intensity of emotions involved had more to do with the political and economic anxieties of various classes of Muslims than with a profound urge to create an Islamic/Muslim State.

The Muslim League's demands summed up the fears and aspirations of the newly emergent professional groups, especially in UP and Bihar—the powerful landed classes in Punjab, Sind and UP, and the industrial magnates of Western and Eastern India. The Muslim divines jumped into the political arena to advance their material well-being, protect their vital landed interests in Punjab and Sind, safeguard religious establishments under their vigil and control, and defend their status as guardians, custodians and interpreters of the Islamic law.

Three important points need attention here. First, the two-nation idea, despite its emotive appeal in some circles, made no sense to the rank and file of Punjab's Unionist Party, Bengal's Krishak Praja Party, or the dominant Muslim party in Sind. It was, moreover, vigorously opposed by a number of Muslim groups and organizations. They spurned religious slogans, rebuffed Jinnah's initiatives, and emphasized that India's Muslim had deep roots in Indian society and were natural inhabitants of an Indian world.

This perspective, combined with the activism of the Jamiyat al-ulama, the Momin Conference, the Khudai Khidmatgar and the Shia Political Conference, enriched the secular content of the nationalist movement. More importantly, their activities disprove the widely accepted notion that the Pakistan movement was unified and ideologically cohesive, or that its progress was unimpeded by the overwhelming enthusiasm of the Muslim masses and the intelligentsia alike.

Leading members of the Jamiyat-al-ulama, who suffered long years of imprisonment and made huge sacrifices for freedom, saw India as a future confederation of two religious and political communities—the Muslim and the Hindu—which would have cooperated successfully against their common enemy, the British.

Thirdly, the Deoband *alim* Maulana Husain Ahmad Madani, in particular, defended full and individual Muslim participation in the freedom struggle by advancing a theory of territorial nationhood for India, a theory sharply rebutted by Iqbal.

The Deoband scholar rejected Jinnah's two-nation idea, arguing that as men's differences in appearances and traits do not come between them and their common humanity, so differences of faith and culture do not come between the inhabitants of India and their association and partnership in their homeland. Solidarity of religious sentiment is not to be expected—indeed Congress itself recognizes—Madani said, that the different religions and cultures in India will need protection from each other after the British withdrawal from India.

Another misconception, one that suits the votaries of both the Hindu nationalists and the protagonists of the two-nation theory, is that the Muslim League's political base and support structure remained unchanged throughout the 1930s and 1940s. This is not true. The entry of individuals and collective formations into the League happened at different points of time and for very different reasons.

We assume that everybody who rallied round the Pakistan flag was uniformly wedded to and inspired by a shared ideal of creating a society based on the Islamic model. No, they were not. Even a cursory look at the Muslim League records reveals intense personal jealousies, caste feuds, Shia-Sunni schisms, and regional discord.

Finally, a number of Muslim theologians at Deoband and Nadwat al-ulama in Lucknow believed that Pakistan divided and weakened the community of Islam in the subcontinent and destroyed the cherished dream of Muslim thinkers of preserving its unity, inner strength, and dynamism. Pakistan symbolized, within their framework, an ill-conceived retreat, one that was fraught with serious consequences for the future of Indian Islam.

Maulana Azad summed up their anxiety when he told the Delhi Muslims on 23 October 1947 that the debacle of India's Muslims was the result of the colossal blunders committed by the League's misguided leadership. He reflected on the same subject in *India Wins Freedom*. Partition, he wrote, weakened the 45 million Muslims who remained in India. 'If we had remained steadfast and refused to accept Partition, I am confident that a safer and more glorious future would have awaited us. History alone will decide whether we have acted wisely and correctly in accepting Partition.'

The judgement of historians or the verdict of history that Azad talked of will differ once the Partition story is demythologized and its complexities unravelled. What is, however, clear is that the very birth of Pakistan destroyed Iqbal's *Naya Shivala*, which was once the ideal of patriots and freedom fighters. It severed or fragmented cultural ties and undermined a vibrant, composite intellectual tradition. So that there was not much to celebrate at the fateful midnight hour or at the dawn of Independence.

In retrospect, what's equally clear is that the colonial government created a religio-political 'community' in its own image. The Muslim League, emboldened by the popular enthusiasm after the Quit India movement, transformed that 'community' into a 'nation'.

Yet neither the 'community' nor the 'nation' were firmly anchored in their respective settings. The 'community' was battered, bruised and fragmented. The 'Muslim nation', on the other hand, was beset with difficulties and deeply fissured right from the day of its birth. H.S. Suhrawardy, whose dream of a united Bengal was shattered long before the actual transfer of power, was anguished. Khaliquzzaman, too, agreed that the two-nation theory 'proved positively injurious to the Muslims of India, and on a long-term basis for Muslims everywhere'.

If this was so, why did they not give serious thought to the fate of Muslims who were going to be left in India? Both Suhrawardy and Khaliquzzaman gave evasive answers.

Whether they knew it or not, the fact is that millions were unwittingly caught up in the crossfire of religious hatred and were indeed hapless victims of a triangular game plan worked out by the British, the Congress, and the League. They were indifferent to the colonial as well as the League's definition of a 'community' or a 'nation'.

They had no commitment to a Hindu nation or fascination for an imaginary Islamic homeland. They did not know whether their villages or towns will remain in Gandhi's India or Jinnah's Pakistan. They had no sense of the newly demarcated frontiers, little knowledge of how Mountbatten's Plan or the Radcliffe Award would change their destinies and tear them apart from their families, friends, and neighbours.

'The English have flung away their raj like a bundle of old straw,' an angry peasant told a civil servant, 'and we have been chopped in pieces like butcher's meat'.

Times of India (Sunday Times), 13 August 1995

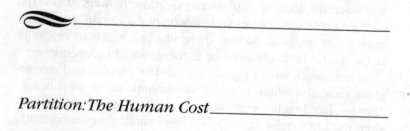

Partition: The Human Cost

The sun had risen fairly high when we reached Amritsar. . . . Every time I visited Amritsar, I felt captivated. But the city this time presented the look of a cremation ghat, eerie and stinking. . . . The silence was so perfect that even the faint hiss of steam from the stationary engine

sounded like a shriek. Only some Sikhs were hanging about, with
unsheathed kirpans which they occasionally brandished. . . . The brief
stoppage seemed to have lingered into eternity till the engine whistled
and gave a gentle pull. . . . We left Chheharta and then Atari and when we
entered Wagah and Harbanspura everyone in the train felt uplifted. A
journey through a virtual came to a halt at Platform No. 2—Lahore, the
moment was as gratifying as the consummation of a dream.

MOHAMMAD SAEED,
Lahore: A Memoir (Lahore, 1989), p. 94

Few writers reveal such poignancy and tragedy of nationally
contrived divisions and borders. India's Partition cast its shadow
over many aspects of State and society. Yet the literature on this
major event is mostly inadequate, impressionistic and lacking in
scholarly rigour. Even after fifty years of Independence and
despite the access to wide-ranging primary source material,
there are no convincing explanations of why and how M.A.
Jinnah's 'two-nation' theory emerged, and why Partition created
millions of refugees and resulted in over a million deaths.
Similarly, it is still not clear whether Partition allowed the fulfilment of legitimate aspirations or represents the mutilation of
historic national entities.

Part of the reason for this flawed frame of reference is the
inclination to draw magisterial conclusions from isolated events
and to construct identities along religious lines. As a result,
discussions tend to be based on statements and manifestos of
leaders and their negotiations with British officials in Lutyens'
Delhi and Whitehall.

The fiftieth year of liberation from colonial rule is an
appropriate moment to question commonly-held assumptions
on Muslim politics, to delineate the ideological strands in the
Pakistan movement, explore its unities and diversities, and plot
its trajectory without preconceived suppositions. Was there
intrinsic merit in religious/Islamic appeals? Does one search for
clues in British policies (which were tilted in favour of the
Muslims to counter the nationalist aspirations) in the ensuing
clash between Hindu and Muslim revivalist movements and in
violent contests over religious symbols (a dispute recently
played out around the Babri Masjid at Ayodhya)? How and why
did the idea of a Muslim nation appeal to the divided and

highly stratified Muslim communities, enabling Jinnah and his lieutenants to launch the crusade for a separate Muslim homeland?

As a starting point, it is necessary to repudiate Jinnah's 'two-nation' theory. Time and again it has been pointed out that the Hindu and Muslim communities lived together for centuries in peace and amity. In fact, their common points of contact and association were based on enduring inter-social connections, cross-cultural exchanges, and shared material interests. Neither the followers of Islam nor of Hinduism were unified or cohesive in themselves. Their histories, along with social, cultural and occupational patterns, varied from class to class, and region to region.

During his tour in 1946-7 the British civil servant Malcolm Darling found, in the tract between the Beas and Sutlej rivers in Punjab, much similarity between Hindus and Muslims. He wondered how Pakistan was to be fitted into these conditions? He was bothered by the same question while passing through the country between the Chenab and Ravi:

> What a hash politics threatens to make of this tract, where Hindu, Muslim and Sikh are as mixed up as the ingredients of a well-made pilau. . . . I noted how often in a village Muslim and Sikh had a common ancestor. It is the same here with Hindu and Muslim Rajputs, and today we passed a village of Hindu and Muslim Gujars. A Hindu Rajput. . . . tells me that where he lives in Karnal to the south, there are fifty Muslim villages converted to Islam in the days of Aurangzeb. They belong to the same clan as he does, and fifteen years ago offered to return to the Hindu fold, on the one condition that their Hindu kinsfolk would give them their daughters in marriage. The condition was refused and they are still Muslim. In this area, even where Hindu and Muslim belong to different clans, they still interchange civilities at marriage, inviting mullah or Brahmin, as the case may be, to share in the feasting.

The search for a political explanation of Partition must begin with the drive for power and political leverage that preoccupied all political parties and their followers during World War II. This accounts for the swiftness with which the two-nation idea succeeded in becoming actualized.

The bitter and violent contest over power sharing reveals a

great deal about the three major themes that have dominated South Asian historiography—colonialism, nationalism and communalism. What it does not reveal, however, is how Partition affected millions, uprooted from home and field and driven by sheer fear of death to seek safety across a line they had neither drawn nor desired.

History books do not record the pain, trauma and sufferings of those who had to part from their kin, friends and neighbours, their deepening nostalgia for places they had lived in for generations, the anguish of devotees removed from their places of worship, and the harrowing experiences of the countless people who boarded trains thinking they will be transported to the realization of their dreams, but of whom not a man, woman or child survived the journey.

Indeed, most Muslims neither understood nor approved of Pakistan, except as a remote place where they will go, as on a pilgrimage. Some left hoping to secure rapid promotion, but not to set up permanent homes there. It did not really matter to the peasants and the mill-workers whether they were physically located in 'India' or 'Pakistan.' Interestingly, for example, the Muslim employees of the East India Railway in a north Indian city decided to stay put in India after having opted for Pakistan, while 8,000 government servants returned to their homes in March 1948, just a few months after they had left for Pakistan.

In other words, most people were indifferent to the newly created geographical entities. They were unclear whether Lahore or Gurdaspur, Delhi or Dhaka will remain in Gandhi's India or Jinnah's Pakistan. The British, the Congress and the Muslim League caught them up in the crossfire of religious hatred—the hapless victims of a triangular game plan masterminded.

Manto captures the mood in 'Toba Tek Singh', one of his finest stories:

As to where Pakistan was located, the inmates knew nothing . . . the mad and the partially mad were unable to decide whether they were now in India or Pakistan. If they were in India where on earth was Pakistan? . . .

Pakistan, a prized trophy for many Muslims, was won, but people on both sides of the fence were tormented by gruesome killings, by the irreparable loss of lives, and by the scale and magnitude of an epic tragedy. Indeed, the birth of freedom on that elevated day—14 August 1947, for Pakistan and 15 August, for India—did not bring India any 'ennobling benediction'. On the contrary, the country was shaken by 'a volcanic eruption'. There was little to celebrate at the fateful midnight hour. In the words of Faiz,

> This is not that long-looked-for break of day
> Not that clear dawn in quest of which those comrades
> Set out, believing that in heaven's wide void
> Somewhere must be the star's last halting place
> Somewhere the verge of night's slow-washing tide,
> Somewhere an anchorage for the ship of heartache.

So, which country did poets like Faiz and writers like Manto belong to? Manto, for one, tried in vain to 'separate India from Pakistan and Pakistan from India'. He asked himself: 'Will Pakistan literature be different—and if so, how? To whom will now belong what had been written in undivided India? Will that be partitioned too?' The uppermost question in his mind was 'Were we really free'?

The silent majority on both sides of the fence, including those 1,000 persons who, after eighteen months of separation, met at the Husainiwala customs barrier in February 1949, shared Manto's anguish and dilemma. They did not pullout daggers and swords but affectionately embraced one another with tears rolling down their cheeks. Their sentiments were reflected neither in the elegant exchanges between the Viceroy and Secretary of State, nor in the unlovely confabulations between the Congress and the League managers.

Today the curtain is drawn on the Husainiwala border; small groups from Pakistan and India congregate at Wagah to witness a colourful military parade that is held every evening to mark the closing of the iron gates on both sides of the fence. Their expressions seem to echo the widespread feeling in the subcontinent that never before in its history did so few divide and decide the fate of so many in so short a time.

'What a world of loneliness lies upon Shabbir (Husain, grandson of the Prophet of Islam) this day!' Everyone who heard these lines in Gangauli village, the setting for the novel *Aadha-Gaon* (Half-a-Village), wept bitterly. They did so to mourn Husain's martyrdom in Karbala centuries ago, but also because 'the cut umbilical cord of Pakistan was around their necks like a noose, and they were all suffocating'. Now they knew what 'a world of loneliness' meant.

Independence and Partition brought varied moods of loneliness. Every individual in Gangauli found himself to be suddenly alone. All of them turned, just as they did every day of their existence, 'to Husain and his seventy-two companions for strength, confidence and spiritual comfort. There was a desire to dream, but what was there safe to dream about?' The atmosphere was foul and murky all around. 'The blood of one's veins was wandering hopelessly in Pakistan, and the relationships and mutual, affections and friendships . . . were breaking, and in place of confidence, a fear and deep suspicion was growing in people's hearts.'

. . .

Today we saw for ourselves something of the stupendous scale of the Punjab upheaval. Even our brief bird's-eye view must have revealed nearly half a million refugees on the roads. At one point during our flight Sikhs and Moslem refugees were moving almost side by side in opposite directions. There was no sign of clash. As though impelled by some deeper instinct, they pushed forward obsessed only with the objective beyond the boundary.

ALAN CAMPBELL-JOHNSON,
Government House, New Delhi,
Sunday, 21 September 1947

The Partition of the subcontinent led to one of the largest ever migrations in world history, with an estimated 12.5 million people (about 3 per cent of undivided India) being displaced or uprooted. In Punjab, the province most affected by violence and killings, 12 million Hindus, Sikhs and Muslims were involved, and migration of some 9 million people began overnight in an area the size of Wales. In UP, nearly 4,000 Muslims a day boarded the train to Pakistan until 1950.

The number of migrants from central and eastern regions

was comparatively small, but the proportion of professional emigrants was relatively high. Educational institutions were depleted of students and teachers overnight. Enrolment figures at the famous seminary in Deoband were down from 1,600 to 1,000 in 1947-8. Income dwindled, as large numbers of students and patrons migrated to Pakistan. The Aligarh Muslim University was rudderless without some of its distinguished teachers who searched for greener pastures in Karachi, the eventual homeland of the *muhajirin* (migrants).

In Bihar, emigration began in November-December 1946 as a sequel to rioting in many places. Peace was soon restored and the movement stopped just before Partition. There was fresh migration after August 1947 mainly for economic reasons and because of the acute food shortage in north Bihar, which had a common frontier with East Pakistan. Migrants totalled 45,00,000, although some returned to their homes during 1950-1.

Hyderabad had received a continuous migration of Muslims in their thousands, particularly since 1857, from the rest of India. In 1947 the numbers increased to hundreds of thousands. Drawn from both the rural and urban areas, there were traders, artisans, domestic and government servants, agriculturists and labourers. However, the influx came to an abrupt end on 13 September 1948, the day the armed forces of India moved into the state in response to the call of the people. Almost immediately a reverse movement started: a number of Hyderabadi Muslims left for Pakistan, while others returned to places they had originally come from.

Elsewhere, nearly 450 Muslims a day continued their trek across the Rajasthan-Sind border. From January to 1 November 1952, 62,467 Muslims went via Khokhropar to Sind in West Pakistan. 'Some hundreds go daily and have been going, in varying numbers, for the last three-and-a-half years', Nehru informed his chief ministers. 'The fact that they go there itself indicates that the conditions they live in are not agreeable to them and the future they envisage for themselves in India is dark.' Established and prosperous professionals from UP, Bihar and the princely states of Hyderabad, Bhopal and Rampur left as well.

Men in government and the professions from Delhi, UP and

Bihar formed the core of *muhajirin*. The Delhi police was depleted of its rank and file because of 'mass desertion'. All the three subordinate judges in the Delhi court rushed to Pakistan. People employed with local and provincial governments opted for Pakistan, although some changed their minds later and returned to India. Poets and writers, Josh Malihabadi being the most prominent, joined the trek at different times. Some landlords, including Jinnah's lieutenant, Nawab Liaquat Ali Khan, were among the *muhajirin*. The Raja of Mahmudabad left his family behind in the sprawling Mahmudabad House in Qaiser Bagh, Lucknow, to undertake the mission of creating an Islamic State and society in Pakistan.

Many prominent Muslims stayed, including those who headed the Muslim League campaign. Landlords like Nawab Mohammad Ismail, Nawab Jamshed Ali Khan, the Nawab of Chattari and the Rajas of Salempur, Nanpara, Kotwara, Pirpur and Jehangirabad clung to their small estates. Ismail was elected to the vice-chancellorship of Aligarh Muslim University in September 1947, but relinquished the post on 14 November 1948. Several others retained their public positions, although they had lost face with their supporters.

Others felt overwhelmed by the climate of hostility, suspicion and distrust. They had a litany of complaints—recurring Hindu-Muslim riots, discrimination in employment and official neglect of Urdu. Syed Mahmud, Nehru's friend and minister in Bihar, protested that Muslims faced harassment and were treated as 'a body of criminals'.

Notably, 31 Muslims were jailed for anti-government activities in addition to many more being detained under the Public Safety Act. Muslims in Agra were required to register themselves with the district magistrate. Their houses were searched and a former Legislative Assembly member, Shaikh Badruddin, was arrested for possessing unlicensed arms. Muslims in Kanpur had to obtain a permit before travelling to Hyderabad; their relatives there had to register at a recognized hotel or a police station in order to visit them.

Muslim officers on the railways in Kanpur, some of whom had served for more than ten years, faced suspicion and dismissal. Aligarh's district magistrate was severe on university students and teachers, who had already incurred the wrath of the local leaders for their involvement in the Pakistan movement. The university, threatened with closure, was eventually saved by Nehru's intervention. Zakir Husain, the newly appointed vice-chancellor, placed it on a firm footing with the active support of Azad, free India's first education minister. Liberal and socialist teachers staged a rearguard action to combat the influence of communal tendencies. In general, however, Mohanlal Gautam, the leading Congressmen touring UP, found 'an all-pervading sense of fear' among the Muslims.

The Evacuee Property Laws restricted business opportunities and disabled large numbers of Muslims. Most Muslims could not easily dispose of their property or carry on trade for fear of the long arm of the property law. A number of old Congressmen continued to send small sums of money to their relatives in Pakistan. They were promptly declared evacuees or prospective evacuees. All this personally distressed Nehru, as he was by the spate of communal violence in UP: 'People die and the fact of killing, though painful, does not upset me. But what does upset one is the complete degradation of human nature and, even more, the attempt to find justification for this.'

By contrast, some of Nehru's colleagues were unrepentant. A powerful section retorted, in answer to the criticism of its murky conduct in handling the civil strife, that the strong anti-Muslim sentiments were generated by bitter and painful memories of Partition. These responses angered Nehru and his liberal and socialist comrades, and dismayed Muslims.

The real pinch was felt in Delhi, UP, Bihar and Hyderabd, the areas most affected by riots, the exodus to Pakistan and the extensive skimming-off from the professional classes. 'Partition was a total catastrophe for Delhi', observed one of the few surviving members of Delhi's Muslim aristocracy. 'Those who were left behind are in misery. Those who are uprooted are in misery. The peace of Delhi is gone. Now it is all gone.' In UP and Bihar very few Muslims were left in the defence services, in the police, the universities, the law courts, or the vast Central Secretariat in Delhi. Large-scale immigration of mostly educated upper-caste Hindus to Lucknow—70 per cent of the total immigrant figure—gradually reduced Muslim influence in government, business, trade, and the professions.

In Hyderabad, Muslims constituted 10 per cent of the population before 1947-8. Muslim government servants held, as in UP, a much higher percentage of posts. But their fortunes dwindled following Hyderabad's merger with the Indian Union. Urdu ceased to be the official language. The abolition of *jagirdari* affected over 11 per cent of the Muslim population, three-quarters of whom inhabited about a dozen urban centres. Smaller *jagirdars*, in particular, faced a bleak future due to retrenchment in government departments, recession in industry after 1951, and a sharp fall in agricultural prices. The old nobles and the absentee landowners started selling their remaining lands and spacious houses to make ends meet.

The dissolution of the princely states impoverished a large percentage, if not the majority, of the upper classes and the bourgeoisie as well as a large number of peasants, artisans and retainers who lost the patronage networks. Nearly half the population of Hyderabad depended on the Nizam for their livelihood, and thus with sources of patronage rapidly drying up this section was worse off.

The rulers of Rampur, Bhopal and Hyderabad were not turned into paupers overnight; they simply lacked the initiative to convert their wealth into more secure and tangible assets. They squandered their inherited resources to maintain their standard of living and allowed properties to be grabbed by unscrupulous land dealers. Their mango orchards, which had yielded vast revenues, were generally converted into uneconomic farmlands. Few ventured into business, trade or industry, or realized which way the wind was blowing. They continued living in their decaying palaces surrounded by a retinue of servants, wives, eunuchs and hangers-on. Wallowing in nostalgia for the bygone era, they cursed the *khadi*-clad politicians for bringing to an end the *angrezi sarkar* (British Raj).

Accustomed to framing their own laws, codes and regulations, they were irked by the presence of local bureaucrats—the district magistrate, superintendent of police and revenue officials—who were visible symbols of political change. Insulated from the populace and blissfully unaware of the changes that were visibly taking place in urban and rural areas, their public contacts were limited to Id celebrations at the close of a month's fast or Muharram observances when the *imambaras* were lit up and the mourners turned up at the desolate Nizam's palace in Hyderabad or the Khas Bagh in Rampur. The memory of the suffering of Husain and his companions at Karbala reminded them of their own trials and tribulations.

The abolition of the *zamindari* system in 1951 stripped the large landlords of the bulk of their estates and awarded the land to the cultivators. The rural influence of the former Muslim landlords was reduced, even more than that of their Hindu counterparts. Many former Hindu rentiers and landowners migrated to places like Kanpur, Gorakhpur and Lucknow in search of new sources of livelihood. Muslim *zamindars* and *taluqdars* were bereft of such ideas. Muslim immigration was a mere 16.28 per cent between 1947-55 from rural areas as compared to 68 per cent among upper and intermediate Hindu castes.

The bigger Muslim *taluqdars* suffered more than their Hindu counterparts because of families being divided, one branch migrating to Pakistan. Such was the fate of the *taluqdari* in Mahmudabad. The Raja left behind his estates in Bara Banki, Sitapur and Bahraich districts to be looked after by his brother. He may have wished to return to his place of birth, but the India-Pakistan war in September 1965 thwarted his plans. His huge assets were declared 'enemy property'.

The Awadh *taluqdars*, accustomed to supporting themselves from the rental income of their estates, were greatly traumatized by *zamindari* abolition. Some left for Pakistan; others retired to anonymity in their villages. Those who stayed found the going hard. 'The abolition of *zamindari* removed our clientele in one fell swoop. All of a sudden the economy changed. And the English customers left. Our shop was "by appointment to several governors of the province".'

Some smaller *zamindars* managed to keep their status intact by moving into nearby towns and cities in search of better opportunities. A few families in the Bara Banki district, living in close proximity to Lucknow, did well. Some reaped the rewards of being close to the Congress. They obtained private and government contracts, licenses and positions. Mubashir Hosain (1898-1959), of Gadia and son of Mushir Hosain Kidwai (b. 1878), the pan-Islamic ideologue in the early 1920s, was a judge at the Allahabad High Court until 1948. Begum Aijaz Rasul, wife of the former *taluqdar* of Sandila in Hardoi district, did quite well for herself. Elected to the UP Assembly and the Rajya Sabha, she held ministerial positions until 1971. There were other successes too.

The small Awadh *taluqdars*, however, lost much of their land to the tenants who acquired legal rights over what they cultivated. They were estranged from the 'new men', rustic and entrepreneurial, who thronged their bazaar and streets and disturbed their social poise and harmony.

For the *zamindars* their universe had suddenly collapsed: they had no 'land left equivalent even to the hub of the great wheels which was once their *zarnindaris*'. In just a few moments they collapsed like the tomb of Nuruddin the martyr, a familiar landmark in Gangauli village. In their prayers they cursed the Congress party. The Syeds, who for centuries had made Gangauli their home, realized that they no longer had any links with the village they had called their own. Whether Pakistan was created or not had no meaning to them, but the abolition of *zamindari* shook them to the core. Now it was all the same whether they lived in Ghazipur or in Karachi.

The *zamindars* of western UP, on the other hand, were not too badly off. Many switched allegiances to the Congress, and some enjoyed a measure of local goodwill because they had implemented certain provisions of agrarian legislation. Most moved to Aligarh to educate their children. They built or renovated their mansions, developed an interest in local politics and used the university—which they treated as an extension of their estates—as a political arena. It satisfied their pride to serve on the university court or the executive council, be involved in the selection of senior office-holders, and turn up dutifully at the railway station to greet visiting dignitaries. But when they retired to the privacy of their homes they recounted the harsh encounters in a world that was not their own.

By the early 1960s some smaller *zamindars* were struggling to eke out a living. There were those who had limited resources to live on; others relied on inherited charitable endowments or even pawned their family jewellery to maintain the facade of high living. Their crumbling houses bear testimony to their steady impoverishment. The luckier ones, such as the Chattari clan, moved out of Aligarh in search of professional careers. The *sherwani*-clad Nawab lost the vigour and determination, which he displayed during his extended public life, now that he had to cope with harsh realities.

Attia Hosain's novel, *Sunlight on the Broken Column*, describes the faded fortunes of the landed aristocracy and captures the sense of an era having passed once and for all:

He [the Raja of Amirpur] lived in retirement at Amirpur, dignified and aloof, bearing the landslide of adversities with courage. His palace in the city had been requisitioned as a government hospital for legislators, and the huge rambling house at the outskirts, with its ornamental gardens divided into building plots, was the centre of the new colonies for the refugees.

The last occasion on which he appeared in public was four years after independence, when he welcomed the President of the Republic to a reception given in his honour by the Taluqdars, There were no illuminations, no fireworks, no champagne, no glitter of precious gems, orders, silks, brocades and ceremonial uniforms. This last reception of the Taluqdars was a staid tea party given by hosts who were soon to have their 'special class' and 'special privileges' abolished.

Dusty portraits and marble statues of stately ex-Presidents of their Associations, and of Imperial representatives, looked down with anachronistic grandeur on tea-tables bearing tea becoming tepid, cakes tasting stale, and Indian savouries growing cold. Guests in Khaddar (loincloth) outnumbered those in more formal attires.

With grace and courtesy Amirpur presided over this swan-song of his order, while those who had habitually bowed before authority hovered round their gentle, dignified guests still hoping for manna from Heaven.

Try another Vantage Point

As the countdown to 15 August 1997 begins, there seems to be unprecedented interest in plotting the history of India's Partition. Why this nostalgia, the revival of individual and collective memories, the celebration of the dead? Why print Manto's 'Toba Tek Singh' repeatedly in scores of newspapers and magazines? Is it because there is not much to celebrate after 50 years of Independence? Or has the occasion itself finally sensitized us to the painful legacy of Partition?

Sure enough, a common refrain in recent writings is that Partition was a colossal tragedy, a catastrophe brought about by politicians who lacked the will and foresight to resolve their disputes over power-sharing, and who failed to grasp the implications of dividing the country on religious lines.

As a result there is much less preoccupation with political parties, their statements and resolutions, and their mutual wrangling in Lutyen's Delhi. For a change, the focus is on the impact of Partition on the common people, and the meanings they attached to happenings in and around their homes, fields and factories.

Such concerns are probably not echoed in Pakistan, where creation of a Muslim state is seen as a legitimate act, the culmination of a logical historical process. Obviously, Partition does not convey the same meanings in Lahore or Islamabad as it does to some of us in Delhi and Calcutta. It is celebrated as a spectacular triumph of Islamic nationalism and not bemoaned as an epic tragedy. True, Manto, Bedi and Krishan Chandar strike a chord among the beleaguered *muhajirs* of Karachi. But why should those living in Punjab or the Frontier region mourn the break-up of India's unity or lament the collapse of a common cultural intellectual inheritance?

The differences in approaches should not, however, stand in the way of developing a common reference point for rewriting the *histories*, and not just the history of Partition. It is possible, despite years of mutual antipathy, for the peoples of India and Pakistan to make sense of Bedi, Kamleshwar, Intizar Husain and

Josh, and to reflect on the trauma of a generation caught in the crossfire of religious sectarianism.

For this to happen, we must first revive the old-fashioned theories on India's syncretic-composite cultural ethos and highlight the shared values and traditions in the making of a subcontinental culture. The urgency must be felt in India as well as Pakistan, where ethnic, linguistic and regional tensions reveal the limits of an Islamic agenda developed around the imaginary notion of Muslim solidarity.

Along with this, scholars and generalists must uncover the complex nature of the Muslim League movement, question its representation as a unified entity, and assess afresh its ideology and mobilization.

By now, the liberal intelligentsia in Pakistan must know that not everyone who rallied round the green flag was uniformly wedded to, and inspired by, a shared ideal of an Islamic society. Many were pushed into religious/Islamic positions; many others used the League platform to promote their material interests. No wonder people hitched their fortunes to the League bandwagon at different points of time and for different reasons. This needs to be underlined to question the exaggerated claims made in the name of Islam by the protagonists of the two-nation theory, and to explore the contradictions in the political and economic trajectory plotted by the rulers of Pakistan.

Consider, too, the intensity of jealousies and internal discord in the League. Are these commensurate with the 'pure' intentions attributed to the League or the romanticized image of its followers? In 1941, Jinnah was told about the influx of undesirable and dubious persons, 'including those who just a few years ago had treated their workers with amused contempt', the regional groupings in the organization, the *Ajlaf-Ashraf* (low and high-born) divide, and Shia-Sunni schisms in several areas.

To put such impressions in perspective and grasp the dynamics of power politics, those critical areas must be probed where the 'faithful' themselves were so hopelessly split. Such an exercise will not reduce the reputation of historic figures or belittle the Pakistan movement but enlarge our understanding of them. If we know our leaders better and question their reading of our shared heritage, we may avoid their error of judgement.

Finally, we must not ignore the role of those Muslims who championed secular nationalism and rejected Jinnah's Pakistan demand. Their perspectives, combined with the activism of several organized formations, disproved the notion that the Pakistan campaign was ideologically cohesive, or that its progress was unimpeded. At the same time, their commitments and orientation communicate forcefully that Muslims had strong secular and nationalist traditions as well which should not be forgotten, and their positions not submerged beneath the rationalization of the 'victors', the founders of Pakistan.

Even if these themes make little sense to some readers, we can still turn to creative writers to reveal the other face of freedom. After all they encapsulate the mood and sensitivity of those aggrieved men and women who had no say in the transfer of power in August 1947. They portray a fragmented and wounded society, even though cynical and self-seeking politicians, impervious to the consequences of their recklessness, ignored their warnings to sign united India's death warrant.

Creative writers expose the inadequacy of numerous narratives on Independence and Partition. They compel us to consider new themes and approaches, and provide a foundation for an alternative to current expositions on inter-community relations in India. Their strength lies in representing a grim and sordid contemporary reality, without drawing religion or a denominational group as the principal reference point. For these reasons, they stir the individual and collective imagination of sensitive readers in the subcontinent.

26 July 1997

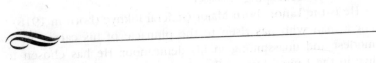

*Witness to a Tumultuous Era*_____

At the time of Independence and Partition, the officers were asked to state in writing their choice of the country they wished to serve. Last week I met someone [in Charlottesville, Virginia] who stated candidly: 'I kept my promise to the Muslim men and volunteered for Pakistan. In fact, I was acting commandant of my regiment and remained with them for six weeks serving under the flag of Pakistan.' This was in the inhospitable terrain of Kohat in the North-West Frontier Province.

Win a couple of million dollars by guessing his name! Win another million by telling me who recommended President Zia-ul-Haq for a regular commission? Let me drop a few hints. Schooled in Shahpur, some 3 miles from the east bank of Jhelum river where Muslim landowners like the Noons and the Tiwanas hold their vast estates, he was among the few hundred pre-War Indian officers to receive a regular commission from King George VI. During World War II, he was the first Indian to join the British officers to go with the regiment for operations in the Middle East and Italy. In free India, he headed an armoured squadron to fight Pakistan's tribal incursion into Kashmir. Later, he became the first person from the Third World to serve as Chief of Staff of the United Nations force deployed in the Sinai after the Suez war. He was appointed Military Advisor to the United Nations Secretary-General, Dag Hammarskjold, whom he met in Gaza way back in 1957. This again was a first. His special assignments carried out for Hammarskjold's successor, U Thant, bolstered his reputation as a key negotiator. In the late-1960s, he was held in high regard for pursuing the United Nations peacekeeping mission.

He is the Lahore-born Major General Rikhye (born in 1918).* For a man who has risen to the pinnacle of his career, he is modest and unassuming in his demeanour. He has chosen to live in the United States after retiring from the United Nations in 1969, but at heart he remains an Indian to the core. Next to

*He has recently published *Trumpets and Tumults: The Memoirs of a Peacemaker* (Delhi: Manohar, 2002).

the *Gita*, his source of inspiration is Gandhi and his voluminous writings. Ironically, it was the Mahatma, an apostle of non-violence, who prevailed upon Indar Jit's father to let him join the army. His father was a medical doctor who died in 1951. His ancestors had close ties with Maharaja Ranjit Singh.

Nurtured in the composite ethos of pre-divided Punjab, Indar Jit does not speak the language of V.S. Naipaul. *Hindutva* or Hindu nationalism militates against his world view. As a fervent votary of India-Pakistan rapprochement, he recalls his friendship with several surviving Pakistani generals.

Not only India and Pakistan are divided but they now seem determined to appear different. If 'Biji' (mother) were alive, she would have said the same. Do you know that we weren't sensitized to the great communal debates in the barracks? At least I wasn't. India's Partition? Nobody talked about it. Not even the Muslim officers.

Much of this conversation was filled with nostalgia and a sense of remorse at the unfortunate turn of events in the summer of 1947. When he visited Pakistan decades later, 'the wounds of Partition and the sacrifices of my family for the price of freedom were still raw under my scars'. This was during Zia-ul-Haq's regime. He reminded me of Amrita Pritam, a remarkable Punjabi writer and poet, who once implored Waris Shah 'to turn the page of the book of love' in a region where 'somebody has mixed poison in all the five rivers'.

Why did the General eventually leave his post at Kohat? Well, Jinnah did not want a Hindu or Sikh officer in the Pakistan army. His inability to remain with the regiment and continue his life in the land of his birth dampened his enthusiasm for Independence. He dreaded the thought of his squadrons being transferred. 'It was a terrible wrench, like losing someone from your family, and that is what we were.' Clearly, the General had no feelings for national borders or the geographical entities that were being laboriously created in 1947. National borders were political constructs, imagined projections of territorial power. They reflected merely the mental images of politicians, lawyers and intellectuals but not the men on the battlefront. Rikhye agreed with me that the cartographic and political divisions constituted by Partition were 'the shadow lines' that the novelist Amitav Ghosh seeks to repudiate.

On a cool and misty morning of 27 September 1947, the train pulled out of the otherwise sleepy Kohat railway station. Escorted by the Pakistan army, some 1,500 men and 500 women and children travelled through the valley of death and destruction to reach their destination. The journey from Kohat to Rawalpindi and Sialkot—from Jinnah's Pakistan to Gandhi's India in Ambala (via Montgomery)—took twenty-one gruelling days. Describing the journey, the General picked up Bapsi Sidhwa's novel *Pakistan Bride* and started reading out a passage he had marked the night before our meeting:

> The earth sealed its clumsy new boundaries in blood as town by town, farm by farm, the border was defined. Trains carrying refugees sped through the darkness at night—Hindus going one way and Muslims the other. They left at odd hours to try to dodge mobs bent on their destruction. Yet trains were ambushed and looted and their fleeing occupants slaughtered.

General Rikhye described to me his engagement in Kashmir, the site of his 'last battle'. He talked about his missions to Congo, Cyprus, Yemen, Cuba and West Asia, his close encounters with Indian politicians, including Indira Gandhi, and his interaction with men of power and influence at the UN Secretariat on the East River in Manhattan and in the far-flung areas of Asia and Africa. To a historian like me, this was a remarkable *tour de force*. International politics is not my cup of tea; yet the General, a witness to a tumultuous era, gave me a taste of it. Let me share with you his meeting with Zia-ul-Haq. 'Why did you hang Bhutto?' Rikhye asked the President. Zia kept quiet for a while. Then, he drew his right hand across the throat and declared, 'It was either him or me.'

Somebody remarked that 'Generals never die, they just fade away.' I beg to disagree. Given his record in India and overseas, the international awards and honours he has received and his list of publications, it is hard to imagine Major General Indar Jit Rikhye fading away.

2 June 2000

Foreignness and the Other Gandhi:
Fear of the Videshi

During India's long and stormy relationship with Great Britain, scores of adventurers and entrepreneurs stepped out of the British Isles to make a fortune in this country. India thus lived under a huge machine that exploited and crushed millions. Wrote Nehru to his daughter, 'This machine was the machine of the new imperialism, the outcome of industrial capitalism.' So that the old-world legend of India's fabled wealth which dazzled poets and beckoned conquerors shrunk, long ago, into an antiquarian puzzle. A concerned Englishman, H.N. Brailsford, commented in 1931: 'Today there confronts us an abyss of poverty so deep that one struggles in vain to plumb it.' A few years later, Verrier Elwin wrote to Bapu: 'I have lost most of my Christian or religious faith. How can a just and good God allow these sufferings of the poor?'

The British set foot on the Indian shores for a variety of reasons. The missionaries were imbued with the mission to civilize a people steeped in barbarism. They desired bringing the Christian West to the East, the land of idolatry par excellence, and 'release some gusts of that dry and searing wind, that bracing scepticism, which swept through Europe after the French Revolution'. All in all, the crude literature of imperialism in India projected a racial ideology that found its most refined expression in Rudyard Kipling.

Yet others studiously explored, not always from an Orientalist perspective, India's culture, religions and civilization and wrote scholarly treatise. They acquired the gift of being interpreters, more trusted by 'the others' even than by their own people. Finally, quite a few official and non-official Britons sympathized with or actively supported India's nationalist aspirations. Allan Octavian Hume (1829-1912) was the 'Father of the Indian National Congress', while his biographer, William Wedderburn, was closely associated with the Bombay branch of the East India Association. His sympathy for India was as real as that of Hume, William Wordsworth, Henry Beveridge and Henry Cotton, men who still retained their faith in cooperation with educated Indians. The Indian branch of the Theosophical Society, founded in 1875, was connected with the formation of the Congress. One of its active members was the Irish woman, Annie Besant. She came to India in 1889, and dedicated her life to the service of her adopted country.

In 1898, Besant founded the Central Hindu College, subsequently the nucleus of the Banaras Hindu University. In 1914, she bought the daily *Madras Standard* and converted it into *New India*. This, together with her weekly *Commonweal* and her religious journals, made her the most formidable press baron in Madras. The Home Rule League (1916), with its branches all over the country, was the brainchild of this energetic woman. It soon gave the British envoy reason to see the organization as an extremely serious threat to the continued existence of the raj. Indeed the Home Rule agitation had so aroused feelings against the government that the governor of Madras interned Besant in mid-1917.

Charles Freer Andrews was another outstanding Briton who, in the words of Tagore, lived 'in our joys and sorrows, our triumphs and misfortunes, identifying himself with a defeated and humiliated people'. He remained, so writes his biographer Hugh Tinker, the unique individual who has stepped out of his position as a foreigner, a stranger to India, into the lives and hearts of Indians in order to show that nationality and race were infinitely less important than brotherhood and love. India bestowed on such a man the title of Deenabandhu.

Andrews' devotion to Indian nationalism was exemplary, his life long friendship with Tagore and Gandhi legendary. The spirit of Santiniketan made him at once restful, and calm and quiet, he told the Gurudev. He wrote before his meeting with Gandhi in South Africa: 'I have a great happiness and blessing in store for me—to see Mohandas Gandhi. No life lived in our day could be more moving than his. My journey will be a pilgrimage to touch his feet.' No wonder, the Mahatma was deeply distressed by his death: 'not only England, not only India, but [also] humanity had lost a true son and servant. . . . I have not known a better man or a better Christian than C.F. Andrews'.

Gandhi's personal charisma and skills of communication attracted a large number of people. Among his devotees were a number of 'foreigners' who made India their home, spent years with him backing his political and social crusade, and lent their wholesome support to the nationalist struggle. Prominent amongst them were Verrier Elwin, Reginald Reynolds, a British Quaker who carried Gandhi's historic letter to the Viceroy on 2 March 1930 announcing the launching of civil disobedience, and Miss Slade, an English Admiral's daughter who had left the life of ease to be with the Mahatma. Mirabehn, as she was famously known, accompanied him on his travels, writing notes and letters, nursing him in jail. She was engaged in a concentrated effort to test and vindicate the Mahatma's programme of village reconstruction and the revival of cottage industries. She joined Gandhi's entourage to London during the 1930 Round Table Conference. Gandhi translated into English a large number of devotional songs for her, which he used in the Sabarmati Ashram prayers.

My problem is how to appropriately describe these dedicated men and women. Should we be concerned with their 'foreign' origin or with their contribution to our public life? Do we invent a special category for them? Should we treat them as videshi—'foreigners'—interfering in our nationalist struggles? Perhaps, we can find answers in the Mahatma's writing. But, then, he was too magnanimous and large-hearted to think in such xenophobic terms.

The majoritarian concept of citizenship, now being advanced in certain political circles for short-term electoral gains, was antithetical to his world view as well as the liberal and accommodating ethos of the nationalist movement.

Returning to my point on citizenship and nationality let me quote what Vallabhbhai Patel said in the Constituent Assembly in 1947: 'there are two ideas about nationality in the modern world, one is broad-based nationality and the other is narrow nationality. Now, in South Africa we claim for Indians born there South African nationality. It is not right for us to take a narrow view.' Remember, he continued, 'the provision about citizenship will be scrutinised all over the world. They are watching what we are doing.' Just as everybody is watching what we are doing now.

It is important to emphasize that the nationalist tradition, ranging from the Congress to the Left, articulated a pluralist and generous conception of nationality and citizenship. No wonder the pluralist vision, nurtured from the last quarter of the nineteenth century onwards, came into sharp conflict with the Hindu nationalists who identified 'India' with the 'Hindus' and 'Hinduism'. No wonder, it was at variance with the two-nation theory. That is why Nehru questioned the rationale of Muslim nationalism in a society anchored in cultural and religious pluralism. He asked Jinnah: 'Why only two I do not know, for if nationality was based on religion, then there were many nations in India. Of two brothers one may be a Hindu, another a Muslim; they would belong to two different nations. These two nations existed in varying proportions in most of the villages in India.'

Whenever a nation is seized with peripheral rather than substantive issues of growth and progress, it is best to invoke the past for the legitimization of a rational approach. For this reason, I once again refer to the Constituent Assembly debate in April 1947 on Clause 3 relating to citizenship. It is for you to decide whether you wish to adhere to the egalitarian norms laid down in the Constitution or get swayed by the narrow definition of citizenship being advocated in certain circles.

KRISHNASWAMY AYYAR: 'In dealing with citizenship we have to remember we are fighting against discrimination and all that against South Africa and other states. It is for you to consider whether our conception of citizenship should be racial or should be sectarian.'

B.R. AMBEDKAR: 'We claim for Indians in South Africa the nationality of that country not merely by birth but by reason of settling there.'

SARDAR PATEL: 'I suggest for your consideration how many foreign men and women come to India for giving birth to children to acquire Indian nationality. It is a curious idea that for that purpose you introduce racial phraseology in our Constitution . . . We will always have a few foreigners coming here. This will be accidental nationality. If by the accident of birth, someone comes and stays here, subject to the proviso which we have enacted, we can control double citizenship by our legislation.'

Sure enough, India belongs to each one of its citizens, regardless of birthplace and each one has rights and obligations attached to the citizenship. My fear is that this controversy may not end here. Tomorrow, somebody may take away my citizenship rights just because my family genealogy, perhaps fabricated, traces our ancestry to a Persian city of the fourteenth-century.

8 and 22 May 1999

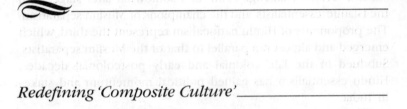

Redefining 'Composite Culture'

The syncretic and synthetic ethos of the Indian civilization—popularly known as India's composite culture—is a pervasive notion as well as a real historical experience shared by many Indians and non-Indians, which has continued in varied forms and meanings across time and space in the region. To them, the genius of India expresses itself in a unique way of accepting, assimilating and synthesizing—rather than rejecting—diverse patterns of beliefs, thoughts and actual living of an infinite variety of people 'and cultures into an inclusive, variegated and complex tapestry of life and culture. This is what is traditionally epitomized as India's 'unity in diversity', and perhaps more meaningfully described as 'living together separately'. In the words of Humayun Kabir, one of the early and best exponents of India's composite culture: 'The story of India's culture unravels the secret of that vitality and that wisdom. It is a story of unity and synthesis, of reconciliation and development, of a perfect fusion of old traditions and new values.'

Professor Asim Roy, scholar at the University of Tasmania in Hobart (Australia), has delineated in a note how in the last couple of hundred years, the syncretistic tradition and perception have been challenged and undermined at times by various contesting ideologies. First, the 'orientalist' scholarship almost exclusively based on Hindu, Buddhist and Islamic religious and other texts constructed and helped to perpetuate exclusive and competing, if not conflicting models of religious-cultural traditions in the region, ignoring the intricate and fascinating processes of interaction of living religions and cultures in India, especially at the level of masses. Orientalism contributed to the construction of barriers among diverse cultural traditions. The second serious challenge came, at a somewhat later stage, from the Islamic 'essentialists' and the champions of Muslim separatism. The proponents of Hindu nationalism represent the third, which emerged and almost ran parallel to that of the Muslim separatists. Subdued in the late colonial and early postcolonial decades, Hindu essentialism has gained political momentum and stakes in India.

The historiography of the 'composite culture' reveals its strong susceptibility and responsiveness to its changing political contexts. The clearest evidence lies in the fact that the bulk of its literature belongs to the last six or seven decades—a period in which the nascent Indian nationalism, liberalism and secularism found themselves seriously engaged and challenged, both intellectually and politically by religious nationalists anchored in either political Islam or political Hinduism or other religious faiths. The colonial context of the imperialists' denigration and opposition to Indian nationalism, prior to the internal challenge and direct intervention on a serious scale, provided a congenial political climate for the persistence and growth of the 'composite culture' as reflected in the shared experiences of millions of Indians. Many nationalist leaders, writers and thinkers as well have contributed to rearing the edifice of this culture.

The political and cultural momentum of Muslim separatism reached its most critical stage in the 1940s. It is not surprising that the year before India's Partition saw the publication, in

1946, of powerful expositions and defence of the composite culture by Nehru, Rajendra Prasad, Asoka Mehta and Achyut Patwardhan, and Humayun Kabir. After a brief lull in the wake of the stunning reality of the Partition, the debate was revived in the early 1960s as a part of the struggle against the communal uses of history from both the Hindu and Muslim viewpoints. Between 1957 and 1961, the Pakistan Historical Society came out with a four-volume edition entitled *A History of the Freedom Movement.* Around the same time the Bharatiya Vidya Bhawan began publishing volumes from a distinctly Hindu point of view. R.C. Majumdar, general editor of the series, echoed the Muslim separatists' assertion that Hindus and Muslims could never come together. All this led to a renewed interest in finding the common grounds in history.

The concept of the 'composite cultures', comments Professor Asim Roy, has been politicized all around. The liberal and Marxist critique, he argues, has found it expedient to use it politically to combat communalism and other forms of sectarian strife, while the Muslim separatists and the champions of political Islam as well as their saffron-robed counterparts of *Hindutva* or political. Hinduism has targeted it to undermine this notion for their own political reasons. 'The chauvinistic claim for a pan-Indian Hindu cultural monolith embodied in *Hindutva*,' he points out, assumes much greater importance today in light of the political power vested in the Hindu-orientated political parties. The argument of pseudo secularism has been deployed by them to sap the foundation of a multi-cultural state. They have appropriated the British divide-and-rule paradigm of Hindus and Muslims as separate civilizational entities that cannot survive together in peace. Doubts have already been expressed in these circles concerning the historical legitimacy of the syncretistic process in the making of India's composite culture, with the corresponding claim made for a reconstructed and exclusive *Hindutva.*

The issue at stake is the role and impact on 'dominance' and intervention relation on culture and its reformulation. What we need to consider, says Professor Roy, are the following questions: Does the syncretic culture have a basis in history?

Or is it a convenient product of India's nationalist aspiration? Imagined or real, can this tradition sustain our cultural continuum through the new millennium? What are the cultural as well as the political fallouts of the possible demise of the syncretic values? How essential is it for the continuance of federal and democratic structure, and for India's viability and survival? Never before has there been so much of urgency in re-examining the historical basis of this culture. Again, this is a Professor Roy's formulation.

Professor Roy has sensitized me to three broad themes. First, the making and development of the composite culture, from ancient through medieval to modern and contemporary times, and the nature, form, content, meaning and symbolizm of the syncretistic traditions at the élite, popular and regional levels; second, we need to scrutinize the historical relationship between the syncretic and other rival traditions in the precolonial, colonial and postcolonial stages and the role and the circumstances of intervention and its cultural and political implications. Finally, according to him, the critical relationship between India's cultural formulation and its political future, with particular reference to democracy and federalism, must command our immediate attention.

26 July 2000

Secularism Revisited

In recent years, the debates on secularism are centred on the arguments outlined in the works of T.N. Madan and Ashis Nandy. The former, a social anthropologist, declared in 1987 that at present secularism in South Asia as a generally shared credo of life is impossible, as a basis for state action impracticable, and as a blueprint for the future impotent. Likewise Ashis Nandy, a noted scholar, argues that both the ideology and politics of secularism have largely exhausted their possibilities and that it was necessary to play around with a different conceptual frame.

These are major interventions and should not be dismissed lightly. More so because the arguments, if not the implications, have secular underpinnings. They must command attention at a time when secularism as a concept and as a state policy is under critical scrutiny.

One thing is clear. Recent debates on secularism, though triggered by the *Hindutva* campaigns, take up the same issues that engaged the Constituent Assembly members after Independence. There was as much confusion then as there is now, about the scope, relevance and meaning of secularism. There was uncertainty and scepticism in the hallowed precincts of the Assembly, just as clouds of doubt hover around academic and political circles today. Secularism was equated with Western liberalism or with minority appeasement. It still is so. Many members argued then, just as they do now, that the 'hegemonic language of secularism' (Nandy) was nothing more than a Western ideal grafted onto a traditional society. The argument is tenable for the Nehruvian era but not thereafter. After all, the secular ideology has steadily declined from the early 1970s and its appeal has diminished even among Nandy's 'Westernised' intellectuals and middle classes.

I return once more to the constitution-makers whose perspective, though nowadays repudiated in some circles, must provide ideological sustenance to the democratic and secular forces. What needs to be underlined is that the issue before many of them was not the European origin of the secular idea but its rightful appropriation in a country of diverse faiths, multiple identities and varied cultural and intellectual norms. Moreover they were not held back, as is the social science fraternity today, by the finer issues of definition, categorization and application of secularism. They wanted to ensure that its essence—the impartiality and neutrality of the State in its relations with the religious institutions and practices of different communities—was not lost on the people. They aimed to prescribe norms for a democratic civil society, foster inter-community relations without reference to scriptures or religious texts, and develop, what was Nehru's great passion, a scientific temper without being encumbered by the weight of scholasticism and traditionalism.

The inspiration came from different sources—from nineteenth-century British liberalism, Fabian socialism, and the revolutionary fervour generated by communism. But the reference point was the Congress-led liberation struggle and its broadly secular goals. Independence, the adoption of a democratic constitution thereafter, and the hegemony of the Congress changed not just the political landscape but also paved the way for marshalling the secular forces.

Most grasped the significance of and accepted the implications of their actions. This was because the major players in the Congress and in the left movement knew full well that the secular model alone could contain centrifugal tendencies threatening to undermine an already fractured social structure after 1947. No wonder secularism, along with 'democratic socialism', occupied a central position in public discourses. It remained, at least in public pronouncements and party manifestos, the foundation on which a progressive modern State could be built for the welfare of the common man.

Secularism itself acquired new meanings and found new modes of expression. This was not something one could decry. An inflexible, static and doctrinaire definition would have inhibited newly emerging social classes and political élites from being closely identified with the values and symbols associated with the changing political climate. In fact, a redeeming feature of the post-Nehruvian era was that these groups did not, as was predicted, shun the secular model. Instead, they enriched its social content. That is how its appeal went far beyond the charmed circle of the élites. This is probably why, what began as a mere experiment in the riot-ravaged and communally polarized India of 1947-9, acquired a fair degree of legitimization in the political, cultural and intellectual discourses of the time.

There is no denying the rise of obscurantist and 'fundamentalist' forces and the gradual weakening of secular tendencies.

This is not surprising, for the dice is loaded against secularism and multiculturalism, not just in India but in many other societies. Yet one must not brush aside the bright spots in our country's tardy progress towards its goal of a secular polity. Instead, it is worth restoring the democratic and secular consensus of the 1950s, maintain the anti-colonial struggle's powerful legacy, and reiterate Nehru's secular agenda. That agenda is not flawless, but it does provide a *raison d'être* for a rapprochement between diverse and conflicting sectarian, and communitarian goals. Perhaps the agenda bears the imprint of ambiguity and needs to be redefined in parts. Perhaps, it needs to be tailored and trimmed to suit the rapidly changing realities of political life. Still, the ideological underpinnings of the democratic and secular consensus envisaged by the architects of India's constitution and assiduously cultivated by the country's first Prime Minister, are as relevant today as they were during his lifetime.

For scholars like Madan the principal question is not whether Indian society will eventually become secularized, as Nehru believed it will, but whether it is desirable that it should. I imagine that the Nehruvian vision is as important as the commitment to the secular ideal.

Notwithstanding the unlovely consequences of the *Hindutva* campaign and the state's passivity in allowing anti-secular forces to run amok, a glimmer of hope lies in the coalition of democratic forces, in the popular revulsion against the excesses or the religious right, and in the sheer diversity of Indian society. If such a coalition receives the electorate's mandate, we can begin to argue confidently that secularism as a general credo of life is possible, as a basis for state action practicable, and as a blueprint for the future desirable.

Revisiting the Jamaat-i Islami _____

One may not know about Islam or the Muslims, but one is well aware of the Jamaat-i Islami (the Islamic Party), an organization identified with Islamism or Muslim fundamentalism. One may not have heard of Syed Ahmad Khan, Ajmal Khan, Maulana Azad and Rafi Ahmed Kidwai, but the mention of Sayyid Abul Ala Mawdudi (b. 1903) raises the spectre of frenzied Muslim fanatics storming into the heartland of the US and Western Europe. That is because Islamic revivalism has evolved around Mawdudi's prolegomenon, and because his interpretation of Islam has influenced contemporary Muslim thinkers from Mindanao to Morocco. In fact he has had an important role in the history and politics of Pakistan, India, Bangladesh, Sri Lanka and the South Asian communities of the Persian Gulf, as well as those living in the West.

For Mawdudi the establishment, realization and pursuit of religion (*iqamat-e din*) means the effort to institute directly the superstructure of social conduct and political action raised on the basis of the divine 'caliphate', the 'divine sovereignty', entirely different from the secular State in all its details and ramifications. Its name is the Islamic State, brought about by the Islamic revolution wrought by a movement, the Jamaat-i Islami, founded in 1941. His stern warning—one that must alert secular republics across the globe—was: 'Whoever really wants to root out mischief and chaos from God's earth . . . should stand up to finish the government run on wrong principles, snatch power from wrongdoers, and establish a government based on correct principles and following a proper system.'

The vagaries of Pakistani politics, in the aftermath of Partition, provided the Jamaat with the opportunity to implement its utopian programme. Initially, the government endeavoured to dismantle the party and diminish its role in politics, but Mawdudi, both in and out of jail, insisted on moving Pakistan in the direction of islamization. The Constitution of 1956 accommodated many of his demands. Ayub Khan gaoled Mawdudi in 1964 and 1967, but was compelled to temper his opposition to Islamic activism. In 1970, the Jamaat participated in national elections, though its hopes were dashed to the ground when the party won only four seats in the National Assembly, and four in the various provincial assemblies.

During Zia-ul-Haq's eleven years rule—from 1977 to 1988—the Jamaat moved from strength to strength, though this was barely reflected in Pakistan's national election of 1985, as also in 1988 and 1999. Yet, the Jamaat has remained a powerful ideological force among politicians, bureaucrats, intellectual leaders, and the armed forces. This does not augur well for the future of secularism in Pakistan. This does not augur well for the prospect of cordial Indo-Pak ties. Though Parvez Musharraf may heed the US clamour to hand over Osama bin Laden and ultimately destroy terrorist outfits, he will have a tough time isolating hot-headed *jehadis*, who subscribe to the Jamaat's ideology of overthrowing liberal and secular regimes. At present, the battlelines are drawn, but the outcome is not easy to predict. It is truly a defining moment for Pakistan, a country finding itself between the devil and the deep sea.

Frédéric Grare, a French scholar, sets out to delineate (*Political Islam in the Indian Subcontinent: The Jamaat-i-Islami*, Centre de Sciences Humaines and Manohar, New Delhi, 2001). The strategies of the Jamaat in Pakistan, a region caught up in the recent tumult caused by the terrorist assault in New York and Washington. This book provides the wider perspective at which he aims—to explore the regional and international strategies of the Jamaat. I do not think he is trying for more in this slim monograph, and what more can a reader on the look-out for a handy book expect? He is painting on a vast canvas, and it is not surprising that the colours are more vivid in some parts than in others.

Grare is persuasive when he writes about the Jamaat acting as the 'torch-bearer of irredendist ambitions'. He is insightful when he argues that the destabilising potential of the Islamist parties generally is much less potent when they are integrated with the nation-wide political or electoral processes. And he is instructive in concluding that Islamism seems essentially to be the problem of failed, and above all, politically deadlocked, Muslim countries.

Quoting approving the scholar Olivier Roy, Grare argues that the strategy of the nation states rather than the existence of a mythical Islamist international outfit explains the place and the action of the Jamaat. This is what the West needs to understand. This is what the protagonists of the clash of civilization thesis need to know.

Who would have thought before September 2001 that terrorists would venture to lay violent hands on a country that claimed invincibility? Who would have said a few years ago that Muslim fundamentalism, though fuelled by America's belligerence in Iraq, Somalia, Sudan and Palestine, would lead inexorably, step by step, to its world-wide legitimacy in many Muslim countries? You may not find answers to some of these questions in this book, but there is much that is refreshingly new.

For me this book has a great deal to recommend it. Grare has a readability I find compelling. His assumptions command today a wide assent and therefore deserve some scrutiny.

Outlook, *1 October 2001*

Hindu Ethos, Muslim Fears

The controversy is not about the flag or the national emblem but the singing of *Vande Mataram*. What is disconcerting is the relative ease with which liberal-left voices have been stifled and the massive task of 'rewriting' history textbooks has been undertaken. What is equally disturbing is how the Gujarat government can get away with the decision, which our 'liberal and moderate' Prime Minister supports, to allow government servants to join the RSS. Reviewing the Constitution at the behest of a party that is not even close to commanding a majority in Parliament, is the last straw. As the erstwhile 'social-ists' in the BJP-NDA alliance remain impervious to what is hap-pening outside their bungalows and office chambers, the country wrestles with long-standing religious, cultural and intellectual disputations. Mercifully, a sagacious President has acted as the custodian of our Constitution with remarkable boldness and tenacity. The silver lining is that we could turn to him for wise counsel and leadership.

Let me return to *Vande Mataram*. Authored by Bankim-chandra Chatterjee, this anthem has triggered some of the great communal debates since the mid-1930s. As the Congress inched its way towards the corridors of power in 1937, the singing of *Vande Mataram* was made mandatory in several schools of UP and Bihar. The Muslim League reacted strongly, though thoughtlessly, to discredit the ministries and catalogue its 'wrongs'. For example, the exaltation of Hindi and the accom-panying attack on Urdu, the exclusion of Muslims from govern-ment service, the introduction of the Wardha and Vidya Mandir schemes, and the concomitant danger to Islamic practices and the traditional system of Muslim education.

In this way the communal cauldron kept boiling and the stage was set for a protracted Hindu-Muslim conflagration. Gene-rally speaking, the Congress was wedded to the view that divi-sive symbols should be kept in abeyance in order to conduct the struggle against colonialism. But, when it came to discussing *Vande Mataram*, some insisted that the song was an integral part of their campaign. Whether or not this is true can be debated, but there can be no doubt that the song inspired many thousands of people, mostly Bengali Hindus, who protested against Bengal's partition in 1905.

Tagore, who set its first stanza to the tune and was the first to sing it at an early session of the Calcutta Congress, maintained that *Vande Mataram* had acquired a separate individuality and an inspiring significance of its own. Yet, Tagore conceded that the poem, read together with its context, was liable to offend Muslim sensibilities. Perhaps he was talking of a Hindu song, reflecting a Hindu ethos in which the country is equated with the mother goddess.

Today, if some leaders of our minority communities express their disquiet, I see no reason why their feelings and sentiments should be brushed aside. At any rate, a secular State has no business to make Muslim, Sikh and Christian students sing any song against their wishes. But, is the song anti-Muslim? Let us discuss it threadbare, instead of exchanging *lathi* blows. Let the priests and politicians congregate in the shadow of the Red Fort and debate their viewpoints, instead of trading charges and counter-charges.

A nationwide consensus is what we need. Once this is achieved, we can move on to sort out the other thorny issues that keep recurring time and again. In the process, we may discover that all these years the Muslim fears have been vastly exaggerated. Or, perhaps, we may convert the protagonists of the *Vande Mataram* to the idea that forcing the song down anybody's throat is against the spirit of the Constitution. But before settling down to an open-ended discussion, let us at least read the poem translated by Aurobindo Ghose. Quite often, ignorance is not bliss.

Mother I bow to thee!
Right with thy hurrying streams,
Bright with thy orchard gleams.
Cool with thy hands of delight./
Dark field waving, Mother of Might, Mother free.

Glory of moonlight dreams
 Over thy branches and lordly streams,
Clad in thy blossoming trees/ Mother, giver of ease,
Laughing low and sweet!/ Mother, I kiss thy feet,
Speaker sweet and low!
Mother, to thee I bow,
With many strengths who are mighty and stored (?)
To thee I call, Mother and Lord!

Thou who savest, arise and save!
To her I cry who ever her foeman drive
Back from plain and sea/ And shook herself free.
Thou art wisdom, thou art law.
Thou art hear, our soul, our breath.
Thou the love divine, the awe
In our hearts that conquers death

Thine the strength that conquers death
Thine the beauty, thine the charm.
Every image made divine/ In our temples is but thine.
Thou art Durga, Lady and Queen (swords of sheen).

With her hands that strike and her
Thou art Lakshmi lotus-throned
And the Muse a hundred-throned.
Pure and perfect without peer/ Mother, lend thine ear,
Rich with thy hurrying streams,
Bright with thy Orchard gleams.
Dark of hue, O candid fair
In thy soul with jewelled hair
And thy glorious smile divine,
Loveliest of all earthly lands,
Showering wealth from well-stored hands,
Mother, Mother, mine!
Mother sweet, I bow to thee,
Mother great and free!

9 February 2000

Sorry, Demolition has no Aesthetics ———————

We flaunt our cities as symbols of composite living. But what if
some of us decide to designate them as Hindu, Muslim, Sikh
and Christian? For one, we will require a visa and a passport to
gain access to them. And if you happen to have a taste of
medieval Indian architecture, you may have to travel to Pakistan
and Afghanistan, for all traces of the *incongruous* mosques,
churches, gurudwaras, synagogues and Sufi shrines would have
been removed from our cities. So, book your rail passage to see
the magnificent synagogue in Calicut before it is moved to
Israel. Travel to Goa at the earliest before the churches are
transported to Nazarelh or Bethlehem.

Lala Har Dayal, the high priest of the Ghadar Party, had an easy way out. Long before Jinnah announced his two-nation theory, the Lala stated in 1925 that the future of the Hindu race, of Hindustan and of Punjab rested on Hindu *sangathan*, Hindu Raj, *shuddhi* of Muslims, and conquest and *shuddhi* of Afghanistan and the frontiers. The Hindu race, he claimed, has but one history and its institutions are homogeneous. 'But the Mussalmans and Christians are far removed from the confines of Hinduism, for their religions are alien and they love Persian, Arab and European institutions. Thus, just as one removes foreign matter from the eye, *shuddhi* must be made of these two religions.'

If I sound alarmist, it is because one is troubled by the argument and implications of an article that appeared in the Friday column of the *Indian Express*. The issue is not whether a mosque in Nazareth or the Vatican City will be out of place or not. That is for the people of those countries to decide. What I dispute emphatically is the view that the three 'disputed' mosques are aesthetically incongruous in Ayodhya, Mathura and Varanasi, and, therefore, 'revolting' for a Hindu. Are we, then, to infer that those who razed the sixteenth century mosque at Ayodhya were moved by aesthetic considerations? No Sir, theirs was not just an 'irrational act' but a brutal assault on the democratic and secular foundations of our society. No Sir, it was not a case of anybody losing his or her 'balance in the heat of politics'. The vandalism at Ayodhya leading to the tragic polarization of our polity and society, was the result of a calculated and well-orchestrated plan.

Nobody I know sings paeans of praise for the iconoclast Mahmud of Ghazni or defends the intolerant policies of the medieval rulers. But the notion of 'hurt' to any community is a typically modern construction. Examining the way communalism has shaped the writing of Indian history, the historian Romila Thapar observed that a major contradiction in our understanding of the entire Indian past is that this understanding derives largely from the interpretations made in the last two hundred years. Yet, some of us carry forth the cultural and ideological baggage inherited from the colonial readings of our past.

The mosque at Ayodhya was not the site of Hindu-Muslim dispute until 1833 and the violent confrontation in 1855. Thereafter, the masjid-mandir dispute remained dormant until 1934 when a riot near Ayodhya, triggered by cow-slaughter, inflamed passions. Again, there was no movement to demand occupation of Ram's birthplace between 1950 and 1984, except for legal actions that are destined to remain endlessly unfruitful.

The other noteworthy point is that when Ayodhya first became an important pilgrimage centre in the eighteenth century, it was as much due to the activities of the Ramanandi *sadhus* as to the patronage of the Awadh nawabs. The diwan of Nawab Safdarjang built and repaired several temples, while Safdarjang himself gave land for building a temple on what is known as Hanumangarhi. Quite a few documents indicate that Muslim officials of the nawabi court gave away gifts for rituals performed by Hindu priests.

I challenge the notion of any of our urban centres having an exclusively *Hindu* or *Muslim* character. Shahjahanabad, the home of the Mughal emperors until 1858, was the capital of the patrimonial-bureaucratic empire, a type of state that characterized the Asian empires from about 1400 to 1750. Despite the mosques and *madaris* dotting its landscape, the capital offered space to diverse and multiple cultural and religious traditions to prosper. 'Its towers are the resting place of the sun. . . . Its avenues are so full of pleasure that its lanes are like the roads of paradise', so wrote Chandar Bhan Brahman of Shahjahanbad (Stephen P. Blake, *Shahjahanbad: The Sovereign City in Mughal India 1639-1739*).

Banaras, occupying that auspicious niche of land where the Ganga and Yamuna rivers meet, has been a model composite city. Beyond the indicators of economic interdependence, we have evidence of Muslim weavers actively participating in public ceremonies expressing a shared civic Banarsi culture, including the marriage of the Laut (Bhairav), Bharat Milap, and the day-to-day observances related to particular figures and shrines.

Nobody can deny the centrality of Banaras and Ayodhya for Hinduism. At the same time, it is worth remembering that many Muslim inhabitants consider these places as their cultural and religious centres as well. The older mosques and shrines in Banaras are all seen as testimony to the legitimacy of the Muslim presence and their contribution to the city's culture. As Nita Kumar's study indicates, both Hindus and Muslims visit the shrines of several saints and martyrs. She points out that, whereas Banaras is the locus of both classical and folk, of both high and low, Hinduism, it is the seat not of classical or orthodox Islam, but only of popular Islam (*The Artisans of Banaras: Popular Culture and Identity, 1880-1986*). It is this vibrancy of popular Islam and its intermixing with local cultures and practices that has made many of our cities pluralist and composite.

To the faithful, a place of worship is not essential for her/his spiritual journey. The desecration of the Golden Temple or the Babri Masjid fortified rather than weakened the faith of the devout and not-so devout Sikhs and Muslims. Critically important for the survival of our multi-religious society are the respect we extend to places of worship, past and present, and the value we attach to them as markers in the evolution of our society. They must not be desecrated or destroyed in the name of aestheticism.

10 December 1998

PART V

History's Many Verdicts

Asymmetrical Nationhood in
India and Pakistan

TE: As an historian, you have written both on the subject of
Partition and on the Muslim community in India. More recently,
you have taken an interest in family histories. How do you see
your own methodological development within your discipline?

MH: The major shift took place immediately after my undergraduate degree at the Aligarh Muslim University in India, where
I had studied medieval Indian history—that is, the period from
the thirteenth to roughly the eighteenth century. I subsequently shifted my research, most of which I started at the
University of Cambridge, to what, in India, we call communal
politics. At the time, in 1974, I was not particularly interested in
the Partition of India: it was not a theme being debated in
academic circles. Besides, the division of the country had not
affected my family or me. I was born after Pakistan was created,
no members of my family had migrated there, so there were no
memories.

My interest in the nationalist movement developed under
my father's influence, a historian of considerable repute. As a
liberal father and a progressive historian, he encouraged us to
debate both historical and contemporary issues. He sensitized
me to the broadly secular and supra communal movements.
And yet he talked about the differences that set Hindus and
Muslims apart and eventually culminated in the bitter, brutal
and violent Partition of the country. As I moved to Delhi to
commence my research—I was only twenty years old—I asked
myself a simple and straightforward question: why did secular
nationalism fail in India? This question assumed some significance particularly because my teachers at Aligarh had written
extensively on the multicultural character of Indian society, the
fusion of Hindu and Muslim cultural traditions, and the pluralist
heritage of our society. Why, then, did everything fall apart?

Turning to the archival materials, one discerned several trends
and tendencies that led various Muslim groups to express their
anxieties, question the claim of the Indian National Congress,

founded in 1885, to represent the nation, and eventually demand a separate Muslim homeland.

My chief contribution, if I may say so, has been to examine the complex role that a whole galaxy of Muslim political leaders, intellectuals and other luminaries have played in the making of modern India. Second, I have questioned, for the first time in a rigorous manner, the very notion of a homogenized, monolithic Muslim community. This line of questioning has important historical and sociological implications. Long before I wrote my first book, sociologists had talked about the social stratification amongst Muslims at a theoretical level, but I worked it out in different regions, in different epochs. Finally, I write firmly from within a nationalist strand of Indian historiography but without the complacencies and conceits of that strand. Rather, I interrogate a number of intersections: between nationalism and communalism, between the communal and secular trends within the national movement, between Muslim nationalists and advocates of the Pakistan movement—and now, increasingly, between political history and literary history as alternative and overlapping modes of access to the social consciousness of an age.

TE: Historically and politically speaking, who benefited from this process of homogenization of the Muslim community that you critiqued?

MH: All said and done, the homogenization of the Muslims as a community or a distinct political category was initially the work of the British government. In a sense, the British created a sense of communitarian identity by asking you what your religion was, what your past was, what your tribe was etc. etc. These were new constructions. The idea of being a Muslim, or being a Brahman, existed in pre-British times—there is no question about that. But their homogenization was a British invention. More important still is that the construction of Muslimness was translated into formal constitutional arrangements. In other words, Muslims were given preferential treatment in the power structures to legitimize their separate and distinct identity.

TE: It may be overstating the case to argue that the British invented it; perhaps colonialism merely provided the framework for it to take place. After all, it was not so much an administrative decision as the social, economic and political context which allowed these latent identities to jel. Do you think this sort of institutionalization of difference could be described as a specific feature of British colonialism?

MH: There is obviously a difference between British colonialism in India and in Malay or Kenya. There is no other country as culturally, socially, ethnically and linguistically diverse as India. The British were obviously struck by this diversity; they were also dealing with a rich civilization. Both the richness and the diversity created enormous problems, from a purely administrative and governmental perspective. And the only way the British could make sense of India was to split it into these arbitrary categories; that is what the census did. The census didn't just remain on paper, by the way. It was translated into practice, into formal institutional arrangements. This is a perfect example of political identity being thrust upon an otherwise diverse, fractured, and stratified community.

TE: In a way, then, the British were fulfilling a need for representation; it was the only way they could deal with reality.

MH: It was a result of British efforts to accommodate the dominant interest groups in Indian society. They proceeded in the same way with the princes, the landowning families, and, though very grudgingly, with the Muslims. Let's not forget that the British representation of the Muslims up until the 1860s or 1870s was a very hostile one—comparable to today's representation of Islam in Europe. But political expediency demanded this negative image to be set aside and draw the Muslims [they made up nearly one-third the population of British India] into the colonial framework.

TE: There has been a shift in French historiography, stemming from the 'new history' movement. This has entailed a shift of interest towards family histories, local history and so on. Though it remains in the field of historiography, this micro-history contributes a whole new quality to the findings, not least of all because the position of the historian shifts, and plays a more modest role. How do you see your methodological shift to family histories?

MH: It is all a part of the same journey, though, at the micro-level, I see family history linked with larger questions of social history and identity. What I want to do is to draw out certain larger, magisterial conclusions. These would make sense not only in understanding the history of a family, but in delineating the contours of its locale.

Subaltern studies have not been come to terms with the sorts of questions that concern me as a political and social historian. The theme of communitarian identity, the theme of ethnicity, the story of Partition has so far eluded most subaltern historians.

TE: When the *fatwa* came down on Salman Rushdie's novel, you took a position against banning books . . .

MH: Yes, my troubles began in April 1992 when I took an unequivocal stand against the banning of books. That triggered violence and agitation; the university was shut, and examinations were postponed. And then the government set up a committee to look into the incident. The committee's report was subsequently placed before Parliament, and on the basis of that report, I returned to the university on 4 December 1992. That is when I was assaulted. I was unable to return to the university for the next four years. I only returned as its officiating vice-chancellor in October 1996, under heavy police protection. After so much agony and suffering, I teach at the same university, write my books, and my fortnightly column in a leading national newspaper. The agitation against me stiffened my resolve to raise my voice against intolerance and religious bigotry.

TE: Do you think your assailants were students of the university or outside elements?

MH: They were students, teachers and professional politicians. Sadly, some of my own colleagues were happy to see me battered and bruised. Yet, I was triumphant; they were made to look silly in the eyes of the world.

TE: Were they sent away?

MH: I was sent away, not them! In our society, the victim is often at the receiving end. I am treated as a 'controversial' figure and not the assailants or the organizers of the ill-advised agitation. The guilty are rewarded, while a person taking a stand consistent with our constitution is dismissed as 'controversial'. This is how the liberal voice in our society gets stifled.

TE: Did you subsequently take a position in favour of other writers faced with the same type of *fatwa*?

MH: I wasn't asked to: once bitten twice shy!

TE: Let's turn to Partition: Independence came about through violence, and two countries were created, though not on the same principle. India is a secular country, whereas Pakistan was created on the basis of a presumed religious identity. Pakistan was premised on the two-nation theory, which was not an Indian idea. It is something of an historical irony that although the two-nation theory was false at the outset (because it did not correspond to the reality of India at the time), after fifty years it has turned out to be a self-fulfilling prophesy. Thus, we are now faced with two asymmetrical nations, different from the Pakistani idea of two nations, in that the Indian Muslims chose to belong to the Indian nation and not to the Muslim nation. India has a Muslim community—120 million people— which is a part and parcel of the Indian nation.

MH: Basically, the movement for Pakistan rested on ill-founded assumptions. Yet, the Pakistan movement was, in the 1940s and not earlier, a massive, popular movement for separation. We must recognize that the two-nation idea was transformed into a reality, a painful one. Immediately after Partition, Mohammad Ali Jinnah made a plea for a secular State. But his plea was a case of too little, too late. Having triggered religious passions, there was no question of Pakistan emerging as a secular society. The important thing is that Pakistan's search for identity has really been constrained by the presence of so many diverse groups and their conflicting interests. It is not the emergence of Bangladesh in 1971 which necessarily disproves the two-nation theory, but rather the way in which Pakistan's journey, beginning 14 August 1947, has been hampered by conflicts and contradictions. Though you can fault the Indian nationalist movement on several counts, the vision nursed by its leaders, from the last quarter of the nineteenth-century onward, was a unified one in which different castes and communities had an equal place.

TE: Could you go into more details about how both these nationalisms failed, and about he failure of Muslim nationalism? MH: Indian nationalism has served as a major catalyst for bridging the gap between different groups, castes, regions and communities. When I talk of the failure of Indian nationalism, I mean the poor representation of the under-classes and their social and economic backwardness; the treatment meted out to women; the growing fears of minority groups; and the slow progress of our economy. Those are clear illustrations of failure. TE: Today, Hindu fundamentalism, which often dons the mask of universalism, points to problems within secular nationalism. But don't we require a more strenuous definition of nationhood? In my understanding, a nation is a community; and a community is a vertical construction, not a democratic one. Whereas a society is secular, a nation—that is, a religious-communitarian construct—is not. Over the long term, the question arises as to how to create a society out of a nation. MH: Secular experimentation in the West was the result of certain tangible social and economic forces. If you look at Britain after the Industrial Revolution, or the French Revolution, or Germany after unification, though individuals may have acted as a catalyst, the whole secular fabric in Europe emerged from these major movements which were not geographically or territorially confined. The process was different in India. Here the creation of a nation was embedded in the nationalist project itself.

India was not yet a nation at the end of the nineteenth century. Yet, what was unique was the blueprint of a major nationalist project. (Obviously the idea of nationalism and nationhood was also the consequence of a perception of exploitation by British colonialism, but that is not an aspect I am touching on here.) Furthermore, to carry out the project, there had to be a recognition of pluralism. The recognition of a multi-cultural society has been the bedrock. Hence, the strength of the nationalist movement. The secret behind Gandhi's enormous popularity, for example, was his ability to communicate the idea of nationhood. He was obviously sensitive to the enormous difficulties in translating this idea into practice, but the moral and political philosophy he developed lay at the heart of his attempt to unify the different segments of the population. In other words, nationalism became a crucial part of the daily experiences of the Indian people, partly because of their suffering under colonialism, and partly because the nationalist leaders placed before them a goal which seemed at once distant, yet realizable.

The problem with this grand project was the failure to accord the communities their just place in the arrangements that were being worked out. The idea was that communities would be integrated into this coherent whole that was assiduously being built—but communities cannot be integrated so easily. The problem with the Muslim communities—and I always use the word in the plural form—was that the nationalist project did not evolve a strategy to accommodate them.

TE: Don't we also have to imagine how to get beyond this communatarian perspective, in order to achieve integration one day?

MH: We should not seek to achieve that *impossible* degree of integration, which is what a lot of people were talking about in the 1920s and 1930s. I think we should talk more in terms of accommodation, more in terms of a social contract between different linguistic, religious, and regional entities. We need a new blueprint for accommodating various interests.

TE: What if I feel my belonging to the society as a whole is more important than my communal belonging? I can't always represent the community, and be defined by it alone; there must be some area where I am more or less than the community. The notion of a social contract implies an arrangement between individuals and not between groups.

MH: The problem arises when communities become homogenized in terms of their mindset, and begin to negotiate with the State, society and polity as a community. The problem, in the context of India, is that the British created a community and that community began to negotiate, first of all with the Congress, then with the British. The British were more than willing—for their own imperial reasons, particularly during the inter-war years, to perpetuate the notion of a community in the political and bureaucratic structures.

TE: How do you see India's ability to prevent communities from becoming homogenous and pursuing this logic of identities fighting against one another?

MH: Much really depends on social and economic developments. A society which is able to equitably distribute its resources, howsoever limited they might be, is likely to develop a much stronger foundation; it is likely to have a better rapport with different segments of society. But a backward society whose resources only certain upper class groups or powerful elements garner, will create greater dissension and conflict. And, in so vast and diverse a country as India, we have seen the kind of discontent which these dissension acquire. So the sense of discrimination, the sense of being left out from the power structures, becomes increasingly accentuated. We need an egalitarian society in the true sense of the word, one that ensures access to resources. Indian society has functioned on a supra-communal basis, more so in rural areas but also significantly enough in urban areas. We need to strengthen these networks. In a growing economy, you would find more and more people relying upon each other, on their mutual expertise, and bridging the gulf. Because of the slow progress of our economy, there has been a rupture within the inter-community, economic networks; once the economy expands, this gulf can be bridged in very significant ways.

TE: How do you respond to your critics who accuse you of making it sound as if it were all the fault of the British?

MH: If your are writing on modern Indian history and are insensitive to the role of colonialism, how can you write about modern India? I don't buy the crude divide-and-rule-policy theory, and yet the colonial narrative and its translation into political arrangements lie at the heart of many important explanations. So it is not an orientalist view that I am putting forward; after all, the colonialist discourse was also internalized by Indians, Muslims and Hindus alike. But, there is merit in the orientalist discourse, because it does establish the connection between knowledge and power. Today, in India, textbooks are being rewritten at the school and college levels: knowledge is being tampered with. Why? The reason is that the protagonists of *Hindutva*, now holding the reins of power, want to nurture a particularist world-view that is divisive. There is an organized attempt to repudiate the Nehruvian vision—liberal, modern and secular. This is, to say the lest, an ominous development.

TE: You have argued that the Muslim community in India was partly homogenized by the first Balkan wars at the beginning of the twentieth century. Did the Balkan wars of the 1990s have a similar effect?

MH: To some degree, they fostered Islamic solidarity. But nothing like at the beginning of the twentieth century, when it was orchestrated effectively by the country's pan-Islamic leaders, who, ironically enough, took sides with the Turks, although Turkey was a colonizing power in the Balkans. And, in fact, there were strong movements within Turkey against the Sultan and the Khalifa. But, there is another dimension to that support, and that is a very powerful anti-colonial sentiment. Pan-Islamism is the greatest fiction that has been perpetuated for more than a century. We, as scholars, need to provide a corrective to it and Muslim societies need to act in such a way that it is shown to be a shibboleth rather than anything tangible and meaningful.

TE: You have claimed that the nationalism in both India and Pakistan have failed, and that the dream of Muslim homogeneity has also failed. You have explained the failure of nationalism in India. Could we now go back to Pakistan and try to see how this failure came about and what it implies for contemporary Islam?

MH: Some leaders orchestrated the pan-Islamic movement, aided and abetted by the British government. It petered out in the mid-1920s. Today, Indian Muslims are anguished by the happenings in Palestine. They are angry with the West for letting Israel pursue its belligerent policies against Palestine. They are angry with the Arabs, especially the governments, for letting down the Palestinians. I am sure the Pakistanis feel equally agonized. But, let me reiterate that Pakistan is caught up in its Islamic rhetoric. That is not conducive to creating a modern nation-state. A modern nation-state cannot be created on the principles of Hindu or Muslim solidarity. Soon after the creation of Pakistan, there developed a strong conflict between the protagonists of modernity and traditionalism. That's because the Jamaat-i Islami developed as a very major political force. Pakistan took nearly eleven years to draft a constitution because there were such hotly contested visions. These contested visions were an important feature of the nation-building exercise—there was never any consensus on creating a secular society. Thus, as early as 1953, the Ahmadis were targeted, and the Jamaat-i Islami instigated sectarian violence. I think the absence of democratic forces in Pakistan society lies at the heart of any explanation of the disintegration of Pakistan in 1971—I mean the succession of Bangladesh—as well as the current turmoil.

TE: Do you see Partition as a single on-going process?

MH: I do not think the resurgence of *Hindutva* in India or Islamic fundamentalism in Pakistan represent the unfinished agenda of Partition. However, even after fifty-three years, Partition continues to cast its shadow over many aspects of our contemporary life and politics. In that sense, Partition remains an important signpost, an important milestone. At the same time, new groups in India are emerging who wish to benefit from globalization, build their own social networks, develop trade and commercial linkages, and create for themselves a better standard of living. Pakistan is, on the other hand, caught up in its search for an identity—an identity that it sometimes defined in relation to West Asia, sometimes in relation to Central Asia. What is sad about Pakistan—what is tragic about Muslim society generally—is the absence of any critiques emerging from those societies. Polemical exchanges do not help the social and economic reconstruction of these societies. In order to hasten the social and economic construction of Muslim societies, what are needed are internal, intellectual critiques, covering both the present and the past.

TE: In that case, it can only stem from the reform of Islam?

MH: The intellectual inertia afflicting most Muslim societies has to be broken by breaching the citadels of orthodoxy. Muslim societies and intellectuals have to develop a critique outside the conventional formats or platforms made available to them. Unless and until this is done, these societies will continue to be undemocratic, discriminate against women, treat the minorities as inferior, and remain ill-equipped to cope with the challenges of this millennium.

(An interview by Rada Ivekovic
at Ghislaine Glasson Deschaumes)

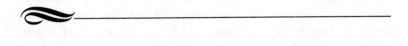

Peace amongst Equals

At the height of his first countrywide movement against the British government, Mahatma Gandhi said: 'what crimes for which we condemn the government as satanic have we not been guilty of towards our untouchable brethren? We make them crawl on their bellies; we have made them rub their noses on the ground; we push them out of railway compartments— what more than this has British rule done?' He referred to the untouchables, often placed outside the four *varnas* and usually found at the lowest economic position and traditionally subject to severe social and civic disabilities. According to the 1981 census, there were 104 million persons belonging to the Scheduled Castes. Most lived in the rural areas.

At the end of 1920, the Indian National Congress, which spearheaded the liberation struggle, made the removal of untouchability an integral part of its political programme. Over two decades later, the architects of India's Constitution provided special benefits to previously disadvantaged groups. Though the Constitution itself does not define the groups that may receive preferences, neither does it provide standards by which such groups are to be designated, reservations were nonetheless made available to Scheduled Castes (untouchables) and Scheduled Tribes and, to a lesser extent, to Backward Classes. According to Marc Galanter's study on 'Competing Equalities', the selection in the delineation of the Scheduled Caste category has proceeded primarily on the basis of ritual untouchability, combined in varying degrees with economic, occupational, educational, residential and religious tests.

There is no denying that the removal of untouchability was high on the national agenda. Gandhiji, for one, gave it unprecedented momentum. Yet he defended the caste system as an organic, unifying and inclusive system that could divest itself of hierarchical ideologies. He viewed caste as a self-governing social unit performing legislative, executive, judicial and other quasi-governmental functions. He therefore defended the caste system on the grounds that it ensured the continuity of hereditary occupation, ordered and structured human relationships and saved India from disintegration during long periods of foreign rule and preserved its religious and cultural traditions. According to Gandhi, the concept of the four stages (*ashramas*) in life—the student, the householder, the member of a community wider than one's family, and renouncer—were useful and 'capable of world-wide application'.

B.R. Ambedkar, the influential leader of the untouchables, condemned such an idealized version of the caste system. Referring to the Mahatma's fast against the government's decision in 1931 to grant separate electorates to the 'untouchables', he remarked, 'the fast was not for the benefit of the untouchables. It was against them and was the worst form of coercion against a helpless people. It was a vile and wicked act. How can the untouchables regard such a man as honest and sincere?'

Though some find India's system of affirmative action or compensatory discriminations unprecedented in scope and extent, the Mahatma's defence of the caste system caused widespread confusion in the nationalist ranks and, in some ways, hindered the postcolonial agenda of dealing with untouchability and other discriminatory practices.

The untouchables cannot still enter some Hindu places of worship. A dramatic rise in caste violence, murder, rape and arson against the untouchables, particularly in rural areas, has taken place since the mid-1960s. But in a number of cases there is just one loud and clear message sent through murder—the untouchables must learn their place in society and in the caste hierarchy.

There is, especially in northern and central India, strong and sustained opposition to affirmative action for the untouchables and the backward classes, a term that first acquired a formal significance in the princely state of Mysore, where the preferential recruitment was instituted in 1921. Hence the violent protest in September–October 1990 against the government's decision to allocate a reservation or quota of 22.5 per cent to the backward classes for government and public sector jobs. More than 160 young people attempted suicide by self-immolation; 63 succeeded. Another 100 people were killed in police firings and clashes that accompanied the widespread protest. 'There is perhaps no issue', commented a writer, 'on which we are such hypocrites as caste. Nor any other which brings out all that is worst in us with such shameful ease.' The moment reservations for the backward castes are announced, 'an avalanche of obscenity hits the country. It carries before it the Press, the universities, and opinion-makers of all kinds.'

The term 'caste' has a variety of meanings and has over the centuries acquired different shades at different levels of society. Between the local caste (i.e. *jati*) hierarchies and the pan-India *varna* ranking lie a bewildering and irregular set of regional and sub-regional groupings of castes and conceptualizations of the caste hierarchy. Moreover, caste groups have changed their relative position because the caste society, as Marc Galanter explains, had mechanisms for incorporating new groups, accommodating changing practices, and legitimating changes in group standing to accord with changing political, economic and socio-ritual attainments.

Yet, while caste sanctions have declined in recent years, particularly among the educated, caste opinion and caste loyalty remains a powerful cohesive and regulatory force. Caste is the natural foci of political mobilization and economic redistribution, as well as the chief marker of social and cultural identity. Invented and institutionalized by the colonial government as an exclusive, social and religious category to foster its 'divide and rule' policies, the caste system is widely identified as the chief source of, and the main cause for, the fractured Indian polity, economic disparities and social fragmentation. Nicholas B. Dirks, the social anthropologist, observed: 'caste may indeed be the most telling reminder of the post-colonial character of India's contemporary predicament, the chilling sign that India's relationship to history and tradition will continue to be necessarily mediated by the colonial past. Even as caste and colonialism in India could not, it seems, have done without each other, they will survive together in India for a long time to come.'

Many parts of the world are deeply divided along ethnic, communal, tribal and racial lines. In South Asia, Pakistan and Sri Lanka are faced with the rising tide of ethnic violence. The secular edifice in India, with its rich cultural, religious and political inheritance and the history of pluralism and tolerance, is strained by the dispute over the Babri Masjid. The Hindu-Muslim violence that followed took a heavy toll of human lives. In another arena, caste allegiances are used both subtly and stridently to either oppose or defend the empowerment of the weaker sections, mostly either outside or at the bottom of caste hierarchies.

The Congress party, having held power after Independence for several decades, used caste as a device to consolidate its electoral gains. The Janata Dal, the ruling party in 1990, pressed into service the Mandal Commission's recommendation for reservations for the backward classes. It did so to form a new coalition of social forces that will erode the electoral base of the Congress and challenge its political hegemony.

In effect, the rhetoric of the leaders strongly reinforced and fortified caste as a major factor in politics, placed the reservation issue high on the national agenda, and unwittingly created the space for caste antagonisms to be sustained. Its most immediate impact was felt in those areas where mobilization along caste lines was already beginning to take place around newly emerged regional based parties. From then on, the ascendancy of caste as a factor in political alignments was firmly established. 'So long as caste remains one of the determinants of property and power', noted a defender of the Mandal Commission recommendations, 'so long as it is used by the rich and the powerful as a means of maintaining and strengthening their domination, it remains the moral right and indeed the political duty of the poor and the deprived to use their caste identity in the struggle for their liberation.'

These tendencies are not to be equated with racism, though some of the traditional structures of division have contributed to social separation and the erection of barriers, of hatred and vengeance between communities. In this sense, the Indian versions of difference, i.e. caste and community, have resonance in different countries. Their politics, as in India, is imbricated in ethnic conflicts and ethnic claims that raise serious and knotty problems of governance.

One India One People (Bombay), *14 August 1997*

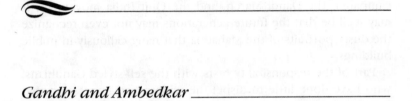

Gandhi and Ambedkar

A leading newsmagazine published excerpts from the well-advertised book of Patrick French (*Liberty or Death: India's journey to independence and division*, London, 1997). Mohandas Karamchand Gandhi was the obvious target. The editor was delighted, but the readers were not amused. From their sharp reactions, it was unmistakably clear that Gandhi still commands widespread respect. Quite a few recounted the high standards of morality set by the Mahatma during his long and eventful public life, and remembered his spirited struggle against colonialism. They invoked the image of a self-sacrificing and devoted leader to draw a comparison with the conduct and performance of the gold-diggers of free India.

This is good news, though not much cause for comfort. Gandhi's charisma does not, after all, work everywhere. He fails to inspire confidence amongst the Muslim intelligentsia owing to his frequent use of Hindu idioms and symbols. The feminist movement does not appropriate him, even though he brought thousands of women into public life and gave them high social and political visibility. His standing among the Dalits has plummeted over the years as more and more evidence is brought to light to establish the limitations of his campaign against untouchability. He is anathema to left-wing groups, though some feeble attempts are underway to assess his role afresh. Hindu nationalists have consistently repudiated his legacy, though for altogether different reasons.

The disconcerting factor is that the young know precious little about the Mahatma. He is a remote, distant, shadowy figure destined to fade into oblivion. No wonder, not many have heard of Kheda, Champaran, Wardha or the Sabarmati Ashram, or are familiar with the Rowlatt Satyagraha, the Non-Cooperation campaign, the Dandi March, and the Quit India movement. It may well be that the future generations may not even recognize the dusty portraits of the Mahatma that hang callously in public buildings.

Part of the responsibility rests with the self-styled Gandhians, who have done little to dispel the widespread impression that Gandhi's legacy is out of place in the 'modern' project of nation-building. By projecting their mentor as a spiritual leader imbued with the mission to transform the world in the traditions of Hindu saints, they diminished his appeal to the generations after Independence. By elevating him to the dizzy heights of a saint and making him appear different from the rest of his contemporaries they have ignored the fact that Gandhi was a 'modern' man with 'modern' goals.

If I sound unduly alarmist, somebody should tell me why college and university students kept quiet when Mayawati [leader of the Bahujan Samaj Party] launched her tirade against the Mahatma? Why the national newspapers failed to highlight the widespread desecration of his statues in Andhra Pradesh on 15 August 1997, in the fiftieth year of Independence? Why is Gandhi not the symbol of popular mobilization against the instruments of oppression and exploitation? Why is the landscape in UP dotted with statues of Ambedkar and not Gandhi?

True, a wide gulf separated the two men. As the supreme

leader of a powerful national organization, Gandhi's chief concern was to weld the different castes and communities into a coherent whole and evolve a nationwide consensus on political and social issues. He acted, though often subtly, as an arbiter of class and caste-based disputes from his own moral and philosophical standpoint. The Socialist or Marxist blueprints did not excite his imagination. Though acutely sensitive to the caste-class contradictions, he was wary of a prescription that would lead to a class war and disturb his vision of a moral order.

Ambedkar was a reformer, an outstanding mobilizer, and a major catalyst for social change in India. But he was no fire-spitting radical. He was comfortable in the council chambers, prepared to negotiate with the colonial government to extract concessions for his constituency, and operate within the institutional framework. He could have easily occupied a pivotal position in the Congress hierarchy had he not been so violently opposed to the Mahatma's spirited defence of the *varna* system. He could well have been an integral part of the Congress establishment had Gandhi not gone on fast against the government's decision to grant separate electorates to the Harijans in 1931. The fast, according to Ambedkar, was the worst form of coercion against a helpless people, 'a vile and wicked act'.

Regardless of such recriminations, Gandhi and Ambedkar were not poles apart. Admittedly, they had different roles to play in the political spectrum. At the same time, they had much the same social agenda, though their perception of the ground realities was at variance with each other. They did not differ vastly in their readings of the transformative processes at work in Indian society. Although they plotted different strategies to deal with social and economic inequities, both were passionately committed to the uplift of the poor and the downtrodden. The difference was that Gandhi appealed to and systematically cultivated a national constituency, whereas Ambedkar was principally concerned with the victims of social degradation, caste violence and discrimination.

Ambedkar's project rested on undermining the traditional

social order, while Gandhi's interest lay in preserving the traditional social equilibrium. The Mahatma raised his determined
voice against all forms of oppression perpetrated by the British
and their collaborators, i.e. the landlord and the moneylender,
energized his countrymen to embark on a programme of national
regeneration, and fostered, as the social scientist Bhikhu Parekh
describes, their cultural and moral autonomy, self-respect and
pride (*Gandhi's Political Philosophy: A Critical Examination*).
Above all, he lifted 'that black pall of fear . . . from the people's
shoulders, not wholly of course, but to an amazing degree'. He
brought about 'a psychological change almost as if some expert
in psychoanalytical methods had probed deep into the patient's
past, found out the origins of his complexes, exposed them to
his view, and thus rid him of that burden' (Nehru).

The task of delineating the nature of Gandhi-Ambedkar
differences should be left to the social historian and to scholars
of Indian nationalism. For the time being, it is possible to benefit
from the perceptions and experiences of both these men. There
is enough space for different voices to be heard. There are
enough people willing to listen to Gandhi as well as Ambedkar.
Why, then, set up one against the other? Why repudiate one in
favour of the other? A dispirited nation can ill-afford to divide
its own rich legacy.

The Mahatma and the Qaid-i-Azam:
A Study in Contrast

And then Gandhi came. He was like a powerful current of fresh
air that made us stretch ourselves and take deep breaths, like a
beam of light that pierced the darkness and removed the scales
from our eyes, like a whirlwind that upset . . . most of all the

working of people's mind. He did not descend from the top; he
seemed to emerge from the millions of India. . . .

JAWAHARLAL NEHRU

In this fiftieth year of Independence, we missed an historic opportunity of reminding ourselves of Gandhi's moral and political
philosophy, his sensitivity to oppression and exploitation, and
his contribution to heightening popular consciousness during
the liberation struggle. One is equally disappointed with the
feeble attempts to understand or interpret the Gandhian legacy,
more so when a beleaguered nation is engaged in fighting simultaneously on political, social and economic fronts.

True, Gandhi's moral and political philosophy had severe
limitations. True, he lost the magic touch after having led and
guided the civil disobedience campaigns. His concern for the
plight of Dalits was genuine but their empowerment, which
would have caused an upper caste backlash, was not his political
agenda. He opposed separate electorates for them. He did not
deal with their leaders, notably Ambedkar, on equal terms.

Gandhi's method of dealing with Muslims was, likewise, based
on mistaken beliefs. He treated them as a distinct pan-Indian
entity and approached them as a monolithic religious group
and not as differentiated cultural, linguistic and economic entities.
He did not turn to the regional Muslim communities or take
cognizance of their regional aspirations. He spent years in the
company of liberal and secular-minded Muslims without being
receptive to their modernist interpretation of Islam. He regarded
the traditionalist view as the more authentic voice of India's
Muslims.

It is easy to disagree with Gandhi and dwell on his inconsistencies and contradictions. Yet, his conception of state and
society, with its emphasis on morality and non-violence, demands
serious attention. Gandhi was a Hindu, but not a Hindu leader.
He deployed Hindu symbols, which appealed to Hindus and
Muslims alike in rural areas, to unite and not to divide his
growing constituency. Indeed, his political engagements developed out of his concern to articulate the interests of the Indian
people. That is why Mohamed Ali [the Aligarh-educated Khilafat

leader] stated in the early-1920s: 'It is Gandhi, Gandhi, Gandhi, that has got to be dinned into the people's ears, because he means Hindu-Muslim unity, non-cooperation, *dharma* and *swaraj.*'

Jinnah did not endorse such a view then or later. One should understand why this was so, though there is no earthly reason to compare his political trajectory with that of Gandhi or publicize his fulmination's against the Mahatma. Why should any book published in the West be the reference point for a Gandhi-Jinnah debate? Is it important to be told that Jinnah spent less than Gandhi on train fares despite travelling first class, since he only had to buy one ticket? Or, that Gandhi believed in the 'increment of human excrement', whereas the elitist Jinnah did not wish 'to soil his carefully scrubbed hands by consorting with the masses.'

At the same time, one is ill served by those who demonize Jinnah or interpret his role from the lofty heights of Indian nationalism. He should not be belittled for rejecting the Congress creed; others did the same more consistently. He should not be singled out as the 'villain', the sole leader responsible for Partition. The nationalist rhetoric can no longer obscure the role of certain key Congress and Hindu Mahasabha players in signing united India's death warrant.

Jinnah's political trajectory can best be studied in relation to the complex interplay of forces that created spaces for the 'Pakistan demand' to gather momentum, the subtle changes in institutional and bureaucratic structures, the shifts in political alignments, and the bitter struggle for gaining access to power, patronage and authority. Still, how did Sarojini Naidu's 'Ambassador of Hindu-Muslim Unity' become Pakistan's Qaid-i Azam? Why did Jinnah repudiate his own liberal and secular creed? How and why did he succeed in mobilizing so many Muslims in such short a time?

The explanations lie elsewhere and not in the pedantic debates centred on the whims and idiosyncrasies of individuals. Jinnah was not a political force when Gandhi launched the Rowlatt Satyagraha and the Non-Cooperation movement. He searched in vain for a role in British politics, while Gandhi led the spectacular Dandi March. During the 1937 elections, he was dismayed to discover that Gandhi's Congress and not his Muslim League was the people's party. Yet, he was not one to lick his wounds. He bounced back and used his bargaining skills to extract major political concessions from a beleaguered war-time government. That was the time when Gandhi, his *bete noire*, languished in British jails.

The two men had little in common. Jinnah, a constitutionalist, relished debating finer points of law and legal processes. He was often impetuous and sometimes reckless in promoting his favourite projects; hence, the use of religion to establish his moral authority on his allies. He was not inclined to define his long-term agenda. He had no blueprint to cope with the demands of a modern nation state. His overall world view failed to transcend the confines of the law courts.

The Mahatma, on the other hand, was a powerful communicator with a sharp and intuitive mind and the ability to marshal his resources towards ends clearly discerned and goals clearly defined. He was an innovator, and a synthesizer of diverse political and philosophical traditions. He developed a political theory grounded in unique experiences and articulated in terms of the indigenous philosophical vocabulary.

Such a man was, alas, reduced to being a figurehead in the Congress hierarchy during 1945-7. Humbled and marginalized by his erstwhile colleagues, he was a lonely figure at the time of Independence. He moved to riot-ravaged areas to provide the healing touch. Here was somebody who practised what he preached. Here was somebody who reminded us through his ideas and actions that a second partition must not be allowed to take place. This is the Mahatma's legacy bequeathed to us.

9 August 1977

Reassessing Nehru:
*Much Maligned by Hindsight*_____

I have no personal memories of Jawaharlal Nehru, free India's first Prime Minister. He was dead when I joined the Aligarh Muslim University in 1964. Yet many of our fellow-students felt then and later that the country had lost a charismatic figure, a man who nursed the vision of free India, and plotted its trajectory with foresight and imagination. We learnt a great deal more about Nehru and the nationalist movement after reading his *Autobiography* and *The Discovery of India*. Published in 1936, the *Autobiography* is a document with hazy ideas but reflecting a strong commitment to a modern, united and secular India. *The Discovery of India* was in the nature of a journey into India's past, a journey that led its author to discover the roots of composite and syncretic ideas and movements. I believe it is hard to find a more lucid exposition of India's composite past.

Nowadays, of course, the tribe of Nehru-baiters has swelled considerably. More and more educated Indians tend to blame the first Prime Minister for the slow and tardy economic progress, the collapse of our most cherished institutions, the erosion of democratic values, and the diminishing importance of values and principles in public life. Surely, we need to place the man and his policies in perspective. We need to examine the break-up of the Nehruvian consensus from the 1960s through to the 1990s, looking in particular at the reasons for the growth of communal activity and the retreat of both Muslims and Hindus into communal political camps. We need to consider, moreover, the political options or choices that were available in 1947-8.

Assessing the contribution of any political leader or statesman at any given moment of history is a tall order. Evaluating Nehru is a particularly awesome task, more so because he occupied centre-stage for so many decades and performed a variety of roles. Starting as an activist in the Congress movements in the early 1920s, he rose to become the Mahatma's political heir. He emerged, thanks to his early exposure to the Bloomsbury group in London, the exponent of socialism within the Congress and the rallying point for scores of radical groups. In the mid-1930s and 1940s, he steered the Congress ship through the rough currents of Indian politics and ensured that the nationalist movement, still guided by Gandhi, did not lose sight of its democratic and secular goals. He was on the move throughout his public life, eager to learn, exhort, mobilize, and leave his imprint on his party and government. That is why he endeared himself to the masses, the minorities and other socially under-privileged groups. In the words of his distinguished biographer, Sarvepalli Gopal: 'To a whole generation of Indians he was not so much a leader as a companion who expressed and made clearer a particular view of the present and vision of the future. The combination of intellectual and moral authority was unique in his time.'

Consider Nehru's role after Independence. India had tasted the fruit of freedom on 15 August 1947, but the country was brutally partitioned, fragmented socially and politically. Under the circumstances, his defence of and justification for a secular ideology seemed unreal and hollow. Yet his personal ingenuity and strong secular commitment, coupled with the weighty secular traditions of the nationalist movement, enabled him to pull through difficult and turbulent times. He and his comrades in the Constituent Assembly kept the secular flag flying in India even though it was being lowered in other newly liberated countries of Asia and Africa.

Nehru's political ideology was much influenced by his up-bringing in Allahabad, a city with a glorious record of cultural and social mingling, his interactions with liberal and left wing groups in England, and the influence of Motilal Nehru. Yet family life and Western education alone do not explain his secular trajectory. After all, the cosmopolitan outlook of the Urdu-speaking élites inspired not everybody who lived in Allahabad. Take the case of Madan Mohan Malaviya, a distinguished citizen of the same city, who was the chief protagonist of Hindu causes and a major critic of Motilal Nehru's eclectic world view. Likewise, Jinnah shared Nehru's social and educational background, but changed course to campaign for a separate Muslim homeland. Whereas Jinnah trimmed and tailored his ideological garb to suit political exigencies, Nehru remained firm in his secular beliefs. He did not waver as Jinnah did.

It is doubtless true that Nehru and Jinnah were not cut out to work harmoniously. The predictable 'parting of ways' took place in 1937-8, when Jinnah launched his tirade against the performance of the Congress ministries in various provinces of British India. The criticism was harsh, as indeed based on flimsy information, but the message was loud and clear. Nehru's secular rhetoric, so implied Jinnah in his letters and speeches, wasn't good enough. The Congress alone couldn't decide India's future political agenda in its negotiations with Pax Britannica; Muslims must have a say and he, as their sole spokesman, had an equally important role in deciding whether India remains united or divided.

Nehru can be faulted for some or his utterances, his reck-lessness, his political miscalculations, his arrogance, and his inability to deal with adversaries on equal terms. Yet, his secular convictions stand in bold relief. When the chips were down, he refused to be swayed by the Muslim League rhetoric or the Hindu propagandist viewpoint; he could not single-handedly stem the communal tide in the 1940s or thereafter. Nor could he prevail upon the Congress to reject the insidious Partition Plan. He could at best provide the healing touch after the bloodbath in 1947, instil confidence in the Muslim communities that remained in India, and create the institutional structures to contain the anti-secular tendencies. This, he did, in ample measure. In so doing, he pursued not a typically Nehruvian goal, but a goal set by the Mahatma, by the secular wing of the Congress, and by the left formations.

Nehru's adversaries in the Congress party's higher echelons did not approve of his sledgehammer efforts to change the fabric of Hindu society, his lenient policy towards Pakistan, and his undue tenderness for the Muslims. But Nehru repudiated such criticism, as he had time and again. 'Whatever the pro-vocation from Pakistan and whatever the indignities and horrors inflicted on non-Muslims there. We have got to deal with this minority in a civilized manner. We must give them security and the rights of citizens in a democratic state. If we fail to do so, we shall have a festering sore which will eventually poison the whole body politic and probably destroy it.'

'For all of us in India', he told the Chief Ministers in May 1950, 'the issue of communal unity and a secular state must be made perfectly clear. We have played about with this idea sufficiently long and moved away from it far enough. We must go back and go back not secretly or apologetically, but openly and aggressively.' The past was a constant reference point. The Prime Minister invoked the Congress record to legitimize its secular discourse after Partition. In this context he pointedly referred to the Mahatma's message of communal peace and his exemplary courage in extinguishing the flames of religious hatred. In so doing, Nehru tried to settle the issue of whether the government and the party were going to adhere to old Congress principles in regard to communalism or whether the country as a whole was going to drift away from them.

This had been the impulse behind Nehru's brainchild, the Muslim Mass Contact Campaign, launched in March 1937. The idea was to approach the Muslims not as a collective fraternity but as a segment of an impoverished population. The principal motivation was to convince them that they did not constitute a 'nation', and that their fortunes were not tied to their Muslim brethren *per se* but to fellow-artisans, peasants and workers in other communities. Nehru carried on a dialogue with Jinnah on these lines, questioned the rationale of Muslim nationalism in a society traditionally anchored in cultural and religious pluralism, and criticized the creation of 'Muslim Identity' in the garb of Islam. He tried in vain delinking issues of proportion and percentages of seats from the more basic contradictions between nationalism and colonialism. He expected Jinnah to draw his constituency into this just and legitimate struggle as co-citizens and not as a preferential religio-political collective.

The basic premise of Nehru's defence of a secular state and society was valid. There was nothing wrong in arguing that religious solidarity should not be the basis for political activism, or that religious symbols of disunity be shunned in public life. He had stated as early as 1927 that 'there can be and should be religious or cultural solidarity. But when we enter the political plane, the solidarity is national, not communal; when we enter the economic plane the solidarity is economic'. The alternative strategy, worked out by B.G.Tilak in Maharashtra or the swadeshi leaders in Bengal, had serious political implications in so far as it created fissures in the liberation struggle, offended Muslims in those regions, and enfeebled the intellectual underpinnings of secular goals set by the Congress.

Nehru was not the sole champion of secular nationalism; yet he, more than anyone else, enriched its content. He provided depth to debates on secularism within the Congress, and in left circles. He introduced complex but relevant historical and contemporary themes drawn from India and other societies. He did not do so on the basis of abstract principles of Western democracy—a charge levelled against him by his detractors—but, because of his own acute understanding of the wider social and political processes in history. There is no reason to believe that his perceptions were flawed, or to doubt his motives or intentions.

As we celebrate fifty years of freedom from colonial rule, we may do well to heed the following lines in Nehru's *Discovery of India*:

Many of us are utterly weary of present conditions in India and are passionately eager to find, some way out. Some are even prepared to clutch at any straw that floats their way in the vague hope that it may afford some momentary relief, some breathing space to a system that has long felt strangled and suffocated. This is very natural. Yet there is danger in these rather hysterical and adventurist approaches to vital problems' affecting the well being of hundreds of millions and the future peace of the world. We live continually on the verge of disaster in India, and indeed the disaster sometime overwhelms us. A divided India, each party trying to help itself and not caring for, or co-operating with the rest, will lead to an aggravation of the disease and a sinking into a welter of hopeless, helpless misery. It is terribly late already and we have to make up for lost time. There are still many people who can think only in terms of political percentages. Of weight ages, of balancing, of checks, of the preservation of privileged groups, or making new groups privileged, of preventing others from advancing because they themselves are not anxious to or are incapable of doing so, of vested interests, of avoiding major social and economic changes, of holding on to the present picture of India with only superficial alterations. That way lies supreme folly.

12 July 1977

After Fifty Years of Indifference: Energize the Idiom

Indian politicians line up at the *samadhis* to pay homage to the freedom fighters and inflict their sermons on their audience. One wonders how many give credence to their pledges or retain confidence in their ability to deliver. Our polity is plagued with contradictions, though the basic malaise is that political parties are unable to instil confidence in their ability to govern. Their leaders win elections without legitimizing their position in the eyes of the electorate.

It was different not so long ago when politicians, regardless of ideological inconsistencies, inspired confidence among their supporters. That is why so many flocked to their meetings. Though the British suppressed public gatherings, the power of language, as evident during Gandhi's Satyagraha against the Rowlatt Bills (1919), prevailed over sterile legislation. For the leaders themselves, words and ideas became the weapons of choice in the context of the non-violent struggle. Yet their control was essential to develop a nation-wide consensus. Words and ideas under control *versus* words and ideas out of control concerned Gandhi more than any another leader.

From the Champaran Satyagraha onwards, Gandhi devised his strategies with skill and dexterity. At the same time, he ensured that a careless speech or an emotionally charged editorial did not undermine his mobilization efforts. The Chauri-Chaura episode (1922) revealed his aversion to violence. He was concerned with a particular social and economic agenda that informed his definition of political freedom.

Nobody had the Mahatma's stature to make the same use of the spoken and the written word. Nehru spoke well, though without being eloquent in the conventional sense. What made him popular was his ability to persuade the multitude that what they passionately desired was attainable, and that he, through his visualization, was the man to attain it. That is probably why the 'tryst with destiny' speech continues to generate such fervour and enthusiasm.

Nehru and his fellow-parliamentarians set high standards in public life. Wit and humour combined well with serious parliamentary deliberations. Regardless of party affiliations, most leaders endeavoured to build something new, something different from the colonial era. Nehru was himself keen on socialism not as some rigid doctrinaire theory, but rather as a broad objective that had to be adapted to India's needs. Others did not share his passion for socialism but were nonetheless committed to the country's socio-economic transformation.

Today, we bemoan the state of public institutions, the party system and the electoral process. We decry the decline in public morality, the rise of corruption in public life, and the noisy and violent scenes in the legislatures. Just a few weeks ago, the Speaker asked: 'Don't you feel sorry to convert Parliament into a street?' Well said, Mr. Speaker. But, alas, not many pay heed to your pleas. What do words mean in the murky world of Indian politics?

The appeal of the written word has, likewise, diminished. Political manifestos are today consigned to the dustbin of history before the electoral battle moves into first gear. The print media does not mould public opinion anymore. Try putting sense into those who have built their support system through family, caste and factional networks. They are convinced that their bandwagon will roll on regardless of adverse public opinion.

Turn to Nehru's temples of learning. Until the 1970s, campus life was alive with teachers and students responding to contemporary affairs, including apartheid, Zionism, colonialism and imperialism. Left-wing journals, in particular, debated major issues. Social scientists reflected on the colonial experience afresh. Ideas still mattered in academic life. Today, the deafening silence in centres of learning is a sign of changing times. Many are wary of disturbing the *status quo*, and indifferent to the ideal that inspired the national leaders to build a democratic, secular and egalitarian society.

Neglect of education has constrained the flow of innovative ideas. We boast of hundreds of universities and thousands of colleges, even though the educational system is crumbling. 'We pay the schoolmaster less than our chaprasi,' Nehru wrote in 1958, 'and expect him to mould our younger generation.' Not much has changed since then. We expect graduates to respond to the winds of change without creating a climate conducive for their intellectual growth.

Consider how ideas are stifled in another area. The reading and interpretation of religious scriptures is mediated, more than ever before, by the priestly class—a class committed to parochial identities. Deviate from the established norms and you invite their wrath. Comment against the banning of books and land up in hospital with a bruised skull. This is Gandhi's and Nehru's India for you.

The Indian State has abdicated its responsibility of defending intellectual freedom and democratic values. I was not allowed to enter my university campus for over four years. After all, the fate of a professor is of no consequence to the higher values we cherish. Just pat the person on his back, especially if he is a Muslim. No point losing sleep over an controversial (?) teacher!

The State has been a mute witness to serious infringements on human rights, and struck deals with communal and parochial groups for electoral gains. Is this because ideas, principles and ideologies are no longer relevant? This is an appropriate moment to invoke the nationalist legacy, energize the nationalist idiom, combat the pernicious influence of religious fundamentalism and intolerance, and impart meaning and purpose to those written and spoken words associated with our secular leaders. For this to happen, we need to:

> Speak, for your two lips are free;
> Speak, your tongue is still your own;
> This straight body still is yours –
> Speak, your life is still your own.

Time enough is this brief hour
Until body and tongue lie dead;
Speak, for truth is living yet–
Speak whatever must be said.

FAIZ AHMAD FAIZ

9 August 1997

The Return of the Congress: Now play out the Ideals

The Indian National Congress has done it again. Having lost its way in the murky world of faction politics for a decade, it has bounced back to re-establish its credentials as a national party. Political analysts, some having prematurely written the Congress obituary, have been proven wrong for the umpteenth time. Though the road to Delhi is still bouncy and strewn with difficulties, the Congress may succeed in wresting the political initiative from the ruling coalition in the near future. Meanwhile, its leaders can draw confidence from their refurbished image and gain comfort from the support extended by the beleaguered minorities, the OBC and Dalit groups.

It is not yet certain whether the outcome of the Assembly elections represents a decisive shift· in politics or not.* What is amply clear is that an alert electorate has checkmated the BJP. Equally, the return of the minorities, the Dalits and the OBCs to the Congress fold is a singularly important development. In case this trend is replicated in UP and Bihar, especially if the Muslims soften their hostility towards the Congress, the Third Front, already fragmented and plagued with personal rivalries, may cease to be a major force in these states. This will bolster, despite the caste configurations, the Congress chances of picking up some seats in UP and Bihar.

In the long run, however, a great deal will depend on how the Congress leadership learns from its mistakes and errors of judgement in the past and, accordingly, responds to its electoral gains in three out of the four states that went to the polls. Ultimately, much will depend on Sonia Gandhi's ability to contain and manage factionalism in the Congress, revive the party's linkages with its traditional allies, energize the organization through democratization, and harness the skills and talent of younger Congress leaders, including the Chief Ministers of Madhya Pradesh and Rajasthan. She should, above all, be wary of the cliques, blasted by her husband in 1985, that enmeshed the living body of the Congress in their net of avarice, their self-aggrandizement, their corrupt ways, their linkages with vested interests—and their sanctimonious posturing. In short, if the Congress is to reposition itself as a major player, it must act, in its new incarnation, as the bulwark against authoritarian and communal tendencies. If it is to sustain its liberal and secular image, badly tarnished during the Emergency, the anti-Sikh riots in 1984 and the Babri Masjid episode, it must act as a left of centre party. The voters will no longer settle for empty slogans.

If the past is taken as the key to the understanding of the present, the Congress recovery, so to speak, is consistent with its record during the liberation struggle. Remember the split at Surat in December 1907 between the so-called moderate and extremist leaders. That split, the first of its kind since 1885, was necessary for the rejuvenation of the Congress. The question, wrote one of its supporters, was to bring the party into contact with the living life of the people.

This came to fruition at the Lucknow Congress in 1916. As a result, a far more unified and revitalized Congress rallied around Gandhi's Rowlatt Satyagraha and the Khilafat and Non-Cooperation movements. Many who worked for the Congress programme during that period lived in a kind of intoxication. 'We were full of excitement and optimism and buoyant enthusiasm', recalled Nehru. Suspension of Civil Disobedience in February 1922 (after the Chauri Chaura incident) caused

*In November 1998, the Congress (I) won impressive victories in Madhya Pradesh, Rajasthan and Delhi.

widespread resentment in many circles, sharpened old communal antipathies, and led to serious internal dissension in the
Congress. For the next six years or so, the Congress, caught
up in its own contradictions, survived in a lackadaisical manner.
Its members reverted, within two years of Gandhi's imprisonment, to their lazy habits, reminiscent of the closed-shop politics of the early Congress, and played out their own struggles
for power, using caste and community as the weapons for
political survival. The Mahatma's own position was weakened.
Some said that his popularity was waning and that he had
become a spent force.

Nehru observed that a leader does not create a mass movement out of nothing, as if by a stroke of the magician's wand.
He can take advantage of the conditions themselves when they
arise; he can prepare for them, but not create them. This
is precisely what Gandhi did when the British government
appointed an all-white Simon Commission in 1927 and when
the Viceroy Linlithgow arbitrarily declared, in 1939, that India
was at war.

The agitations that followed, i.e. the Salt Satyagraha of 1930
and the individual satyagraha campaign of 1940-1, revived the
dwindling fortunes of the Congress, gave its activists a new
sense of unity, and placed the party at the head of political life.
As the Liberal leader Tej Bahadur Sapru commented: 'In the
first place the Congress has got a powerful organization. It has
got energy and has got money and manpower and it does
appeal to the imagination of the people firstly because it
professes to represent the forces of freedom and secondly
because it has gone through some suffering.'

The dawn of freedom did not sensitize most Congressmen
to the massive task of national reconstruction. Having spurned
the Mahatma's plea to wind up their organization, the leaders,
fired with dreams of achieving office, became part of an unwieldy
club, embroiled in intrigue and factionalism to control the levers
of power. Our energies, Nehru wrote in 1949, are concentrated
in disruption and destruction.

As weeks and months roll on, one will have to wait and see
which way the wind is blowing, and whether the Congress will
make the best of the opportunity and not allow itself to fade

away before our eyes. One can only hope that its leaders will pay heed to the admonition by Mira Behn, one of Gandhi's favourite disciples. The Congress, she had stated in 1952, should recognize that it was the ideals that conquered, and it is those ideals alone that can successfully overcome the difficulties and dangers that surround us today from all sides.

5 December 1998

The Congress and Coalitions

Regardless of exit polls, the BJP leadership seems jittery. The feeling is that Kargil and Sonia Gandhi's 'foreign origin' has not worked to the party's advantage. Even the Prime Minister's charisma appears to be fading in the heat and dust of the elections.* Admittedly the BJP will win enough seats to cobble together a coalition, but it is unlikely to occupy the same vantagepoint in our polity. If the NDA performs better than expected, the BJP may well rue its decisions to take on on board so many of its notoriously fickle-minded constituents.

The Congress will not have enough seats to head a government, but its fortunes have improved dramatically in recent weeks. All said and done, the Italian-born Sonia Gandhi has made the difference. She has revived a dormant party and instilled confidence in its rank and file. Next time round, she may well return to 7 Race Course with a comfortable majority. I believe the alarm bells are beginning to ring in Jhandewalan.

The Congress would have much greater cause to celebrate if

---

*The thirteenth general election—the third election in three years—yielded a decisive mandate to the BJP and its 23 regional allies. And yet the coalition took a beating in Karnataka, Punjab and Uttar Pradesh.

Sharad Pawar [senior Congress leader from Maharashtra] had stayed put in the party. His exit may well turn out to be the party's nightmare. For this, one will blame the tall poppies in the party hierarchy; a judicious mixture of buffets and boons should have quietened him. Their other monumental failure, for which the Congress may have to pay a heavy price, preceded Sharad Pawar's exit. This was the political message from Pachmarhi, way back in September 1998, to its potential allies. It was ill timed and ill advised, because there was no objective reason for the Congress to exude that kind of confidence so soon after Sonia Gandhi's entry into the political arena. At that juncture, as indeed after the Assembly elections, an open-ended policy on coalition may have served the Congress better.

By closing its doors on like-minded parties, the Congress dimmed its prospects in several crucial states, notably UP. Agreed, Mulayam Singh Yadav is a hard nut to crack. Agreed, the logic of caste and community politics makes the distribution of seats so much more difficult. Yet, the Congress had no business to occupy the high moral ground and drive him into the 'enemy' camp, so to speak. He should have been forgiven, in the interest of a secular front, for his numerous political indiscretions. Likewise the Congress should have worked towards an alliance with the Bahujan Samaj Party in order to refurbish its secular and pro-poor image.

The controversy over the coalition issue has dogged the Congress for decades. It surfaced in 1937, sparking off a major Congress-Muslim League row. Times have changed since; so have the players. But the Congress ambivalence on coalition politics continues to plague its leadership. In 1937, Nehru took the lead in opposing a Congress League ministry in UP. More than six decades later, a member of the same family is trying to cope with, though in a different context, much the same legacy. They say history repeats itself. Who can deny this bald assertion?

The Congress truculence over a coalition with the League was a political miscalculation, for it created the space for the League's revival, offered Jinnah the chance to establish his hold in UP, a province where his initial overtures were repeatedly spurned, and bolstered his claim to represent 'Muslim India'.

Bringing the League into government may have accentuated inter-party feuds, but rejecting its representatives created a far broader unity among the League factions and greatly hardened their stance thereafter.

The Pachmarhi declaration proceeded on the assumption that the Congress will romp home on its own. The Congress success in the 1937 elections led its leaders to reach a similar conclusion. Thus Nehru explained the 'breach of faith' in terms of the unexpectedly large Congress majority in the elections, which made all talk of a coalition indefensible. I believe the optimism then, and now at Pachmarhi, was misplaced. True, the Congress ministries survived until the outbreak of World War II, but the coalition issue cast an ugly shadow over its performance in UP and elsewhere. Congress' democratic and secular ideology featured in the 1937 campaign, and was underlined in the Pachmarhi manifesto as well. But it has repeatedly erred in acting as the sole custodian of democracy and secularism. That is why it tends to construct the image of the other and, for this reason, refuses to accommodate other interest groups.

In this light, consider the Muslim League's status in 1937 and its relationship with the Congress. Their election manifesto had a great deal in common, and their workers campaigned for the same candidate in quite a few constituencies. Their differences, though exaggerated in public pronouncements, were by no means irreconcilable. This is why Jinnah talked of a 'united front' when the Congress accepted office in March 1937. There is no difference, he proclaimed in September, between the ideals of the Muslim League and the Congress.

If so, it was a mistake to portray the League as a political adversary or a counter force. It was right to make clear the Congress discourse on nationhood; equally, to expose the League's predominantly feudal character, its links with government and with the conservative social classes. What was, however, lost sight of was that not everybody was swayed by the League's communal claptrap at that juncture. A coalition ministry may have weaned away such elements from the League and sapped its organizational strength. Second, berating élite forms of compromise hatching was legitimate, though inconsistent with the Congress' record of pacts with the Muslim League (in December 1916), and with other sectional groups, such as the Akalis in Punjab. Lastly, it is hard to make sense of Nehru's unwarranted rhetoric, in 1937, against the League. After all, he was the one who had told a Muslim Leaguer: 'I do not quite know what our differences are in politics. I had imagined that they were not great.'

In effect, a Congress-League coalition failed to materialize for reasons that had little to do with lofty ideals. Otherwise, Nehru would not have referred to the feeling in Congress circles that without the League they will be freer to quarrel with UP's governor, and break with him on his own terms. One will await the historian's judgement on the consequences of the Pachmarhi stand on coalition.

25 September 1999

And Then There will be
No One Left to Speak

We are a mouthful they can *never* digest!

AKBAR ALLAHABADI

A friendly phone call on a Saturday morning, the day when my column appears in print, revives my spirits. I end the day hoping that my intervention will convey some sense to somebody living far away from the metropolis, somebody open to reason and free inquiry, somebody wedded to decent and civilized norms and values, somebody who isn't busy desecrating churches, digging cricket pitches, or targeting the weaker sections of our society. This is, after all, the *raison d'être* for producing a column every fortnight.

This week was different. I wondered if it was at all worth writing and adding my voice to the legion of comments on the spurt of violence, including the murder of G.S. Staines and his two sons in Orissa, described by the President as 'a monumental aberration' from our traditions of tolerance and humanity.

Many of us are distressed by the crisis of governance, the inter-party feuds, the civil strife in society taking an ugly turn in parts of Gujarat, Karnataka and Bihar, and the display of religious fanaticism by some of our co-citizens. There is something in the air, regardless of what the urban élites may say, that makes us feel uneasy and restless. Still, I was not sufficiently motivated to write.

It was not clear whether I should comment on the confusing signals emanating from the recently concluded Congress Working Committee meeting or the vandalism of the Shiv Sainiks. Or, perhaps, the desecration of churches and the brutal killing of Staines and his children, the gruesome murder of 23 Dalits in Jehanabad district, the martyrdom of the Mahatma on 30 January which is all but forgotten nowadays? Or, should one coolly ignore such unpleasant happenings and comment, instead, on the pomp and pageantry of the Republic Day parade, the awesome display of sophisticated missiles?

This is the appropriate occasion to invoke, as does Bal Thackeray, our civilizational heritage. This is the moment to celebrate, as the VHP and the Bajrang Dal activists tell you, our long-standing traditions of tolerance. The Constitution of the Republic 50 years ago symbolized our commitment to freedom, democracy and social justice. It was a momentous event, an occasion to remember, rejoice and celebrate. Watching the Republic Day parade in 1955, the country's first Prime Minister had a sense of fulfilment 'in the air and of confidence in our future destiny'. Two years later, Nehru told the Chief Ministers:

If we look about to various countries which have recently attained freedom . . . India compares favourably with them, both in regard to our stability and the progress we have made in these last 10 years. The record is a creditable one, and this is increasingly recognised by other countries of the world.

I wonder what the present Indian Prime Minister would

have said or written to his friends and colleagues on 26 January. Surely, he would not have repeated the claim made by one of his most distinguished predecessors nearly 40 years ago. If anything, he may have bemoaned the lack of political stability, the degradation in public life, the and overall drift in our polity. He may have even commented on his differences with his ministers, his coalition partners, and his mentors in the RSS. If he were sensitive he would have discussed the atrocities against women and Dalits, the harsh realities of life encountered by the vast majority of our people, and the ever-increasing gap between the rich and the poor.

He could have gone along with the die-hards or the self-proclaimed defenders of India's national/strategic interests on the nuclear issue. But he way have also echoed the views of his no less patriotic citizens who believe that the nuclear explosion at Pokharan has tarnished our image in the comity of nations and that, in the long run, we may end up paying a heavy price for our impetuousness.

The Prime Minister would have had many important things to write to his chief ministers. Yet one assumes that he would have taken notice of, and expressed his uneasiness with, the growing militancy and stridency of his own comrades. Posterity would like to know his views on the happenings in Gujarat, western Karnataka and Orissa, though one hopes that these incidents, accurately and sensibly reported in the media, are not treated by him as sporadic and isolated or the result of a so-called international conspiracy.

As a veteran politician, he must know that the issues at hand are not conversion or the inflow of foreign funds for missionary activities, but whether he and his government possess the political will to save the Republic from the onslaughts of proto-fascist organizations. Some of his trusted lieutenants may think differently but he, one hopes, will fulfil the mandate given to him by the electorate to conduct the affairs of the state not merely as the leader of a political party but as India's Prime Minister.

A ban on the activities of the Shiv Sena, VHP and the Bajrang Dal is no solution, but those connected with such outfits must be tamed and humbled before they tear apart the social fabric of our society. The politics of hate which they preach and practise (they don't have to be in power to do so; they don't need MPs and ministers to pursue their goals) must be countered, while their misguided passions, invariably directed against the minorities, must be curbed. Hooligans masquerading as defenders of faith cannot be allowed to ransack cinema halls, persecute creative writers, artists and historians, and destroy or desecrate places of worship. The likes of Bal Thackeray must be told in no uncertain terms that enough is enough. Someone must call his bluff before it is too late.

Let us remember what the poet Martin Niemoler (1892-1984) wrote:

In Germany the Nazis came
first for the Communists.
And I did not speak because I was not a Communist.
And then they came for the Jews
And I did not speak because I was not a Jew.
Then they came for the Trade Unions.
And I did not speak up
because I was not a Trade Unionist.
Then they came for the Catholics.
And I was a Protestant and so I did not speak up.
Then they came for me.
And by that time there was no one left to speak for anyone.

30 January 1999

Where are the Healers?

'While you are in India', V.S. Naipaul admonished his sister in 1949, 'you should keep our eyes open.' More than five decades later, we still need to keep our eyes as well as our ears open. Today, millions of people grope in the dark, as they have done for so long, in search of food, water, shelter and health care. Indeed, the problems afflicting the nation are no different from what they were in the first year of the millennium. What is different now is the renewed threat to communal peace from scores of sants and sadhus, backed by the VHP-RSS combine, who have raised the communal temperature over the construction of the Ram temple at Ayodhya.

Historians are no prophets, but the writing on the wall is for everybody to see. Social and political grievances will be heightened across the board because of farmer's unrest, the feverish pace of liberalization, resurgence of militancy in Kashmir, and the erosion in the popularity of the BJP-led National Democratic Alliance on account of its poor record of governance. To add to the growing uncertainties, new alignments and a massive mobilization of caste and communal sentiments will precede the Assembly elections that will take place in five states this year. In short, we are in for a prolonged summer of discontent.

Is India basking in the glory of 'spectacular political stability' for the past 15 months? This is surely not the perception of the 17,461 interviewees (conducted by *India Today*-Org-Marg) spread across 514 parliamentary constituencies in 16 states. Apart from their scepticism over the so-called idyllic stability of the Vajpayee government, the mere fact of a fragile coalition being held together by the Prime Minister brings no comfort to, among others, the Dalits, the backward castes, and the minorities. The persecution of Christians in certain pockets continues unabated, whereas the Sikh establishment is up in arms against the activities of the RSS in Punjab. Here, too, there is potential for Hindu-Sikh animus being aggravated. Whether it is Kashmir, Punjab or the North-east, majoritarianism in any garb will lend weight to divisive forces and add credence to the belief that *Hindutva* is the new mantra of civil society.

In short, the hope and optimism that had brought Atal Behari Vajpayee to centrestage have been belied by the lack-lustre performance of his ministers. His own strenuous efforts to project himself as a liberal no longer carry conviction. Starting with his ill-fated plea for a nation-wide debate on conversion and culminating in his ill-advised remarks on the so-called 'national sentiment' over the building of the Ram temple, the Prime Minister has not been able to break free from the RSS strangle-hold. If anything, he has time and time again proclaimed his loyalty to an organization that is unabashedly wedded to the idea of a Hindu nation. If on occasions he has ignored the dictate from Jhandewalan, it is because he does not want the coalition government to collapse. Who knows, next time round he may, if the electorate favours the BJP, dispense with his uncomfortable coalition partners and pay heed to his buddies in the RSS.

Surely, a diverse and disparate nation needs be anchored in an ideological frame provided by the Constitution. If so, the systematic and energetic efforts to tinker with the Constitution must cause widespread consternation. Sonia Gandhi struck the right note in pointing to the danger from within, from those elements that challenge the very basis of the social character and social sacrament that was put together by the architects of the constitution.

Higher education has been the prime casualty over the last 15 months. Doubtless, we require major structural reforms, but there is no reason why the state should retreat from its long-standing commitment to supporting higher education. By all means ensure the flow of private funds, but please do not make it a norm to be enforced in all disciplines and in every college and university dotted on the map of India. It is true that middle class opinion has largely veered around the idea of privatization, but its legitimization, which is inherently based on the exclusion of the less privileged sections of society, may well turn out to be the country's nightmare.

Perspectives on education, as indeed on other social sectors, must not be determined by market forces but informed by an understanding of the needs of a developing society and the empowerment of its backward segments. My sense is that the politician-bureaucrat combination in Shastri Bhawan does not adequately recognize its own role in bringing about a major socialization of our society. Having frittered away the opportunity to learn from past mistakes and initiate corrective measures, they have chosen to seek refuge in fanciful ideas and theories that reflect the idiosyncrasies of an individual or two.

A weary Republic, caught up in the quagmire of politicians, needs symbols of unity and harmony not to paper over the existing divisions but to nurture the vision envisaged by its founding fathers. Instead, we invoke sectarian leaders who preached hatred, bigotry and intolerance. Indeed, we may well confer upon them the highest national honour. This is not all. Recently, Amartya Sen talked of India's tradition of scepticism and the expression of hereticism and heterodoxy. To the very protagonists of our cherished 'ancient' traditions, these values seem to have lost their relevance when it comes to extending patronage, funding research projects, rewriting history textbooks, or not letting the 'Towards Freedom' volumes to be published. By all means consign the Marxists and 'pseudo-secularists' to the dustbin of history, but spare some thought for a generation that needs to rise above sectarian prejudices and beyond the painful historical memories that are revived to create a climate of hate, violence and aggression. A cry goes out from the ramparts of the Red Fort where the National Flag was first hoisted: 'Somebody has to provide the healing touch to a beleaguered nation.'

26 January will be yet another day in the life of a nation, though perhaps a little more cloudy and misty than the previous year. It is important to salute the memory of the freedom fighters, and yet we must not forget what a poet, far removed from the corridors of power, wrote at 'Freedom's Dawn':

> Where did that fine breeze, that the wayside lamp
> Has not once felt, blow from—where has it fled?
> Night's heaviness is unlessened still, the hour
> Of mind and spirit's ransom has not struck;
> Let us go on, our goal is not yet reached yet.

24 January 2000

From the Ramparts of the Red Fort

Any momentous occasion, whether it is the Republic Day parade or the celebration of Independence, must prompt people to think about who they want to be, what values they want to actualize, what their legacy will be. This has been the message of our thoughtful and energetic President, K.R. Narayanan. No wonder, on the eve of the Golden Jubilee of the Republic, he called for an 'honest self-analysis and self-questioning about where we, as a people and a society, are headed?' Drawing attention to the sullen resentment among the masses against their condition, he cautioned that these voices of resentment should not go unheard. 'The unabashed, vulgar indulgence in conspicuous consumption by the *nouveau riche* has left the underclass seething in frustration . . . Our three-way fast lane of liberalization, privatization and globalization must provide safe pedestrian crossings for the unempowered India also.'

The President talked of the raw deal given to women—'our greatest national shame'—and the indifference towards the Dalits. Last fortnight, the President spoke yet again of the 'dark clouds of prejudice and callous unconcern' over the problem of rape and atrocities against women and suggested rewriting of laws to deter such crimes. In a tone that bears the imprint of his strong personality, the President observed that democratically elected governments should assert their authority over the daredevil heroes of crime and banditry. One wonders if the Chief Ministers of Tamil Nadu and Karnataka are listening!

Vajpayee's first speech in this millennium (as Prime Minister) from the nation's most hallowed pulpit can be interpreted as his personal manifesto for the forthcoming talks with the American establishment. If so, his statesman-like tone may have sent out signals of moderation and reasonableness abroad. While the Prime Minister enhanced his personal stature and bolstered his liberal image in Washington, the *Sangh Parivar*, already feeling rudderless and demoralized by the declining fortunes of the BJP in UP, will be fuming and fretting over his references to India's liberal culture, his plea for religious tolerance, and his criticism of creating 'imaginary enemies'. Besides, the *Sangh*

Parivar's grandiose plans of building a Ram temple in Ayodhya may well have been grounded after the Prime Minister's observations. This calls for celebration.

Yes Prime Minister, borders cannot be redrawn either in the name of religion or on the strength of the sword. Your criticism of the two-nation theory is well taken. I am sure you have heard of Manto, who eloquently and poignantly captured these themes in his story *'Toba Tek Singh'*. But please convey your strong sentiments to the American establishment as well. Let them know that the state of Israel must choose the path of compromise and accommodation and not ride roughshod over the legitimate aspirations of the Palestinian people. Let the American President, who brokered the Camp David summit, know that our philosophy militates against coercion and the misuse of religion to serve territorial ambitions. This, Prime Minister, will vindicate our own stand on Kashmir.

You rightly underlined the need for reconciliation: healing the wounds by the larger canons of *insaniyat* (humanity) is a noble thought. But, Sir, consider translating this idea into practice. I venture to suggest, first of all, that a false national pride should not stand in the way of engaging Pakistan on the Kashmir imbroglio. If reconciliation is the hallmark of your strategy, why not talk to our chief adversary and expose the hollowness of its stand on Kashmir? Second, the beleaguered people of Kashmir expect tangible material prosperity and not empty promises. Militancy is largely caused by underdevelopment, and thrives on exploiting popular discontent. You cannot therefore create a haven of peace unless you remove the causes of disaffection in the wounded valley. The ball is in your court at 7 Race Court Road. Let us know what you think when you return to the Red Fort next year.

Pandit ko bhi salam hai aur maulvi ko bhi
Mazhab na chahiye mujhe iimaan chahiye

Away with pandits and with maulvis too
I do not want religion, I want faith.

23 August 2000

The Candid Camera has Said it All

The NDA government kindled hopes of a better future in certain circles. A weary nation, having experienced the rise and fall of the not so united fronts, turned to Vajpayee for political stability. He was the new icon, idolized by not just his followers but his erstwhile detractors as well, ushering the rule of the saints in an area of darkness.

The politically untidy socialists, led by the stormy petrel of the Emergency days, chose to leap in the dark by joining the RIP bandwagon. So did several other leaders who had built up their reputation in the United Front government by espousing secular causes. They preferred unity to acrimony, and agreed to share power with the BJP at the Centre and the states. They realized that there was something to be gained by declaiming socialist/secular slogans. For all their previous scorn of *Hindutva* and for the BJP, they were now beggars and not choosers.

The spurious unities worked for a while. The Prime Minister's personal charisma, assiduously promoted by the media, served to cement the NDA partners and convey to the electorate a semblance of political stability at the Centre. The opposition parties being weak, divided and dispirited reinforced this factor. The Congress, enfeebled by its diminishing influence in UP, was riven with dissension over Sonia Gandhi's leadership that ultimately led to Sharad Pawar's exit. And then came the war in Kargil, a blessing in disguise for the BJP-led government. Though the conduct and performance of our Defence Minister raised questions, the media sang paeans of praise for the Prime Minister and catalogued his skills as a leader of peace and war. Some discovered in him the qualities of a Lloyd George and Winston Churchill.

Ultimately, though, this regime has managed to survive owing to the personal loyalty of its coalition partners to the Prime Minister. Such is their fondness and obsessive devotion to him that they seem unaware of the larger developments unfolding in the country, including the impact of ill-conceived economic reforms on the underclass. They are not even at odds with the extremists busy rewriting the country's secular agenda. They were unmoved by the murder of a Christian priest and the desecration of churches. They assail the Congress, perhaps justifiably, but not the *Hindutva* brigade. Their sensitivities numbed, they have turned a blind eye to the climate of intolerance created by the VHP-Bajrang Dal, the saffronization of education, and the vilification campaign against liberal-left academics.

By George, the past has ceased to be a reference point for the followers of Ram Manohar Lohia and Acharya Narendra Dev.

What, in brief, explains the palpable gap between what they claimed to represent and what they really stand for at the beginning of this millennium? The answer is simple enough. What moved George Fernandes & Co. were not ideological niceties and the socialist turns of phrase but electoral needs, and these demanded a hard line against, say, the Rabri Devi government. They needed to capture Bihar, in the way the East India Company seized control of Bengal. And with the BJP's support, they had the ideal weapon in hand. This is what bonded them and determined the nature of their relations with the BJP.

Now, of course, the plot to overthrow a democratically elected government in Bihar has been aborted by an act of indiscretion committed at 3 Krishna Menon Marg by a friend and ally of George Fernandes. The end result is for everybody to see. Rabri Devi has gained a fresh lease of life. The coalition is under threat following Mamata Banerjee's noisy departure to Kolkata. The PMO is in disarray, with Brajesh Mishra placed in the dock by the Samata Party itself. RSS leaders fume and fret. And a tired-looking Prime Minister is caught in the nutcracker.

Corruption in public life is endemic but not all pervasive, the unblemished record of the Left Front governments in Bengal, Kerala and Tripura illustrates this. Elsewhere, though, one era of corruption succeeds another, and the victory of one party merely spurs the other into making a new bid for control of the fruits of office. Regardless of the BJP's own self-image, nurtured by the hollow pretensions of the RSS, power corrupts and absolute power corrupts absolutely. Having formed a government at the Centre for the first time after decades of job-hunting, the predictable has happened. Today, the myth of a clean party or a party with a difference lies shattered; in fact, party stalwarts, having been torn between loyalty to the RSS creed and the compelling demands of governance, may find it increasingly difficult to control the damage done to their image. Corruption in the party is rampant, and, for this reason, Bangaru Laxman should have done his homework and taken a few lessons from his more enterprising BJP friends in Lucknow or Ahmedabad. He should not have settled for so little.

For an average voter, the crucial point is that Bangaru Laxman has unwittingly demonstrated that even a *swayamsewak*, imbued with a divine mission, is not only a unabashed scrambler for advantage at the top but is also prone to accepting rupees and dollars. All this may not spell the end of the golden days of the government, but the balance has tilted against the BJP, so self-righteous in style, so corrupt in practice. This may not be the beginning of the end for the BJP. India's political gold-diggers don't give in that easily to retire voluntarily to Kashi or Badrinath. They will still want to impart value-based education to us so that we eschew, for the health and wealth of the nation, materialism and reach the commanding heights of spirituality. They will continue to proclaim, after having compromised our national interests, their loyalty to the nation and their commitment to value-based politics. They will repeat ad nauseam how foreign agencies have tried destabilizing the nation in order to thwart the steady march towards globalization. By George, this will not carry conviction.

I trust Arun Shourie, the crusader against corruption in public life, will agree, and that his sphinx-like silence will not be interpreted as an endorsement of the recent murky happenings. There is nothing to probe. Judicial commissions yield nothing. They take time, use up scarce resources, and then their findings get consigned to the dustbin. Those guilty of demolishing the Babri Masjid are at large; those guilty of instigating the horrific riots in Mumbai still call the shots. In this case, though, the candid camera has said it all. Only a new leadership and a new political combination can salvage something from the wreck.

21 March 2001

PART VI

India Votes: Assembly Elections

Is incumbency likely to pose problems for Laloo Prasad Yadav? And will the BJP-Samata Party alliance be the beneficiary? These questions seemed irrelevant to the electorate in rural Bihar, which was the impression we gathered. But come to the urban centres like Patna and Ranchi and you will discover that the query is posed with unfailing regularity.

The incumbency factor has been reinforced in recent weeks by the Samata Party-BJP entente. More importantly, because the BJP, having won over 41 seats in the 1995 Assembly elections, acquired a high profile in some urban constituencies. For instance, the party won three of the six seats in Patna. Likewise, Ranchi, Jamshedpur, Kishanganj, Katihar and Bhagalpur indicated a preference for saffron. And because the BJP performed well after five years of Janata Dal rule, it was widely assumed that incumbency was impeding the juggernaut.

The question is, however, tinged with a degree of wishful thinking on the part of the urban-based upper castes. This is what we were told by some scholars at the prestigious A.N. Sinha Institute in Patna. Even though the BJP wrested two seats from the Janata Dal in 1995, these scholars do not recognize incumbency as a plausible explanation.

With caste-based politics coming into play, caste has become a unit of mobilization. There is little space for community-based politics. This is why *Hindutva* has not struck a chord in Bihar. The explanation for the BJP's success lies elsewhere—in the post-Mandal churning process begun in the summer of 1990—and the sharp caste polarization that took place in UP and Bihar. In this scenario, the traditional upper caste support for the Congress defected to the BJP which, in months prior to the elections, was violently opposed to reservations for the backward castes in government jobs. This is the single most important factor that helped the BJP, though its appeal was still limited to only some urban constituencies.

Elsewhere in Bihar, Laloo Yadav improved his tally from 115 in 1991 to 165 in 1995. In other words, much more is being read into the BJP's limited electoral success than the facts indicate. Time and again, we were told not to draw our conclusions on the strength of the verdict of the relatively high-profile urban sectors.

Let us now turn to the Samata party's disengagement from the Janata Dal and its eventual attachment to the BJP. For one, the combination is engaged in an electoral combat for the first time so that they convey mixed and often confusing signals to their potential supporters. Second, in Bihar's exclusively caste-ridden parties, this *entente cordiale* does not reflect the complex social currents coming together. It represents, at best, simple caste arithmetic. Finally, the Samata Party leaders, chiefly Nitish Kumar and George Fernandes, have pinned their hopes on the Kurmis, the progressive and prosperous agricultural caste in central Bihar, notably in Patna, Nalanda and adjoining districts. They may find an important ally amongst the dominant Bhumihars who, in the absence of any organized caste formation of their own and the diminishing appeal of the Congress, may willy-nilly rally around the Samata Party to break Laloo Yadav's caste coalition. Yet, the strategy may not work. The party may pick up a few seats without being able to disturb the *status quo*. The Yadav-Muslim alliance, masterminded by the Chief Minister, has come to stay for some time and is most likely to erode the Samata-BJP combination. Laloo Yadav has, moreover, mobilized the Rajputs, many of whom are still tied to the Janata Dal and are loyal to V.P. Singh. In many constituencies Rajputs are pitted against the Samata Party candidates.

Nitish Kumar, chief architect of the alliance with the BJP and representing the interests of the Kurmi agro-capitalists, has charisma but not much credibility. According to Dr. Saibal Gupta of the Asian Development Research Institute, he is 'yet to have a proclivity to be an organic leader of his caste/class. He feels shy even to be their organic intellectual.'

Both in Patna and Ranchi there are mixed reactions to the BJP's electoral fortunes. One thing is clear. The RSS and the BJP have enlarged their support base in south Bihar since 1967 when their cadres earned much goodwill among the famine-stricken people of the region. Since then they have gained a foothold on the strength of their newly created non-Christian Dalit constituencies. At the same time, they have incurred the wrath of the Christians and the Muslims.

In 1991, the BJP returned five candidates from the south Bihar constituencies. Three years later, Samata Party legislators broke away from the Janata Dal and only eight of them returned to the Vidhan Sabha in the 1995 elections. In brief, the Samata-BJP combination is an untested one and their gains, jointly, are unlikely to exceed beyond four seats. So, if the BJP could win five seats, the alliance will not be able to send more than seven to nine MPs to Delhi.

So what accounts for the relative weakness of the BJP in Bihar as against UP, where the party has gathered momentum after the agitation over the Babri Masjid. For one, UP, land of Aryavarta, has been the focal point of Hindu communal mobilization from the last quarter of the nineteenth century. Not so Bihar. In addition, the Kisan Sabhas and the Socialist movement weakened the communal tendencies in the state.

Professor Sachidanand, former director of the A.N. Sinha Institute, brought another important factor to our attention. The support base of the BJP in UP, he pointed out, was drawn from the small and large urban-based trading communities, that is, the Aggarwals, Banias and Mittals in central and western UP. These groups, with their ideological concerns anchored in the *Hindutva* traditions, are not so numerous in Bihar.

Finally, scholars commented on the limitation of the Congress movement in Bihar and its dominance by the Bhumihars and the Rajputs with their powerful landed interests. That is why Sri Krishna Sinha, a Bhumihar, became the first Chief Minister after Independence. He was Nehru's chief political ally. On the other hand, A.N. Sinha, a Rajput, was patronized by Rajendra Prasad, the first President of the Indian Republic.

Now, with caste-based alliances coming into play both at the centre and the state, it was not surprising that caste became a unit of political mobilization in the localities. Consequently, there was little space for community-based politics. This is why the *Hindutva* ideology has not struck a favourable chord in Bihar, an otherwise volatile state.

In UP, on the other hand, there were serious fissures in the Congress movement. A section was no doubt wedded to Nehru's vision of a secular and socialist society, but the Brahmin-dominated Congress leadership had different ideas. Thus, the consolidation of the Hindu vote started with Pandit Govind Ballabh Pant, its first Chief Minister. The Hindi agitation and the cow slaughter movement were conducted under the aegis of the Congress. It is no coincidence that the Ram idol was placed in the Babri Masjid in 1949, with Pant still at the helm of affairs. Years later the *shilanyas* was performed under Congress auspices. In other words, the Congress on its own offered sufficient space to the BJP to organize its mobilization campaign.

Scholars and administrators alike dwell on the absence of land reforms in Bihar. This fact alone has enabled the left movement, though weak and fragmented, to act as a bulwark against communal and revisionist trends. In UP, by contrast, the CPI or CPI(M) have not made much headway. This is because their agenda was, to some extent, appropriated by the Congress (abolition of *zamindari* in 1954) and by non-Congress governments led by, notably, Charan Singh. The SVD and the Lok Dal forged cross-communal alliances, especially in western UP, but it was not easy to either stem the communal tide or to erode the base of the Jan Sangh/BJP.

If the contrast between UP and Bihar is real, how does one explain the recurrence of communal riots in Bihar? Clearly, one must not put the blame squarely on the BJP. After all, the Bhagalpur riots of 1984 took place with the Congress in power. An inept administration watched helplessly as 2,000 Muslims were murdered, their property looted or burnt down. Everyone we spoke to argue that the Bhagalpur riots constitute a watershed in so far as the Muslims, regardless of caste and class, abandoned the Congress. It symbolized said, Qazi Mujahidul Islam Qasimi, head of the *Imarat-e-Shariah* in Phulwari Sharif, the 'parting of ways.'

The Muslim disenchantment coincided with the groundswell of the backward caste, lower caste support for leaders carrying the Mandal banner, taking advantage of the enthusiasm and the hopes generated by V.P. Singh. Laloo Yadav forged, with dexterity, a solid Muslim-Yadav combination.

It was a year after the Bhagalpur riots that Laloo came to power in Patna with 115 seats. By 1995, he had dramatically improved his tally to 165 seats. And in the current parliamentary elections, the logical expectation is that Laloo will gain new ground or at least maintain the tally of the 1991 parliamentary elections.

To understand Laloo's appeal, one has to follow him on the campaign trail. There are no promises of major projects, what Nehru called the new temples of India, no unwrapping of a spectacular economic package. He comes across as a man-next-door from the village, who has cast himself as a wandering mendicant, one who beckons the poorest of the poor, the wretched of the earth to join hands and 'march on Delhi' to 'capture the Red Fort'. He adds: 'We have had enough tea at the Islampur street corner; let us now have tea in New Delhi's Connaught Place.' In this conversational manner, without promising anything of substance, Laloo conjures up a vision of the inclusion of Bihar's poor in the governance of Delhi. The surprise is that this huge promise does not ring hollow when it comes from Laloo because he rattles off the list of communities who in the past had to keep their heads bowed in the village and who are now represented in the Assembly, the Legislative Council and Parliament. His recent list of nominees to the council includes a Bind (earth digger), Tauti (weaver), Kumhar (potter), Lohar (blacksmith), Amat (landless labourer) and so on.

'In the past five years of Laloo's reign,' comments Dr. Saibal Gupta, 'the most oppressed and suppressed have been imparted a new consciousness, confidence and social identity'. A comparison with Mulayam Singh will be misplaced. The Samajwadi Party leader, insists Gupta, operates within the parameters set by Charan Singh's agrarian politics and is thus part of the 'vernacular elite'. Laloo starts from a base similar to Mulayam but reaches out to new, sometimes obscure groups at the lower extremity of the caste ladder—rat catchers, scavengers and worse off castes.

In this, Gupta finds a striking resemblance in Laloo's methodology of communication with Sagina Mahato, a celebrated cellu-
loid character of the 1970s immortalized as an indomitable
union leader by thespian Dilip Kumar. He makes intelligent use
of his homespun nickname and refers to himself in the third
person. '*Darna mat; Laloo tumhare saath khara hua hai*' (Don't
be afraid, Laloo is with you).

By reaching out to an ever-increasing constituency beyond
the pale, Laloo has invested his personality with a charisma of
inexhaustible potential. His larger-than-life image has been able
to cushion the animal husbandry scam. 'It is an upper-caste
plan to tarnish his image', murmurs Charan Das, a tea-owner in
Jehanabad. 'He is appealing to those on the fringes of the market
or those outside the market', says Gupta. 'This is a gigantic
coalition of the dispossessed.'

Secularism is another constant theme in Laloo's speeches:
'*Hindustan ke char sipahi: Hindu, Muslim, Sikh, Isai*' (The
four soldiers protecting Hindustan are Hindus, Muslims, Sikhs
and Christians). 'Muslims in the state are almost 100 per cent
with Laloo', declares Qazi Mujahidul Islam Qasimi. This assessment probably leaves out the Muslims traditionally tied to the
Congress or the various left formations. 'What Laloo Prasadji
has been able to ensure for us is the security of our lives and
property', says Qazi M.O. Siddiqui, a minister in Laloo's cabinet.
'Traditionally, secular Hindu leaders visited Muslims to console
them or give them protection. Laloo is the first Hindu leader
who reached out to the Hindu masses to convince them that
the communal divide will weaken the cause of the poor', he
adds.

Begum Abid Reza Bedar, a middle-class Muslim housewife in
Patna, recalls the genesis of it: 'we saw with our own eye how
Laloo was always on the spot to control the riots that broke out
after the fall of the Babri Masjid. And the self-respect he has
given to the poor is something no Indian leader has been able
to give the country's oppressed.'

Laloo travels either by a privately hired helicopter or by his
'*garib chetna rath*'. The consequent 'awakening' is a source of
considerable anxiety even to the two Communist Parties. An

influential communist leader said: 'Just look at the leadership of the CPI and CPI(M) in the state. It is packed with the upper castes. If we do not mend our ways and the Laloo juggernaut is not checked, our cadres will desert us and join the Janata Dal.'

For the BJP-Samata alliance Laloo's unorthodox methods of lower caste mobilization presents a frightful prospect. 'He is the most corrupt politician the country has ever known', bellows George Fernandes. Fernandes will probably win because the caste arithmetic in Nalanda—Kurmi, Koeri and Bhumihar—may be able to neutralize the Janata Dal caste alliance backed by Yadav militancy. This militancy is a very real factor in these elections. The Yadavs have been made to feel that their man is about to go to Delhi as Prime Minister (this is the refrain in all of Laloo's election meetings). Says Professor Sachidanand: 'They feel that their caste pride is at stake.'

When we asked Laloo if he planned to be 'kingmaker or king', he laughed: 'He who has the numbers will be heard. I expect to get 50 seats along with the left allies.' Obtaining 50 out 54 seats is absolute exaggeration and Laloo knows it. Yes, 40 seats are not unthinkable.

Laloo's projection of himself as a Prime Ministerial candidate is clearly designed to enhance his vote-catching ability. But this projection runs into minor difficulties in a constituency like Hajipur where, Ram Vilas Paswan too is seen as Prime Ministerial material. 'Supposing the LF-NF combine emerges as the largest single party, who else will join you to give you the majority?' we asked him. 'The Congress will break, he said without batting an eyelid.

It is being whispered in political circles that Laloo may deliberately have fielded weak candidates against those Congressmen who will be inclined to join the LF-NF combine after the elections. For instance, Tariq Anwar, the Congress candidate from Katihar, is not expected to have difficulties against Mufti Mohammad Sayeed of the Janata Dal.

Even the suspicion that Laloo may be cultivating a core of pro-Janata Dal Congressmen has the potential of complicating the intra-Dal politics. Sayeed is, after all, a former president of the Janata Dal. In brief, Laloo's ever-expanding base will stand him in good stead in the current elections. Problems will surface later when intra-Janata Dal conflicts break out and when within his own state the newly awakened social groups begin to seek economic returns, an area where Laloo gives no evidence of being in possession of a blueprint.

At present there is hope in some circles that Laloo may fabricate a new class coalition with the same dexterity with which he has woven caste alliances. Indeed, a unique feature of the election is that for the first time after Independence, Bihar has an autonomous political agenda quite independent of the perception of national priorities.

Hindi Heartland: Caste is the Vote

Lucknow
8 May 1996

'It is my faith, my religious duty to vote for the BJP', declares Rajendra Kumar Goswami with disarming candour, seated on a wooden bench outside his modest food grain shop near the Barabanki bus stop. 'Casteism is a danger to Hinduism . . . the BJP is the answer', he adds. Ravi Shankar Tewari at a Rudauli tea stall, Ashok Mishra in Kanpur—all are emphatic in their support for the BJP. But talk to the Muslims, Yadavs, Dalits, and they are guarded in their response—they don't spell out their electoral preferences quite so easily. For itinerant observers, it's exceedingly tempting to give weightage to the five who were emphatic in their support for the BJP, as against the fifty who hemmed and hawed and didn't show their hand. But this is elementary caste behaviour in the Hindi heartland—the upper castes are vocal in their electoral support. The lower castes and the minorities are less so.

This is one of the lessons we learnt as we travelled through the Hindi heartland in UP. The noise and excitement associated with electioneering were missing. Posters, banners and hoardings were tucked away in party offices, not displayed on the streets and bazaars. In Qaiserganj and adjoining Bahraich, just a handful of people huddled together in party offices. In Kanpur, where the police had conducted an eight-hour operation to remove posters and banners at the Election Commission's behest, there was no sign of a vibrant campaign. Subhashini Ali, the CPI(M) candidate, was asleep when we visited her office at 4 p.m. 'The stringent conditions imposed by the EC have dampened our enthusiasm', a Congress activist stated. 'It's not good for democracy.'

Given the inglorious record of communal riots in UP, we expected some degree of intense communal activity. This was not so. Such polarization may take place in riot-prone cities like Kanpur, but the principal preoccupation is with caste, not religion. People talk of socio-economic empowerment and of castewise representation, of quotas, local bodies and programmes. Mandal rather than mandir tops the political agenda in UP. You can sense the deep caste schisms and rivalries, sharpened by Mandal. It's hard to imagine how this divide is ever going to be bridged; every party is trying to create or enlarge its constituency among various castes and sub-castes. Nobody in this backward state talks about illiteracy, massive urban unemployment, land reforms or rural development.

'Communalism is not an issue this time', said a senior state bureaucrat. 'The communalists have no goods to sell in the market.' Traditional cross-community linkages, we were told, are intact in the hinterland. The impact of Ayodhya seems much less pronounced in the areas we visited. In other words, we found no significant upsurge in the BJP's favour. Yet there is no denying its presence across the state—in the 1993-5 polls, the BJP had consolidated its dramatic gains in the 1989 and 1991 Lok Sabha polls. Its leaders draw comfort from disciplined cadres committed to the *Hindutva* world view. Moreover, they are confident of consolidating the upper caste vote—Brahmins exceed 15 per cent of the population in 34 out of the 85 Lok Sabha constituencies.

The Rajputs are more ambivalent because of their loyalty to V.P. Singh, but not everywhere. In most constituencies they are sure to vote in increasing numbers for the BJP. And the BJP, having wrested control of the influential Kurmi Mahasabha, has gained a firm foothold in the Kurmi territory in central UP. Much the same has happened in Bihar where the Kurmis, led by Nitish Kumar, are a significant component of the BJP-Samata combination. Thus, the BJP's support base is not confined to the Brahmins, Rajputs, Banias and Kayasths. It includes the Kurmis, Gujjars and Lodhs in western districts. After all, in the 1991 Lok Sabha and the 1993 Assembly polls, the Kurmis helped the BJP win in Bareilly, Sitapur, Shahjahanpur, Pilibhit and Hardoi. Such facts alone acquire salience in the complex caste arithmetic. More so if the Muslim vote is split between the Bahujan Samaj Party and the National Front-Left combine.

Every single Brahmin we met was loyal to the BJP. 'The BJP is a defender of the Hindu faith', said a schoolteacher in Bara Banki. At a roadside tea shop off Kanpur, the BJP was seen to be ideologically equipped to combat the divisive forces. In Kishore-ganj, where the Brahmins dominate the 35 per cent upper caste voters, the consensus was in BJP's favour though its candidate may still not win because of the large Muslim (mostly Momins) and OBC population. 'The BJP is the answer to the onslaught of the Mayawatis', declared a Brahmin shopkeeper. 'How can we tolerate a Harijanized administration?' asked an angry postal official.

These are symptoms of a deeper malaise. Equally, they are pointers to which way the wind is blowing. Yet, they don't reveal the whole story. The picture here is much less clear than in Bihar where Laloo Prasad Yadav has masterminded an extraordinary Dalit-Muslim-OBC coalition. Such a coalition has paid rich dividends, though its future efficacy rests on a wide range of factors, including the political will to translate poll promises into practice. The important theme in Bihar today is not its chronic poverty and backwardness but the empowerment of the lower castes. The real story, which is yet to be unfolded, is the dextrous manner in which Laloo has undermined the traditional Congress base and has thus removed his chief rival from the electoral fray. He has, above all, weakened the political hegemony of the Brahmins and the Bhumihars and, at the same time, dimmed the BJP's prospects.

The battlelines in UP are less clearly demarcated. For one, the caste arithmetic is different. The upper castes are a much larger group and have greater control over the rural and urban levers of power. The complex caste divides in the political domain are also more apparent. That's why former Chief Minister Kalyan Singh could create fissures amongst the Yadavs, and the Kurmi Mahasabha could plot a trajectory independent of the Yadavs.

Finally, the Dalit-Muslim-OBC combine dominates the Bihar political landscape; similar endeavours in UP have not clicked. The fragile SP-BSP alliance collapsed for a variety of reasons, though the main difficulty was that each party tried to cut into the other's caste base. So that in the local bodies' polls, as in Etawah, the BSP marshalled all its resources to defeat the SP man.

As the countdown began, people in Lucknow wondered whether the BJP will draw mileage out of this situation. One thing is clear. Although the Third Force has expanded due to the recent democratic upsurge, its appeal amongst the Dalits has greatly diminished. Nobody bemoans this fact more than the Muslims. Having hitched their fortunes with Mulayam Singh Yadav and Kanshi Ram, they seem confused now. 'We feel let down by this tragic parting of ways', said a professor at the Aligarh Muslim University. Asked whom she will vote for, a *burqa*-clad woman in Nakhaas retorted 'How do I know? You tell me, Kanshi Ram is a spoiler. He is aiding and abetting the BJP cause.' In the end she may be proven right.

Such reactions are crucial in gauging the mood in Muslim circles. But the 'Muslim dilemma', as it is described in university and journalist circles, is a figment of the imagination. One can hear murmurs in some quarters, but no clear pattern of alignment has emerged. Most educated Muslims eschew serious political talk, though they unequivocally condemn the Congress. The

Muslim divine we spoke to remained non-committal. At the Dewa Sharif shrine in Bara Banki, we were politely told not to discuss politics. The only person who spoke to us said he will vote BJP. Why? Because the Congress had let them down. 'We want to make peace with the most powerful force in UP', he declared.

Making peace with the BJP is hardly anybody's agenda. If anything, the prime concern everywhere is to defeat the BJP even if it means backing the Congress in places. As the campaign gathers steam, the consensus among community leaders, some of whom still exercise influence, will veer around Mulayam Singh. Not because they are necessarily averse to Kanshi Ram, but because they don't see the BSP as a 'winner'. This was told to us in Qaiserganj where the elders meet every evening to take stock of day-to-day developments, and in the predominantly Shia locality of Sheesh Mahal in Lucknow, Kalb-e-Sadiq, the influential Shia leader, has already hitched his fortunes with Mulayam Singh.

This is a disturbing element in the BJP's strategy. If the 'Muslim vote' is not split between the BSP and the SP, it may not be easy for the BJP to recover lost ground in UP. Hence, strenuous efforts are under way to project the party's secular image. Its leader in Bahraich took pains to explain that the BJP was not against the minorities. He dwelt on cordial Hindu-Muslim relations and on composite cultural and religious traditions in the area. 'All this is an eyewash', said the poll manager of Arif Mohammed Khan, the high-profile independent candidate in Bahraich. Most Muslims in Bahraich, Kanpur and Lucknow pay no heed to the BJP's secular rhetoric. Mulayam would hope this is so. With the erosion of his own caste-based coalition, he can't just rely on the nearly 24 per cent OBC voters. More so because they are so hopelessly divided. The 7.6 per cent Yadav vote is not good enough. What he needs is to mobilize the Muslims, who account for nearly 14.5 per cent of UP's population. Then, the Third Front may well taste victory without the BSP. 'That may well be our finest hour', observed an Urdu newspaper editor in Badaun.

What if it does? This brings us to the significance of these elections in UP and their national impact. With 85 seats in the

Lok Sabha, the state occupies a vantage point in shaping future alignments at the Centre. People are sensitive to this reality. 'In the final analysis,' declared a banker in Kanpur, 'the UP voter will leave an imprint on the Indian nation's emerging personality.' Interest is, of course, centred on the SP and the BSP, their un-lovely struggle to take advantage of caste polarities, and on Muslim disenchantment with the Congress. For, this election will decide the Dalit-Muslim-OBC combine's future. And it may yet have a longer lease of life than the BJP's attempt at Hindu consolidation.

The future of the Congress rests in UP, the familiar turf of leading figures during the freedom struggle and of successive Prime Ministers from Nehru to Rajiv Gandhi. Can the Congress check the deep and enduring erosion in its base? Can it recover the ground it had so comprehensively lost in the 1993-5 elections?

The story is a familiar one. In the 1993-5 polls, the Congress was relegated to the rank of the third party in UP, Bihar and Karnataka. Both in UP and Bihar its vote share had fallen well below the 20 per cent mark. 'In these states', said a political analyst, 'the Congress stands on the receiving end of the logic of the plurality system which might further hasten its decline.'

Ramesh Dikshit, Congress party spokesman in Lucknow, is hopeful of a recovery, though the disarray in the rank and file belies his optimism. There is no attempt to refurbish its image, no drive to win. Having failed to represent the people's demo-cratic urges, the Congress in UP has lost its *raison d'être*. The Muslims will rather choose, as in Bihar and Maharashtra, any party but the Congress. The Dalits and the OBCs have abandoned it and channelled their aspirations through caste-based formations. And the Brahmins have slowly but steadily shifted allegiance to the BJP. The Congress may bag a few seats in places like Pratapgarh, Amethi, Baghpat and Rampur, but its fate in UP, its main stronghold for decades, is manifestly sealed this time. It is hard to make predictions, but we were told time and again that the party, bereft of any vision or social strategy to deal with caste cleavage, is heading for it lowest ever vote share in any Lok Sabha election.

This election will decide the fate of the *Hindutva* campaign, triggered off in its most recent incarnation by the Ayodhya issue. In other words, UP matters a great deal more in the post-Ayodhya period because of the way in which the 'politics of difference', the cultural heterogeneity and the intellectual diversities will be played out. Ultimately, India's most populous state will tilt the balance in deciding whether the country remains 'secular' or not. After all, even the restrained behaviour of the BJP in the course of this campaign is a bonus for secularism.

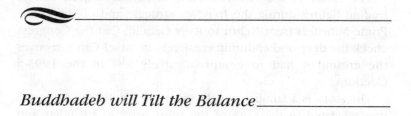

Buddhadeb will Tilt the Balance

Kolkata
3 May 2001

I would certainly vote, but my vote is a secret, said Abdul Ahad, a van-puller in the Muslim majority village of Mallikpur in 24 Paraganas district. This cautionary note cuts across the 48,123,469 voters in Bengal who will elect their 294 MLAs next week. Much of this is the result of inter-party violence that has led to deaths and marred the campaign in certain areas. 'Political cleansing is the order of the day; civil society has ceased to exist', says Ms. Krishna Bose, Trinamul Congress member of Parliament from Jadavpur. Left activists, who accuse her party of instigating violence, hotly contest her view.

The election fever is sweeping Bengal. Flags flutter from shops and houses, though streets everywhere were deserted on May Day. In areas where community TV sets do not exist, people gather around the central square of their village to discuss how best to ensure a better future for themselves. 'Politicians come and go, but we have to think of a party that can serve our present and safeguard our future', says an emaciated peasant in Kalikapur village.

The coming election is important not only for this peasant but for the future of the CPI(M)-led government and its most formidable adversary, Ms. Mamata Banerjee. For the Marxists the battle lines are clearly drawn. A clear-cut victory would be interpreted as a vote of confidence after the exit of Jyoti Basu, who relinquished power after nearly 24 years. More importantly, it will bolster the stature of his successor, Buddhadeb Bhattacharjee. Already, the CPI(M) is sensing victory, following weeks of confusion and uncertainty.

Perceptions matter more than policies. Bhattacharjee, a Presidency College graduate, is attracting huge crowds at his election rallies, and has successfully established himself as a pragmatic and accessible public figure. He is not merely Basu's successor, but is widely regarded as someone who has so quickly left his personality imprint on this campaign. The hope is that his economic blueprint, more in tune with the demands for liberalization, will rescue Bengal from underdevelopment and industrial stagnation, though sections of the party claim that such a blueprint already exists and it is being implemented.

What has made the difference to Mr. Bhattacharjee's stature is the attitude of the urban élite, who have shifted their political allegiances from time to time in the past, and for whom land reforms or anti-poverty programmes count for nothing. After weeks of dithering, they grudgingly concede that the present Chief Minister inspires confidence in trade and business circles, and in the absence of a viable alternative, the Left Front is their best bet.

Over and above everything else, Mr. Bhattacharjee's image of a caring, upright, fair minded and affable leader is a major political asset. His message is simple, but different. His style, hallmark of a *bhadralok* culture, is endearing and reassuring. This factor counts more in Bengal than anywhere else in the country. In a society where caste polarization has not taken place, this cultivated image of the Chief Minister will bolster the fortunes of the CPI(M) in the elections. Indeed, the balance will be tilted by the presence of the 56-year-old Bhattacharjee rather than the party's own past record or the energy of the cadres. Party officials at the Muzaffar Ahmed Bhawan on Alimuddin Street may not concede, but at this juncture he is their main trump card.

Yet, the going will be tough, if one considers the rapid decline in the Left Front's share of votes from 54.52 per cent in the 1980 Parliamentary elections to 47.35 per cent in 1996, and 47.35 in 1998. In the Assembly elections, too, its share of votes has plummeted from 51.6 per cent in 1982 to 48.02 per cent in 1996.

Anil Biswas, state secretary of the CPI(M) attributes the discontent towards the Left Front to the rising expectations of the expanding bourgeoisie and the government's failure to fulfil all their needs. Fair enough. But, then, why should such people now repose their confidence in a party that has failed to deliver during the last 24 years? Especially since the state has made no rapid strides during the Left Front's last 5-year term.

On the plus side, land reforms have been this government's major contribution towards changing the balance of power in rural Bengal. But public memory is notoriously short. 'The young have sadly erased the revolutionary struggles from their memory; they have forgotten, moreover, years of Congress misrule', says Biswas. But, on the other hand, the Left is unlikely to abandon its commitment to social justice and equality. The import of their message is all but lost to the Opposition parties. Today, the Congress is gasping for breath and its chances of winning are limited to its traditional strongholds. Ghani Khan Choudhury is flexing his muscles in Malda, whereas the Congress-backed Independents, described by Pranab Mukherjee, as 'unbridled horses', are up in arms in Murshidabad. This is bad news for a party that is devoid of any programme that will put it back on the rails. It is already fragmented and weakened by a divided leadership.

The BJP may corner a few seats on the strength of the un-settled conditions on the Indo-Bangladesh border, but its long-term survival on Bengal's political landscape is at best a remote possibility. Although the BJP vote shot up to 11.36 per cent in the 1991 Assembly polls owing to the *Hindutva* wave, it dropped to 6.45 per cent in 1996. This time round its share of votes may plummet further.

In effect, what keeps the midnight oil burning at Alimuddin Street is the upsurge of support for the Trinamool. Fiery and passionate, though impetuous, Ms. Banerjee has successfully assailed some of the communist strongholds: 'Didi aschke, CPI (M) bhay pacche' (The CPI(M) is scared as Didi comes on) was the cry at a Trinamul rally in Calcutta on May Day. Yet her decision to withdraw from the NDA, followed by her hurriedly concluded pact with the Congress, has dampened the enthusiasm of her supporters.

Even if she succeeds in rallying round her supporters in the days to come and splits the Left Front votes, caused by the PDS, she will need to do well in Birbhum, Burdwan, Bankura, Purulia, Hoogly and Midnapore. These districts account for as many as 118 seats or approximately 40 per cent of the total seats. If the outcome of the 1996 Assembly and the 1999 Parliamentary elections is any guide, the Left is sure to press home its advantage. In the event, Ms. Banerjee's political fate will be sealed in Bengal, her principal political akhara and her diminishing role in State politics will affect her bargaining position in New Delhi.

The elections in West Bengal are poised for an interesting countdown. Whether the people endorse Mr. Bhattacharjee's dictum, 'the only alternative to the left is a new, improved left', or accept Ms. Banerjee's call 'for change', will be known on 13 May when electronic voting machines from 61,542 voting centres produce the results. Whatever the verdict, the results will have far-reaching implications for Bengal as well for the future of coalition politics at the Centre.

Bengalis are Liberal:
*Buddhadeb Bhattacharjee*_____

Kolkata
3 May 2001

For a historian of Indian nationalism, Muzaffar Ahmad Bhawan
on Alimuddin Street evokes memories of Bengali revolutionary
past. I stepped into the building hoping to get a sense of that
past.

The Chief Minister, Buddhadeb Bhattacharjee, was relaxed,
courteous and affable. He talked to me in a room with portraits
of Marx, Lenin, Stalin and other revolutionaries hanging pre-
cariously in the background. Bengal is changing; so are the
Marxist ideologues. Buddhadeb Bhattacharjee symbolizes this
change. He represents the face of communism in the twenty-
first century Bengal a state which is crying out for economic
regeneration.

MH: How does it feel to be a communist in 2001?
BB: Like Fidel Castro I think there is a worldwide current against
us after the debacle in the Soviet Union and Eastern Europe.
But capitalism cannot be the last chapter of humanity. There are
some people who talk about the end of communism, but I say
no. The world is now badly divided into rich and poor countries;
poor countries are now trying to consolidate. And Communist
Parties throughout the world are trying to understand what
is going on. We have to adopt a proper strategy. Socialism is
historically inevitable.
MH: What was the feeling when you entered the Chief Minister's
office?
BB: I had already been a member of the Left Front Cabinet. But
the new position meant additional responsibility. It is like a
crown of thorns.
MH: Do you think a change of leadership should have taken
place earlier?
BB: No. The party correctly decided the timing. I wanted Jyoti

Babu to continue. Jyoti Babu had considerable ability and knowledge to govern which has helped me to take over and work effectively.

MH: You have managed to strike a chord with the electorate. How?

BB: This is partly due to the fact that in recent times the middle class in urban and semi-urban areas and the youth have started supporting us. The industrial and commercial houses feel that the Left Front government is able to create a congenial climate for business and industry. They feel that an alternative to Left Front will spell disaster for this state. They want a rule of law, which we have provided.

MH: What's the new style you have introduced?

BB: I am trying to perform in my own way. I am trying to reach out to the masses directly. I want to know their problems. The common man wants to see the politician in their midst, and I am not only accessible but also willing to redress their grievances.

MH: What is there in your background or personal style that has made you popular in so short a time?

BB: I was a student of literature. Literature was my first love and from literature I came to politics. I plunged into the world of communism from this vantage point. Therefore, I try to communicate with the people through literature. The Bengali middle class loves his literature.

MH: Is there any particular programme you wish to prioritize?

BB: The challenge is obviously rapid industrialization. We are a late starter in this field. But our 1994 industrial policy has brought about some changes. New areas are opening up— petrochemicals, agro-based industries, electronics, and IT. We would like to tap the knowledge of our boys and girls in computer technology, electronics, and biotechnology. We have formulated a clear strategy of developing knowledge-based industry in West Bengal.

MH: But some would say this strategy goes against the spirit of socialism?

BB: No. Side-by-side we are trying to develop small and medium scale industries to create more job opportunities. Twenty-five per cent of the people in West Bengal live below the poverty

line, although this percentage is lowest in the country. We have
to address their needs by creating more jobs opportunities in
our traditional sectors like handloom, sericulture and hosiery.

MH: It is said that the Bengali middle class is provincial, and that
they need to develop a pan-Indian outlook. Do you agree?

BB: What I'm trying to say is that we are Bengalis no doubt, but
we are Indians. I just addressed a public meeting in Burrabazar,
which is Calcutta's trading centre and is inhabited mostly by
Marwaris, Gujaratis and other non-Bengalis. I told them that the
Gujaratis and Marwaris and other non-Bengali communities have
played an important role in Bengali life. Bengalis are not
chauvinists. They are liberals. We are proud of our liberal tradition.
Bengal is a mini India and all communities live in Bengal
harmoniously. There are Biharis, Bengalis, Marwaris, Gujaratis,
Madrasis—you can find all colours of the rainbow in Bengal.

MH: What is it that we can invoke from our recent past to create
a liberal, tolerant and secular society?

BB: The situation in the country as a whole is complicated.
Parties like the BJP are trying to saffronize all our ideas and
cultural norms. But our state is absolutely secular. As I told you
in our metropolitan cities, many communities live together and
we are trying to maintain the secular fabric of our society. Our
writers, dramatists, film makers have contributed to the maintenance of communal peace in this state. I can humbly state
that the BJP brigade *Sangh Parivar* has not been able to penetrate
our academic and cultural life.

MH: In a broad sense whom do you invoke from the nationalist
movement?

BB: We are Communists. We criticize Gandhi for many things.
But we cannot deny that when he was saying 'Iswar Allah Tero
Naam, Sabko Summati De Bhagwan' he was invoking a secular
concept for India. During the Second World War, we were
criticized for helping the British, but Jawaharlal Nehru's ideas
were similar to ours. I'm reminded of a story where the Indians
were felicitating a Spanish Communist leader in London.
Jawaharlal attended the programme supporting the International
Brigade in Spain and presented a bouquet to the Spanish leader.
Jyoti Babu complimented him. Jawaharlal said that it was just a

mere gesture. He supported the Spanish people against Franco from the core of his heart. Jawaharlal also studied developments in the Soviet Union, their planning, and their ideas of reconstruction. We have to understand in proper perspective the ideas of Gandhiji, Nehru and Netaji.

MH: I wanted to ask you about developments along the Bangladesh border?

BB: Very unfortunate! The government of India is now talking at the highest level.

MH: Does the government of India not consult you on this?

BB: No. This is the External Affair's Ministry's concern. But I'm concerned with what happened in Meghalaya. We have a long border with Bangladesh. But from what I read in the newspapers, the government had no knowledge of what was happening on the border. It was the doing of the Bangladesh military. But the government of India should not overreact, because Bangladesh is no threat to us. We have a friendly government in Bangladesh and we should try to improve our relationship with it. I have requested the central government to deploy more BSF personnel on our border, particularly during the elections.

MH: Are you confident of victory?

BB: Certainly. What I say to the public is that the alternative to the Left Front is a more organized, more dynamic and more responsive Left Front.

4 May 2001

We still have a Long Way to Go,
*says Jyoti Basu*_____

Kolkata
4 May 2001

Sections of the Calcutta *bhadralok* resent him for what he is
and what he is not. In rural Bengal, though, he is a household
name. He is their saviour, the man who changed their destiny
by giving them land. I discovered in Matiya Burj, the site of
Nawab Wajid Ali's ignominious exile, that the Muslims hold
him in high regard. He is the 87-year old Jyoti Basu.

Politicians often retire in disgrace, but Jyoti Basu, bubbling
with energy and enthusiasm, is cast in a different mould. Sceptics
may say what they like, but he is assured of an honourable
place in history. Despite his shortcomings, allegedly exploited
by family and friends, he has ushered in an era of transformation
in this region and restored dignity to parliamentary democracy.
All said and done, he is a politician *par excellence.*

A quintessential Communist, a breed that is fast disappearing,
he has covered nearly 2,500 km travelling from Jalpaiguri to
Purulia during this election campaign. For me, a historian of
modern India, it was a delight to meet him at his official
residence in Salt Lake. Wearing a white half-sleeve shirt on his
dhoti, he smiled and laughed as we covered a wide gamut of
issues. He was patient, reflective, and generous.

MH: Do you spend more time with your family?
JB: Not yet (smiles broadly).
MH: But, you do look forward to? Don't you?
JB: Probably after the elections.
MH: Do you get time to read books?
JB: I read books before going to bed.
MH: What sort of books?
JB: Novels, detective stories, and serious books. I get hold of

them from people who know about literature, like my present Chief Minister. He recommends books to me.

MH: Have you read Arundhati Roy's novel?

JB: Yes, yes. Recently, I also read Sagarika Ghose's novel. I was impressed. Then, there is Shobha De. I once met her in Calcutta.

MH: Do you have an icon?

JB: No, no. I believe in Marxism-Leninism. No particular individuals I can think of (laughs sheepishly).

MH: Who is your favourite historian? I bet it's not me.

JB: My favourite historian is, of course, Marx and Engels. I can't mention any other name (bursts into laughter).

MH: You have kept the left flag flying for the last 24 years. How does it feel after relinquishing office?

JB: Because of my ill health I have been asking my party for the last one year to allow me to step down.

MH: But is there a sense of fulfilment?

JB: Yes, 24-years in office is a record. I hope we will win this election again. So it will be another record. But we have a long way to go. I am reminded of a meeting with Chou-'En-lai in China long ago. We had gone as part of a trade union delegation to the People's Republic of China. We were not in government. During the meeting, we told Chou'En-lai how we were very impressed with China's development. Chou'En-lai remarked, 'if you came back after one thousand years, then also there would be something to be done'. I think he was absolutely correct.

MH: Do you regret not being the Prime Minister?

JB: Yes. I still think it was a historical blunder. History would not give us such an opportunity. Imagine 10-12 bourgeois but progressive parties asking me to be the PM. We were in a minority, and yet this opportunity would have helped us in the long run. It was worth running the government even for a year. Our budget would have demonstrated to the people that we did not blindly follow the World Bank and the IMF regulations. Agreed, we cannot ignore the impact of liberalization and globalization, but we should ensure that they do not adversely affect the interests of the poor and underprivileged sections of our society.

MH: In the event of this government collapsing, there is still talk of you being the consensus opposition candidate for Prime Ministership.

JB: No, no. We are trying to forge a Third Front. The Congress is a secular party no doubt, but it surrenders to communal forces. They need to be self-critical and introspective. So we conceived the idea of a Third Front. Now that regional parties have become powerful, we are trying to contact them as well. But the meeting of leaders will not yield significant results. We have to launch political struggles. We need to tell the people how the central government policies were destroying our country and making us dependent on others. Take, for example, the latest import-export policy. Already our industries are suffering from foreign competition. Even industrialists supportive of the BJP tell me that the RSS itself is deeply resentful of this government's economic policies. Those who once talked of *swadeshi*, are doing *bideshi* (smiles).

MH: Any dramatic moment in your life?

JB: I can't recount any particular experience. But I draw satisfaction from the restoration of parliamentary democracy in West Bengal. People here have created history by voting my party and me to power for 24 long years. This has never happened in India. I'm satisfied with this. I joined politics after returning from London, and I've been a whole-timer thereafter. I have led a busy life. It gets hectic at times.

MH: Are you saddened by the fact that the promised revolution has eluded you and your comrades?

JB: No, no. As I told you, the Soviet Union was for us a big show-piece for what socialism could attain. But, unfortunately, we have experienced a major setback. Sadly, the younger generation is no longer interested in socialism. Still, our party has expanded at all levels in urban as well as rural areas. Yet, as a political party we cannot do everything on our own. There are constraints; so we need everybody's support—businessmen, industrialists and traders.

MH: What is the future of Marxism?

JB: Marxism is a science. Sometimes we move forward, sometimes backwards, depending upon specific conditions. But ultimately Marxism is the answer for us. There had been so much propaganda that capitalism is the last word for human civilization. But that has not happened. Already, a big crisis is brewing in the US. You know what happened in Seattle and in London on 1 May. Don't you? The American working class is organizing huge demonstrations owing to the closure of factories.

MH: As the architect of an industrial policy, you surely don't want Bengal to go the Andhra or Karnataka way. Do you?

JB: Whether it is Karnataka or Andhra or any advanced capitalist state, there is a negative side to their progress. They have done nothing for the landless labourers or peasantry. This sort of lop-sided economic growth will not do.

MH: At the national level, caste and communal formations have gained crowd and isolated the left movement. Is that right?

JB: You are quite right. Earlier, we did not take note of the negative traits of Hindu religion. The caste system has its problem. Untouchability is still prevalent. So, while we try to develop class-consciousness we should have also looked at social practices. As I said, we did not do this in the past. Recently, though, we have started to address this problem.

MH: You have achieved so much during the last 24 years. And yet opposition to the Left Front is mounting in Bengal?

JB: Initially, we received a little more than 50 per cent of the votes, and then our vote share declined. Some positive things have happened, such as land reforms and the introduction of *panchayati raj*. But unemployment is still a serious problem, particularly in urban areas. Earlier, people in the villages demanded land, now they want electricity. We now have a programme that will satisfy the people's rising aspirations.

But, we are already first in so many spheres. We have made primary education free. The Congress ruled for 27 years, but nothing was done in this area. In other areas, too, we started rather late. But now we have 13 new engineering colleges. A year ago, we established the National University in Juridical Sciences in Kolkata. That is doing very well. But sometimes people do not understand. For example, West Bengal alone cannot solve the unemployment problem. We are not a republic, but a part of the Government of India. So we cannot pursue a socialist programme independently.

We feel sorry on one count. We wanted the agrarian and the industrial sectors to develop independently, but we fell back on the industrial front. Industrially, we are in third or fourth position, although we were at the top at the time of Independence. Nowadays things are changing. We've received applications for industrial investment of Rs. 48,000 crore from industrialists based in India and abroad. We have built the biggest petrochemical complex at Haldia; already, we have captured 50 per cent of the market in the eastern region. In Salt Lake, we are trying to develop an electronic and IT complex. We urged Indira Gandhi to help us, but she did not respond. So we went ahead on our own. Our universities are teaching computers, electronics and modern sciences. So, we are coming up. That's all what I can say.

MH: How do you react to the saffronization of education? Why are the apparently secular parties in the NDA quiet?

JB: No, no. Those people have completely changed. George Fernandes was a labour leader when we knew him. He was in V.P. Singh's cabinet. But all that has changed. If people change this way, what can be done? But people change in other ways as well. That we know from our own experience in West Bengal. In 1946 there were only three Communist MLAs here. For the last 24 years, we have been the ruling party. During this period, people from other parties have joined us.

As for saffronization, it is terrible. Not only saffronization of education but everything is wrong with this government— their political and economic policies. This government has adopted the path of barbarism and uncivilized conduct. But, anyway, this combine enjoys a majority in Parliament; the BJP alone secured 25 per cent votes in the last election.

There is not only saffronization of education, but in every sphere of life the rulers in Delhi are trying to divide the people along religious lines. The method they adopted to demolish the Babri Masjid was uncivilized and barbaric. The Liberhan Commission summoned me. I had to appear twice. I told them that I had nothing much to say, except that I have in my possession the recorded speech of Kalyan Singh in Kolkata. He had stated that, while the contractors would have taken to pull down the mosque in one-and-a-half month, the *karsevaks* accomplished the task in five minutes.

Now, the Trinamul has brought the BJP into Bengal, although the Hindu Mahasabha leader Dr. Syama Prasad Mookerjee was from this state. Now, some voters have shifted their allegiance to the BJP, though only in one or two parliamentary constituencies. I am deeply saddened by the resurgence of communalism.

But we should remember that the United Front failed at the centre. We supported the UF government, but that experiment failed. That is not our fault. The left parties are running at least three state governments, and we have strong mass organizations. But we are not politically powerful at the national level. We are now trying to find allies. So, a new People's Front has been formed. But this is still leaders' front. On the ground, nothing much has happened yet. We still await the outcome of the elections.

MH: What it is like being a communist after the collapse of the Soviet Union?

JB: We felt very sad about something that we thought would never happen, i.e. the demise of the Soviet Union. But, then, we are Marxists. Marxism is a science. How long it would take to establish socialism or communism we do not know. Nobody can predict. But we are satisfied that China—the largest country in terms of population—bases itself on Marxism-Leninism. And, then, countries like Cuba, Vietnam, Kampuchea and Laos are also socialistic. We feel encouraged by them. But we must draw lessons from the failure of socialism. As Marxists, we have to be realistic. We derive lessons from the failures as well as the successes of the working of socialism in the contemporary world.

5 May 2001

Performance, not Ideology, Counts _____

Kolkata
5 May 2001

Driving along the Eastern Metropolitan bypass towards the southern reaches of Kolkata, we were reminded of the Bengali novelist Gajendra Kumar Mitra's novel—*Kolkatar Kache*—describing the area as a large swamp interspersed with small settlements. Predominantly rural, this locality offered, in 1947, refuge to the evacuees from East Bengal.

Now, of course, the electric suburban railway network that connects the district with the Calcutta metropolis replaces the steam engine. Though thatched mud-built huts still predominate, the urban build-ups along the main thoroughfare have all the marks of concrete jungle with shopping arcades, cinema halls and STD/ISD booths. What West Bengal thinks today may not influence the rest of the country, but this state is most certainly catching up with other metropolitan cities. To be sure, a signboard on the road to the Netaji Subhas Chandra Bose airport announces: 'Women, Learn English and Social Manners: Contact. . . .'

Our first halt was Jagatdal, a sleepy village in Sonarpur. This is a Scheduled Caste constituency with a large concentration of Poundiyas, the local caste name being Pod. Once a riverbed, Sonarpur is now inhabited by 6,000 people, mostly agriculturists. Sitting with Debiprasad Chakrabarty, a retired schoolteacher, we recounted the history of this village, its landscape dotted by ancient Shiva temples, old but dilapidated houses, and beautiful bamboo and palm trees. The numerous ponds lend colour and depth to the calm atmosphere prevalent in this tiny hamlet.

After Independence, this region was profoundly affected by the Tebagha movement (1947-8), and by the first United Front government's decision to get rid of the *jotedars* belonging to the Nashkar and Bag families. Jagatdal, with its lush vegetation, provides a perfect setting for writing a novel. Today, the social profile of this village, as indeed the constituency as a whole, has changed. Many of its 2,07,500 voters are not 'locals', but middle class professionals. They have chosen to live in Jagatdal rather than in Kolkata's crowded localities.

The air is clean, but the political climate is fouled by the intense struggle between the ruling Left Front and its chief adversary, the Trinamul Congress. Although a Left stronghold since 1952, the CPI(M) has performed poorly in the last two Parliamentary elections, the margin in 1999 being as high as 30,000. Sure enough, Mamata Banerjee's bandwagon rolls on in Sonarpur, which is part of her South Calcutta Parliamentary constituency. She has won many a heart; her vision of removing the 'red menace' is, indeed, shared by her adherents. Mohammad Shan, cycling to her rally last week, sang paeans of praise for a leader who, according to him, was upright with an unblemished political record. A Muslim widow in the neighbouring village headed towards the same site. Her grievance—the CPI(M) had done nothing whatsoever to alleviate her sufferings after the death of her husband in a car accident. Like many others, she is indifferent to the fall out of the *tehelka.com* episode or the consequences of Mamata's alliance with the Congress.

What accounts for the change? The trend here, which must worry the CPI(M) candidate Abha Mandal, is no different from most other constituencies where performance rather than ideology matters most. In Sonarpur, however, the dialectics of economic growth and development is crucially important. From the 1980s, improved communication and enlarged economic opportunities, resulting from land reclamation, agricultural farming and pisciculture, have drawn migrants to this area from the Sunderbans, a large concentration of water mass and forests in the Gangetic delta. Many of them happen to be the erstwhile *jotedars*, who had been pushed out of their holdings during Operation Barga. It is indeed this social group that forms the nucleus of the current anti-Left opposition. As a matter of fact, one can see this factor being important in several other constituencies as well where the *jotedars*, now impoverished owners of 4 or 5 *bighas*, are beginning to recover some of their lost prestige and influence. Part of their resurgence is attributed to their involvement in local communal and anti-Left politics.

The recent erosion in the vote bank of the Left is attributed to the Left's failure to educate the younger generation, many of whom have only faded memories of the Left's revolutionary past. As a result, the Left is widely perceived as an establishment-oriented political force clinging to power and distributing patronage to its clients. The local Left political activists admit this, as does Anil Biswas, secretary of the state unit of the CPI(M). The fact is that the Left, commonly designated as a 'bourgeoisie' party by its detractors, has achieved a great deal more than the centrist or the Left of centre formations in the rest of India.

The contest in neighbouring Baruipur is also poised for an interesting finish. In 1991 and 1996, the Congress won with a narrow margin. But, in the 1998 by-election, the CPI(M) youth leader, Sujan Chakrabarti, wrested the seat. So far so good. Regardless of the party's success in winning 29 out of the 33 wards in the municipality, left activists are now concerned with the TMC's improved showing in the last Parliamentary election. Consequently Sujan Chakrabarti, with a doctorate in Pharmacy from the Jadavpur University, can hope to draw political mileage only from the disillusionment with the TMC's performance in the constituency, and from its ill-advised fraternization with Sonia Gandhi's Congress. He is confident that he has achieved much during his tenure, but all the voters may not accept his claims. We sensed this in Mallikpur, a traditional Congress stronghold. A classic example of civic neglect, Mallikpur village, with its large concentration of Bengali and Bihari Muslims, reminds you of the poverty and misery of fellow-citizens living in rural India. This could be any village—in eastern UP or north Bihar.

Generally speaking, trends in Muslim vote will be similar to the trends in the rest of the population, i.e. it will be based on their perception of the Left Front's ability to deliver. Unilke UP and Bihar, the minorities have benefited as a result of land reforms and rural development programmes, along with other groups in rural Bengal. Till September 2000, 10.45 lakh acres of agricultural land have been distributed among 25.44 lakh beneficiaries, of whom a considerable number belong to the minorities, especially in the Malda, Murshidabad and Nadia districts. No wonder, academic surveys have indicated that the Muslim voters generally function as a class rather than a religious community.

However, Sonarpur, owing to its proximity to Calcutta, may well turn out to be an exception. In the constituency as a whole, Muslims constitute 25 per cent of the population. Many of them are disillusioned with Mamata Banerjee for having joined the BJP-led coalition at the Centre, though Thursday's public rally, addressed by Sonia Gandhi and Mamata Banerjee in Burdwan, attracted large numbers of Muslims. Possibly, they turned up to assess the prospects of the Trinamul-Congress *entente*. The fact is that the people we talked to invoke quite passionately, the demolition of the Babri Masjid and the recent episode in Kanpur, which triggered a massive communal riot. Time and again they gave vent to their anger, in our presence, against the *Sangh Parivar* and its former ally, the TMC.

Again, you can hear such voices all over West Bengal. Muslim voters, having rallied round Mamata for a brief spell, wonder if it is at all worth reposing their confidence in the TMC. Perhaps, the CPI(M) was a far more dependable ally. 'It has provided, after all, security of life and property to the Muslims', says Justice K.M. Yusuf, chairman of the West Bengal Minorities' Commission. Maybe, Sujan Chakrabarti derives his confidence, nay exuberance, from such sentiments in his own constituency. At the same time, he knows well enough that both the Sonarpur and the Baruipur seats would be prized possessions in the race for crossing the magic figure of 147 in the 294 strong West Bengal Assembly.

All said and done, electioneering in Sonarpur and the Baruipur, as indeed in the peri-urban areas around the metropolis are low-keyed. High decibel election meetings are a rarity in this election. In the suburban trains moving to and from the city, commuters seem to be tight-lipped. This is in sharp contrast to the enthusiasm generated by previous elections. The reason is that people are generally wary of, and fed up with, the frequency of elections. The reason is also that they are distrustful of politicians. Arguably, this breeds cynicism. The reason could well be that the electorate is, for once, unsure of which way the wind is blowing. This is probably what has led to violence in some areas. Our impression is that, in a highly polarized pre-poll scenario, the electorate has already made up its mind about whom to vote for. As the Bengali song goes:

Pathe ebar namo sathi
Pathei hobe path chena

Comrades, step on to the streets,
Only then will you know your streets.

6 May 2001

Catching the Breeze in Rural Bengal_____

New Delhi
16 May 2001

'One should be grateful', wrote Mirza Ghalib in 1827, 'that such a city exists. Where else in the world is there a city so refreshing. To sit in the dust of Calcutta is better than to grace the throne of another dominion. By God, had I not been a family man. . . I would have cut myself free and made my way there. . . . How delightful are its cool breezes, and how pleasant is its water! How excellent are its pure wines and its ripe fruits!' With its land vegetation and huge expanses of water, rural Bengal is equally enchanting. Let me give you a sense of my journey in another area, far removed from Haryana, where people speak Bangla and not Haryanvi, live differently, and relate to their world differently.

We travelled for approximately seventy kilometres on the

Kona Expressway, took a left turn at Bagnan, reached the crossroads at Shyampur before heading for Gadiara in Howrah district. Unlike most parts of UP, the land of Aryavarta, and Bihar, where a prince became a mendicant more than 2,500 years ago to find an answer to human suffering, we saw clear signs of progress and prosperity. In sharp contrast to eastern UP, there weren't many mud and thatched houses. Instead, the rural landscape is dotted with schools, health centres, roadside shops, and STD/ISD telephone booths. Nuntia village, for instance, has a Gramin Bank, a primary school, a junior high school, and a hospital at Mugkalyam, just 2 km away. Part of the Bagra Assembly constituency, it has 38 per cent Muslims, mostly masons, agriculturists and artisans.

One did not encounter, as one does driving to Aligarh, children—mostly naked, with hair matted and faces caked with dirt—standing listlessly at the *dhabas* on the Grand Trunk Road. I did not see emaciated peasants or thin women wearing tattered clothes. Stubborn critics may say what they like, but Operation Barga has truly transformed rural Bengal's lifestyle. The CPI(M), now in power for another five-year term, has faltered on many counts. At the same time, it has been the chief catalyst for a major revolution in rural areas. Given the party's record, its electoral victory in last week's election was not surprising. Performance, based on ideology, has ultimately paid off in this election.

Gadiara is on the confluence of the Ganga and Rupnagar rivers. Its dilapidated Shikargah (hunting house), the only surviving monument, is a reminder of the days when the rajas of Mahishadal exercised sway over this *zamindari* settlement. The crumbling structure of what was once a rice mill, started in 1938, is symbolic of West Bengal's industrial decline precipitated by the rationing and cordoning that took place, in 1963-4, under the aegis of the then Chief Minister, Ajoy Mukherjee. The combined strength of the rice mill-owners and the *jotedars* ultimately led to his ministry's downfall.

Today, the staff of the tourist lodge occupies the building that housed the mill office. The erstwhile rajas are, on the other hand, lost in the mists of history, though their nineteenth century palace and temple is intact across the river in Mahishadal. The eighteenth century palace of Rani Janaki is in ruins. A popular myth is that she was a relentless anti-British crusader. Another local legend is that the British built a fort with an underground tunnel, and that these are still to be seen, despite the level agricultural land, when the water recedes during low tide.

Gadiara, a place with 122 households (approximately 2,000 people), is inhabited by a dozen Brahmin families who live at the edge of the village, the Majhis and Bagdis (Scheduled Castes), and the Mahishyas (earlier known as Kaivarta), the principal agricultural caste in south-west Bengal. At the turn of the nineteenth century, many local Mahishya associations mushroomed in different districts to assert their identity. By the 1920s, they had been mobilized on the issue of social status. Once this was achieved, it became easy for the Mahishyas to resist unpopular government measures and stake their claim in power structures. Their leader was a Mahishya lawyer from Contai, Birendranath Sasmal, and a close lieutenant of C.R. Das.

Today, the Mahishyas are economically well placed in Gadiara. They own the boats that carry wood from the Sundarbans, a journey that can take up to a week. They employ the Scheduled Caste Bagdis to perform this arduous task. With improved river communication and the introduction of launchers and steamers eight years ago, the wheel of fortune has swung their way.

Being the principal landowners in the area, the Mahishyas benefit from the rotation of two rice crops. For them the great breakthrough has been the spring rice crops, with average yields of 6/7quintals. No wonder, price of agricultural land has increased phenomenally over the last couple of decades—from Rs. 6,000 to 30,000. You may have to shell out as much as Rs. 5 lakh for a *bigha* anywhere between the bus stand and the tourist lodge. The road link to Kolkata—it did not exist in the early-1970s—has not only enhanced the value of land but opened up new markets for the agricultural produce.

All this means greater social cohesion in village life. It means that every householder has enough rice to eat. Even the landless, mostly Bagdis, can lease out land from the Mahishyas for Rs. 1,000, invest twice the amount on fertilizers, and expect a yield of 7/8 quintals that will fetch a market price of Rs. 5,000. This arrangement works out amicably. 'Earlier', Mahaim Majhi explained to us, 'caste taboos existed, but now we break bread with the Mahishyas. We worship at the temple. Fifteen years ago it was not possible.' A bearer at the tourist lodge, he earns up to Rs. 5,000 a month. His four daughters and son go to school. No wonder, he sings paeans of praise for the CPI(M) government. Incidentally, this tiny village has a primary health centre, a primary school, a high school and a girl's school, just three kilometres from Gadiara.

As the night descended on this village, the brightly-lit Falta in the distant horizon offered a spectacular view from Gadiara. Now a free port, the British had taken refuge at Falta in 1756, following Nawab Siraj ud-Daulah's seizure of Kolkata and re-naming it as Alinagar. It was time to return to the modern, noisy and dusty city of Alinagar.

Mahaim Majhi joined us on a short ride. Noticing the *khadi* bag he carried, I asked: 'Have you heard of Subhas Bose?' 'Yes', came the prompt reply. 'And Gandhiji?' 'No', he said before stepping on the street clasping his *khadi jhola*. I was speechless.

16 May 2001

PART VII

In the Corridors of Academia

Representation of an Intellectual

Antonio Gramsci, the Italian Marxist imprisoned by Mussolini between 1926 and 1937, wrote in his Prison *Note-books* that, 'all men are intellectuals, but not all men have in society the function of intellectuals'. The career of several individuals in our long and chequered history exemplifies the role he ascribed to the intellectual.

I shall not trace their career but merely clarify two points. First, I do not presume that the intellectuals, now or before, have ever constituted a unified and homogeneous group; second, a well-known definition of an intellectual is one who works in any field connected with the production or distribution of knowledge. Edward Said's argument is that intellectuals are individuals with a vocation for the art of representing, whether that is talking, writing, teaching, appearing on television. And that vocation is important to the extent that it is publicly recognizable and involves commitment and risk, boldness and vulnerability.

Over the last many centuries, we have had an unbroken record of celebrated and energetic dissenters—from Gautam Buddha to the eclectic Bhakti saints, the nonconformist Sufis, and scores of writers and poets. Nineteenth-century reform movements and the rise of nationalism sustained this long-standing tradition. Its main carriers were the intellectuals, 'the fathers and mothers of movements, and of course sons and daughters, even nephews and nieces'. Starting with Rammohun Roy and the Brahmo Samaj, the reformist landscape bore the imprint of many ideas that flowed from diverse traditions and perspectives. Quite often the reformers neither spoke nor acted in unison; yet they critiqued their own society and its values so as to construct a social order that will harmonize with their own world view and with the currents of change and enlightenment. They indicted many aspects of colonialism and highlighted its exploitative character.

The dawn of freedom precipitated the fragmentation of the intellectual élites. The most creative and vocal group amongst them, notably the Marxists, found it increasingly difficult to reconcile their ideology with what they thought was a bourgeois and oppressive postcolonial state. Some remained dogged in their opposition, while many others, moved by Nehru's socialist rhetoric, lent legitimacy to his authority and backed his nation-building enterprises.

The same process was at work nearly a decade later during Indira Gandhi's tenure as Prime Minister. More and more liberal-left intellectuals, overwhelmed by her populist measures, including the abolition of privy purses, joined the Congress bandwagon. Though most did so for ideological rather than personal reasons, it was nonetheless an ill-advised and ill-fated decision. This, they discovered, the hard way. Having pressed them into service to bolster her personal authority in the Congress party, Mrs. Gandhi discarded them when it politically suited her to do so.

At the same time, most liberal-left intellectuals did not make their peace with the establishment. All said and done, we still have our share of Jean Paul Sartres, Noam Chomskys, Gore Vidals and Edward Saids. So many of them have stepped into the public arena to debate some of the contentious issues over the last decade or so, the nuclear explosion being the latest. Historians, R.S. Sharma, Irfan Habib and Romila Thapar included, have intervened in civil society at considerable personal risk, though their erudition is derided and their secular credo is assailed in certain circles. Now that the balance of power has shifted from the centre to the right, a campaign is underway to damn the liberal-left intellectuals by removing them from centres of learning. They are being replaced, without any consideration for merit, by a fresh breed of intellectual managers-cum-ideologues.

Pockets of resistance to the attempted ideological homogenization of our intellectual life exist. But, in general, there is much greater acquiescence in, and acceptance, of authoritarian trends. Premier universities, once the focal point of feverish political activity, have become the bastions of political conservatism. If somebody wants to breach the citadel of orthodoxy in educational institutions, he or she must be prepared to pay a heavy price. Today, as the radical currents have been swept aside by the winds of right-wing discourses, at least momentarily, not many heed the Saidian dictum that 'nothing disfigures the intellectuals' public performance as much as trimming, careful silence, patriotic bluster, and retrospective and self-dramatising prophecy'.

The print media has lost its independent spirit, and is often hand in glove with the political establishment. Enterprising journalists travel far and wide to install new icons to gain favours from them. All that matters are slot in Doordarshan, an overseas trip with the Prime Ministerial entourage, and free housing. This does not augur well for democracy. Any kind of allegiance to the state is itself problematic, more so when it invariably leads to distorted perspectives.

Where do we go from here? I am not presumptuous enough to suggest a course of action for the intellectuals. Generally speaking, I believe that an intellectual cannot enjoy credibility without raising embarrassing questions, without confronting orthodoxy and dogma, rather than producing them, and without representing all those people and issues that are routinely forgotten or swept under the rug. Edward Said, whose views I have just quoted, should know better. He is my idea of an intellectual *par excellence*.

3 September 1999

Exploring Intellectual Self-doubt

Nobody seems interested in a serious appraisal of the deep and endemic problems afflicting higher education. Education-ists comment on the declining academic standards, cynical journalists take delight in covering campus violence, and aggrieved teachers complain of low salaries, poor housing, and unsatisfactory working conditions.

Yes, we have been wronged, but must share the blame for the current crisis in our educational system. We agitate for higher wages but do little to promote higher and innovative standards of teaching and research. We promote our material interests but do not take a principled stand on what threatens to divide and weaken our society. We seek promotions without concern for academic norms and qualifications. Learning and research in our universities is less important now than ever before. In university teaching, what is important is knowledge of one's subject and keenness about what is being done in it. I believe many of my colleagues are not sensitive to this fact.

Shelley describes the day's work of a poet as follows:

> He will watch from dawn to gloom
> The lake-reflected sun illumine
> The honeybees in the ivy bloom,
> Nor heed nor see what things they be.

These habits are praiseworthy in a poet but not, shall we say, in a teacher. We cannot frame our education, as Bertrand Russell pointed out in his eminently readable book *On Education*, with a view to giving everyone the temperament of a poet. Yet some of the characteristics he elucidated are universally desirable and apply to poet and teacher alike. Let me therefore turn to a Hindi novel published recently. I do so because the storyline centres on the literati, their hierarchies, jealousies, factions, and insecurities. The novel brings out the fears and anxieties of educated men and women, and uncovers their reactions and responses in a riot-stricken town.

Geetanjali Shree, the author, wrestles with many ideas, some conventional, others bearing the mark of originality. If read as an intellectual statement, *Hamara Shahar Us Baras* underlines the anxieties of the intelligentsia. The characters, mainly located in a familiar environment, speak intelligibly and voice concerns all too well known in academic circles. The author's own claim is that she 'wanted to write a novel on a subject repeated ad nauseam, expressing new doubts and fears, seeking some clarity, and in a style so easy that it will even be discursive'.

Hamara Shahar Us Baras deals with many facets of university life, some of which are obscured by the rhetoric typical of many a teacher's association. The demolition of the Babri Masjid and its bloody aftermath is the principal reference point; the communal scene prevalent in much of north India through the 1980s unfolds in the novel. The town is a microcosm of heightened communal feeling in the national and provincial arena. Something sinister is creeping into the atmosphere, revealing itself not just in the bloody outbursts but also in the language and discourse gaining currency among the educated. A 'new' person appears with a project to divide people. The propagandists to undermine composite living invent a new identity.

Some characters, living on the fringes of a volatile urban life, reflect on riots, discuss the dynamics of religiosity and religious politics, and think of dealing with the communal menace. They are engaged with the nation and the notions of identity politics in contemporary India. But this exercise, like many intellectual exegeses, does not take them very far. Some have inherited prejudices towards the other and are susceptible to communal propaganda. That is why the stereotypical image of a Muslim, bigoted, intolerant and *kasai ka kaam karte hain* (dealing with blood and gore), recurs throughout. That is why history is being rewritten in the bazar and the *dhaba* to detail how Muslim rulers defiled temples and forcibly converted people.

In the end, these intellectuals emerge confused, helpless and fearful of tearing themselves from their social and cultural upbringing. *Hamara Shahar Us Baras* traces the contours of this fearful confusion, fearful because 'we cannot understand, but we must understand, or else we are just going to be swamped under'. The invisible and undefined narrator records their words, thoughts, feelings, and actions. The novel becomes a collage of apparently disjointed fragments, reflecting the trauma and agony of the 'town in that year'.

Don't look for the town on the map or its description in the gazetteer. That town, bruised and battered by the doings of unreconstructed communalists with an insatiable appetite for killing and destruction, is everywhere in India. 'That year' too is not specific. The threat to communal peace does not recede in that town or, for that matter, in any other town.

The 'I' unravels the lives of four principal characters—Hanif,

Shruti, Sharad and Daddu—who live under the same roof. Daddu is a venerable landlord, a father figure; Sharad, his son, teaches at a university; Hanif is Sharad's friend and colleague; Shruti is a writer married to Hanif. Each one of them is anguished by worsening Hindu-Muslim relations and eventually drawn into the vortex of communal politics. Hanif, in particular, feels insecure in his own faculty. Even radical and liberal colleagues sensitize him to his 'Muslim' identity. Why, wonders Sharad. What's this glib talk of secularism on the campus? Why victimize Hanif? Doubts, doubts and more doubts. Shruti is convinced that Hanif has been wronged. How is Hanif different from her when they share a common identity? Daddu is different. He does not share such feelings. He isn't overwhelmed by the escalation of violence.

The novel ends where it begins. Daddu, the ever-joyous old cynic, retreats into silence. Torn by conflicting loyalties, Hanif and Sharad drift apart. Shruti is seen visiting Sharad and Daddu. *Hamara Shahar Us Baras* is a collage of life in 'unnatural times', a 'consciousness' which is scary. A life and consciousness one must begin to understand.

3 October 1998

Murder of a Language:
Time for an Epitaph

'Hindi Divas' was celebrated last week, though without much fanfare. There was much cause to celebrate, for Hindi has progressed over the last couple of decades despite the initial hiccups. It flourishes in and outside the 'cow belt'. It has gained legitimacy, quite justifiably, as the national language. This was the message that former Prime Minister H.D. Deve Gowda tried to communicate from the ramparts of the Red Fort on 15 August 1996.

Yet such symbolic gestures are not good enough. There are still powerful linguistic groups who are arrayed against Hindi, though their resistance is much less pronounced now than before. Some sections continue to identify Hindi with Hindu revivalism and the *Hindutva* ideology, though the correlation is often stretched a bit too far. Let us not forget that secular nationalism was expressed through this language. Let us not forget that Hindi prose and poetry are not devoid of eclectic and composite ideas and refined sensibilities. That is one of the many reasons why it is the language of the subaltern classes, particularly in UP, Rajasthan, Madhya Pradesh and Bihar. Members of various religious communities also speak it. Not only do Muslims speak the language, but have enriched its literature. Have we, for example, forgotten the creative genius of Jaisi, Rahim and Raskhan? Or the contributions of Rahi Masoom Reza, Badiuzzaman and Abdul Bismillah in our own times?

Still, it is frequently argued that the vocal protagonists of Hindi have, through their insularity and conservatism, reinforced their image of being 'Hindu' in orientation, aggressive in approach, and intolerant towards other languages. There is an element of exaggeration in such representations, but this is not what I want to contest in this article. What is perhaps worth pointing out in passing is that Hindi's future rests with the Hindi-wallahs and their willingness to distance, if not delink, their language from its exclusive 'Hindu' specificity. Slogans like *Hind, Hindu, Hindi—yeh tin hamare liye ek hain* (Hindi, or India, Hindu and the Hindi language are the same for us) *or Hindi suchmuch Ram Rajya ki bhasha hai* (Hindi is truly the language of Ram-Rajya) can hardly serve the cause of Hindi. It is important to accept, howsoever belatedly, the richness and variety of other literary and cultural traditions. The present signs are not encouraging.

Consider the anti-Urdu campaigns spearheaded by the Hindi Sahitya Sammelan before and after Independence. Its leaders were instinctively hostile to any trace of Muslim or Islamic inheritance, and hence Hindustani, which they saw as a mask for Urdu, was anathema to them. They depicted Urdu as a

Muslim language, which it was not, identified it with the Pakistan movement, and claimed that its style was distinctly 'unnational', if not anti-national. The position of Hindi was assured after the Constituent Assembly declared it as the national language, Urdu was not its rival. Yet, active and aggressive campaigns were mounted to suppress the language of Mir and Ghalib, spoken by millions of people of all religious creeds and a vital and graceful aspect of a vibrant composite tradition in the Indo-Gangetic belt.

Not much has changed over the last five decades. The establishment-oriented Urdu speakers boast of numerous Urdu Academies and Translation Bureaus, housed in elegant buildings with plenty of funds to dole out to friends and admirers. Some take pride in Urdu being the language of Bollywood; others draw satisfaction from awards and scholarships given to literary figures in the glittering halls of the Raj Bhawans and the Rashtrapati Bhawan. Some derive comfort from the mere fact that *mushairas*, where sections of the audience pronounce Ghalib as Galib and applaud poor quality romantic 'poetry', attract larger audiences than *kavi sammelans*.

In reality, Urdu has been marginalized in the country as a whole. Even the democratic and secular forces have not shown much inclination to defend a language that symbolizes our composite heritage. In UP, the then Chief Minister, V.P. Singh, after failing to act on repeated promises, finally issued an ordinance in 1982 granting Urdu the status of a 'second language' (not second official language). His government did not convert the ordinance into legislation. Five years later when the Vidhan Sabha adopted the Official Language (Amendment) Bill in 1989 amid unruly scenes, the BJP MLAs stormed into the well and raised slogans like *Urdu Bill Murdabad* (Death to the Urdu Bill) and *Ek Rajya, ek Bhasha, nahi chahiye dusri Bhasha* (One state, one language, a second language is not required).

Urdu survives lazily in the alleys and by-lanes of Muslim localities. It has lost its position in Osmania University, Hyderabad, Delhi's Jamia Millia, and the Aligarh Muslim University. An Urdu University' languishes in Aligarh; another one is in the making at Hyderabad. Except for some districts in UP and Bihar, Urdu has ceased to be the language of administration, the judiciary, and the police. Even symbolic attempts to promote Urdu have led to a violent backlash. Thus, riots were triggered when the UP government decided to make Urdu the state's second official language in 1989. Ten-minute Urdu television news bulletin in Bangalore led to riots in October 1994, leaving 30 dead.

Urdu poetry? 'How can there be Urdu poetry when there is no Urdu language left? It is dead, finished. The defeat of the Mughals by the British threw a noose over its head, and the defeat of the British by the Hindi-wallahs tightened it. So now you see its corpse lying here, waiting to be buried.' This is not just the anguish of a living Urdu poet in Anita Desai's novel, but a summation of the grievance of Urdu-speakers all over the country. The story of a weak, gasping poet in *In Custody* is, indeed, the story of Urdu language and poetry.

Urdu is necessary to promote multiculturalism. Its creative potential must be encouraged and not stifled in the interest of a nation-wide literary and cultural Renaissance and the flowering of our languages. The Indian State should, in this fiftieth year of Independence, take tangible steps to establish Urdu schools and colleges and train Urdu teachers who are in short supply. One hopes I.K. Gujral and S.R. Bommai, friends of Urdu, are listening.

20 September 1997

Save Education from Bigots

Education is the key to the New World; indeed, the essence of a vibrant democracy lies in a long-term, well-conceived and coherent education policy. Coherence is the keyword, for a country like ours can ill-afford to drastically amend or subordinate its educational strategies to suit the ideology of the ruling élites.

Politicians and political parties may understand what constitutes good education, but they should avoid imposing their ideological preferences on a culturally and linguistically diverse population. The teacher, like the artist, the philosopher, and the man of letters, can only perform her work adequately if she feels herself to be an individual directed by an inner creative impulse, not dominated and fettered by an outside authority. We have made rapid strides in the realm of higher education, but the progress in basic education has been unsatisfactory. Many goals set out at the time of Independence have yet to be realized. The Constitution laid down that within a period of 10 years there should be universal, free and compulsory education for all children until the age of 14 years, but it is manifestly beyond our capacity to fulfil this directive principle for years to come.

The growing gap between higher education and elementary education led the Nobel Laureate Amartya Sen to argue that the inequalities in education in India are, in fact, a reflection of inequalities of economic and social powers of different groups. Finally, education planners had hoped that education will help to draw out the best in child and man—body, mind and spirit. This too has not been translated into practice, as is demonstrated by the crisis faced by our education system. Some of these areas require attention and prompt remedial measures.

Instead, politicians and bureaucrats dissipate their energies raking up fresh controversies. The task of placing a fragile education system on a sound footing is periodically deferred in response to the changing political climate. Scores of reports and recommendations drafted by eminent educationists, are wilfully ignored. Even if rescued from the dusty shelves, they will make little sense unless we have some conception of the kind of citizen we wish to produce. Appropriately enough, Gandhi wrote the following in the context of his reflections on the dowry system:

There is something radically wrong in the system of education that fails to arm girls and boys to fight against social or other evils. That education alone is of value which draws out the faculties of a student so as to enable him or her to solve correctly the problems of life in every department.

Education, as the Mahatma's comment illustrates, concerned the nationalist leaders and was integral to their vision of transforming India as a whole. Gandhi, for one, mooted a scheme known as 'Basic Education', to counter the ill effects of the Western-style education, which produced generations of students, whose main ambition was to obtain a secure job. The Wardha scheme enshrined many of the ideals and innovations the Mahatma had worked out. Interestingly enough, the scheme omitted, presumably with Gandhi's approval, any provision for formal religious instruction, leaving this to parents.

Though a devout Hindu, he did not want his own world view to be reflected in the curriculum. Education was, after all, the instrument to unite people and not to widen areas of religio-cultural conflicts. His overriding concern in public life was to weld different castes and communities into a coherent whole so as to create a strong and unified nation. And his real strength lay in not harbouring bitterness or hatred for anyone. Nehru, who was sensitive to the Gandhian legacy, laid stress on providing a moral and ethical tone to education.

Arguing that being a secular state did not imply disregard for moral values or India's rich spiritual heritage, he desired an ethical content in instruction imparted in schools and colleges. He did not, however, want this to be done without reference to any particular religion. This message, which captured the secular character of the liberation struggle, was not lost on the framers of the Constitution. They recognized, even after Partition, the intrinsic connections between democracy, multiculturalism, and the obligation to protect minority rights.

Thus Articles 29 and 30 of the Constitution summed up the position of the minority groups and delineated howsoever ambiguously, their relationship with the secular state. Amending such provisions will militate against the tone and tenor of the Constitution, raise cultural and religious fears, alienate the minorities, and make them more susceptible to communal propaganda. A national government needs to address itself to the challenge of national reconstruction and not reduce itself to being an ideologue of a particular viewpoint. It must endeavour to evolve and sustain a consensus around symbols of national unity and national regeneration, and avoid messing around with religious and cultural susceptibilities. The issue is not the appeasement of minorities, which should at any rate be eschewed. What are at stake are the future of secular democracy and the preservation of our multicultural inheritance. The recent controversies around culture, nationalism and history writing are of a complex nature and cannot be resolved through polemical exchanges or the denigration of individuals.

Men who talk of Hindu culture, Nehru told the Nagpur University students in 1950, miss the basic human culture and show a narrow, barren, and limited outlook on life. They are completely against the assimilating and absorbing nature of India's ancient and glorious culture. He was surprised that, in the complicated and fascinating world of today, with a hundred varieties of principles and experiences, there were people talking in the narrowest, in the most limited way of nationalism and of India. 'Anybody will tell you that India has shown an amazing capacity to assimilate and absorb other ideas. A people who can do so must have inner strength provided, of course, they are not swept away by any poisonous wind that blows.' But, as Nehru told the same audience, 'keep your windows and doors of your mind always open. Let all winds from the four corners of the earth blow in to refresh your mind, to give you ideas, to strengthen you. . . .' In other words, Nehru envisaged that a change in the political regime will not jettison the consensus reached in the Constituent Assembly on democracy, secularism, and the educational and religious rights of the minorities. The need for that consensus to survive is greater now than ever before.

31 October 1998

Something's Foul in the Corridors of Academia

At a time when our own institutions starve of funds, we go around distributing largesse to some well-endowed universities overseas. At a time when primary/secondary education needs greater state support, the central universities siphon off scarce resources allocated to education. At a time when the world is trying to harmonize sectarian differences and create a forward-looking and enlightened world view, our latest blueprint for education seems potentially divisive. Even part-time education-ists have joined in the cacophony of noises, making serious demands on the teaching fraternity to 'perform'. Some have taken upon themselves the responsibility of devising strict codes of conduct not for themselves but for us.

A favourite pastime is to bemoan the presence of delinquent teachers in our ranks. Sadly enough, nobody records scores of brilliant students produced by their own colleagues. Our temples of learning continue to have large numbers of prayer leaders and learners, but their single-minded devotion rarely figures in the voluminous educational reports that are periodic-ally compiled only to be consigned to the dustbin of history. According to the vice-chancellor of Jawaharlal Nehru Uni-versity, 90 per cent of the teachers take their classes regularly; the faculty published 300 books and 1,700 research articles between 1995 and 1999. It is not just JNU that keeps the academic publishing industry in business; other institutions too have contributed their bit to scholarship.

Mind you, the performance of prayer leaders and their adherents is all the more significant because they operate in a system where reward for, or recognition of, merit rarely exists. Remember, too, that these persons, who have virtually no access to state *daan*, continue to publish books, write research papers and, in the process, raise our intellectual profile in the temples of learning located in the rest of the world.

If, on the other hand, educational standards have declined drastically, it is because the state has invested so little in primary and secondary education. Please chide political parties for fouling the corridors of learning with their blatant and unwanted interference in appointment and selection procedures. Please criticize the government for defiling our temples of learning by entrusting to undeserved men and women the responsibility of administering them, and our educational planners for messing around with education for so long and with such tenacity. It will not do to find alibis for their own lack of vision and foresight.

True, our own conduct is not exemplary; indeed, we have much to answer for. Besides suffering from a degree of intellectual inertia, many of us have failed to reform our teaching methods or revise our curriculum from time to time. Indeed, teacher's associations and student's unions do not generate a serious debate on restructuring and modernizing our educational system. As a result, the initiative rests with the government and not the academia. Finally, many of us have insulated ourselves from our neighbourhoods and localities, and abdicated our civic/social responsibilities. It is thus commonplace to defend the *status quo* and jockey for positions in the college/university hierarchy.

Yet, the fraternity of teachers should not be singled out for acts of omission, and harsh standards of judgement should not be applied to them alone. Accountability, a recurring theme in current debates, is a noble ideal. At the same time, other privileged sections of our society should be made accountable to somebody or the other. Politicians go scot-free for five long years before the electorate punishes them, whereas we are berated for demanding our due share.

I believe the conduct of principals, rectors and vice-chancellors be henceforth monitored by a public agency, and not just by ineffectual bodies like the Academic Council and Executive Council. Once this is done, you may well find that some amongst them have, in collusion with vested interests, contributed to the ills that plague our educational life. Some have even encouraged mediocrity, created a coterie of advisers around them, and stifled independent research. Increasingly, they turn to international funding agencies—sometimes without the concurrence of university bodies—to gain political leverage in their institution. Yet, they pontificate from a high moral ground, knowing full well that their stakes in improving higher education is limited to their personal career advancement. The way out is to identify persons with experience and administrative flair, and devise rigorous methods to exclude political nominees.

The ill-conceived merit promotion scheme illustrates how those wielding power used their authority to distribute patronage without any consideration for talent or merit. A bizarre drama of partisanship has been enacted—from Kashmir to Kanyakumari—with academic bodies colluding with the heads of institutions. By a single stroke of pen, the distinction between brilliance and mediocrity was done away with. Again, the solution lies not in reversing a well-established trend, but in providing academic incentives to motivated teachers.

What is disconcerting is the undue government interference. In this respect, two points merit consideration. First, the idea of a uniform curriculum for schools being mooted in certain quarters must be resisted, for it threatens to destroy the multireligious and multicultural character of our society. Second, government agencies should not be allowed to impose their agendas on the already fragile educational structures; indeed, the need to seek autonomy *vis-à-vis* the University Grants Commission and Shastri Bhawan, the home of educational bureaucrats, is greater now than ever before. For this reason, the proposal to depute UGC-appointed 'observers' to Selection Committee meetings betrays a lack of confidence in the vice-chancellor, the nominee of the Visitor, and, above all, the subject experts (two in the case of lecturers/readers, and three for professors).

The current trend to ignore statutory bodies, except when it is convenient to validate a decision, is a recipe for disaster. As an old-fashioned teacher, I repose faith in the mature judgement of my colleagues manning college/university bodies. Some tend to be populist, but most are not. Some may be out of place in the profession, but most are well equipped to perform their duties. That is why they are entitled to a free hand in deciding on matters concerning teaching/research. Independence and autonomy, the hallmark of our educational experimentation, cannot be taken away by idiosyncratic politicians and bureaucrats.

13 December 2000

Academics in Despair: Clutching at CVs

What if, after completing their education, somebody in Great Britain had offered employment to Gandhi, Nehru, Jinnah and Bose? Would they have stayed or returned home, as they eventually did, for personal, professional or ideological reasons? You may insist that serving the British empire was anathema to some of them. On the other hand, somebody else may argue that so many Indians did, after all, journey to London to qualify for the civil service in order to join the 'heaven-born'.

Long ago the 'steel frame' of the empire disappeared but other openings for the young and enterprising graduates grew as Western economy recovered from the effects of World War II. From the early 1970s, scores of students, trained and tutored in our highly subsidized educational system, set their eyes on a career in the West and, more particularly, the United States. Thus, the exodus—call it brain drain, if you like—of doctors, engineers and computer scientists gathered momentum. Believe it or not, some jobs are up for grabs even in social sciences.

So book your passage for Chicago, the venue of the Association of Asian Studies (AAS) meeting next year (2001). Just turn up at this grand annual *tamasha* with your *curriculum vitae* and get yourself interviewed by a selection committee. I did not carry mine to San Diego this year and, therefore, missed the golden opportunity. But I saw young historians and political scientists flocking to the Convention Centre. Basking in the glorious California sunshine, they were trying their luck in this land of milk and honey. In the list of AAS members, I noticed the significant presence of Indian social scientists occupying professorial positions in prestigious American universities. This did something to soothe my national pride. I believe several others from the academia, including a couple of fellow-historians, await the bell to ring from Chicago, Berkeley and Minnesota.

From this distance I can only say *bon voyage* to them. I have no problem at all with those in search of greener pastures. Nor do I support the move, being contemplated in some quarters, of imposing curbs on their settling in the West. In this age, we can surely share the wisdom of Amartya Sen, Ranajit Guha and Gyatri Spivak sitting in Ballia or Basti. There are no consolation prizes or bonus points for those travelling by our city buses to access research libraries, drinking Kutti's tea at the Nehru Memorial Museum & Library, or eating greasy omelettes and *samosas* at Delhi's National Archives *en route* to the unlikely prospect of achieving academic stardom. But, one is still curious to learn why our young and senior scholars left and, more importantly, why others are still going. Why should a professor in Jawaharlal Nehru University or the Delhi School of Economics settle for a similar position in the US? Is it the lure of the crisp American dollars, or the search for a secure and vibrant academic enclave? Is it for children's education, or pure and simple personal career advancement? Perhaps, the HRD Ministry will take time off its mindless ideological crusade and consider the long-term implications of brain drain.

Whatever the reasons, America's gain is India's loss. Nehru's temples of learning are located outside and not within India. The net result is that educational centres are gradually depleted of our best social scientists and, in the process, weakening the intellectual edifice so assiduously built in the 1950s and 1960s. In my own discipline, several eminent historians have either emigrated or declared their intention to do so in the near future. I miss them and bemoan their absence.

How does one account for the loss of academic talent? I do not claim to know the answer, but I do believe that some of our outstanding men and women are simply driven out by the inertia of the system. The long-awaited restructuring in our system, which would have improved the performance of our universities, has not taken place. Instead, we divert the already scarce resources from the universities to research centres. In our universities themselves, we legitimize, thanks to the ill advised 'merit promotion' scheme, mediocrity in the corridors of knowledge. We recognize differentiation in other areas, but we treat, in a spirit of equanimity, good and bad teachers/ researchers alike. Such is our benevolence that we promote teachers regardless of merit and allow them a voice in the decision-making bodies. Such is our commitment to the oral tradition that we appoint professors without expecting them to write a book. It is infuriating when such persons quote French/ German scholars, many of whom are not read in their own countries, and pontificate on how history should or should not be written.

Our system accords no recognition to merit; consequently, delinquents get suitably rewarded with academic promotions and the riches of administrative office. Diligent scholars, on the other hand, find themselves at the receiving end. What this does to the enthusiasm of younger scholars is anybody's guess. A case in point is the relentless persecution of Imtiaz Ahmad, a sociologist at Delhi's Jawaharlal Nehru University. He would have contributed so much more had his colleagues rallied around him to isolate his detractors. By the time they did, he had lost years of his creative life.

For those accustomed to intellectual freedom during the past five decades, barring the Emergency, the disconcerting element is the rise of intolerance, as illustrated by the attack on Asghar Ali Engineer, the resurgence of religious bigotry, and systematic attempts to stifle dissent in civil society. Attacks on the minorities, notably the Christians, the bizarre ICHR episode, and vandalism in places like Kanpur and Varanasi are symptomatic of a deeper malady in society.

Enough is enough. Somebody must draw the proverbial *Lakshman Rekha* and ensure that hoodlums do not destroy freedom and democracy.

Somebody has to tell them that the upsurge of ugly *Hindutva* will destroy the creative energies of our people. Somebody has to remind them of the damage they do to themselves by targeting the likes of M.F. Husain, Dilip Kumar, Deepa Mehta, and Shabana Azmi. We must, instead, value such persons and their contributions. If, on the other hand, the self-styled custodians of knowledge, art and culture do not heed the voice of reason and moderation, many more scholars, aware of what happened in Nazi Germany, will seek refuge in the salubrious climes of the West.

22 March 2000

Lost Causes, Faded Credo

Visiting the *Dar al-ulum* at Deoband last year, we found the atmosphere tense. Students and teachers alike were stricken with fear due to police harassment. One teacher told us, 'in the past we were aligned with the Congress and spearheaded the campaign against the Muslim League. Today, we are targeted as pro-Pakistan agents. This is free India's reward to our sacrifices during the liberation struggle.' Likewise, the Nadwat-al ulama in Lucknow, another Muslim centre with impeccable credentials, has been targeted, more recently by Bajrang Dal activists. Some years ago, the police raided its premises: the mission was to flush out suspected Kashmiris holding Pakistani passport. And now it is the turn of the Jamia, 'a lusty child of the Non-Cooperation' (Nehru).

Innocent students have been brutally assaulted by the police and stigmatized as 'ISI agents', 'Pakistanis', 'anti-nation'. They were rounded up and put in Tihar jail. How can one remind the cops lodged in Shrinivaspuri and Lajpat Nagar police stations of Jamia's nationalist record and its contribution to the freedom struggle? Who is there to tell them that Gandhi, the father of the nation, was one of its founders? Who will list its innumerable architects—Ajmal Khan, Ansari, Devdas Gandhi, A.M. Khwaja, Zakir Husain and A.J. Kidwai?

When founded in October 1920 during the heady days of the Khilafat and non-cooperation days, the Jamia encapsulated two dominant trends. One was reflected in the anti-colonial activism of Muslim theologians; the other stream represented the politically radical segments of the Western-educated intelligentsia. They were the ones who rejected the Aligarh Muslim University's pro-British proclivities and gravitated towards Gandhi and the Congress. In 1935, the Turkish author, Halide Edib, visited the campus in Okhla. Do you know what she found? She noticed the Jamia to be much nearer to the Gandhian movement than any other Muslim institution. Whether others agreed or not, the Jamia *biradari* (fraternity) was convinced of its quintessential role as a national institution, destined to contribute to the shaping of modern India. 'In name Jamia was also a university . . . but in fact it was a camp of the satyagraha volunteers', recalled the Marxist historian K.M. Ashraf who left Aligarh to join Jamia.

Though founded by Muslims, Jamia was Muslim only in name. The atmosphere was mixed and cosmopolitan, thanks to the presence of several Hindu and Christian teachers, including a few from Germany, where the young Zakir Husain, Mohammad Mujeeb and Abid Husain (as also Lohia) learnt their first lessons in nationalism and developed their antipathy towards British colonialism. The theological disputations, which marred campus life in Aligarh, were alien to Jamia's spirit. The communal debates, which turned Aligarh University into 'an arsenal of Muslim India', did not stir passions in Jamia. The consensus was that India's Muslims had deep roots in Indian society, were natural inhabitants of an Indian world, and had much in common with other communities 'in fundamental, religious and moral consciousness, social structure, family life and the general way of living that can easily fit into any national pattern' (Abid Husain).

Jamia's education programme bore the Gandhian imprint

and incorporated some of Tagore's innovations at Santiniketan. Its liberal orientation owed much to Syed Ahmad Khan, the outstanding Aligarh reformer. And Maulana Azad's neo-intellectual modernism, religious universalism and commitment to composite nationalism represented Jamia's essence. No wonder, the Jamia fraternity was deeply disturbed by Iqbal's plea for a Muslim state in north-western India. Do you know what the vice-chancellor, Mohammad Mujeeb, told the chairperson of that meeting, Iqbal? The Muslims, he stated, must live and work with non-Muslims to realize common ideals of citizenship and culture.

Jamia's *raison d'être* was to promote cultural integration, foster composite and syncretic values, and strengthen inter-community ties. As the first chancellor, Ajmal Khan expected students to know each other's culture: 'the firm foundation of a united Indian nationhood depends on this mutual understanding'. Dr. Ansari, Congress president in 1927 and Jamia's chancellor for many years, often said that the future of India must be a field of cooperation between the followers of different faiths. He considered the brotherhood of man as the only real tie, and partition based on religion was, to his mind, artificial and arbitrary. He did not believe in a politically separate community. According to him, people must live by the moral dictates of a religious creed, but theological subtleties and contrived political distinctions must not disturb harmonious living.

Jinnah's agenda ran contrary to the Ajmal-Ansari (or Gandhi-Nehru) project. The Jamia *biradari* lionized Gandhi, their chief benefactor, admired Nehru's vision, and regarded both as models of impeccable political conduct. In the 1930s and 1940s, they accepted Gandhi's guidance in working for an institution free of British control, and promoted his constructive programme without being lured by office, power, and authority. Not surprisingly, the Muslim League in the 1940s rebuked Zakir Husain and his band of followers for turning Jamia into a 'Hindu stronghold' and 'Hinduizing Muslims' through the Wardha scheme of education prepared under the supervision of Gandhi, the 'most astute and cunning hypocrite of all time'.

An institution with a secular and nationalist record could not escape the mob fury that struck terror in Delhi during the 1947 communal holocaust. Jamia's property in Karol Bagh was looted and destroyed. There were other tragedies as well; yet Jamia survived such harrowing times, in Gandhi's opinion, 'like an oasis in the Sahara'.

In its search for moral and political support, Jamia could have turned quasi-religious or quasi-communal after Independence. Nothing of the sort happened. It remained secular and nationalist to the core. Jamia remained true to its ideals partly because men like Zakir Husain and Mujeeb never capitulated before the forces of reaction. This is the legacy the Jamia *biradari* must cherish most. Having been traumatized by an ill-advised agitation in 1992, Jamia must live up to the traditions of Ajmal Khan and Ansari. More recently, it must derive inspiration from men like Anwar Jamal Kidwai, who placed Jamia on the intellectual map of India.

The political landscape of many universities has changed in recent years; the Jawaharlal Nehru University is no longer the bastion of the left; The Visva Bharati is not what it was during Tagore's lifetime. But the Jamia, though troubled, has remained secular and nationalist to the core. 'I look on this,' claimed Mujeeb proudly, 'as a secular school.' Over the decades, its essential character and orientation have remained intact despite the recent fundamentalist murmuring.

As a central university, the Jamia adheres to the guidelines of the UGC in matters of recruitment and admission. Engineering, law, art, education, mass communication and scores of other disciplines are taught there. We, too, have our share of modern and traditional scholars. Please don't conjure up the image of an Islamic institution where *purdah* is prescribed and theology is thrust down everybody's throat. Who knows, such images may have led the police department and its managers in the Home Ministry to treat the Jamia students differently and to use the *lathi* more freely.

Although persecuted and my entry to the university was 'banned' for almost four years by religious zealots, I find most colleagues and students ideologically no different from their counterparts in other centres of learning. There are right wing as well as liberal and left elements; there is space for 'modernists' as well as traditionalists. This being the case, the Delhi police and its patrons in the political establishment will not succeed in their ill-conceived design to destroy the morale of the Jamia community.

Jamia will doubtless overcome the present crisis. True, it will probably take a while for the wounds to be healed. This is not the time to heed the communal rhetoric, and to allow unscrupulous politicians to dirty their hands in the muddy waters. Let the new vice-chancellor settle in and raise the university's academic profile, an agenda neglected by some of his predecessors. For this, he will need everybody's support and cooperation. In the long run, the fate of an institution depends on how well its faculty negotiates with worldwide currents of intellectual development. As somebody who has a stake in the future of the institution, I hasten to add that the Jamia must therefore remain part of and not isolated from the intellectual mainstream. Nehru once said: 'Few institutions succeed in retaining for long the impress of the ideal that gave them birth. They tend to become humdrum affairs, perhaps a little more efficient, but without the enthusiasm that gives life. Jamia, more I think than any other institution I can think of, retained some of the old inspiration and enthusiasm.'

8 November 1995 and *17 May 2000*

*Wailings of an Alumnus*_____

Driving out of Jawaharlal Nehru University in the early hours of the morning last Sunday, I saw scores of policemen walking up and down the street. Four hours later I was in Aligarh Muslim University, 150 km away, to attend my first meeting of the University Court. Here, too, armed policemen escorted me to the conference centre. I hold the old-fashioned view that the university is still a sacred space and must not be violated, except in exceptional circumstances, by the police presence. And, I believe, the onus of redressing the grievances of the students and teachers rests with the university administration. We need imaginative persons at the helm of affairs, who are patient and tactful in dealing with agitations and angry demonstrations. Above all, we need administrators committed to not using the big stick at the slightest provocation. Regardless of their ideology, they must not be allowed to stifle protest and dissent on our campuses.

The Aligarh experience was an eye-opener for other reasons as well. The first startling fact is the monstrous growth in the non-teaching staff—as many as 5,899 (as against 1,457 teachers) to serve 21,105 students. Any kind of pruning may not be possible in the foreseeable future, but the dangers of bureaucratization are too obvious to go unnoticed. Ill-planned expansion of the non-teaching sector will ultimately impose severe strains on the scarce monetary resources, and impede the university's academic growth.

Another disconcerting fact is that this recognized national centre of excellence has ceased to draw students from most parts of the country. Out of its 17,954 Indian students, as many as 13,155 are drawn from UP. Additional 2,912 students come from Bihar. Evidently, the university's regional as well as social profile has changed in recent years owing to the massive influx of so many from the two northern states. True, this change is not confined to Aligarh; indeed the character of numerous educational centres is being gradually transformed owing to reservations and the growing pulls and pressures of regionalization. Yet Aligarh must learn to transcend, if not disregard, some of these considerations. It must construct its 'national' identity and pursue an agenda that will serve the educational needs of the Muslim communities cutting across regional boundaries. For this to happen, the university will need to rise above regional, local and parochial considerations, and broaden rather than narrow its recruitment base.

The regionalization of the university has contributed to

declining academic standards. The university's annual report highlights numerous gains, but the overall impression is of intellectual stagnancy. This is not because of poor housing, or the lack of research and other facilities. If anything, Aligarh's sprawling and attractive campus offers an ideal setting for teaching and serious research engagements. Yet the fraternity of teachers has failed to marshal its intellectual resources adequately and leave its imprint on the country's intellectual life. They have not even taken the lead in training students for the civil service and other competitive examinations. Last year, nobody qualified for the IAS; only two made it to the UP PSC. Out of 60 students coached for the post of subordinate *naib tehsildar*, not a single student made it to the final round. The figures are no less dismal in the JRF/NET examinations conducted by the University Grants Commission.

The reason for this poor showing is neither discrimination nor the marginalization of the university in terms of accessibility of state resources. The real cause is intellectual inertia that has set in. The university, having been pampered by the politics of minorityism, has become a spoilt child in the nursery of the educational system. Ideally, teachers and students should be accountable to themselves for their performance or lack of it, in Aligarh and elsewhere, but in reality they are not. The point is that if so few qualify for the competitive tests, it is easy to understand why Muslims are so poorly represented in government. Indeed, if the present trend continues, Muslims are likely to remain outside the area of state employment and find themselves predominantly in the unorganized sector either as workers or as self-employed bourgeoisie. If so, this is bad news. The way out is not to insist on reservations but to equip oneself to compete in the wider world. Here, Aligarh's university has to play a pioneering role. This was, after all, its *raison d'être*.

Aligarh's large community will congregate on 17 October under the shadow of Stratchey Hall to pay tribute to their sage, Syed Ahmad. On that occasion, they will do well to reflect on their recent past and, perhaps, consider ways and means of pioneering an intellectual renaissance that will transform the

lives and fortunes of their less privileged brethren. This is an
earnest plea from one of its most undistinguished alumni.

9 October 1999

Power as an End in Itself:
The Crisis of Our Times

In 1953, *Encounter's* first issue carried an article on India that
concluded on the following note: 'Between a past reduced to
practical impotence but offering a resistance to depth, and a
future only skin-deep, India's present seems to lack substance.'
Today, almost all rank-and-file Indian politicians will disagree,
for there is no limit to their imagined triumphs. The stark
reality—illustrated by the country's appalling state of affairs—is
that the shadows of doubts and uncertainties move among us;
almost too many to count and sometimes even hard to name.

The BJP-led regime—its life span extended by unprincipled
alliances in the shadowy world of politics—has lost credibility
in the eyes of the people as well as amongst its erstwhile supporters in the print media. Change is the crying need of the
hour, but this may not happen at the centre simply because the
NDA partners, having lost the public trust they enjoyed, are
unprepared to face the electorate. They will even swallow the
bitter pill administered by the Prime Minister in last week's
cabinet reshuffle.

A series of events during the last fortnight, including the
shameful conduct of the Shiv Sainiks in Thane [suburb of
Mumbai], must alert us to the crisis of our times in all their
fullness, their concreteness, and their reality. The Prime Minister
must be aware of the intolerableness of hunger, starvation and

degradation in a country that seems to have the resources to remove them. He should know that, close on the heels of the *tehelka* expose, his party's image has been irreparably damaged by the UTI [Unit Trust of India] scandal. And yet the Finance Minister stays put, while Jagmohan, a man of integrity and efficiency, is ousted [later appointed as Minister of Tourism] ostensibly under pressure from the land mafia and its BJP patrons. The Prime Minister is, surely, informed of the indictment of the BJP government in Gujarat by the CAG report, and the steady erosion of public institutions in UP where his party holds the reins of office. Love of power (as opposed to lust), in various limited forms, is almost universal. There is, however, a great difference between power desired as a means and power desired as an end in itself.

The BJP's crisis of political and moral legitimacy is partly the result of opportunist politics, but mainly the consequence of its own contradictions. Failure to evolve a national agenda is its major weakness; hence the widening chasm between the posturing of leaders and their narrow and sectarian goals. What contributed to the BJP's electoral success was its ability to convince the electorate that it stood for certain principles. Even if one does not scan those principles sceptically, the fact is that they have been willy-nilly consigned to the dustbin of history. Again, this is illustrated by the cabinet reshuffle.

If democracy is to be workable, our ministers must respond to public opinion even when it goes against them. Hence my appeal to the HRD minister to consider the mounting criticism of his pet projects. He is free to use the *Sangh Parivar* platform to disseminate his novel ideas, but not from Shastri Bhawan where he heads the country's ministry of human resource development. He shoulders a huge responsibility—preparing a blueprint for this millennium and, at the same time, preserving the rich legacy he has inherited from his predecessors, the most distinguished being Maulana Azad, free India's first Education Minister.

Our system of education should seek to promote rationality, independent thinking, somewhat sceptical and wholly scientific, and preserve the composite values of this society. This, wrote

Bertrand Russell long ago, was the task of modern liberal education: to give a sense of the value of things other than domination, to help to create wise citizens of a free community, and through the combination of citizenship with liberty in individual creativeness to enable men to give to human life that splendour which so few have shown that it can achieve.

Doubtless, the educational system is deficient in many ways. Doubtless, history textbooks should be updated. But this task should have been assigned to the historians themselves and not to those who will, I suspect, produce works to further the *Hindutva* agenda. Yes, reform and restructure, but not without wide-ranging consultations at various levels. The lead should have been taken by school, college and university teachers and not by bureaucrats. This is the essential difference between the liberal outlook and that of the totalitarian state. There is no mechanism to tame bureaucrats, except for the boards of studies and the academic council to assert their autonomy. So far, they have abjectly capitulated without insisting on their own right to be heard. Their empowerment alone is the sole guarantor of our educational centre's independence and freedom.

We recognize the need to update the curriculum, introduce new courses, and improve methods of instruction. And yet we are not attuned to the revival of antiquated notions, obsolete ideas, and irrational beliefs. The issue is not whether or not Vedic astrology or mathematics is the current rage in overseas universities (why, at any rate, should a fervent proponent of 'indigenism' imitate overseas universities?), but its value for a society pregnant with new ideas of change and innovation. Leading scientists have spoken in unison against the introduction of Vedic 'sciences'. So have scores of social scientists and parliamentarians cutting across party lines. The HRD Minister will do well to heed their views.

Design education to breakdown caste and communal barriers, create a liberal ethos, and nurture a sense of togetherness in an already fractured nation. Conduct the teaching of history in a similar spirit. Saffronization, the mantra of the HRD ministry, is the antithesis of what constitutes liberal education, for it seeks to instil a set of beliefs into the minds of the young before they are capable of thinking and exercising their independent judgement. And when two opposite groups are taught in this fashion, they produce two armies which clash, not two parties that can discuss.

Saffronization breeds fanaticism, heightens caste and communal consciousness, and stifles the natural inclination of a student to cultivate a balanced and cautious judgement. This is bad news for a country trying to rewrite the colonial agenda. This is ominously alarming for a country endeavouring to link up with the global economy.

Is there a breath of fresh air drifting through the pollution that we have been accustomed to take from our normal atmosphere? In 1953, the *Encounter* editorial struck the right note: 'after the apocalypse come—another day. Just another day. But our own.' I wish one could conclude with the same optimism in the year 2001.

5 September 2001

PART VIII

Know Thy Neighbour

A Reality Check on Pakistan _____

Information is power. That is certainly what the colonial powers believed in. From Francis Buchanan's survey of Mysore and eastern India to the last census in 1941, the British developed a vast corpus of knowledge about the 'natives'. They conducted census operations to create social categories by which India was ordered for administrative purposes, and studied language and literature as part of the colonial project of control and command. The very Oriental imagination that led to the antiquarian collection and archaeological finds were in fact forms of constructing an India that could be better packaged, inferiorized, and ruled (Bernard S. Cohn). In short, colonial knowledge both enabled conquest and was produced by it; in certain important ways, knowledge was what colonialism was all about (Nicholas B. Dirks).

The relationship between knowledge and power changed after World War II, but not in significant ways. In the 1950s and 1960s, the United States and its allies competed with the Soviet bloc to buttress their claims in the newly liberated countries of Asia, Africa, and Latin America. Their bitter confrontation led to the revival and establishment of several 'academic' bodies in different parts of the world. The project of such institutions, though tailored and trimmed to suit the postcolonial world, was not very different from what was conceived and implemented by the erstwhile colonialists in the late eighteenth and nineteenth centuries. In some ways, the activities of various US 'educational' agencies, especially in Latin America, would have put the likes of Warren Hastings and Curzon to shame.

In a democratic set up like ours, information and knowledge have a different role to play both in the domestic sphere as well as in dealing with the rest of the world. At least in one particular area, we have the resources, though meagre compared with the West, and yet we have failed to develop the wherewithal to study and understand our neighbours.

How much do we know about Bangladesh, a country we helped liberate in 1971? How much do we know about Sri

Lanka, except that the Tamils and the Sinhalese have disfigured that serene and beautiful island through acts of violence and aggression? Surely, not enough to develop a viable strategy to resolve long-standing differences with the people and government of that country. Our knowledge of Nepal society and polity is, to say the least, appalling. One would have expected our universities to produce renowned specialists on Pakistan, our *bete noire* in the region. Sadly, this has not happened.

Thanks to the Institute of Defence Studies, we monitor merely Pakistan's military strength and strategy with ease. Thanks to the Ministry of External Affairs, we are well up on that country's diplomatic manoeuvres. What do we make of the people and society in Pakistan? Most of us draw a blank on that score. That is what our image or images of Pakistan rest on—preconceived notions and mistaken assumptions. We think we know, though the reality is that what we know is not always right.

Consider our media—print and TV—and its projection of Pakistan as traditional, oppressive, backward looking and, to top it all, Islamist. These magisterial generalizations do not end at that. Women, we are told, are kept in seclusion, while the men folk go around their business with their flowing beards. Such impressions conform to our own conception of a typically Islamic ethos. One can dismiss all this as utter rubbish, but what does one do with the false images, now part of our national psyche after Kargil, created and sedulously cultivated by politicians?

The real problem is this: by portraying Pakistan as an archetype of a highly traditional and unchanging society, we demarcate sharp boundaries between 'us' and 'them'. The reality is that the resurgence of democracy has emboldened the Pakistani intelligentsia to strike a discordant note, to lead sustained campaigns in defence of civil rights, women's empowerment, nuclear disarmament, and in opposition to political Islam. Today, the voices of dissent and protest can be heard loud and clear on the streets of Islamabad, Karachi, and Lahore. Today, the democratic forces, even though bruised and battered by General Zia-ul-Haq, call the shots at different levels of Pakistan society.

The election results indicate that the Jamaat-i Islami's project of creating an Islamic State and society has very few takers. The lessons of the Khomeini revolutions in Iran, followed by the seemingly endless war in Afghanistan, have not been lost on the voters. They realize that the militant Taliban and their allies in Pakistan pose a serious threat to regional peace, and that the ideology and movement of the Taliban-Jamaat combine will ultimately retard the progress of Pakistan society, and lead to its fragmentation.

Pakistani intellectuals, having survived the nightmare of Zia-ul-Haq's rule, are now beginning to ask some new and some awkward questions. Ayesha Jalal, better known for her seminal study of M.A. Jinnah, has talked of the hollowness of civil society, the weakness of the institutions of the State, and the ideological contradiction in the self-projections and self-perceptions of the State. The real problem in Pakistan, she points out, is that the structures inherited from the colonial State were not realigned with the dominant conceptions which had fired the Muslim struggle for equality, solidarity, and freedom. So that Iqbal's lofty equation of Islam and civil society has been lost sight of in the litany of confusion surrounding conceptions of national identity and state sovereignty (Victoria Schofield, ed., *Old Roads New Highways*, 1997).

Ayesha Jalal calls for sustained debates on citizenship rights towards forging a collective ethos as a nation state, and a national dialogue to create the necessary consensus to begin rebuilding anew.

We, in the Indian academia, must follow such debates with care, and, in the process, disperse the clouds of ignorance about our neighbouring country. With India fast emerging as a major player in Asia, the need to do so is much greater now than ever before.

21 August 1999

Pakistan in Past Tense

An important political statement on the ideological foundation of Pakistan was made by the British archaeologist Sir Mortimer Wheeler when he titled his book *Five Thousand Years of Pakistan*. Likewise, the multi-volume *History of the Freedom Movement in Pakistan* invented a unified and continuous historical tradition starting with 1707, the year of Aurangzeb's death. Indeed, the intellectual challenge for the Pakistani historians in the 1950s and 1960s was to lend weight and historical legitimacy to Muslim nationalism and its fruition in the birth of a Muslim nation. Their task, as the editors of the *Freedom Movement* volumes stated in 1957, was to tell the 'remarkable story of their [Muslim] survival and their attainment of sovereign status as the emblem of their freedom'.

Historians, some having taught in Indian universities, had to shift gears after reaching Pakistan. Scholars like I.H. Qureshi, having taught at St. Stephen's College and the University of Delhi before their trek to Pakistan, had to rewrite their own histories. They had to construct a new past, one that was at variance with their earlier exploration. They had to search for heroes and martyrs, invoke new symbols and traditions, and discover milestones, such as the 1857 revolt, to trace the historical antecedents of Pakistan. The scholar Shaikh Ahmad Sirhindi, a contemporary of Jahangir, was pressed into service. So were Shah Waliullah, a leading eighteenth century thinker, and Syed Ahmad Barelwi, who led sporadic movements in mid-nineteenth century against the British. In their relentless search, the historian finally turned to Syed Ahmad Khan, the major catalyst for social and educational reforms among Muslims, in order to trace the 'two-nation' theory.

The issue was not just the defence of Partition or *Independence* from Pakistan's vantagepoint, but a different reading of the past involving, among other things, the rejection of a diverse but vibrant composite cultural and intellectual legacy. The legitimization of a Muslim homeland required, first of all, conjuring up the image of the Muslims as a monolithic entity acting in unison and committed to specifically Islamic values and norms. Second, it was necessary to portray them as a beleaguered religious entity. Hence the following observation: 'with the debris of the constructive effort of centuries around them, the Muslims of the subcontinent stood alone. They were weak, disorganized and backward, hardly equipped for a great struggle, standing on the cross-roads of destiny without knowing in which direction safety lay and yet determined to fight for their right of existence and freedom.'

At the heart of such a formulation is the tendency to demonize the Hindus, more than the British, and to attribute Muslim social and educational backwardness to the unremitting, overwhelming power and prejudice of the Hindus. On the other hand, no salience is attached to nearly two centuries of British rule, and to the exploitative nature of colonialism. We are, instead, introduced to a society where the colonial government's actions seem to make no difference whatsoever to the fortunes or misfortunes of the people, Muslims included. In sum, the mythology of Muslim nationalism has been built on the belligerence and hostility of the non-Muslims towards the Muslims. The historian's project has been to present an image of an always enlightened, largely innocent Muslim community.

Though the agenda of fellow-historians in India has changed over the decades, in neighbouring Pakistan conservative die-hards continue to base their arguments on the incompatibility of Islam and Hinduism, the cornerstone of Jinnah's two-nation theory. Yet some new, though muted, voices are being heard: the fiftieth year of Independence may have just about given impetus to a re-evaluation of old theories and assumptions.

The US-based historian, Ayesha Jalal, has charted an independent intellectual trajectory, freeing herself from the ideological claptrap in Pakistan historiography. Likewise, a book published by the Oxford University Press in Karachi introduces a regional dimension to Pakistan's history. What is lost sight of in the controversy surrounding the two-nation theory, argues its author J. Hussain, 'is the basic geographic good sense [sic] of an agricultural nation centred on the great Indus Valley river system'.

Finally, the same publishing house may have dithered some years ago in publishing *Common Heritage*, a collection of essays by Indian and Pakistani writers on common affinities, a common past, and old friendships. But nowadays, the intellectual ambience has changed. So has the political climate after Zia-ul-Haq's death. The intelligentsia continues its search for unity and cohesion in a country torn apart by regional, ethnic, and sectarian fissures.

We must not be apprehensive of this exercise, for Pakistan's stability and survival as a democracy must remain central to our concerns. The sporting exchanges augur well for the future. The bus diplomacy [initiated by the Indian Prime Minister] is a sign of political wisdom and maturity. Never before did so momentous an event take place in the history of India-Pakistan relations.

As the bus to Lahore rolls on today, it is hard to predict the outcome of so important an event. One simply hopes that frequent contacts and regular interactions will sensitize the people of India and Pakistan to each other's fears and anxieties. The demarcation of boundaries is a settled and irrevocable fact, and yet borders, as the post-war European experience demonstrates, can foster unity as well. Mutual distrust apart, we can still build bridges of understanding and learn to live as civilized neighbours. My wish is that fellow-historians here and in Pakistan will sit together and revisit the old-fashioned theories on pluralism, and detail the shared traditions that had enabled Hindus and Muslims to live harmoniously for centuries.

Hopefully, someday I will cross the Wagah border with my colleagues. This time not to watch cricket, but on a mission to bridge the intellectual gulf that separates the scholarly community in the subcontinent.

Ours is a dark age; men have lost trace of love and loyalty.
In former days it was not so; these things were second nature then.

MIR TAQI MIR

3 January 2001

The Islamization of Pakistan_____

The importance of Islamic language, ideas and imagery to the legitimization of political rule is underlined by recent developments in Pakistan. Still, despite the implicit consciousness of shared beliefs, Islamic political language, symbols and values require a broader conceptualization. Muslim politics, too, must be placed into multiple and shifting contexts. We must recognize, as a recent book by Dale F. Eikelman and James Piscatori suggests, that Muslim politics constitute the field in which an intricate pattern of cooperation and contest over form, practice, and interpretation takes place.

Such a recognition enables us to establish the relationship between doctrinal prescriptions and practice in Muslim societies, trace the linkage of religion and politics, and challenge the unreflective presumptions that go into the making of many dated and deeply flawed theories. A number of critical issues, some relating to the efficacy of a secular polity in a Muslim milieu, figured in Pakistan's National Assembly debate last week. Personally, I did not draw comfort from what was said either in support of or in opposition to the Islamic *Sharia* Code Bill.

Notwithstanding the eloquent speeches, the criticisms offered by opposition leaders, mainly from Benazir Bhutto's Pakistan's People Party, failed to carry much conviction to television viewers like me. Most speakers, guarded and defensive in their approach, should have taken their cue from the NGOs and human rights groups and challenged the underlying assumptions that go into the making of such a legislation. They did nothing of the sort. Nor did they invoke the alternative frameworks within the Islamic tradition that have lent a fair degree of political and institutional stability in more than forty Muslims countries.

In short, liberal and modernist voices, heard loud and clear in Turkey, Iraq, Syria, Algeria and Egypt, were muted in the Pakistan Assembly. Surely, the issue at stake in South Asia generally is to promote multiculturalism, secularize politics, demarcate the religious boundaries from the public domain, and prevent the cynical use of religious symbols by the priest-politician combine.

The stark choice is to either create or adhere to a theocratic State or secularize society on the strength of a liberal and enlightened secular discourse. I believe Nawaz Sharif's government, still haunted by the shadow of Zia-ul-Haq's ill-conceived Islamization fervour, has taken the first step towards the creation of a theocratic State. If the current predictions about the Islamist bandwagon rolling on in Pakistan come true, history may not exonerate Nawaz Sharif for his grave error of judgement.

In opting for a *Sharia*-based polity, Nawaz Sharif traverses a rough and unwieldy terrain. But what prompted him to do so? Does he not head a stable government? Did he need the Bill to buttress his otherwise unassailable political position? Was he obliged to make concessions to the Islamists, many of whom stand discredited in the eyes of the people? The reality is that his government had no immediate domestic compulsions to flaunt its Muslimness. Nobody accepts his own claim that the Bill's provisions will restore law and order, end sectarian and ethnic strife, and resolve the deepening economic crisis.

On balance, in addition to betraying the people's democratic aspirations, Nawaz Sharif has created space for strident Islamists to impose their old-fashioned codes on the people. What he and the 151 out of the 217 Assembly members have embarked upon is not a modern but a retrograde project. By taking recourse to the age-old practice of using religion for political legitimization, Nawaz Sharif has ignored the warning that fundamentalism is an inherently divisive ideology. For the time being, he may have weakened both the opposition and, in the wake of General Karamat's resignation, the military establishment. But religious rhetoric, as one of his unfortunate predecessors would have discovered on the gallows, often backfires. He must know that religio-political fundamentalism devours its own protagonists.

Islam is and will remain a way of life for the Muslim communities. Indeed, Islam offers 'agency' to its adherents in the sense that sociologist Anthony Giddens uses the terms 'an individual's' or 'group's capability' to intervene, or to refrain from intervening, in a series of events so as to influence their course. But fundamentalism, often nurtured by the West to serve its own ends, has ceased to be a dominant and all-pervasive force in today's world. This is a cause to celebrate.

Though secularism is still a far cry and Afghanistan's militarism and fanaticism remains a disturbing element, fundamentalist stirrings of the Khomeni brand has of late lost some of its fervour. The Shia orthodoxy in Iran has been tamed, though not humbled. The Islamic-oriented Welfare party in Turkey has lost some of its élan, while the Muslim Brotherhood in Egypt and the FLN in Algeria, having captured newspaper headlines in the past, are gasping for breath. The CSIS countries are unmoved by the rhetoric of the mullah. Pakistan's electorate, too, repudiated Zia's religious legacy, though they have every reason to feel disappointed that the turbaned men with flowing beards are back in business with their sermons and *fatawa* (religious decrees).

Predictably, Pakistan's dwindling minorities and human rights activists have fulminated against the Bill. What augurs ill for their future is that only 16 Assembly members voted against it: the rest stared at the peril without knowing what to do to avert it. Why? For decades the country's dilemma is to either carve out its place as a modern nation state or assert its distinct Islamic identity. Quite simply, the uneasy tension between the protagonists of these two distinct world views is unlikely to be resolved by the Islamic Bill. A possible outcome, one that must alert us in India, is that Sunni fundamentalism may well gain a fresh lease of life in neighbouring Pakistan. In such a scenario, we can ill-afford to ignore Mirza Ghalib's warning:

Ub kaha jaeya ga sailaab-i bala mere baad

Where else is this deluge of misfortune to go after I've gone!

Meanwhile, Pakistan's citizens must wonder if their interests were safe in the hands of a ruling élite that deploys religion merely to gain political leverage. Their nightmare, beginning with Zia's inglorious regime, is not yet over. Already, reports suggest that the Big Brother has arrived with his rabble-rousers, judges and executioners, ready to strike down any one who dares to deviate from the legislated code of conduct. If so, their feelings find expression in what Ghalib wrote more than a century ago:

> I go some way with every man I see advancing swiftly.
> So far I see no man whom I can take to be my guide.

17 October 1998

Mindless Militarism

Now that the dust has settled in the Pokharan desert, it is time to consider the implications of the dangerous course plotted by India and Pakistan. Sober reflection and not nationalistic claptrap is what we require.

Political analysts have already told you all you need to know. What they have not explained is why the ordinary citizen in Delhi or Islamabad was dancing to the nuclear tune. How and why did the deafening sound of explosions awaken national pride and national sensibilities? Why the euphoria over a seemingly intangible gain? Was this 'explosion of self-esteem', an idea invented by a newspaper editor, an expression of alienation and deep-rooted frustration over the non-performance of previous and existing political regimes? If not, why are we insensitive to the enormous cost and consequences of an arms race in South Asia? Why, in the name of nationalism and patriotism, do governments and sections of the media lose sight of the more pressing socio-economic problems?

Maybe, the nineteenth century poet Mirza Ghalib would have brushed aside these questions and said:

> The world is like a children's playground
> A *tamasha* unfolds itself before me from morning to dusk.

We are truly a great nation with a rich heritage, bequeathed by men of piety, art, culture and literature. Poverty and destitution apart, we have managed to create a pluralist and democratic society. That is why we command world-wide respect, though cynics like Nirad Chaudhuri and V.S. Naipaul decry our gains. Why tarnish this image? At any rate, whom are we trying to impress by flexing our muscles? If the intention is to secure a berth in the Security Council, one must ask whether it is worthwhile joining a debating society that has invariably acted against the interests of the Third World? Who knows, the gamble may pay off, but at what cost?

As we enter the next millennium, it would be silly to ignore the world-wide currents of change sweeping across Europe. Starting with the collapse of communism in the countries of the former Warsaw Pact, followed by the dramatic fall of the Berlin Wall in 1989 and the reunification of Germany, the political landscape of this continent has changed in just a few years.

Take Germany. As past enmities, ideological and otherwise, recede into the background, more than 80 million Germans surge ahead to establish their monetary, institutional, and diplomatic ascendancy in Europe. The emotional and psychological trauma of the Nazi regime does not deter them from building a powerful and unified nation. The Brandenburg Gate in Berlin symbolized the division of the country; today, it is a vibrant symbol of unity and progress.

The end of communism paved the way for the Treaty of Maastricht and the commitment by the member states, save England and Denmark, to introduce a single currency by 1999. Past rivalries and prolonged hostilities have been set aside to foreground a European agenda and set in motion an irreversible move towards real federation. In the process, the history of Europe is being re-written for future generations. Today, the European Union represents the largest single unit in the world economy. It has a GNP of about $6 trillion, compared with $5 million for the US and $3 trillion for Japan. Its total population, now over 360 million, approaches that of the United States and Japan combine.

Why state the obvious? Merely to underline the reasons why

we should do our utmost to bury the past and start on a clean slate. If we cannot draw lessons from Vietnam, Germany, or Korea, we must learn from our own experiences since Independence. Regardless of Pakistan's repeated aggression against India and its nefarious role in Punjab and Kashmir, the country's leadership, notwithstanding its political complexion, should demonstrate greater sagacity, wisdom, and statesmanship in breaking the present impasse. Having joined the nuclear club, now is the time to initiate a peace process. Having proven our scientific, technological and military superiority, this is the moment to resolve our outstanding disputes with our neighbours, China and Bangladesh included. The 'explosion of self-esteem' must not stand in the way of a meaningful dialogue.

I realize this is easier said than done. But, then, what is the way out? Should we carry the burden of the past and fritter away our energies and limited resources? Should we remain in a state of military readiness and celebrate this mindless military build-up? No, no, we cannot allow this to go on forever. Enough is enough.

I don't have much of a blueprint, but I believe that a handful of bureaucrats and military 'experts' should not be the arbiters of our destiny. Nor is their definition and meaning of 'national security' infallible. Instead, concerned and informed citizens should formulate their own ideas, monitor what is being said or done in the establishment to promote a particular world view, and warn the public about the dangers of a nuclear conflagration. This should combine with a massive disarmament campaign to counter the self-styled custodians of 'national' interests and security. We cannot take responsibility for the rest of the world, but should guarantee a nuclear-free South Asia for the generations to come.

In other words, it is imperative to initiate a national debate, and not get carried away by our own rhetoric. Those who dissent from the so-called national consensus must be allowed to speak and write. They are, after all, the only people who stand for democracy and secularism as well. It is an unforgivable sin to question their credentials or their loyalty.

Time and time again the people of India and Pakistan must

be reminded of their strong ethnic, cultural, religious, and linguistic bonds. People in Europe can travel without a visa and passport. Why can't we create similar conditions in the subcontinent? For this to happen, we must explore and widen areas of unity and cooperation in our private and public discourse.

Let me join the poet Ali Sardar Jafri in echoing the following plea:

Tum aao Gulshan-i Lahore se chaman-bardosh
Hum ayen Subh-i Banaras ki raushni lekar
Himalaya ki hawaon ki taazgi lekar
Phir uske baad ye puchain ke kaun dushman hai?

You come covered with flowers from the garden of Lahore.
We bring to you the light and radiance of the morning of Banaras,
The freshness of the winds of Himalaya
And then we ask who the enemy is.

Pakistan Repudiates Democracy

Pakistan's political leadership has done it again. Once more religion has been pressed into service to serve the political interests of the ruling establishment, legitimize a weak-kneed government that has failed to deliver, and heighten tensions in the region. Once more the Muslim divines, waiting in the wings, will endeavour to Islamicize the State and society. In the process, the people of Pakistan, having repudiated the fundamentalist legacy of Zia-ul-Haq and voted in a secular coalition, remain at the receiving end. The electorate is once more left high and dry in Pakistan's fractured democratic experience.

The scholar Fazlur Rahman pointed out in the early 1980s that the slogan, 'in Islam religion and politics are inseparable, is employed to dupe the common man into accepting that, instead of politics or the state serving the long-range objectives of Islam, Islam should come to serve the immediate and myopic objectives of party politics'. This is an apt comment on contemporary politics in neighbouring Pakistan. The liberal and secular élites, outraged by Nawaz Sharif's enthusiasm for Islamization (Fifteenth Amendment Bill introduced in the National Assembly on 28 August), have promptly aired their disquiet and dissent. But, are they strong enough to win the day? True, their influence in Pakistan society has grown in recent years, but it is not easy to deal with the well-entrenched religious establishment. The strength of their detractors in the 'secular' as well as the 'traditional' groups is compounded by the unresolved tension, one that plagues various Muslim societies, between the Islamic notions of community and State and the compulsions of running a modern nation state. Admittedly the neo-fundamentalist parties have fared poorly in electoral politics but their popular appeal has not diminished. The ultimate success of the secularists-modernists combine will henceforth depend on their ability to isolate the protagonists of 'political Islam' in the Jamaat-i Islami and such other organizations.

Jinnah, in a broadcast in February 1948, stated: 'Islam and its idealism have taught us democracy. It has taught equality of man, justice and fair-play to everybody. . . . In any case Pakistan is not going to be a theocratic state—to be ruled by priests with a divine mission.' Equally, some leaders and intellectuals when asked about 'the nightmare of Pakistan's going back to a rigid, backward, narrow country', responded 'For us, the intellectuals, the problem is that Pakistan shall not go back. That it should not become simply an extension of Afghanistan. It is a nightmare for us. The danger of the mullahs coming to power is serious; it will be calamitous. This is the terror.'

Yet, the secular project was not a part of the political discourse during the early decades of Pakistan's existence. Hence, liberal and secular voices remained feeble and fragmented. The political élites, drawing sustenance from the two-nation theory, continued to make concessions to neo-fundamentalist groups. Thus the *ulama* wanted the State to be declared Islamic, which the first Constitution, adopted in 1956, declared it to be. Later, they attacked the progressive Muslim Family Laws Ordinance, promulgated by Ayub Khan on 2 March 1961. In the first Amendment Act of 1964, the name of the country was again changed from the Republic of Pakistan to the Islamic Republic of Pakistan. The Pakistan People's Party, led by Zulfiqar Ali Bhutto, fared no better. As a practitioner of realpolitik and moving according to the conception of what was most advantageous in the gaining and maintaining of power, Bhutto cultivated the conservative and religious parties. The most significant concession was granted in 1974, when the Qadianis [Ahmadiyas] were declared a non-Muslim sect. The PPP banned alcohol, gambling and nightclubs, as well as replacing Sunday with Friday as the weekly holiday. Liberal Muslims, unable to question these measures which are backed by the authority of the *Sharia*, had to swallow the bitter pill.

Zia-ul-Haq's Islamization programme covered judicial reforms, the introduction of an Islamic penal code, the creation of a federal *Sharia* court, and a new educational policy incorporating 'Islamic tenets'. These measures legitimized the power of the *ulama*, institutionalized theocracy against the wishes of most people, and, in the process, increased the divisions, ruptures and bitterness within an already insecure nation. 'Military dictatorships, even without divine missions, are bad enough. When they are imbued with the spirit of religious fundamentalism, an atmosphere of ideological oppression suffocates the creative impulses of a society', wrote Omar Noman in *Pakistan: Political & Economic History Since 1947*. Though Nawaz Sharif has been committed to the Islamization Bill since assuming office in February 1997, there were no immediate political compulsions, regardless of America's cruise missile attack on Afghanistan, to take recourse to an ill-advised move. If Pakistan's economy is in tatters, how is the Islamization Bill going to help?

As a democratically elected leader, Nawaz Sharif should have learnt his lesson from his country's bitter experiences of the past. He should have known that the essence of a democratic order lies in letting people follow their moral and religious codes, and that state authority should not be extended into the private domain or used to prescribe, in the light of a religious text, what is right and to forbid what is wrong. The Muslims no doubt created Pakistan for the Muslims. But more than fifty years later the State can no longer afford to either nurture or acquire the role of a vanguard for a fundamentalist vision of Islam. A modern State, after all, cannot be structured, as some of the West Asian countries have belatedly discovered, on the indivisibility of the *din wa-dawla*, 'religion and state'.

The debate will go on ceaselessly. Meanwhile, consider Nazib Ayubi's observation that some of the heat in the fundamentalist cause will be taken away once the Islamists are permitted to air their views, in the open, and once they are allowed to compete, succeed, and fail. The last point is particularly important, for the more Irans and Sudans you get, the less impressive and appealing the Islamists' call will become.

19 September 1998

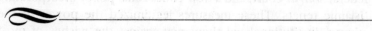

The Democratic Dream Remains

Its business as usual in Karachi. A democratically elected Prime Minister is in custody, paying for his 'sins' in the eyes of the self-appointed guardians of the State.* His descent from power has proved to be as precipitous and quick as his ascent had been two years earlier. The Parliament, where he enjoyed a two-thirds majority, is locked up, while the Constitution is put in cold storage. As Washington prepares to do business with yet another dictator, the sound and fury against the coup has

*General Pervez Musharraf staged a coup on 12 October 'to prevent any further destabilization'.

quietened down. This is how it has always been since October 1958, when Ayub Khan took over as Martial Law Administrator. 'The Himalayas will weep, if I am harmed', Z.A. Bhutto told his prosecutor in jail. But the mountains did not cry when Zia-ul-Haq signed his death warrant.

Army Chief Pervez Musharraf knows this, though he may not send the deposed Prime Minister to the gallows. With American tanks stationed at strategic points, he can afford to take time off to pose before cameramen. Journalists, finding him agreeable and engaging, carried the same impression of Zia, the general who unleashed a reign of terror from 1977 to 1988.

What explains the latest assault on democracy? A commonly aired opinion is that democracy has not struck roots; hence the people's muted response to yet another military takeover. Pakistan's brief and tumultuous experience with democracy belies this view. Besides, silence should not be construed as acquiescence. Turn the pages of history to discover that, time and time again, our neighbours have celebrated the demise of tyrants and the return to civilian rule. It was their enthusiasm that contributed to Bhutto's ascent to power, to his 36-year-old daughter's victory after her triumphal return to Pakistan in 1986, and again in 1993.

It is a different matter that the democratically elected leaders squandered the opportunity to reshape Pakistan, to break the stranglehold of the military-bureaucratic regime, and to create a multi-party system that will aggregate and synthesize the interests of many diverse groups. Zulfi promised much but delivered little; Benazir's legacy was a country torn apart by provincialism, Shia-Sunni violence, and by growing ethnic strife. When Nawaz Sharif jumped into the fray in 1997, the electorate seemed to be saying to him:

The wind has blown away the dust of men
Unnumbered from your lane;
Yet your true lovers are not daunted men
Come to your threshold still.

No wonder he won a landslide victory. Overwhelmed by the popular mandate, he declared his intention to keep faith with the people. But he proved to be a reckless country politician with no sensitivity to even the elementary lessons of govern-ance. At a time when he should have concentrated on economic discontent and a recession unprecedented in Pakistan's history, he chose to go nuclear. Washington responded angrily; Nawaz Sharif lost face with his people. At a time when he should have dealt with growing sectarian/ethnic unrest, he used the rhetoric of Islamization to buy peace. If he had read his country's history, he would have realized the merit in what Iskander Mirza said not so long ago, 'We can't run wild on Islam; it is Pakistan first and last.'

When Bhutto was caught up in his own quagmire, he resorted to repression. Nawaz Sharif did the same, though at a time when, thanks to the efforts of people like Asma Jahangir, civil liberty as an issue has gained salience in Pakistan society. Beset with internal and external problems, he acted more as a despot than a democratically elected leader. This is probably why much of the confidence he generated at the time of his election, dissipated. In a nutshell, this has been the fate of all elected governments in Pakistan; their record of governance contributing to their inglorious collapse.

Do we then trace the origin of the present turmoil to the two-nation theory? This standard explanation is unacceptable for the simple reason that Pakistan's civilian and military rulers have not been guided by the contested vision of Iqbal, Jinnah, or the Jamaat-i Islami chief Maududi. Yes, the arenas of conflict and strife have enlarged over the last five decades. But the ex-planation lies not in any serious ideological stirring in Pakistan, but in the abysmal failure of the state to pay adequate attention to illiteracy, social empowerment, and regional economic dis-parities.

Today, the central issue is the intense struggle and competition to access scarce resources, rather than an imaginary ideological contest, say between the Pakistan's People's Party and the Jamaat-i Islami, taking place in civil society. This is what the Muhajir-Sindhi conflict is all about. On the other hand, if the Jamaat's dismal electoral showing is any indication, then the signs are that the bulk of the electorate has shed its Islamic cloak and opted for a secular (not the Nehruvian kind) and democratic polity. It will be a mistake to ignore this important consensus emerging in Pakistan, or to rule out the prospect of yet another campaign for the restoration of democracy,

Pakistanis, the historian Ayesha Jalal reminds us, have the 'state' if not quite the nation of their collective imaginings. The real problem, according to her, is that those wielding despotic power in the name of Islam have done precious little for the principles of equality, solidarity, or freedom. According to her, the absence of sustained debate on citizenship rights, not just political but also social and economic, that has hindered the growth of civil society and the creation of a collective ethos as a nation state.

Added to this is the absence of a social coalition of the three main segments—the underprivileged, the middle class, and the élite. For this, the ruling élites must share the blame. They have left the Pakistani ship adrift in turbulent waters. For decades they have consolidated their own gains, leaving the common man on the streets of Karachi or Lahore awaiting the realization of the promises made by Bhutto's election manifesto of 1970.

The endurance of the long-standing tie-up between the military and the bureaucracy is at the heart of the present and previous crises in Pakistan. Nawaz Sharif did not try to break loose; instead, he systematically subverted established political institutions. He tried taking on the army, but came a cropper. In the end, he was consumed by his overweening ambition. Meanwhile the common man may have to wait long enough for the fulfilment of his dream. As Mir Taqi Mir wrote:

> Have you not heard what happened to Mansur?
> Here, if you speak the truth, they crucify you.

23 October 1999

The Night of the Generals

Tim Sebastian, of *Hard Talk* fame, needs a dressing down from his boss in London. Normally pleasant and gracious towards his guests, his tone and temper tend to change while interviewing Third World personalities. He conducts an inquisition rather than a dialogue with them. This was illustrated in his conversation with Hasan Sharif, son of the deposed Pakistani Prime Minister. Tim tried to extract a confession of sorts that the coup evoked support rather than condemnation, that Hasan's father presided over a massively corrupt empire, and that he himself lived like a prince in a rented Mayfair Garden flat that was paid for by two off-shore companies. Added to this was Hasan Sharif's own weak defence of his father's misconduct in public life. The celebrated interviewer, using his vast experience and skills, managed to bludgeon a young student into submission.

The problem with Tim Sebastian was that he did not address himself to the more fundamental issues of governance in Pakistan. Perhaps, he chose the wrong person to talk to. Perhaps, he is not well informed about the ill effects of a fractured polity and the gravity of the economic crisis in Pakistan. If so, I will not blame Tim Sebastian. In recent weeks, Pakistan watchers in India and elsewhere have focused more on the causes rather than the consequences of the military takeover. For me the key question is not the enormity of corruption in Pakistan (was it any less at any other time?), but the legitimacy of a military government and the future of democracy. Likewise the un- mistakable unpopularity of Nawaz Sharif is not central to my concerns.

The real challenge is to explain how and why an elected government was removed with such ease. Some might say the predictable has happened. I am not quite sure if I agree. Military dictators have their own way, their own ambitions, and their own style of functioning. Whether in Pakistan or elsewhere, they are not in the habit of relinquishing power. I doubt if General Musharraf will prove to be an exception to this rule. The early signals are disconcerting though quite in keeping with the tradition pioneered by Yahya Khan and Zia-ul-Haq.

Having usurped power from an elected government, Musharraf chose a site in Saudi Arabia to announce that the restoration of democracy might take as many as three years. Whatever opposition parties might say at present for fear of persecution or reprisals, they must know that the general's intentions are far from clear. If they are not alerted to this fact at the earliest, they may well bemoan Musharraf's reign as an epic tragedy. When their brief honeymoon with the existing regime is over, they may well regret their ill-advised decision not to defend democracy.

For India, the choices are not so simple as they appear to be. For one, the general, emboldened by the short-lived support he has, may well turn out to be a hard nut to crack. Second, India's experience with previous generals has not been a happy one. We cannot forget the military aggression of Yahya Khan and his brutal repression of the people's movement in Bangladesh. We cannot ignore that the recent unprovoked aggression in Kargil was the handiwork of the military government. Surely if this is Pakistan's army record, we cannot expect an *entente cordiale* with the Pakistan establishment in future. One suspects that once Pervez Musharraf tightens his grip, he may well decide to heighten anti-India sentiments to legitimize his authority among the people.

If the past is a guide, we can expect this to happen sooner than later. Time and again both military and civilian rulers have whipped up anti-Indian feelings to diffuse discontent and opposition against their authority. A wise general like Musharraf must know that this strategy paid off in the past. There is no reason why it should not work as long as he controls the levers of power.

It is nobody's case that civilian governments, starting with Zulfiqar Ali Bhutto, were friendly towards India. But this does not mean that we legitimize military rule. There can be no doubt that the US will do business with the Pakistani general but not Saddam Hussain, President of a beleaguered nation. Doubtless, the IMF and the World Bank, having produced the familiar noises, will soon pour in their dollars to rescue Pakistan from bankruptcy. Equally, the Commonwealth, having occupied the high moral ground for a week after the coup, appears to have abdicated its commitment to democracy in Pakistan. This is what international diplomacy is all about. This is what morality in politics amounts to. Still, if the international community's ambivalence towards this regime continues, the return of democracy in Pakistan may take much longer than expected. In the long run, this may not suit the freedom-loving countries of the West.

We must act differently if India wants to leave its imprint on the twentieth century. As the largest and one of the most successful democracies, we have a moral responsibility towards the restoration of the democracy in our neighbouring country. The spirit of the Lahore Accord, though violated by Sharif and his generals, should continue to guide our relations with their successors. This is because our long-term interest lies in stable democratic governments in South Asia.

This point needs reiteration owing to the growing Taliban menace. The last thing we want is to allow a bunch of misguided religious zealots to take advantage of political uncertainties in Pakistan, cross over our western borders, and stir up trouble in the already wounded Kashmir Valley. Regardless of India's experiences with Zulfiqar Ali Bhutto, his daughter, Benazir Bhutto, and Nawaz Sharif, a democratic Pakistan alone can act as a bulwark against the fundamentalist tide. When the night of the generals is over and the dawn of freedom arrives, the democratic forces will have to ensure that no general will ever place an elected Prime Minister in custody, lock up Parliament, and suspend the Constitution.

For the moment, Pakistan's political élites seem to have accepted the *status quo*. Even the more enlightened sections are resigned to their fate. This augurs ill for their own future. If they have a stake in democracy, they can ill-afford to give precedence to their personal or party preferences over established constitutional norms. Today, Nawaz Sharif languishes in custody; tomorrow it could be the turn of elected representatives.

6 November 1999

*Defending the Indefensible*_____

Clad only in two unstitched white cotton sheets, he joined, in April this year, the tidal wave of humanity that sweeps across Saudi Arabia during the Haj. He prayed for humanity, his long-suffering country, and for peace with honour with India. For himself, he added,'I asked only for strength to play my designated part in the cleansing of the nation.' But it seems Allah did not take too kindly to his prayers. The General in Islamabad was not impressed. His critics made Socrates drink poison. The generals in Pakistan deal with their adversaries differently.

They either dethrone them or send them to the gallows. Just a few months after his publicized appointment as Pakistan's High Commissioner to London, S. Akbar Ahmed, the civil servant turned scholar, received the marching orders from Islamabad. I did not see it coming when I met him a few days before his final denouement. I did not realize that my meeting with him will turn out to be my first and, perhaps, my last visit to Pakistan's High Commission in London's fashionable Knightsbridge district.

What an inglorious end to an otherwise promising career! I can see the 57-year-old Akbar Ahmed pacing up and down his room turning to M.A. Jinnah's portrait for solace and comfort. Why was he fired? Though beleaguered by a spate of controversies owing to his film-making enterprises and embroiled in at least two alleged financial scandals, he could not have become a liability for the military government in such a short time. Having defended the coup before his appointment, he had emerged, much to the chagrin of his admirers, a staunch and vocal supporter of Pervez Musharraf. 'He supported the military dictator General Zia, then Benazir Bhutto and Nawaz Sharif, and now he is the greatest fan of another military dictator', writes M. Anwar Khan, chairman of the Jammu Kashmir Peace Committee. That was Akbar Ahmed's fatal error. A man committed to liberal and democratic values had no business accepting an assignment under a military government.

He is an excellent communicator and wields a powerful pen. Author of scores of books he wrote during his stay at

Cambridge, his friends fail to understand why he abandoned the secure world of scholarship to legitimize a military junta. Was he a victim of his own personal ambitions? The jury is out in the open. Anyhow, I turned to the High Commissioner for his views on Indo-Pakistan relations. Sadly, he skimped on his own vision. Instead, he bashed India for 'behaving like a bully on the block and for being stuck in an anti-Muslim mindset. The virulence and arrogance of the statements emerging from Delhi threatening to wipe out Pakistan are disappointing.'

His views obscured the fact that what he had to say substantively differed little from what is being repeated *ad nauseam* by his countrymen. When I pointed out that not everybody in India was a Pakistan-baiter, he turned to me angrily: 'Where are the people of goodwill and the people of good sense in India? Why are they allowing those with hatred in their hearts to poison the South Asian atmosphere?'

This rhetoric failed to carry conviction. In fact, one was saddened, if not disappointed, to discover that a man with a scholarly background was unable to steer an independent course in formulating his world view. Often, this is what happens to some people who, having been catapulted into prominence, stray into the world of international diplomacy. Are you not obsessed with India? I asked.

Yes, I am. Every Pakistani is. India is, after all, active in promoting Pakistan's negative image. This has a resonance in the West. Remember, India cannot hope for its much-vaunted take off with 400 million people living below the poverty line and its resources being diverted to a full-scale military confrontation with Pakistan.

I reminded him that his country had waged war against us, and aided and abetted terrorism in Punjab and Kashmir. At that point Akbar Ahmed quickly changed the subject to proclaim:

Pakistan's destiny is the vision of Qaid-i Azam, a vision based on human rights, women's rights, respect for the minorities and integrity in public and private life. Jinnah's Pakistan will be alive as long as there are Muslims who feel for the dignity, the identity and the destiny of other Muslims, and who care for the oppressed and the minorities in their midst.

I wanted to tell him that a stable and democratic Pakistan

suited India, but Akbar Ahmed was in no mood to listen. How, then, does Kashmir fit into his scheme of things?

The core issue is Kashmir. It is widely felt in Pakistan that Mountbatten and his allies in the Congress cheated Pakistan by depriving the newly created nation of Kashmir. Today, Kashmir must not be seen only as a political problem between the two countries. There is, in addition, the human rights dimension of thousands and thousands of ordinary people who lost their lives and properties. They have become the victims of geo-politics, the victims of history and they must not be forgotten.

This was too simplistic a view for me to pay attention to.

What made sense in Akbar Ahmed's conversation with me was his plea that the countries of South Asia should build cultural bridges and forge strong economic ties. 'If South Asians can overcome their political, ethnic and religious divisions they can fulfil their destiny in a short period; if not, it is a bleak future and they will be lodged at the bottom of the world league.' He underlined, moreover, the need to emphasize the cultural richness and diversity of the region. The stature and quality of the founding fathers, he added, are unrivalled anywhere in the world. Mercifully, Ahmed's list had the names of Gandhi, Nehru, Patel, Bose, Ambedkar and Azad.

For years Akbar Ahmed has alternated between the realm of scholarship and the open-ended world of diplomacy. Suddenly, his world has been turned topsy-turvy by the military regime. It will not be easy for him to negotiate his position *vis-à-vis* the scholarly community: already, the financial scandals have damaged his reputation. At the same time, the decree from Islamabad has clipped his wings and may have brought to an end his career as a diplomat. Perhaps, when he performs the Haj next year, he will receive the inspiration to lead the life of a scholar. He can then tell his friends: 'I had a feeling of duty done, of serenity acquired—and a new sense of perspective that is still with me.'

14 June 2000

Goodwill Hunting

In war both interests and ideas are pushed aside; hence, as an exception to the rule, the great individuals then triumph. This is the essence of what has gone on in the subcontinent since Independence.

Enough is enough. That's the common refrain in private and public discussions. More than a fortnight ago, we had a taste of the people's sentiments in Agra. Talking to people who came to the *dhaba* next to a graveyard on Fatehbad Road, the road leading to Amarvilas Hotel, I found the non-élitist segments of our society much less susceptible to sabre-rattling. Two young graduates and an office clerk working in Amarvilas Hotel expressed their yearnings for peace and an immediate end to conflicts. He reminded me of Ali Sardar Jafri's moving lines— *Khuda kare ke ye shabnam yuhi barasti rahe/zameen hamesha lahu ke liye tarasti rahe* (May it become the Earth's lot to be wet with dew/by denying it human blood forever).

Why just the men at the *dhaba*? Indians and Pakistanis expressed similar sentiments at the People's summit at Delhi's India International Centre. This is not all. Amongst the 170-odd guests at the Taj Palace Hotel on Saturday, I noticed a glimmer of hope and optimist. Faces lit up as Dilip Kumar broke the ice, so to speak. My bonus was sharing a table with Shahrukh Khan, and getting his autograph for a non-existent autograph book.

The Prime Minister seemed calm and relaxed as he left the banquet hall with his guest. He had reasons to feel that way. Having realized long ago that the RSS dream of an *Akhand Bharat* was long outmoded, he set the tone for a dialogue with Pakistan. He invited the President and hoped that goodwill on his part would be reciprocated by the other—a hope fulfilled. Despite the criticisms of the diplomatic muddles during the bus ride to Lahore, the Kargil war and Sushma Swaraj's [government's spokesperson] *faux pas* at Agra, he is the one who has most certainly turned the President's visit into a major event.

The two leaders met without breaking the impasse. But, then, why get upset by their failure to produce a joint declaration?

Why get unduly perturbed by the intransigence of some politicians and bureaucrats? It takes time to resolve issues of war and peace. It takes time to size up friends and foes. The silver lining is that the peace process initiated by the Prime Minister and his Foreign Minister, who are unfairly placed in the dock by self-appointed guardians of our national interests, is irreversible. They and their Pakistani counterparts will meet again not to thrash out the terms of a Versailles or Sevres-like treaty, but to negotiate the subcontinent's future on equal terms. When that happens, it will be time to keep one's fingers crossed.

Never before in South Asian history has the fate of so many rested in the hands of so few. President K.R. Narayanan is wise and sagacious. He put across this idea elegantly. 'Tomorrow', he told the Pakistani President, 'when you and the Prime Minister of India, sit together in Agra . . . I hope the face of the poorest person in the subcontinent will be before you.'

Whatever the implications of the Agra Summit—no prizes for guessing at this stage—Vajpayee and Musharraf have assured their respective places in history. Compared to what they have accomplished, the efforts of the architects of the Shimla Accord fade into insignificance. In 1971, India was flushed with victory. Pakistani prestige, on the other hand, was at its lowest ebb. Z.A. Bhutto bought peace to gain mileage back home: a weary Indira Gandhi obliged.

All said and done, the clouds of war have dispersed. For a variety of reasons, the American pressure being one of them, the climate is much more conducive for a dialogue on several thorny issues that have bedevilled Indo-Pak relations. This opportunity must not be allowed to fritter away.

The steady men of solid principle and mind, wrote the British historian A.J.P. Taylor years ago, are the ones who achieve effective success. At Rajghat, Musharraf extolled Mahatma Gandhi's devotion to non-violence and peace. 'Never has the requirement of these ideals been more severely felt than today, especially in the context of Pakistan-Indian relations.' Recognizing this painful reality, howsoever belatedly, augurs well for the future of India-Pakistan talks.

As a footnote, let me add that never before did any Pakistani head of state express such warm sentiments for the Father of the Nation. Let me also add that he struck the right note ruling out a military solution to the vexed Kashmir issue, though he now has to take firm measures to check cross border-terrorism. It was also politically correct to invoke M.A. Jinnah's vision of fostering good neighbourly relations. Yes Sir, we must overcome the burden of history. Others have done it. Yes, Mr. President, we too must do so. You and our Prime Minister!

Our prime minister has conducted himself in a statesman-like manner, shown magnanimity towards Pakistan, and revived the eclectic spirit of the Mahatma and Jawaharlal Nehru, a spirit that has remained dormant for decades. Once the exponent of India's strength—hence the nuclear explosion at Pokharan—Vajpayee has proved to be too strong a character, though en-feebled by two recent operations, to be swamped by cantanker-ous patriotism even in old age. Although some of his belligerent and irrepressible BJP colleagues have not been reined in on vital domestic issues, it is quite clear that he, as the leader of an otherwise unwieldy coalition, does not want to look back to the past but anticipate the future. On the issue of forging friendly ties with Pakistan, in particular, he has shown himself to be too individual, too full of personality to be fitted into a party-pattern.

Today, the key issue is to sustain the momentum gathered by Musharraf's visit. Raking up old issues will not do; a change in mutual perceptions is required. Making political capital out of who was invited where and, for what reason, will not cut much ice. Believe me, the presence of Hurriyat leaders [militant outfit in Kashmir] at the Pakistan High Commissioner's tea party was a non-event. We hardly noticed their entry and exit. Yet, it is silly to leave them out in the cold. India's options have been narrowed by the ill-advised governments moves in the past that has led to the political death of the JKLF (Jammu and Kashmir Liberation Front) and other secular forces in Kashmir. Having created spaces for the Hurriyat men to garner support, they have become the guarantors of peace in the Valley. Talk, or isolate them politically.

25 July 2001

PART IX

Remembering 11 September

Wrestling with Shadows

The events of the past week have been a colossal human tragedy in every sense of the term. There is a certain numbing, surreal quality about what we witnessed as lived experience for those in New York and Washington, the living and dead, and those of us who share their trauma, whether in India or America. More generally it is a worrying situation for us in South Asia, which will doubtless bear the brunt of retaliation. It is a defining moment for Pakistan; it has an opportunity to cleanse itself of the abhorrent trend of terrorism and fundamentalism.

Terrorism endangers all countries, but the answer to this menace is not to nurture a monster, i.e. Osama bin Laden or the Taliban in Afghanistan, but to evolve a counter-ideology to weaken the very forces that give rise to extremism. For this to succeed, the US, having thrown its weight behind feudal, military and authoritarian regimes in West Asia in yesteryears, will need to define afresh its national interests and international agenda. In a unipolar world the US will remain invincible, for its military might and economic hegemony is likely to engender resentment in areas afflicted with poverty, disease and social strife. Indeed, Americans will feel increasingly vulnerable unless they mount pressure on their republican government to fortify liberal, secular and democratic ideologies around the globe. An alternative strategy may not avert such disasters.

In other words, the US should do what it does in its own backyard. What is good for America cannot be bad for the rest of us. The sense of loss will, doubtless, push many to seek revenge. And yet, there are numerous sensible voices in US cautioning against retaliation. They realize that increased defence spending and world-wide coalitions against terrorism will not buy peace now or in the future. Certainly, the fight against terrorism and fundamentalist ideologies must be pursued relentlessly, but punitive action will only deepen anxieties and enlarge arenas of tension in the Arab world, Iran, Central Asia, and the Horn of Africa, notably Somalia.

In the long run, President Bush and his sober Secretary of State must curb the belligerence of the Zionist lobby in Israel and put to a halt its almost natural inclination to hurt and humiliate the Palestinians. They will have to alleviate the enormous sufferings of the Iraqi people, whose leader was once a great favourite with the American establishment. Mr President, even the dead—infant children and women—talk. Believe me Sir, they do. Oil and gas will continue to flow from the wells in the Arab peninsula and numerous World Trade Centres will mushroom in your vibrant country, but global peace will be an elusive goal without a Palestinian homeland free of Israel's aggression.

The US anger is justified, but directing its anger against Islam or the Muslims is hardly an antidote to terrorism. Millions of Muslims are not in a state of readiness to wage *jehad* against all and sundry. They live, as do followers of other religious creeds, within the moral and spiritual realm defined by Islam. They must not be stigmatized or targeted by the fury of 'Christendom'. The Archbishop of Canterbury, having allowed his imagination to run amok, must know that there is no clash of civilization. The irrepressible V.S. Naipul must realize that, contrary to his assertion, there is no clash between Islamdom and Christendom. At a time when passions are running high, it is extremely irresponsible for the leading lights in religion and literature to fuel such ill feelings.

Regardless of Islamist rhetoric, *jehad* is at best a moral doctrine representing the civilizational urges of a people to order their lives in the light of the Koranic teachings. This is evidenced by such a verse as the following: 'He who exerts himself, exerts himself only for his own soul,' which expressed the *jehad* in terms of the salvation of the soul rather than a struggle for proselytization.

Surely, the meanings of *jehad* have changed over the centuries, and hotheaded individuals and groups cannot invoke it in the present world order. Instead of taking recourse to such diabolical means, Muslims groups need to marshal their intellectual resources to strengthen socialist and secular ideologies. That is how the people in Palestine, Iraq and Kosovo can secure justice in an otherwise unjust world. That is how we can also break the stranglehold of autocratic and military regimes in Muslim countries.

Instant reaction is no substitute for sober reflection. Quite apart from the fact that the attack on strategic centres in New York and Washington were acts of terrorism, let us pause for a moment and consider defining (outside the formalistic legal codes) terrorism. It is not going to be easy, unless we endorse the definition handed down by Western governments and the Western media.

If, on the other hand, the unified American definition is patented, you will find many voices of dissent being aired in international bodies. This will, surely, make the task of destroying the shadowy and murky den of terrorism so much more difficult. In effect, it will not help to tighten procedures, forge elaborate espionage networks, and monitor the movements of suspected individuals/groups. What may help is a consensus that will distinguish popular struggles against oppressive regimes from brazen acts of intimidation and violence directed against innocent civilians.

Who is a terrorist? Chapekar brothers, Chandershekhar Azad, Madan Lal Dhingra, Bhagat Singh? If you had lived in colonial India and acted in unison with like-minded people to overthrow British rule, your action would have been described conspiratorial. Hence the 'Silk Letter Conspiracy' in 1915-16, the 'Meerut Conspiracy', and the Kakori 'Dacoity Case'. And if you were reckless enough to take up arms, you would have been hauled up, gaoled and executed. Even Gandhi, the symbol of the liberation struggle, would not have come to your aid. He did not, for example, secure clemency for Bhagat Singh. The idolization of Bhagat Singh after his execution, wrote Gandhi in *Harijan* (3 July 1931), had done incalculable damage to the country.

In our own times, it is hard to characterize the activities of Al-Hamas, the Maoists in Nepal, the Naxalites, the Christian groups in the Indonesian Archipelago, the Kosovans, and the Chechnyans. Is Yaseer Arafat a terrorist? The Israel Prime Minister, who has blood on his hands from the days of Israel's

occupation of Lebanon, would like us to believe that he is. It is
his judgement against mine. Why is he, one might ask, not a
terrorist? George W. Bush might know.

If they lean to peace, then lean thou also to it . . .

Koran, VIII, 63.

19 September 2001

Jehad: *On My Behalf?*

Terrorism has no sanction in religion, morality and international
law. It follows therefore that whosoever struck at the citadel of
America's economic and military might has committed an act
of barbarism. Yet, today, its long-term consequences are far more
important than the precise identity, religious or ethnic, of the
terrorists.

Terrorism is bad news for us and the rest of the world. It
represents, though not in official parlance, the collective fury
and indignation of a people against the Other. For this, as indeed
for other reasons, it has to be taken seriously. At the same time
it must be combated not by targeting a leader—Osama bin
Laden for example—but by coming to terms with the collective
anger of the people spread across the continents.

Military pacts and hollow moral posturing will not do.
Regardless of domestic compulsions, stronger nations need to
address themselves to the long-standing grievances of the
Palestinians and the beleaguered Iraqis. Talking in terms of 'a
monumental struggle of good versus evil' (President Bush) may
move audiences, but such imaginary and self-righteous
constructions typify a mindset that will preclude a lasting
solution of outstanding international disputes. Henry Kissinger

has rightly called for a systemic approach to deal with the terror tactics directed against his country.

The stability of American democracy is close to our heart, but then White House has to think and act differently in relation to Iraq, Palestine, and other vulnerable nations across the globe. It cannot hope to remain secure by making concessions to Zionism. It cannot occupy a high moral ground by legitimizing monarchical and military regimes. If this monumental human tragedy turns out to be the defining moment in the reappraisal of priorities, we hope the American people will recognize that their national interests lie in fortifying the values enshrined in their constitution. They have known that the essence of the American way of life is freedom and democracy: if so, the great American dream cannot be realized without discarding the Zionist, racist, and anti-democratic ideologies of their allies.

In the long run, the strength and durability of Islamist movements and their ideological impact has to be blunted. Immediately, punishment must be meted out to those involved in this utterly despicable apocalypse-like carnage. At the same time, restraint rather than punitive action against an entire nation will serve the global interests of the US better. Terrorists have no nation, no territorial loyalty, and no permanent bonding with their fellow-countrymen. Though imbued with a mission, their methods run contrary to norms of civilized conduct.

At the time of writing this article, some arrests have taken places in Boston, but the main culprits are still at large in the shadowy world of conspiracies. Osama bin Laden may well have masterminded this war-like operation, though he has denied involvement. So has Al-Hamas. Yet the knives are already out in the open pointing to the so-called Islamic conspiracy of international dimension. Islam, already stigmatized in the Western Hemisphere, is once more being equated with fundamentalism and terrorism. Some journalists talk of a worldwide Muslim-inspired *jehad* against the West, echoing Samuel Huntington's notoriously ill-founded thesis on the clash of civilizations.

Already, I am inundated with scores of requests to speak and write on Islam and fundamentalism. Is it because the views of a professional historian will enhance the quality of debate? Or, is it simply because I bear a Muslim name and, therefore, must account for the conduct of my co-religionists from Morocco to Malaysia?

It is utterly gibberish to construe last week's tragedy as an assault on Christendom: the Islamic rhetoric and the live images of some Palestinians celebrating the havoc caused by the terrorists are peripheral to a complex configuration of factors— notably, cultural anxieties, mounting political disillusionment, and national identity. It is equally preposterous to draw Islam into this debate, for no religious creed sanctions violence. I need not invoke the Koranic verses to establish the validity of my argument: this task may well be assigned to Muslim divines or the Muslim spokesmen. My own reading is that Islam's civilizational rhythm flows from its explicit recognition of tolerance, social equality, and high moral order and spiritual depth. Its philosophical roots, too, rest on the same principles. This factor, rather than the orthodox Judaeo-Christian inter-pretations that some people cling to, has enabled Islam to survive through the vicissitudes of history.

Doubtless, political Islam exists; in fact, the reality of mostly semi-feudal and undemocratic Muslim countries contributes to a climate in which the influence of Islamic activists will in-crease rather than diminish. Doubtless, fundamentalist ideas— exemplified by the imposition of obsolete moral, social and religious codes, and the brazen vandalism at Bamiyan in Afghanistan—inspire certain segments of the Muslim com-munities. But, then, how do such elements alone represent Islam's authoritative voice? Why categorize, define and essentialize their stridency, and not the poise and equanimity of the silent majority? Is my Muslim barber wielding a lathi ready to attack his next 'Hindu' customer? Do the school-going children on Bombay's Mohammad Ali Road carry the green flag with the intention to attack their Hindu or Christian neighbourhood?

Why lend credence to the notion of *jehad*, a doctrine that has undergone changes in its meaning to suit the changing circumstances of life? The change in the conception of *jehad* in the tenth century—from active to dormant war—marked, according to Ibn Khaldun (d.1406), the great Muslim thinker, the change in the character of the nation from the warlike to the civilized stage. Today, the call for *jehad* is merely a weak component of the Islamist rhetoric. It has few takers among Muslims.

We must reflect on these issues, for they are relevant to Kashmir and our relationship with Pakistan. As for the US, the sober advice of the American scholar John L. Esposito merits consideration: 'Guided by our stated ideals and goals of freedom ... the West has an ideal vantage point for appreciating the aspirations of many in the Muslim world as they seek to define new paths for their future.'

Outlook (cover story), *24 September 2001*

Repeal Evil with Good

On 13 September 1931, two days before Gandhi arrived in England, the Columbia Broadcasting System arranged for him to deliver a radio address to the American people. Gandhi approached the microphone with curiosity and asked, 'Do I have to speak into that thing?' He was already on the air and these were the first words his listeners on the other side of the Atlantic heard. Three minutes before his time was to be up, a note was passed to him saying that his voice would be cut off in New York in three minutes. Unruffled, he began to bring his impromptu speech to a conclusion. After the engineer signaled him to stop, he commented, 'Well, that's over.' These words, too, were carried across the Atlantic.

What would the Mahatma have said or done at this juncture? For one, this apostle of non-violence would have deplored the perpetrators of violence, as he so often did in his own country. He expressed no sympathy for the revolutionaries, i.e. terrorists, in colonial vocabulary. Instead, he asked them to desist from the path of violence: 'If you must kill English officials, why not kill me instead?'

For Gandhi non-violence consisted in refraining from exercising the power to hit back and was a virtue of the brave. Those lacking in courage and bravery could be no more non-violent than a mouse in its relation to the cat. He would have therefore appealed to the American people to eschew the path of retribution. What good does it serve to target people of Middle Eastern and South Asian descent to track down suspects in the terrorist attack? What good does it serve to direct the American ire against the Palestinians, the Afghans, the Iranians and the Iraqis—all having suffered long enough at the hands of the US and its allies. 'Please don't prolong their agony. Please don't punish them all for the mistakes of a few. Enough is enough', he would have said to George W. Bush, Jr., and his administration.

Who knows, Gandhi may have added in his low voice that the intention of the otherwise dreaded terrorists in US was 'to make the deaf hear' (statement attributed to Bhagat Singh and B.K. Datt). He may well have repeated what he had said in 1940. When asked about the practice of democracy in America, he replied:

My notion of democracy is that under it the weakest should have the same opportunity as the strongest. That can never happen except through non-violence. No country in the world today shows any but patronizing regard for the weak. The weakest, you say, go to the wall. Take you own case. Your land is owned by a few capitalist owners. . . . These large holdings cannot be sustained except by violence, veiled if not open. . . . *Your wars will never ensure safety for democracy.* (emphasis mine)

Throughout his public life, Gandhi invoked the Indian tradition of violence and explored both the sources of and alternative to the dominant forms of violence in modern society. He did not believe, a point detailed by the social philosopher Bhikhu Parekh, that non-violence had taken deep root among the Indian people, as otherwise they would have shown compassion in their treatment of the poor, the lower castes, and the untouchables. Major

Hindu scriptures sanctioned violence; so did some thinkers. Shankaracharya, for example, used 'unspeakable cruelty in banishing Buddhism out of India'.

Gandhi's method of dealing with individual and collective violence varied from time to time. After violence broke out in Chauri Chaura (1922), he called off civil disobedience. In September 1947, he went on a fast unto death in Calcutta to make the people 'purge themselves of the communal violence'. In Noakhali, he put to test his *ahimsa* by providing the healing touch to the victims of Hindu-Muslim riots. On 13 January, he began his fast in Delhi 'to find peace in the midst of turmoil, light in the midst of darkness, hope in despair'. The inner peace was shattered as soon as the fasts ended. 'From calm, I have entered storm', he told a friend after the Delhi fast.

One earnestly hopes that the American people, traumatized by the 11 September experience, will begin their quest for world-wide peace by choosing a different path from the one chosen since the dropping of atom bombs on Hiroshima and Nagasaki. The Americans have the right to protect their way of life from external aggression, but they must respect the Indian, Chinese and Mexican way of life as well. The US administration has drawn up a list of 'rogue states', but does that include Israel? If not, why? 'Lighting strikes, always, the beleaguered Muslims' (*Barq girti hai to bechare Mussalmanon par*), said Mohammad Iqbal long ago. The US government backs the freedom struggle in Chechnya, but not in Palestine. Why? The US champions freedom and democracy everywhere except in Egypt, Saudi Arabia, Kuwait, and the Gulf States. Why? To ensure the flow of oil, and protect the 'American way of life'?

If Gandhi were alive, he would have certainly raised such questions not on the Columbia Broadcasting System but on our own TV network. He would have participated in the *Big Fight* or the programme *We The People*, airing the anxieties of the weak nations. At the same time he would have chided their autocratic and feudal governments, expressed concern at the spread of Islamist ideas, and warned against 'their imposition, such as the enforcement of *purdah* in parts of Kashmir.

Gandhi's own respectful responses to Islam were not a matter of political pragmatism, but far beyond—to a philosophical understanding of the very essence of Islam. He approvingly quoted the Koranic line—Repeal evil with that which is best, to underline the value of personal and political morality. He would have urged the regressive Taliban regime—guilty of many excesses in the past—to pay heed to the Koranic values and eschew the rhetoric of *jehad*. He would have asked the Pakistan-aided militants in Kashmir's mountainous pass to pack their bags and let India and Pakistan resolve their disputes amicably. Hopefully, no Nathuram Godse would have sprung from somewhere to silence his voice.

Gandhi once told a correspondent why he had stopped talking of aspiring to the age of 125: 'I have lost the hope because of the terrible happenings in the world. I don't want to live in darkness.' One hopes that the war clouds will disperse and the sane voices of restraint and moderation will be heard across the globe. Maybe then, we, Indians, Afghans, Arabs, Pakistanis and Americans, can aspire to live for another 125 years!

3 October 2001

Muslim Rage is for Real

The 'Muslim rage' goes unnoticed unless expressed stridently. I wish to point to the manifestations of seething discontents not only in daring acts of terrorism, but also in peaceful and unobtrusive endeavours to restore a moral and spiritual order corrupted by authoritarian Muslim regimes. Based on the premise that the Koran provides answers to contemporary dilemmas and predicaments, Muslim movements fortify their belief structures through outward assertions of their identity—mosques, *madrasas*, the Arabic language, the headgear, the *purdah*.

You may pour scorn at these trends, but they will remain powerful and highly evocative symbols of protest against the depraved Muslim governments and their external adaptation to the mores of the West. Have we forgotten the political storm that broke out with full fury in February 1979 against the Shah of Iran? Today, the ferment generated by Ayatollah Khomeini still provides, despite its Shia colouring, a model for a revolution in the modern world. So that the debate is not whether such a model is worth emulating or not, but its effectiveness in adapting Islam to changed circumstances within an orthodox-Islamic frame.

What the Khomeini revolution achieved was to broaden the meaning of *jehad*, and place it on a par with the modern concept of revolution. In effect, the religious signification of *jehad* coalesced with the concept of *inqilab*—i.e. activism— leading to a political transition and not just a moral revolution. Let's get a sense of the background. After Second World War, the Muslim communities were freed from the colonial stranglehold and its collaborators, the indigenous political élites. Decolonization opened to them the opportunity to ensure their cultural and religious survival on the strength of existing intellectual and spiritual resources. Wherever the Western powers allowed the transition to proceed smoothly, Muslim leaders tried, as in Egypt under Nasser and in Syria and Iraq under the Baath Socialist Party, to reform society or community without reference to Islam. But whenever the US occupied the space vacated by the previous colonizers, especially after the discovery of oil in the desert, they installed or backed feudal, conservative, or Islamist regimes.

The result was two-fold. First, secular regimes, trying to break free from their colonial past, found it difficult to face external aggression, i.e. the overthrow of Musaddiq in Iran and the invasion of the Suez Canal. They resorted to political repression as a countermeasure, and gradually lost the moral ground occupied during the anti-colonial struggles. In the process, democratic forces received a decent burial paving the way for the emergence of dictators like Anwar Sadat and the resurgence of the Ikhwan al-Muslimeen in Egypt. Second, with the credibility of Arab states eroded and a Zionist state implanted in Israel, the Americans were firmly established in the Middle East. Unlike the lazy colonial administrators who retreated to their country houses or chateaux, their successors—proud inheritors of Thomas Jefferson's wisdom—stayed put in the region with their heavy military equipment and coarse cultural baggage. Firmly ensconced, they instilled in the sheikhdoms a false sense of security, regulated oil prices, and ensured its regular flow across the Atlantic to preserve the American way of life. What the rich Arabs earn through royalties is stashed away in UK/US banks. What they spend at London's Harrods or at the casinos in Las Vegas keeps the American dream alive.

These bare facts, rather than the sterile debate over Islam *versus* democracy, need to be underlined to explain the absence of democracy in Muslim countries. These bare facts need reiteration also to discover the roots of the present Muslim rage. The roots lie in an oppressive past constructed by the West to colonize the body and mind, and an equally oppressive present where deadly missiles are fired only at the Palestinians, Iraqis, and Afghans. New generations have grown up with the knowledge of the past and present: the past is no longer buried under the debris but repeatedly invoked in the context of the events in erstwhile Yugoslavia, Somalia, Sudan, Chechnya, Palestine, Iraq, Kosovo, and Afghanistan.

Having wrestled with these memories without finding answers to current anxieties, Islamic militants have broken free from the shackles of the past in order to rebuild a world free of Western aggression and exploitation. Doubtless, their perspectives are often distorted. Doubtless, their emphasis on *taqlid* (strict adherence to the letter of the law) stifles internal dissent, dims the chances of innovation and interpretation (*jehad*), and impedes the emancipation of women. At the same time, they are not the rustic Bedouins to be herded by a Lawrence of Arabia, but skilled, sophisticated, urbanized professionals (invisible, of course, in India) trained in the metropolis. For right or wrong reasons, they offer hope to a tormented *millat-i-Islamia* (community of Islam). It is this self-perception, of being beleaguered, that needs to be addressed before taking recourse to the familiar stereotyping of Islam and its followers. The Muslim rage is real and not confined to the canonical texts prescribed in Egypt's Al-Azhar, Iran's Qum, or Deoband's Dar-al-ulum. It is directed not against Christendom or the West *per se*, but towards the inconsistency and injustice displayed by the US administration—Democratic and Republican—in dealing with Arab sentiments and popular aspirations.The rage is directed not against Judaism, but against Zionism and Israel. It is for these reasons, mostly secular in spirit and impulse, that the anger cuts across territorial boundaries and the ideological divide. Today, the West is faced with a challenge, the first of its kind after one of them, Adolf Hitler, burst on the scene threatening to destroy the foundations of Western civilization.The West was able to overcome that challenge—and thank God for that—but this is a different game altogether. Here the players will come and go without offering respite to their wearisome adversaries. The enemy is invisible, lurking in the shadows and waiting for the next best opportunity to strike. If so, banning terrorist outfits will prove to be an ineffective exercise unless backed by the creation of a Palestinian state, lifting of sanctions against Iraq, and withdrawal of US support to anti-democratic regimes in the Middle East.

Guns are silenced; mountains flattened.And yet the US appears to have lost round one of the battle. Victory in the next round depends on how best American policy-makers combine their military and political strategies to recognize the desire for change and progress in Muslim countries. Already, Osama bin Laden, the *enfant terrible* of the Muslim world, is on the way to achieving martyrdom. Dead or alive, he will be perceived as a hero.

18 October 2001

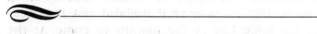

The Task Ahead

A grievous error of judgement on September 11 led to a colossal human tragedy—the death of innocent civilians in US, followed by the massive air strikes in Afghanistan. The action of the *jehadis* or terrorists is unpardonable, but so is the disproportionate reaction of the US administration. Having exercised restraint for nearly a month, the Bush administration, responding to the popular and justifiable revulsion against the terrorists, relented. In consequence, Osama bin Laden, firmly in the crosshairs of American rage, has become some sort of a messianic figure. Dead or alive, he will inspire the *jehadis* across the globe. An alternative approach—one that's still worth pursuing—is to forge an *ideological* rather than a military coalition.

This is a no-win situation. The death of Osama or Mulla Omar will achieve nothing; they will be well on their way to martyrdom. The relentless bombing of Afghanistan will, on the other hand, stiffen the resolve of the *jehadis* to wage future wars again the US. Drawing lessons from the Soviet experience, the US should get out of Afghanistan as fast as possible, and let its people sort out their mess. They cannot win this war. The US policy makers can, however, develop a long term agenda— to foster, *with the active support of the Muslim countries*, a counterculture and a counter ideology that will isolate the likes of Osama bin Laden. This, rather than the pounding of the Afghan mountains, is the way out of the present crisis.

The way out of the current predicament is not to punish the entire Afghan nation for the misdeeds of an individual and his Taliban followers. Cities like Kabul, Kandhar, and Herat form part of the historical memory of the Muslims: their bombing hurts and leads them to wonder if Baghdad and Damascus could meet the same fate in the months to come. At the beginning of the last century Shibli Numani, a reformist scholar, was outraged by Western imperialism directed against the Muslim countries. This is what he wrote:

Will someone ask, ye teachers of civilization,

How long these cruelties, these atrocities—how long?
How long this provoking hurricane of injustice and trouble?
This delight at wailing and crying—how long?
How long will ye take vengeance for the victory of Ayyub?
Ye will show us the sight of the crusaders—how long?
Shibli! Should you long to migrate, where can you go now?
Syria or Najd or Cyrene are sanctuaries—how long?

At the beginning of this millennium the same apprehensions are voiced from Cairo to Jakarta. Muslim fears, though exaggerated, will not be assuaged in the face of the West marshalling its enormous military and intellectual forces against the Muslim nations. If anything, their anxieties are heightened by the media's systematic attempt to conjure up the image of Islam as the number one threat to the West. Already, several writers have drawn the battle-lines between Islam and Christendom. The bosses in Stockholm have rewarded one of them, V.S. Naipaul, an Islam-baiter.

It is easy critiquing the West and offering guidance to Bush & Co. as to what they should do. Their conduct in Iran, Somalia, Sudan, and the Middle East deserves loud and strong criticism. Yet, the lamentation must cease and give way to self-introspection, to a reappraisal of the crisis that afflicts Muslim societies, and to a careful reordering of priorities. The survival of Islam is not at stake, the progress and prosperity of the Muslims is. Self-delusion and misplaced confidence—and that may well be the unfortunate outcome of the 'successful' September 11 attack—can only make their position more awkward and vulnerable.

Moving away from the anti-Western rhetoric, it is important to highlight the dismal failure of the Muslim nations to meet the very minimum standards of good governance. Somebody has to explain why Osama bin Laden and the Taliban target the West and not the regimes in the Middle East. Somebody has to analyse the absence or weakness of democratic movements in Muslim countries. Somebody has to tell us, furthermore, about the passive role of the Muslim intelligentsia and its acquiescence in political repression. What one needs is a powerful internal critique, free of religious rhetoric, which will set the Muslim societies on the right course and free their people from the stranglehold of oppressive governments. One thing is sure: no longer can the West be a convenient scapegoat for the ills that plague their countries.

In theory, the Muslim communities are not answerable to anybody else; in practice, their conduct is under close scrutiny. They must get their act together not because others want them to, but because sooner or later the forces of reaction and bigotry within their own ranks will overwhelm them. The enemy lies within the boundaries of a nation-state, acquiring a transnational dimension only in specific situations. The enemy is not Samuel Huntington, Salman Rushdie or Naipaul, but those who destroy statutes at Bamiyan, impose dress codes, and enforce a version of Islam that goes against the spirit and letter of the Koran. The enemies are those who flout the Prophet's following injunction:

O believers, be you secures of justice, witnesses for God, even though it be against yourselves, or your parents and kinsmen, whether it concerns rich or poor, for God, even though it be against yourselves, or your parents and kinsmen, whether it concerns rich or poor, for God is nearer to you than both. And do not follow caprice, so as to swerve (from the truth).

It is this search for truth and justice that must go on, in the traditions pioneered by the Sufis. The elusive notion of *umma* (international community) or the political ideology of pan-Islamism need not sway a Muslim. The finer definition of what constitutes *Sharia* need not be his sole concern. He needs to hold, rather than abrogate, his right to hold an independent opinion about right and wrong, good and evil. What he needs is to act according to his conscience and remind himself that he must be 'securers of justice' not only for his brethren but the whole international community, of Muslims and non-Muslims to which we belong.

Historical situations in which certain deductions are made from the Koran are no longer relevant; the Mutazalites in Baghdad, and Syed Ahmad Khan and Maulana Azad in our own country, repudiated them long ago. The Urdu poet Akbar Allahabadi ridiculed the type of casuistry practised by the ulama:

You can wear these souls and shoes
And make love to Miss D'Souze

If only you fast and pray
You can live and love as you choose.

Doubtless, the Muslims are inheritors of a great and glorious civilization. Indeed, nobody can deny to them the right to lead their lives in accordance with the injunctions of the Koran, the highest authority, and to regard the Prophet of Islam as the model of a Perfect Man. At the same time they cannot regard themselves as the sole possessor and upholder of true belief without coming into conflict with other religious traditions. Central to the of idea of Unity of Existence (*wahdatal-wujud*), expounded by the great thinker Ibn Arabi, is the acknowledgement of a Muslim community accepting the right of non-Muslims to profess their own faith. Taking our cue from the Sufi saints and the Persian and Urdu poets in India, we have every reason to reinforce and popularize such ideas.

A change in the mindset of the Islamists, in particular, will make the categories of *darul-Islam* and *darul-harb* irrelevant. That is when *jehad* in the modern world, in the sense in which Osama bin Laden or the terrorists in Kashmir use it, will loose its popular appeal. In the world of today, a secular idiom, as indeed secular goals, can be the sole *raison d'être* for waging war against the internal and external enemy. Expressions like *jehad* and *jehadis* are used rhetorically, with disastrous effects, to legitimize non-secular goals and ideologies. This is exemplified by the Taliban or the Pakistan-funded mercenaries in Kashmir.

Admittedly, some Western scholars are prejudiced, but the traditional presentations of Islam are woefully inadequate. The point to stress is that 'The West' is neither a unified entity nor is it inimical to Islam. Conversely, the ideology of Islam is not antithetical to Western ideas and institutions. Still, in the aftermath of the September 11 happenings, a great deal needs to be done to build bridges not between Islam and the West but between the Muslim countries and the rest of the world. When that happens we will not have to light candles to mourn the victims of terrorism.

The Hindu, *15 October 2001*

*Shahi Imam You've Got Mail*_____

Dear Imam Sahib, *As-salam-o-Alaikum*:
   You occupy an exalted position as the custodian of Dilli's
Jama Masjid. You are the prayer leader, the moral guide of the
thousands who pray at the great masjid. At the same time, the
faithful expect you to interpret the Holy Koran and the traditions
of our great Prophet and not to make political pronouncements.
The sweet sound of the *Azan* (call for prayer) from the minaret,
rather than the call for *jehad* from the pulpit is what they want
to hear.
   Scores of mosques, shrines and traditional schools dot our
landscape. Yet, we do not hear *fatawa* emanating from, say the
Fatehpuri mosque, situated so close to where you hold court.
Similarly, we observe piety on its knees at the sacred shrines in
Nizamuddin and Mehrauli, and not politicians lining up to pay
homage to their *sajjada-nashin*. These long-standing institutions
wield influence and command allegiance, and yet they are not
susceptible to political influences. Please follow their example,
eschew politics, and avoid turning our great masjid into a
political *akhara*. You will then find many more faithful being
drawn to you and the mosque. Piety, devotion, and humanity
are the essence of the Islamic faith.
   There is no Pope, priest or bishop in Islam. Islam also does
not recognize any form of social and religious hierarchy, *Ek hi
saf me khare ho gaye Mahmud-o-Ayaz* (the King and the slave
pray together), said the poet Iqbal. Doubtless, you have *inherited*
a position, and, for this reason, occupy a vantagepoint in the
lanes and by-lanes of old Dilli. But, surely, this does not give you
the right to be the sole spokesman of 120 million Indian Muslims.
Do the Shias accept your verdict? Do the Barelwis follow your
diktat? Do the Muslim farmers in Assam or the fishermen on the
Kerala coast know you? No, they don't. Can you deliver votes
for any political party from the Mallapuram district? No Imam
Sahib, you can't.
   If so, how do you represent the authentic voice of Islam in
India? Somebody must answer. My explanation is this: our

political classes repeat the mistakes made in the past. By negotiating with priests and politicians whose organizational base and political stature are by no means assured, they perpetuate their legitimacy as spokespersons of the whole community. Rather than forcing them into a situation where they are required to demonstrate their implied support, they refuse to draw out the conditions for such a confrontation. In the process the weight of orthodoxy stifles the liberal voices among Muslims. This was exemplified by the Shah Bano affair, and by my own personal experience at the Jamia Millia Islamia. In the event, the conservative Muslims establishment, backed by the non-left formations, tasted the fruits of 'victory'.

Let me turn to terrorism and to the relentless US bombing of Afghanistan. First of all, silence should not be construed as acquiescence in violence against the civilian population. Second, you should draw comfort from the strong body of opinion in this country—spearheaded not by the Muslims but by vocal liberal-left groups—that has lambasted America policies in Palestine and Iraq, and protested against the loss of civilian lives in Afghanistan. Instead, you raise the battle cry from the safety of the great mosque. Why? Some years ago, you committed a colossal blunder by asking Muslims to boycott the Republic Day celebrations. Now, your monumental folly is to call for *jehad* against the Anglo-Saxon world.

It is distasteful to talk of 'holy' wars in this day and age. What, if the *sangh parivar* declares *dharmayug* for 'liberating' their sacred sites? You and I will run for cover. The usage of expressions like *kafir* is equally unacceptable. Surely, the future of a great religion does not depend on taking recourse to such offensive categories. Surely, the Islamic personality of an individual can be developed and refined without conjuring up the false image of 'unbelievers' ready to strike at the faithful.

Imam Sahib, soothe rather than inflame passions. Develop a different vocabulary to convey the community's fears and aspirations, and reject, once and for all, the binary opposition inherent in the idea of *dar al-Islam* and *dar al-harb*. Have you heard of the call for *hijrat* (migration) to Afghanistan, the so-called *dar al-Islam*, during the Khilafat movement in the early

1920s? It was an adventurist campaign with disastrous results. While the divines stayed put in their homes digging into the *qorma* and *biryani*, scores of their Muslim brethren died of hunger and cold during their trek through the rugged mountains. Incidentally, their Afghan hosts put them in jail before sending them back to India.

An ideal world envisioned by the scriptures is out of our reach. And yet let's create a better world for ourselves by popularizing the idea of a *dar al-aman* (land of peace). Let Islam flourish along with other religious creeds. For us, the Muslim intelligentsia, the real challenge is to move beyond the somewhat simplistic approach of deploring and denouncing the West. In the present-day worldwide context, let us be vigilantly self-critical and aware of our historical and political situatedness. Let us challenge many obsolete ideas and concepts that impede progress, and espouse the cause of democracy, human rights, empowerment of women, and equal rights to the minorities. If we shirk our responsibility, you and I will become unwitting collaborators in Islamist ideologies whose costs to Muslim societies have been no less brutal than those of colonial domination.

Please do not stand in the way of those Muslims who wish to pursue, without impediment, the full development of their capacities and to contribute to their societies in all domains. I respectfully reiterate that we need to develop a variety of subtle analytical perspectives and positions in order to address problems afflicting Muslim societies—poverty, illiteracy, obscurantism, and the exploitation and social confinement of Muslims women. If public opinion is mobilized, it must be directed against feudal/monarchical regimes that seek legitimacy from Islam.

Admittedly, many of us, Hindus and Muslims alike, feel agitated over certain issues. So do you. When that happens, walk up to Maulana Azad's mausoleum or the shrine of Sarmad, the Sufi martyr of Aurangzeb's reign. Learn from them the values of liberal humanism and tolerance and consider the following verse Azad quoted in his essay on Sarmad:

Zuhiri's breast is full to the brim with the love of the beloved.

No place is left in my heart for hating my rivals.

Meanwhile let the cameras stop clicking, and let the tape-recorders be switched off at the Jama Masjid.

Khuda Hafiz!

31 October 2001

The Indian Muslim and the Loyalty Test

Edward Said points out how, in the global panorama of cultures, not all peoples are granted the equal right to narration and representation. This is more true of the Muslim communities the world over. Hence the appalling ignorance displayed in the media after September 11, the confusion created about the meanings of Islamic symbolism, and the tendency to conjure up the image of militant Islamic forces seizing control of the 'civilized' world.

At another level an utterly futile counter exercise continued unabated—to prove that terrorism has no sanction in Islam, that it is a peace-loving religion, and that the clash of civilization theory is totally unfounded. Added to this cacophony is the assertion that every Indian Muslim must pass the loyalty test prescribed by self-proclaimed patriots. Otherwise, their silence will be construed as acquiescence in terrorism.

Like Gabriel who brought Allah's message to his Prophet with the prefatory remark 'say', India's Muslims are told to condemn Pakistan's invasion of Kargil, terrorism in Kashmir and the US. And when they reiterate what they believe in, somebody comes up with the startling revelation that liberal Muslims hardly represent the community—only the Jama Masjid's

Imam does. So the task assigned to Javed Akhtar [poet and writer] & Co. is to dispel this impression. Believe me or not, it's hell of a difficult task, time-consuming, and too demanding for the establishment of one's nationalist credentials.

Life goes on with the finger of accusation perpetually pointed at the Muslims, regardless whether one is an atheist or a believer, a secularist or an Islamist, a Marxist or a Congressman. But, then, why should anybody trust us? Our ancestors destroyed and desecrated temples: hence our public figures remind us of our collective guilt by visiting the Somnath mandir. Muslim leaders partitioned the country; hence we must live in Bharat-varsha according to the *Sangh Parivar's* terms. Our brethren assassinated Mahatma Gandhi, Indira Gandhi, and Rajiv Gandhi, and other leaders. Our co-religionists instigate caste/class violence in different states. They foment terrorism in Punjab, Kashmir and the North-East, and not the Sikhs, Christians or Afghan mercenaries. And our educational institutions—not the Gurukuls and the RSS schools—disseminate 'mischief', and produce unpatriotic men and women like Badruddin Tyabji, Azad, Ajmal Ali Khan, Ansari, Rafi Ahmed Kidwai, Zakir Husain, Amjad Ali Khan, Ustad Bismillah Khan, Begum Akhtar, Azim Premji, Abdul Kalam, Shabana Azmi, and the Nawab of Pataudi.

We are a threat to India's unity. Why? Because we constitute a monolithic entity, marry four or more times, cheer the Pakistan cricket team, go to Saudi Arabia for Haj, read and recite Urdu poetry, and valorize terrorists like Osama bin Laden. This is how over 120 million people speaking different languages, following different customs, and owing allegiance to different parties, are located, categorized and described. To cap it all, Osama reminds everybody of the strength of the pan-Islamic sentiment. Besides the 'Islamic bomb' stored somewhere, Islamic terror is knock-ing at our doorsteps. No wonder, politicians gird up their loin to perform their patriotic deed! SIMI is banned; the POTO ordinance [ostensibly, to curb terrorism] is in place. Freedom is in peril: three cheers for its defence by the *Sangh Parivar*.

A balanced appraisal is required in these unsettling times. Let us not regard the Muslims as a homogenous entity, but as disparate and differentiated. Let us concede that the inter-pretation of Islam has changed over time, and that powerful pluralist visions shape Muslim communities. Let us spell out the Islamist and modernist movements without prior assumptions, discuss the contested terrain of who represents Muslims in State and society, the nature of the political and religious leadership, and the leadership's ability to connect with the varied experiences of Muslim societies.

Let us also recognize the emergence of a trans-national community, new phenomenon of increasing importance. Its social and economic profile is different from the previous unwieldy coalition of Islamist formations. It is upwardly mobile, self-confident, and in tune with the changes ushered in by globalization. Although this constituency carries some of the baggage from the past, its members mostly draw upon the range of contemporary experiences not from one but different locations. Why, they ask, are their co-religionists victimized in Bosnia, Somalia, Chechnya, Palestine, and Iraq? These sites confirm their belief that something is fundamentally wrong with the world they live in. It is this contemporary reality, rather than any Islamic doctrine, that contributes to the collective reaction.

My intention here is not to present an image of perpetually enlightened, largely innocent Muslim communities—more 'sinned against' than 'sinning'; nor to suggest that their fortunes or misfortunes can be explained solely in terms of unremitting power and prejudice of the West. I believe sections of the Muslim intelligentsia have constructed their own history at least as much as others have made it for them—and the reality is that they have caused more harm than good. The interface between certain kinds of Western writings and certain kinds of Islamic ones, and their re-surfacing in various forms of subsequent articulations, is something that neither Edward Said's diktat nor the idea of 'colonial discourse' can ever accommodate.

The Muslim intelligentsia—from the days of Shah Waliullah in the eighteenth century to Iqbal in the 1920s and 1930s—dialogued with itself and not with others. This has limited its political and religious engagements. The intervention of Muslim scholars seldom went beyond the communitarian frame, and, instead of re-writing their script in the light of ever-changing context and situations, they allowed ill-conceived theories and ill-founded assumptions to dominate the intellectual landscape.

Today, it is easy to notice the scholarly inertia in Muslim institutions, and the absence of protest, dissent and political activism. Lamentation rather than self-introspection are the dominant refrain. Outside medieval Indian history and Urdu literature, not much has been done to interpret Islam and analyse Muslim societies. The few Muslim intellectuals who have done so are, invariably, tied to flawed frameworks. They use Islam lazily to validate or refute different theories, and draw comfort from the limited intellectual resources provided by unoriginal thinkers.

Let me conclude on a different note—pointing to Muslim societies not being attuned to creating icons. Political heroes are scarcely remembered. On the other hand, martyrs, fighting on behalf of the oppressed souls, form part of a nation's memory. While the West has to guard itself against them, it must not ignore those Muslims who wish to fashion their lives differently from their ancestors and who, as co-citizens of an international community, seek havens of peace and justice.

Meanwhile, my countrymen please let me know, once and for all, if I have passed your loyalty test.

14 November 2001

Writing the Obituary of Political Islam

This Ramzan is different from the previous ones. Probably the celebration of Id-ul Fitr, a few days from now, will be equally muted. The US attacks on Afghanistan and the consequent loss of so many innocent lives sadden many. Islam's ceaseless demonization, despite Muslim countries joining the coalition against terrorism, hurts the faithful. And many are, of course, deeply shocked by the US acquiescence in Israel's assault on Palestine. The *Shab-i Qadr*—the night (twenty-third day of Ramzan) of the Prophet's ascension to heaven from the great mosque in Jerusalem—is over, but the Israeli State, prolongs the agony of the Palestinians.

Maybe the martyrdom of Hazrat Ali, the Prophet's cousin, which took place on the twenty-first day of Ramzan, would bear fruit next year when the Palestinians will achieve freedom from Jewish bondage. Maybe, this year's prayers on *Shab-i Qadr* will be answered next year. Maybe, rewriting the script for Afghanistan—the customary play on paper with ideas unconnected with the people's aspirations—will augur well for that war-ravaged country. Perhaps, a secular leadership is the panacea for the ills that plague over fifty Muslim countries.

One thing is for sure. Now nestling in their hideouts, the Taliban leaders are exposed as petty, short-sighted politicians who only used obscurantist ideas and religious and anti-Western rhetoric to bolster their political designs. In the end, they brought ruin and misery to their people, tarnished Islam's image, and made its followers vulnerable to the attacks of xenophobic elements in the West.

This is, sadly, how it has been for sometime—starting with Jamaluddin Afghani, the roving pan-Islamist in the last quarter of the nineteenth-century, continuing with Saddam Husain's ill-fated invasion of Kuwait, and culminating in Osama's silly and messy manoeuvres. Such adventurists, I repeat, serve neither the faith nor the people. If anything, their world-view is a sure recipe for self-destruction. Given the Iran, Pakistan and Afghan experience, it is time to write the obituary of political Islam.

Islamist ideologues have no business playing around with the lives of innocent people. They must be countered with the aid of liberal and secular ideologies that have been experimented with for centuries in Muslim societies across the globe. Religious zealots, on the other hand, must not be allowed to stalk our lands. Flowing beards and gowns do not necessarily represent true Islam; the spirit and temper of the faith does. Outward rituals are not good enough; spiritual journey begins from within, reaching commanding heights through individual exertion. One is a good Muslim—and that is Islam's quintessential message—

without wielding a gun and striking at 'enemy' targets.

The fact is that militant fanatics, nurtured to bolster US machinations in the region, did not carry much conviction outside their limited spheres of influence. Where are the militant Muslim armies overrunning the territories of their neighbours? Where is the great 'Islamic bomb'? Perhaps, lying in the cold storage at London's Harrod's! Where are the *jehadis* who were expected to burst forth from mosques/*madrasas* to wage war against the West? The bubble of Talibanization has burst sooner than later. Bamiyan's Buddha has seen it all. He, a victim of its brutal manifestation, knows that the Western media exaggerated the Taliban influence in the region.

The decapitated Buddha is smiling. He is also aware of the hollowness of pan-Islamism. The anguish over civilian deaths apart, neither the governments nor the Muslim communities are emergized to back the Taliban cause. Domestic unrest rather than Muslim solidarity caused the initial furore in Indonesia; Pakistan chickened out, hoping to make a few extra bucks; Bangladesh remained largely quiescent. And, thank goodness, the 120 million Indian Muslims offered no excuse to the *Sangh Parivar* to raise the spectre of a green menace.

Historically, tribal and ethnic identities have shaped the contours of Muslim societies. After the French Revolution (1789), the ideology of nation-states and nationalism have had greater appeal than the romantic notion of *umma*. Hence, the historic contest between competing Arab, Persian and Turkish identities. After World War I, Arab nationalism cut across the religious divide, despite rumblings in certain quarters, to develop on broadly secular lines. Similarly Palestinian nationalism, pitted against Zionism, has welded the Muslim and Christian communities in its struggle against Israel's occupation.

Although Islam binds peoples through its essential tenets, the ebb and flow of Muslim societies has not rested on divine commandments. Muslim nations are, consequently, split vertically and horizontally. So that pan-Islamism has been a vague idea, a grievance, a mere sentiment that is not translatable into a unified world-wide movement. Despite the essentialized image, lack of unity and coherence have been the hallmarks of Muslim societies;

hence, the multiple ideological strands and the diverse social and cultural practices.

Please, therefore, do not be swayed by Islamic symbolism. On close reflection, you will find your Muslim neighbour thinking and acting like you. Just as you, a practising Hindu, will not heed the demand for building a temple at the disputed site in Ayodhya, he, a devout Muslim, will not know the meaning of *jehad*. If, on the other hand, you ask him to wage *jehad* against your common oppressor, he may follow your lead.

In Islam's early days, *jehad* was the war cry of a tribal-ridden society. Later, rulers employed this emotive slogan to justify military expansion. Today, *jehad* is the weapon of the strong— military dictators and monarchs—and bears no resonance in the minds of the poor and the weak. That is precisely why its meaning must reflect contemporary realities. If the Muslim communities insist on *jehad* as a spiritual asset, they may consider incorporating some of the values embodied in Asoka's *dhamma*, in Sufi thought, or in Akbar's *Din-i Illahi*.

If they wish to nurture *mujahids* in the true ecumenical spirit of Islam, they will need to draw on democratic and socialist theories that have made this world a better place to live in. Indeed, Urdu writers and publicists have argued in the past that socialism means an organized and harmonious co-operation of individuals with a view to securing universal well-being. The Urdu poet, Hasrat Mohani, commended the crusade against exploitation and oppression by the socialists. Do you know that the same Hasrat, an otherwise devout Muslim, visited Mathura each year to take part in the Janamashtami celebrations? He followed the well-established eclectic Sufi tradition, pioneered by Amir Khusro and creatively expressed in the poetry of Jaisi, Rahim and Raskhan, of revering Hindu gods and participating in Diwali celebrations. This is, for you, another version of Islam observed in the subcontinent.

12 December 2001

Islam and Fundamentalism

Mushirul Hasan speaks to Manish Chand demystifying the 'Islamic ogre', debunking popular notions of *jehad* and *ummah*, and the fashionable but dangerous theory of clash of civilizations.

MC: How do you see the US whipping up the spectre of Islamic fundamentalism?

MH: There is no denying the existence of Muslim fundamentalism. Just as there is no denying of Christian fundamentalism or Hindu fundamentalism or, for that matter, Buddhist fundamentalism in Sri Lanka. So, fundamentalism is of all varieties. Just as one doesn't equate the events leading to the demolition of the Babri Masjid with Hinduism, or with the Hindu community, likewise, one should refrain from equating such trends and tendencies with any particular religion, the way Islam has been linked with all this.

The point to remember is that the essentializing of religions doesn't help to understand the dynamics of the problem. Nor does it help to arrive at a solution to the problem. I don't think there is an Islamic injunction that endorses acts of violence directed against civilians. So, the effort to discover the roots of terrorism in Islam is not only an exercise in futility, but also a very dangerous exercise at that.

MC: Why is there this pronounced tendency to find the roots of terror in Islam?

MH: This has happened for reasons that not many people have spoken of. There has been, for centuries, a conflict between Islam and Christendom. Now, Christianity knew how to come to terms with Islam *per se*. But it didn't know how to come to terms with political Islam. And with the rise of the Ottoman empire, Christendom faced a huge problem, which was aggravated by the character of political Islam. Political Islam, in any situation, is linked with the territorial expansion of the Muslim community. Now, if you come to the first half of the twentieth-century, the Western Hemisphere did all it could to thwart socialism and communist ideas. And with the self-destruction of communism and socialism in the 1990s, the spectre of the 'Other Enemy' had to be found. So, the whole lot of theories, of which Samuel Huntington's book is a classic exposition, were revived.

MC: You don't believe in Huntington's 'clash of civilizations' theory?

MH: It's a monumental myth reminiscent of the Crusades. Its founded on the superiority of the Western world. It not only reflects anxieties towards the Islamic world, but also serves to preserve the so-called superiority of the Western culture and civilization. There can be no inherent clash between civilizations. The Arabs live in the US, and work in the US. The Arabs live in Europe and work in Europe. The clash, if there is one at all, is an invented one.

MC: What is it about political Islam that inevitably puts it in opposition to the West?

MH: I am making a distinction between Islam and political Islam because, now, some Arabs and some South-East Asian countries have wealth and resources. This is not something the West is comfortable with. To begin with, the extremely important thing is that the West thought that liberal democracies as expressions of national identity were at variance with Islam and inconsistent with the needs of Muslim societies.

That's why Gamal Abdul Nasser had to be checkmated; likewise, the democratic and socialist upsurge in Algeria, Syria, Iraq, and Lebanon had to be countered. Why? In order to preserve the *status quo* in the Gulf region, Saudi Arabia, Kuwait and other Arab-Muslim countries. This is where you find the roots of anger. This is why you find that large sections of the Muslim community all over the world are seething with anger and discontent. The point is, you can quell democratic aspirations for a while, but they are bound to surface again and again.

MC: Are you trying to say that even if there was no Osama bin Laden, the West needed to invent him?

MH: He is an invention! Bin Laden is an invention. He has been nurtured by the US. The Taliban is a creation of the West. No one can justify terrorism. What is happening in Kashmir, the kind of terrorism aided and abetted by Pakistan, is not acceptable.

Nobody is gong to support it. But then how do you find a solution? The solution doesn't lie in just targeting one individual or one community or one country. Earlier, it was Saddam Hussain and Iraq. Before that it was (Yasser) Arafat and the Palestinians. And now it is bin Laden and the Taliban.

Hence, this strategy of marshalling resources and rhetoric to the destruction of the 'Other'. This is dangerous. One thing is clear: you can destroy Osama and the Taliban, but this will not bring security and eliminate terrorism. The retaliation will only produce more Osama bin Ladens.

This approach of inquiring into the roots of terror has attracted a lot of flak from the hard-liner lobby, who see it as a veiled apologia by intellectuals. Just because it's advocated by intellectuals doesn't make the exercise any less relevant. Sober reflection and a long-term perspective are what one needs in a crisis-ridden situation. To be swayed by emotions or any kind of jingoism is no solution. The US' sense of rage and anger is understandable, and the world identifies with that rage and anger. But the world must go on. And the world must go on with the Muslim communities and with the Arab nations. And they must figure in not always as enemies but as those representing a different culture, who have different aspirations and desires. And if America wants to fulfil the desires of its own people, it must be sensitive to the Arab people. What is uppermost in the minds of the Arab people? It is Palestine. Surely, the creation of the Palestine state is a legitimate demand.
MC: There are powerful emotions invested in the Palestinian cause, and these emotions, mingled with a sense of profound injustice, are often cited as one of the reasons for these attacks. Do you see any concrete changes in the US policy in West Asia?
MH: There will be a change. Once the dust settles down, there will be a fair amount of reappraisal. There will be a reappraisal of the invincibility of the US. And there will be introspection about what has led to such violent expressions of deep-seated anger by a group of people. And there will be a reappraisal about where the US has gone wrong. I have a strong feeling that something good and lasting will emerge out of this colossal tragedy.

MC: Why is there so much hatred towards America?

MH: In a bipolar world, there were many targets against which the anger of a group could be directed. It is directed against the US because the US is the key player. Its like a cricket team. The skipper has to take the rap for whatever the rest of the team does. If the US does recognize the aspirations of the Arab people in the way Clinton did, I am sure frayed tempers can be soothed.

MC: The concept of a transnational Muslim community haunts the US and the West. How far are these anxieties justified?

MH: The idea of the *ummah* (community) is the greatest myth perpetrated by theologians. There is no unified vision nor is there a single goal among the Muslims that goads them to act in unison. The Taliban, for instance, is seen as a retrogressive force by many Afghans and many Muslims the world over, and not just by the rest of the world. As enunciated in the Koran, the *ummah* is a very progressive idea. In its original form, it struck at the roots of parochialism and nationalism. It was an effort to create a Muslim personality that would not bear the lineage of race, language, colour and other parochial denominations. However, and this is the unfortunate part, its construction in the later centuries was designed to foster not an inclusive notion of Islam, but an exclusive notion. That's where the distortion takes over.

MC: There is this elaborate mythology of *jehad* being used by radical Islamist groups to justify their existence and terror tactics. What was the original meaning of *jehad*?

MH: Like the *ummah*, the meaning and import of the word *jehad* has changed drastically over the years. The Islamic world view divided the world between *Dar-ul-Islam* (the land of the pure) and *Dar-ul-harb* (the land of the enemy). In the Koran, there is a distinction between the 'the land of the peace' and 'the land of the enemy'. But this distinction made sense at a time when the Muslims communities were trying to evolve a code *vis-à-vis* the rest of the world.

However, once Muslim expansion reached the heartland of Europe, the distinction became difficult to sustain. Historically, *jehad* was used rhetorically by the imperialist powers to justify their worldly expansionist designs. In its original sense, *jehad* was more of an inner moral cleansing for the community. This was called *Jehad-e-Akbar* (The Great *Jehad*). But now, the whole notion of *jehad* is being used as an instrument for legitimizing militaristic, monarchic and dictatorial regimes. As for these radical Islamist groups, *jehad* is being used as a cynical ruse to whip up religious fervour for their cause.

MC: Khomeini called America 'The Great Satan' reflecting the popular feelings in the Arab world. And the US calls bin Laden, and the ideology he represents, America's 'Enemy No. 1'.

How do you see these rival demonologies? And is there a way out of it?

MH: The denigration of imperialistic power is at the heart of liberation struggles. For instance, Gandhi called the British empire the 'Satanic Empire'. As a way out of the perceived ideological enmities, you have to create a counter-ideology by invoking the liberal, eclectic and Sufi strain of Islam. Any other course of action is a recipe for disaster. There is a need for moral and ethical cleansing, just as there is a need for creating a political order that can only fulfil the aspirations of the people. The myth propagated by the US and some Western powers that Islam and democracy are not compatible has to be exposed and shown up to be dangerous in its implications. On the contrary, the US should try to strengthen democratic regimes in the Arab world. What is good for America can also be good for the Persian Gulf.

There has been pervasive stereotyping of Islam and the Muslims as a certain kind of people. Why do negative images proliferate in public perception and in the media? The negative images are there because of deeply entrenched biases and a failure to understand a different culture and its belief systems. But even as there are negative images, the dominant images after the September 11 attacks are that of Pakistan offering all help to the US in its war against terrorism. Not only Pakistan but most Central Asian and South-East Asian countries are offering support to the US. And most Arab nations have rallied around this global war on terrorism. The dominant image is that of the Indonesian President Megawati Sukarnoputri in Washington pledging her country's support to the US President. It is important to project these images to expose the myth of the *jehad* and the *ummah*. The concept of *jehad*, as has been used by the Taliban, is not the one most Muslim societies subscribe to. But myths stay despite live images. Popular stereotypes proliferate despite objective evidence to the contrary. That's the sad and distressing part.

MC: The way Arab-Americans have been targeted in the aftermath of these attacks, don't you think America's distrust of the 'Outsider' will only be accentuated in the coming days?

MH: Increasingly, the Arab-Americans will occupy the same space as the Turks in Germany. They will not be treated as an outsider, but will also be perceived as a byword for an entire constellation of negative traits. On the other hand, such is the dynamic of the American society that it can't afford to allow such tendencies to persist for long.

MC: As a liberal Muslim, how do you see all this impacting on Indian Muslims?

MH: On one level, the Indian Muslims lives in security provided by a secular regime. They enjoy and exercise the prerogative of dissent. I can talk to you freely and criticize the Bharatiya Janata Party (BJP) government for its saffronization agenda, and yet can feel secure that such views will not affect our relationship. At another level, cultural anxieties of Indian Muslims are heightened by majoritarian tendencies, as reflected in attempts at rewriting of history and the so-called 'saffronization of education'. However, in this war against terrorism, Indian Muslims are one with the Indian government's point of view.

MC: You spoke about something good emerging from this colossal tragedy. Do you see America and the world changing after these attacks?

MH: America will never be the same again. Neither will the world. There has to a major realignment of perceptions. If that realignment doesn't take place, there is nothing to save us. There is really no other choice. Americans will be more sensitized towards the world. America is not the world. And the Americans better wake up to this reality. They carry the burden of translating this idea of justice, not through military strikes, but through other means. The US government feels that they are accountable only to the American people. And, therefore, whatever actions they take enjoy their support. Increasingly, they will be accountable to the international community as well. The actions of the American government are going to be under increased global scrutiny.

MC: America has called the war against terrorism 'Operation Infinite Justice'. Don't you think the code name itself bristles with ironies?

MH: Yes, the irony of America's claim to deliver justice can't be lost. But let's hope they are serious and sincere this time and seen thus by the rest of the world. America has to understand that, as the only superpower, it has to behave in an even-handed and just manner. Justice is the key word here. Any other course of action will only lead to meaningless death and destruction.

Tehelka.com. *22 September 2001*

PART X

Gujarat Ablaze

It is one thing to write about death and reflect upon its implications on society, and quite another to experience personal loss, despair, grief, desolation and the failure to comprehend the death of a person near to oneself. An ethnography of dying—which is yet to be written—would have to include the emotional involvement of the dying and the bereaved. It would have to cope with the silence before death, besides considering concepts of death and the cultural practices related to it. I quote these lines as a poignant comment on Gujarat's bloody record in recent weeks.

While the affected families mourn the dead, Navratri is being celebrated throughout the country. But this Navratri is different from the previous ones. An anguished mother goddess travels from north to south and east to west, appalled by the conduct of some of her devotees in Gujarat who gang-raped, abducted and burnt alive Muslim women. As her numerous devotees flock to her temples with cries of *Jai Mata Di*, she turns around, pain writ large on her face, exhorting them to maintain and foster inter-faith harmony.

The omnipresent *Mata* stands amidst the debris of mosques and *dargahs*, bemoaning the loss of the nation's priceless heritage. This kind of vandalism is truly unprecedented in free India. Indeed, if Lord Rama had his way, he would return from Ayodhya, in the august company of Lord Hanuman, to rebuild the *dargah* of Wali Dakhini and Ustad Fayyaz Khan, and repair the damage caused to mosques, shrines, and *madrasas*. Given a chance, he would have waged war against the Ravanas in Gujarat.

Invoking the *Gita* or the *Ramayana* will cut no ice with the practitioners of hate and violence. They have done irreparable damage to their faith, and their Hindu heritage. There are other signs of degradation as well. A political party that adheres to no moral or ethical values governs us. Besides violating constitutional norms, it forges unprincipled alliances to stay in power. Now, of course, it is out in the open with its dagger pointed at not just the Muslims and Christians but all those who swear by the Constitution of India.

The BJP, the prime culprit, has seized the political initiative from its NDA partners, who were caught napping, to plot its own independent trajectory. With its declining electoral fortunes and the resurgence of the Congress, it has decided to shed its ideological inhibitions clamours for a Hindu *Rashtra*. The gamble may not pay off, especially if the Congress, now holding office in 14 states, gives up its lazy habits and resorts to mass mobilization on a continental scale. The message from Guwahati offers some hope and comfort.

Meanwhile, left parties must abandon their doctrinaire approach *vis-à-vis* one another, raise the level of popular consciousness, and act in unison with NGO's in order to forge an effective front against the beastly communal forces. Otherwise, the BJP-RSS-Shiv Sena combine will, uninhibitedly, invent yet another divisive issue to further polarize communal sentiments across the board. In that event, the left, already fatigued by its excessive reliance on parliamentary processes to the exclusion of mass mobilization, will be further marginalized. Moreover, we will be back to the dark days when L.K. Advani's *Rath Yatra* left, in its wake, death and destruction.

In this context, it is important to underline, first of all, that the Prime Minister's speech in Panaji provides a blueprint for his party's manifesto, and a guide to the BJP-RSS cadres to deepen their hostilities against the minorities. Second, he has seemingly abrogated his role as the country's Prime Minister and, instead, acted as the spokesperson of the BJP-RSS combine. Finally, by raising the spectre of a green menace and, in addition, expressing some unfriendly comments about the Muslims, he has implicitly but nebulously endorsed the 'two-nation theory'. It is for opposition parties, as indeed the NDA partners, to debate the 'dangerous streak of duplicity' in such utterances. Though the immediate issue is the fate of the Modi government, their conclusions will have a bearing on the survival of India's democratic and secular polity.

Clearly, statements emanating from Panaji and elsewhere are designed to undermine the confidence of the minorities, and instill in them a sense of fear and panic. What, then, is the way out? While the minorities should unequivocally reject the communal rhetoric and eschew the path of violence and confrontation, they need to emerge from the safe confines of legislatures, classrooms, and law courts to fight for their civic rights. They must act in unison with secular forces for fostering secular and democratic goals. Fear, complacency and passivity at this juncture will be construed as admission of defeat. Hence, the sphinx-like silence on the campuses at Aligarh, Jamia Millia, and Jamia Hamdard will not do.

Those habituated to agitating over religious issues should read the writing on the wall and draw a lesson or two from what happened in Italy and Germany. Meanwhile, the Prime Minister should be reminded of what Maulana Azad said at the Congress session in 1940: 'I am proud of being an Indian. I am part of the indivisible unity that is Indian nationality. I am indispensable to this noble edifice and without me this splendid structure of India is incomplete. I am an essential element which has gone to build India. I can never surrender this claim.' Dr. M.A. Ansari, another *jehadi* Muslim who presided over the Congress session in 1927, had this to say:

I consider the brotherhood of man as the only real tie, and partitions based on race or religion are, to my mind, artificial and arbitrary, leading to divisions and factious fights. Nationalism of a general and liberal type I can appreciate, but not the jingo nationalism of the German or the Italian type.

Today, we experience the jingo nationalism of the *Hindutva* variety. So, Durga Ma, I appeal to you to descend on this land and offer the hand of peace and reconciliation. Victory, as always, is yours for the asking. When politicians turn demons, we seek your intercession.

17 April 2002

We Know who Lit the Fire

'It would be intellectually satisfying if, in some ways, this book is regarded as a personal manifesto, a statement through the history of Partition and its aftermath, of the values which India's Muslims should cherish, of the national priorities they should promote.' This is what I wrote in 1997 introducing *Legacy of a Divided Nation: India's Muslims since Independence*. My conclusions were, then, based on the delineation of secular ideologies, the cross-communal networks in Indian society, and the social and cultural values shared by urban India's Urdu-speaking élites.

Today, India stands partitioned—not territorially, but in terms of the polarization that has taken place across the board. The swing of the electoral fortunes may temporarily reverse this process, but that may not bring about the meeting of minds and the mending of hearts. After Gujarat, second Partition has occurred, exposing the weakness of secular goals and policies. Recovering the secular ground is, admittedly, a compelling necessity, but the turf, vandalized by the *Sangh Parivar*, is at present, not easy to negotiate.

When asked to revisit *Legacy of a Divided Nation* at a conference held a fortnight ago at the Oberlin College, USA, it was difficult to define, with the BJP and its allies occupying the commanding heights of power, 'national priorities'. I was at pains to explain that the task of the liberal Muslim was even harder in the aftermath of the carnage in Gujarat. By all means, mouth secular slogans, write against fundamentalism, and exhort the Muslims to reform family laws. But, who is listening? Certainly, not the victims in Gujarat or the fear-stricken Muslims elsewhere. Sadly, in a highly polarized society even the fuzzy liberal agenda appears to have been irretrievably lost.

Many professional historians underlined the presence of just three parties in colonial India—the British, the Congress and the Muslim League—and, consequently, focused on a triangular narrative. As a result, we lost sight of the rising tide of Hindu nationalism, a powerful force that was beginning to mould attitudes and influence public opinion from the last quarter of the nineteenth-century. What is important is the emergence of this force, exemplified, for example, in the Arya Samaj movement, independent of colonial policies and the stridency of the political claims advanced by Muslim organizations. Today, the power, strength and appeal of this force in Gujarat needs serious probing in the context of the evolution of the ideology of Hindu nationalism.

Rooted in the ideas and movements of the late-nineteenth-century reformism, and essentially designed to demonize the Muslims and Islam, Hindu nationalism released its own energy to capture the minds of its potential adherents in urban areas. Seemingly dormant owing to the Congress' hegemonic presence, it surfaced in the 1940s to counter the Pakistan idea, an idea the RSS, the Hindu Mahasabha, and the Arya Samaj had itself cultivated by imaging the Muslims as 'the Other'. With its cultural and religious baggage gifted by the Orientalist scholars, Hindu nationalism gained a fresh lease of life in the late 1880s, directing its anger, once again, against the minorities. The pogrom organized in Gujarat has, from the standpoint of its votaries, advanced the project pioneered by none other than the Gujarat-born, Dayanand Saraswati. His book, *Satyarth Prakash*, is a classic exposition of the blatantly divisive ideas that are now being articulated in *Hindutva* circles.

Legacy, I repeat, was a personal manifesto of an individual born in free India, brought up in a liberal household where one read Ghalib rather than religious scriptures, heard Faiz, Majrooh and Firaq, and received lessons in history from leading Marxist historians like Irfan Habib and Athar Ali. Personally, I did not require a neat theoretical construct to put in place the working of different ideas and movements after Independence. To my generation, it was abundantly clear that secularism was a typically *Indian* goal; hence, its legitimation during the nationalist struggle and in the political processes thereafter.

It is true that the secular project suffered from certain ambiguities; equally, a secular constitution and state did not necessarily create a secular society. Yet, a secular blueprint offered by the

Constitution mirrored, historically speaking, India's trajectory during the colonial and postcolonial periods. In 1947, an alternative blueprint would have spelt disaster to the nascent Indian project.

Yes, we read Faiz and Firaq and revelled in the poetry of Sahir, Sardar Jafri and Kaifi Azmi. Today, many turn to Iqbal, the poet whose populism in the 1940s provided a grand ideology, a phantasmagoria in which some Muslims could find their image. Moved by the images from Afghanistan, Iraq, Palestine, and Gujarat, many read his poem 'Shikwa' (Complaint to God), or Altaf Husain Hali's 'The Ebb and Flow of Islam'. Comparing the catastrophe in Gujarat with Hulagu's invasion of Baghdad centuries ago, there is even talk of closing ranks, shunning *ijtehad* (interpretation), and following, both in letter and spirit, the Koranic injunctions.

Nursing such defeatist ideas will not do. Islam is not just a religion but a tremendous civilizational force; it will remain so despite the massacre of Palestinians, the plight of the Iraqis, and the trauma of Gujarati Muslims. Secularism, though assailed by the votaries of *Hindutva*, is not yet a defeated idea in civil society. It still commands, the allegiance of the non-BJP political classes. Let me also reiterate that a secular polity is the sole guarantor of our survival as a community and the nation. We have a stake in the secular project for a variety of reasons. One of them is that we don't want children to be burnt alive, women to be gang-raped amidst cries of *Jai Bajrangbali ki*, and mosques and shrines to be destroyed and desecretated.

So, when the battlelines are already drawn and the *trishuls* are out, it is important to defend our secular institutions and not retreat from the battleground. The fire of mutual hatred that is ablaze has to be extinguished by us. We know who lit the fire, and how it was lighted. The fire is blazing; it has to be put out. When that happens, we may not have to burn candles to mourn our dead, or bemoan the demise of secularism.

Let me conclude with Gandhi's message to the Muslims in 1921: 'They must not be irritated by the acts of irresponsible or ignorant but fanatical Hindus. He who exercises restraint under provocation wins the battle. Let them know and feel sure that responsible Hindus are not on their side in their trial in any bargaining spirit. . . India, for they are even as blood brothers, born of the same mother—*Bharat Mata.*'

1 May 2002

The Unthinkable has happened in Gujarat

The unthinkable happened a few days ago. An otherwise quiet evening on the Jawaharlal Nehru University campus in New Delhi was rented by the cries of *Babur ki aulad hosh me aon, hosh me aon*. Standing outside 139 Uttarakhand and watching the 200-strong students' march with hate and anger writ large on their face, I wondered what had gone wrong. Why raise provocative slogans at my doorstep? Have we, as teachers, failed to inculcate the values of tolerance and decency in our students? Why the erosion of secular and radical values? Where, if I might ask, are the new Yechuris (Sitaram) and Karats (Prakash) at the beginning of this millennium?

I sought and secured the University Rector's intervention, but what about the hapless victims in Gujarat? They are trapped in a world that is clearly not their own. Strangers in the land they have inhabited for centuries, nobody responds to the cries or comes to rescue them from the clutches of rampaging mobs. The tragic story of Ahsan Jaffrey's brutal murder is the story of every Gujarati Muslim—lonely, isolated and vulnerable to more attacks. Today, the army has reined in the VHP goons; tomorrow, they will return armed with swords and trishuls to attack the descendants of Babur. The army will buy 'peace', but it will not be easy to heal the wounds inflicted by so few on so many.

Today, the chief minister quotes Newton's third law—'every

action has an equal and opposite reaction'—to virtually justify the carnage in his own State. Tomorrow, he may pursue the game of brinkmanship and find an alibi for his inaction and criminal negligence. Yes, Mr. Prime Minister, Narendra Modi is a blot (*kalank*) on the nation's image. He has unleashed a reign of terror, and his deeds and public pronouncements merit unequivocal condemnation. Although the BJP government has itself forfeited the moral right to remain in power in Gujarat, you will do well to sack the Chief Minister, an irresponsible *sangh pracharak*, as a first step towards the restoration of peace in Gujarat. This may offer some consolation to the bereaved families.

At the outset let me reiterate—a view widely expressed by the Muslim leaders and Muslim organizations—that the brutal attack on the Sabarmati Express on 27 February is both regrettable and condemnable. Such an occurrence should never have taken place for the simple reason that mindless acts of minority violence invariably invite retribution and brutal reprisals. Yet, a newspaper editor construes silence, in some quarters, as acquiescence in the brutal murder of the *karsevaks* in Godhra. The VHP's General Secretary pours venom against the Muslims on a television network, while the Union Law Minister, instead of ridiculing him, pontificates on the virtues of self-censorship in reporting the ghastly happenings in Gujarat.

Admittedly, the murderous assault on the *karsevaks* was planned in advance, and the Godhra incident, caused by some Muslim miscreants, triggered the violence in other parts of Gujarat. Still, the Muslim complicity explains neither the conduct of the Chief Minister, the Home Minister and the police force nor the brutal retaliation of the Hindu mobs. When the authorities do not act decisively to contain and control riots, it is not because they do not have the means to do so, but because, for political reasons, they choose not to do so.

Let us not forget that the assembly elections in Gujarat will take place in January 2003. The BJP's state unit, headed by a hotheaded member of the *Sangh Parivar*, may well benefit from the riots as the protector of one community against the alleged threats of the other and may seek to present their political rivals, i.e. the Congress as protectors of the other community.

In this context, four issues need to be addressed: first, the criminal negligence of the administration; the level of intensity, destruction, and murder in particular times and places; the promptness and efficiency displayed by a mixture of lumpen elements and others in systematically destroying Muslim owned commercial establishments, hotels, restaurants and housing societies; and finally, the sources and causes of the deep-seated hatred and hostility towards the Muslims.

The persistence of Hindu-Muslim riots is not unusual. What is new is the rapid spread of the cult of violence aimed at the intimidation of Muslims, their selective killing, and the destruction of their properties. In this cult of violence, the Muslims continue to be portrayed as the aggressors, the Hindus as defenders. Somebody has to set the record straight.

Social and economic explanations exist, but, in addition, something is fundamentally amiss in Gujarat's history and contemporary polity that makes it prone to the recurrence of large-scale violence. At the heart of the explanation, past and present, is the fact that the social and cultural bonding—once the hallmark of that society—have weakened over the decades. Pride in a Gujarati identity, based on language and region, has disappeared leading to the formation and crystallization of sharply demarcated communitarian identities. It is easy to sow the seeds of dissension in a house divided.

In 1969, extensive Hindu-Muslim violence at Ahmedabad fractured Gujarat's polity and breached the citadel of composite living. Though the state limped back to some degree of normalcy, there was no attempt to channel the conflicts and violence through political and policy changes, and changes in leadership, institutions, and structures. Instead, the BJP turned the official secular ideology on its head by making a case, albeit a flawed one, for a Hindu *Rashtra*.

In the late-1980s, Hindu nationalism, riding on the crest of a popular wave, widened the existing cleavage. L.K. Advani's *Rath Yatra* from Somnath was the last straw. The intensification of Hindu-Muslim ill-will during the Ramjanmabhumi movement was part of a political design to create a new Hindu community. The very nature of that exercise was profoundly divisive. The roots of the present violent conflagration lie in the evocative symbols deployed by the BJP to enlarge its political constituency.

The pogrom in Gujarat epitomizes the tragedy of a weary nation caught up in the quagmire of ethnic, caste and communal conflicts. Today, the Prime Minister terms the Gujarat carnage as a 'blot on the nation's image'; tomorrow, the international community may well challenge our claims over Kashmir and the high moral ground we occupy in being part of the world-wide coalition against terrorism.

The project of building the temple must be abandoned in the interest of the Indian nation and its citizens. This will, surely, restore the dignity of our country. Above all, it is certain to bring peace and comfort to Lord Rama.

6 March 2002

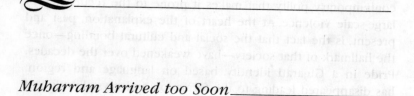

Muharram Arrived too Soon

The Gujarati Muslims—a fair mix of Khoja, Bohra and Memon communities—are markedly different from us, in U.P. and Bihar. Follow their social habits and cultural traits, and the depth of their integration with local society may well surprise you. They neither spearheaded nor actively supported the Pakistan movement. They speak Gujarati and not Urdu. They are religious without being swayed by Muslim orthodoxies. Their cultural symbols, mostly secular, lie in Gujarat and not in the volatile Indo-Gangetic belt. In short, they are quintessentially Indian. This makes the story of their genocide so much more poignant.

The Muslims observe Muharram with usual solemnity. Processions are underway mourning the martyrdom of Imam

Husain, the grandson of the Prophet of Islam, and his family. For the Muslims of Gujarat, Muharram (month of mourning) arrived a bit too soon. Their lives are shattered by the orgy of violence. Burnt houses and commercial establishments and the debris of shrines and mosques, including the one built in the sixteenth century, mutely witness the horrors perpetrated in the land of Gandhi.

Survivors mourn their dead, the hapless victims of unprecedented hate and aggression. The dead cannot tell their tale, but the living do. The tragedy of Karbala took place in AD 680 on the bank of the Euphrates in Iraq; it was re-enacted on the Sabarmati river a few weeks ago. For the Gujarati Muslim, every evening is the *Sham-i Ghariban* (the night of the mournful). The crack of dawn raises little hope of a safe and secure future. Darkness envelops the lives of the rich and the poor, the urban dweller and the rural folk.

Rat aur subh bahut der gale milte-rahe.

Daybreak and night lay long in each other's arms.

True, Hindu-Muslim violence has rocked Gujarat before, but this carnage has turned its major cities into a graveyard of secular nationalism. M.A. Jinnah talked of two-nations in the 1940s. Presumably, he erred in his judgement. Yet, those of us who harp on composite culture as the principal feature of Indian society need to leave Gujarat out of our frame. Those of us who celebrate secular nationalism, as opposed to the two-nation theory, need to arrive at a more nuanced understanding of the past. The 'Unity in Diversity' claptrap will not do.

As in Tel Aviv where the UN Charter lies in tatters, Gujarat has become a live testimony to the utter contempt that the Indian Constitution and the rule of law have been reduced to by the BJP's elected representatives and their VHP and RSS allies. Yet, the Chief Minister remains in office despite the countrywide demand for his resignation, and receives, from the country's Home Minister, a testimonial of good conduct. Long live the *Sangh Parivar's* solidarity! The Police Commissioner's appalling conduct and indiscreet statements must be comforting to scores of senior police officers prone to wielding the big stick against the minorities, Dalits included, and trade union leaders. Even if indicted by a commission, he will go scot-free. The government-appointed commission is itself an alibi for inaction and a massive cover up operation.

A few months back, SIMI, an organization of a couple of hundred misguided youth, was banned to please George W. Bush. But has Uncle Sam directed this government not to ban the VHP and the Bajrang Dal? Many of their members, masquerading as *karsevaks* or *Rambhakts*, adopt terrorist methods to kill, loot and intimidate the Muslim and Christian minorities. More than anything else, the storm-troopers of the BJP-RSS have tarnished Hinduism's tolerant and eclectic image. In an ugly display of violence, they have now attacked the citadel of democracy in Orissa. All in the name of the benign Lord Rama! Somebody has to call their bluff; otherwise, they may cause incalculable damage to our polity and society.

Provisions of POTO and TADA have been pressed into service to nab 'terrorists', though the perpetrators of the worst possible crimes against innocent civilians are still at large. Their knives are still out in the open. Only the Muslims—already battered and bruised—find themselves at the receiving end. They continue to suffer, their agony prolonged by the apathy and criminal neglect of the Gujarat administration.

> Bury me, oh my country, under your pavement,
> Where no man now dare walk with head held high,
> Where your true lovers bringing you their homage
> Must go in furtive fear of life or limb;
> For new-style law and order are in use,
> Good men learn,—'Stones locked up, and dogs turned loose'.

Written in Lahore jail in the 1950s by Faiz Ahmad Faiz, these lines sum up the sense of loss, tragedy and humiliation of India's Muslims in 2002.

Violence continues sporadically, spreading to the tribal belt. People flee their villages only to become refugees in their own place of birth. Relief camps are inadequately equipped; yet the practitioners of modern hate, having performed their brutal operations with meticulous care and planning, prevent food and medicines from reaching the victims. Reminiscent of what happened during the dark days preceding the transfer of power, they have called for the social and economic boycott of the Muslims.

Scores of politicians, having heard and seen it all, do precious little to mount pressure on the Central government to provide relief. Why don't they observe a symbolic fast, the traditional but effective Gandhian method, as an act of penance? Previous Prime Ministers visited sites of violence and brought some comfort to affected families; the present one has not moved out of 7 Race Course.

The NDA allies produce the familiar noises without rocking this government's boat. Kashmir's chief minister growls but to no avail. Self-proclaimed disciples of Rammanohar Lohia and Acharya Narendra Dev do the same. Eventually the socialists in the NDA, too, will make their peace with the establishment and remain firmly ensconced in their ministerial benches.

Love of power, in various limited forms, is almost universal. There is, however, a great difference between power desired as a means and power desired as an end in itself. Only in myth can Shiva drive a straight path through the opposition with his trident affairs. In politics, the NDA partners, free India's gold-diggers, will bow before political exigencies.

In Gujarat's bloody landscape, the Muslims cannot be expected to pay heed to liberal and secular exhortations. Yet, they must eschew any form of retaliation. The nation's glory lies in our hands, in fostering reconciliation and promoting camaraderie between the religious communities. This is a moment of trial not just for the Muslims, but for the Indian nation. Freedom is in peril; let's defend it with all our might.

20 March 2002

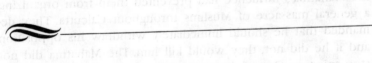

2002: A Sad Odyssey

I share with you the following reminiscences of encounters with Mahatma Gandhi and Jawaharlal Nehru. I found these in the A.P. Benthall papers at the Centre for South Asian Studies, Cambridge.

SCENE I

In the autumn of 1947 Gandhi arrived in Calcutta and stayed in a tumble-down house on the outskirts of Calcutta, near one of the scenes of the worst Hindu-Muslim riots. Soon, he realized that one of the principal causes of the rioting was the poverty of the people and the terrible conditions under which some of them lived. Hundreds of thousands of people had no roof over their heads at all, and millions lived in slums of the worst description. He therefore summoned leading businessmen of all descriptions in order to rebuild Calcutta. He wanted the project to be completed within two years.

Benthall, vice-president of the Bengal Chamber of Commerce, set off to the rendezvous, but on the way encountered a riot. 'Bombs were exploding and guns were being fired, and the streets were littered with glass and stones', he wrote. When he reached the house, he found Gandhi sitting on a low wooden platform, spinning, and wearing only a loincloth. A small girl was sitting on the platform near him, apparently learning to spin, or perhaps ministering to his needs.

Twenty minutes after the Gandhi-Benthall meeting, a mob of young Hindus broke into the house. They were furious because the Mahatma's influence had prevented them from organizing a general massacre of Muslims throughout Calcutta. They demanded that he should immediately withdraw his opposition and if he did not, they would kill him. The Mahatma did not stop spinning. One of the young men then aimed a blow at his head with a *lathi*. The little girl sitting beside him caught the blow on her arm. Gandhi continued to spin.

Nobody else in the crowd then had the courage to strike the

Mahatma again. They merely vented their fury on the building, pulled the window frames out of the walls, smashed the doors, and reduced the scanty furniture to matchwood. And yet, from the moment when the little girl saved the Mahatma's life, the rioting in Calcutta ceased, and nothing of the sort occurred in the city for a good many months.

SCENE II

From 1947 to 1950 Benthall represented on numerous occasions the Bengal Chamber of Commerce and the Associated Chambers of Commerce of India. In these capacities he had numerous meetings with Nehru, sometimes in company with others, and sometimes alone. He recalled his visit to Calcutta, soon after Independence, to combat the rioting and massacres that were taking place in Bengal. The Prime Minister sat at a desk which had on it a large inkpot, some pens and pencils, and the weighty volume of *Thacker's Indian Directory*.

A discussion took place about how best to combat the communal ill feeling. It proceeded on sensible lines for some time, but after a bit some Marwaris made an impassioned appeal for the Indian Army to go into East Pakistan to rescue the Hindus, who, it was alleged, were being massacred there.

Nehru listened for a short time, but then suddenly appeared to lose his temper. He picked up the directory, raised it to the full length of his arms above his head, and brought it smashing down on the desk. This action he repeated three or four times, with greater and greater force. The ink-pot, pens, etc., scattered on to the floor. He accused the Marwaris of deliberately planning a war and a massacre of Muslims, though they themselves were prevented by their Jain religion from taking up arms or even crushing a mosquito. He continued with extraordinary eloquence until the Marwaris slunk out of the room, leaving only people from other communities to listen to the Prime Minister. Shortly after that the discussion returned to a minor key, and the meeting dispersed.

In fact, added Benthall to his description, no Hindus were massacred in East Bengal at that time, though hundreds of thousands were driven out to take refuge in West Bengal. Nehru was of course right in refusing to send the army across the new frontier, and his violent reactions to such a suggestion was typical of the man.

SCENE III

This is a brief trail of what happened in Calcutta after Independence and Partition, and the long downward spiral since. Gujarat 2002 is different. The nature of the times, of leadership, and of communal riots itself, has changed. Narendra Modi, who has virtually written the script of murder, death and destruction, holds the reins of office in that State. His targets have been so utterly mundane. A pregnant Muslim woman. School children. A housing colony. Worst of all, the very idea of inter-community peace has been destroyed by the Chief Minister and his VHP-Bajrang Dal goons. Their narratives, inspired by the evil-minded ideologues of the RSS, continue to feed hatred and prejudices. His presence is the greatest threat to Gujarat's well being. Already, the fact of the violence permeates daily life in its cities. Hence, his return to the *shakhas* in Delhi as an ordinary *swayamsevak* may be the only way back to hope.

While the print and electronic media broadcast a steady stream of reports on Muslims under fire, their homes and commercial establishments destroyed, their children killed, the Prime Minister chooses to holiday. He should have been in Ahmedabad providing the healing touch, and not in Nainital. The attitude of his lieutenant, George Fernandes, continues to be opportunistic. Having given Modi the clean chit (remember, how he shamelessly exonerated the administration after the murder of Staines) now deserves, not a knighthood or an O.B.E., but a pair of khaki shorts from the RSS headquarters. He has the unique distinction of presiding over the liquidation of what little is left of Ram Manohar Lohia's legacy.

Meanwhile, the RSS diatribe against the Muslims goes on, with its chief asking them to fall in line. His is an ominous warning. What, if they don't? A repeat of the Gujarat carnage? I hear Ariel Sharon saying the same sort of nasty things in Tel

Aviv. Clearly, there is a residue of the old fascist attitudes that spawned the RSS policies in the 1930s and 1940s which ultimately led to the assassination of Gandhi.

The silver lining in this otherwise dismal picture is the role of the media and the activism of the secular forces, led by Left-wing parties and groups. The Congress, too, has given up its lazy habits, and the Italy-born Sonia Gandhi is, indeed, perceived as the guarantor of secular peace in this country.

3 April 2002

PART XI

From Overseas

The Miracle in Giridih:
Daktarlog, *Come Again*_____

Nobody in India will confer upon them any honours. The media will neither cover their arrival nor detail their activities. Yet, year after year they travel to a region, where even the gods have failed to perform a medical mission. No guard of honour to announce their arrival, no photo sessions, and no welcome speeches. Just a handful of earnest Rotarians at Calcutta's refurbished international airport take them to Dhanbad, the coalfield, *en route* to their destination.

They work hard—from dawn to dusk—bringing relief to scores of sick people. And then, after a week or ten days when the sun begins to set early and the wintry winds sweep the paddy fields, the word spreads far and wide that the *daktarlog* (doctors) and *daktarnis* (lady doctors) were going home. Saddened at the prospect of their *mai-baap* leaving, they assemble outside the crumbling boundary wall of the Bagheria Hospital with folded hands, their turbans placed on the ground. Soon, a noisy jeep emitting smoke and contaminated diesel emerges from the hospital gate on its trek to Dhanbad.

For the rural poor the uppermost thought is whether the *daktarlog* and *daktarnis* will return next year to perform what they consider to be reconstructive miracles. It is a hope they have lived with for several years. Yes, they will.

The Virginia Children's Connection, formed in 1989 as a voluntary body, has acquired a respectable profile for its outstanding work over the years. Nowadays it receives wholesome support from individuals and organizations. This year (1999) the Northwest Airlines took care of international transportation, while the Merck and Roche pharmaceutical houses provided medicine. I found the VCC members, including my Charlottesville dentist, well and truly committed. I sensed the fervour (not evangelical, mind you), enthusiasm and commitment that move people like them the world over to serve fellow human beings.

Victims of war, famine, diseases and natural calamities can

hardly afford to wait endlessly for revolutions to transform their lives. They are beholden to anyone and everyone who can bring to them immediate relief. Mention Bihar, and you may be treated to a sigh, a yawn, or even a roll of the eyes. But members of the VCC are undeterred by what goes on in Patna's murky political world. At the beginning of this millennium, three plastic surgeons, three anaesthesiologists, two dentists, a paediatrician, a medical student, six nurses, a physical therapist and a photographer travelled from Charlottesville, an attractive university town (population: 45,000-50,000) located in the heart of Thomas Jefferson country. Giridih was their destination. Their mission—to correct cleft lips and palates caused mainly by Vitamin B deficiencies, and facial scars resulting from burns. There are of course other volunteer medical groups working in India, but few focus on children and fewer still on the reconstructive surgery performed by the VCC.

Their leader is the affable 39-year old Dr. Thomas J. Gampper, a plastic surgeon at the University of Virginia Medical Centre in Charlottesville. When I met him, he told me, 'It's amazing to me. You can change a child's life in an hour.' Reflecting on what he and his team had accomplished during their January visit, he said that the beauty of the experience came from knowing that they had changed a child's life forever. How much will it cost to perform such operations in the United States? 'Three crores', replied Dr. Gampper.

I realized that the payoff for the team members was not in dollars or rupees, but in the affection and gratitude of those children of Giridih whose lives were transformed.

Frankly I had not heard of Giridih. So I turned to Professor Walter Hauser, an eminent historian of South Asia who has guided researches on Bihar in the twentieth-century. He tells me that a large Adivasi population inhabits the district, in the heart of south Bihar's mining region (Chotanagpur or Jharkhand). Though the region produces coal, as do other areas in Chotanagpur, the district is a major producer of mined mica. Topographically and economically, Hauser compared Giridih to Appalachia in West Virginia, and Kentucky. It is something of a rough, tough 'frontier' environment. Not exactly the kind of place, I said to myself, where you'll find people making sparkling conversation.

As I said, it began in 1989 when two surgeons—Dr. John Persing and Dr. John T. Lettieri—from the University of Virginia Health Sciences Centre devoted two weeks of their time repairing congenital and traumatic deformities. Why Giridih? Simply because Dr Lettieri's in-laws had lived there for about 38 years as missionaries and saw a need. Remember, the VCC made the gruelling trek not as evangelists but as professional surgeons who believed in serving not only those in needs at home but also those abroad. They received no monetary compensation, but were rewarded in other ways.

Dr. Mark Harris, the paediatric anaesthesiologist on the 1990 team, stated, 'You get a tremendous amount of personal satisfaction from providing care to people who otherwise wouldn't receive it. But for every child you help, there are thousands upon thousands you can't help. This is frustrating.' Focusing on younger children was intentional, because socially 'they have the greatest potential for getting on with normal lives', to quote Dr. Persing. Today, the team was building more than lips and palates. They were building self-esteem.

Rough and tough the place may be, but the 1,00,000-plus inhabitants of Giridih have been crying out for medical help for decades. We have excellent doctors and surgeons in the country but they end up in private clinics and multinational-sponsored hospitals. Happily some people, living some 10,000 miles away, offer care and comfort to the rural poor in depressed areas like Giridih. They make their own modest contribution to what is a massive task of building a decent health system. But sooner or later, the state and central governments will have to do some quick thinking.

Rewriting history textbooks or tampering with the Constitution can scarcely take us very far. Providing adequate medical facilities to our people alone will create a strong and healthy nation. Who do I say this to? Is anyone listening? As the poet (courtesy: noted Malayalam poet, K. Satchidanandan) said:

Nothing had changed
When I woke up after twenty years, I am going to bed.
Rouse me when it changes.
I shall then tell you how the world was
In such a way that
You would long to go back there.

23 February 2000

Musings of an Arab Scholar

Hur ek baat pe kehte ho tum ke tu kya hai
tumhi kaho ke ye andaaz-e guftugu kya hai

GHALIB

Quite a few Orientalists could well be repeating these lines to
Professor Aziz Al-Azmeh, a leading Arab intellectual located in
the Western Hemisphere. Though not so widely read in India,
his powerful critique of the scholarship on Islam has brought
name and fame to the Syrian-born and Oxford-educated historian.
Consider the title of his famous book, *Islams and Modernites*,
and his comment:

The very premises of Islamic studies are radically and thoroughly
unsound; their very foundation, the identification and the construal of
relevant facts, is based upon a political and cultural imagination. . . .
Any proper writing of Islamic history has to rest on the dissolution of
Islam as an orientalist category. . . . It has to liberate itself from
Islam. . . . Only then will Islam be disassociated and reconstituted as
historical categories amenable to historical study.

Professor Azmeh, who was invited to India a year ago by the
Indian Council for Historical Research and will travel to Delhi
again next February, agreed to discuss some contemporary issues

with me at the Institute of Advanced Study in Berlin, where he runs a major project on Islam. He began by telling me how he admired India's liberation struggle and how, as a graduate at Oxford, he was inspired to read about the secular and democratic institutions of the Nehruvian era. He is both surprised and impressed that those structures, especially those regulating the management of culture, survive and continue to flourish.

What an achievement! India is one of the very few Third World countries that have produced an indigenous high culture, including academic culture, of a very high order. Indian economists, historians and sociologists are widely respected in the international community of scholars. Sadly, the Arab world has not managed to crystallize processes of the same kind.

Some Arab countries have, moreover, not succeeded in preserving their secular values and traditions. Today, secularism is endangered not in Algeria but in Egypt, where 'Islamic phraseology is taking over almost the entirety of public life. Even secular figures are seeking ratification from Koranic verses.' The Egyptian government plays a double game, projecting itself as secular to the Western world but making concessions to Islamicists who have a strong presence in the state machinery. Elsewhere, there are ascendant Islamicist ideological/political forces; some are indigenous but most are inspired by, or act at the behest of, Saudi Arabia.

The Islamicists have developed a sophisticated organizational, information and educational infrastructure in the last three decades. The impetus to their activities was provided by the cultural section of the Truman doctrine, and by the Americans and the Saudis who were jointly pitted against Syria and Egypt in the 1960s. Still the 'fundamentalists' remained dormant until the Salman Rushdie affair. 'The controversy over *The Satanic Verses* gave them a concrete and tangible sense of purpose; indeed, they became effective and influential thereafter.'

Asked if the unresolved Palestinian issue offered a *raison d'être* to fundamentalists, Professor Azmeh opined:

Remember, Hamas is an effective and sophisticated political movement with a coherent anti-colonial agenda. At the same time, it endeavours to revolutionize and resocialize the entire Muslim world from within.

The Hizbullah in Lebanon has the same project, though much less interested in imposing its agenda on the entire population. Having said this, I must emphasize that the Palestinian question no longer plays such a pivotal role. Today, its role is one of lamentation and not encouragement.

I went on to discuss the 'crisis' in the Arab world: the repudiation of Gamal Abdul Nasser's secular legacy, the reasons for the collapse of the left and democratic front, and the factors leading to the growing cynicism among the educated classes. Professor Azmeh underlined how the Western Powers, led by the United States, had aligned themselves with despotic and authoritarian governments to suppress liberation movements, how the collapse of socialism and communism weakened the Arab cause and bolstered Israel's position, and how the acute socio-economic crisis facing the Arab world may prove to be the last straw. With people trying to make ends meet, where is the time for revolution or meaningful political engagement? 'The disappearance of the middle classes, the lazy habits of quietism and compromise instituted by despotic regimes, and the lack of internal class structuration [except in Morocco] have changed the course and direction of Arab society and politics.'

As our discussion came to a close, I noticed an element of despair and despondency in some of these formulations. Professor Azmeh seemed visibly moved when talking about the uncertain future of the Arab States in the comity of nations. I asked if my impression was right. He picked up his umbrella, looked at the dark clouds hovering above the Institute, and stood silent. When I pressed, he said:

I take the view that we should accept the existing regimes in the Arab World, create areas of political opening and avoid engaging the State directly or frontally. Engaging the State has two drawbacks. First, it is bound to lead to the persecution and repression of the activists. Second, it will strengthen the hands of the Islamicists who, with the active backing and patronage of the NGOs, have latched on to the international civil rights agenda in order to undermine the State. The Arab State is a positive historical acquisition; we must not let it be undermined.

Is the future grim? 'Not necessarily. The Arab regimes, having learnt a few lessons from their past mistakes, are opening up culturally and economically.' Do we, in India, need to learn from the Arab experience after Abdul Nasser? 'Not at all. We must benefit from the Indian experience, rather than the other way round.'

I stepped out of the Institute secure in the conviction that India's image in the Arab world, tarnished by Pakistan's propaganda during the mandir-masjid controversy, can be vastly improved if we renew our intellectual and cultural links with the intelligentsia. Instead of looking to the West all the time, let us try and understand the fears and aspirations of the democratic and secular elements in Arab societies and strengthen our ties with them. Our future lies in closer cooperation with them and our neighbours.

29 November 1997

The West Asian Peace Talks: Riven on the Inside

History, politics and international diplomacy have been repeatedly cruel to the Palestinians. For several decades the erstwhile colonial powers, having divided people and territories before and after decolonization, ignored their legitimate claims. Battered and bruised for more than thirty years and driven out of their homes—since the Six-Day War—they discern no immediate silver lining.

As darkness descends on the holy city of Palestine, hopes turn into despair. Patience turns into anger as the Israeli government flouts the Oslo Accord without inviting the wrath of international opinion.

The major irritant is the continued construction of settlements and by-pass roads through territories that Israel still recognizes as Palestinian. The Palestinian Authority is reduced to a minor player. Yasser Arafat, who has announced that he will proclaim a State on 4 May 1999, is the head of a 'nation' that does not exist in reality. His credibility is low, for many in the Arab world accuse him of a 'sell out'. The Al-Hamas gathers momentum, as hopes of a Palestinian state recede with every passing day.

On the other hand, Israelis have every reason to rejoice in the half century of the existence of their State. It has friends all around the world, particularly in the US and Europe where people recall, with a sense of guilt, their betrayal of the Jews during the Holocaust. You cannot convince people in, say, Amsterdam or Berlin of the just Palestinian cause.

Now the home of about one in three of the worlds' 15 million or so Jews, the country is on the move. Its GDP per head is $17,000, putting it within striking distance of many West European countries. More importantly, a State carved out of a great insult of people sentenced to be the horrifying symbol of the foreign and cursed, has survived and prospered. As David Grossman wrote in *The New Yorker*, Israel is the only place in which a Jewish person can live with vital ingredients of the history and culture and mental life of all the generations of Jews that have preceded him, and can realize them in the creation of a new and modern reality.

Fair enough. Yet Israel is today riven with disputes between the Ashkenazim (Western Jews) and Sephardim (Oriental Jews), and by conflicting perceptions about the unfinished Zionist business. Tension is mounting between the ultra-orthodox, the inheritors of the legacy bequeathed by David Ben-Gurion, and the 'secularists' who feel uncomfortable with rabbinical authority and the rising voice and power of orthodoxy. There is a sharp cleavage between the protagonists of peace and the hardliners in different parties, including Likud, who have turned 'national security' into an obsession. Yitzhak Rabin's assassination symbolized the great divide in Israeli society.

Gabriel R. Wardburg, former member of a left-wing socialist group, founding vice-chancellor of Haifa University and a scholar of international repute, has no individual and collective memory of the Holocaust. His family had emigrated from Germany well before Hitler's naked aggression against the Jews. But he was inspired, as were millions, to return to the Promised Land and contribute his bit to the making of a nation.

Wardburg, 71, is an intellectual with a difference, though his reasoned voice, once muted in Tel Aviv and Jerusalem, is much more widely heard now than ever before. He speaks slowly but firmly. When asked if Israel was an illegitimate child of British colonialism, he reminded me that the birth of Israel is the natural culmination of Zionism, started in late nineteenth-century. The British, he insisted, were nowhere in the picture until the Balfour Declaration (1917) supported its objectives.

Today, the Arabs do not question the legitimacy of the State of Israel. Wardburg is no exception. At the same time, he is candid in criticising government policies. He invokes the Declaration of Independence (15 May 1948) to reiterate that Israel should treat its million Palestinian citizens—almost a fifth of the population—as equal and not as second-class citizens. 'Israel's story is unfinished, its dreams have not been realized. I hope realpolitik will force the party in power to build a just society and achieve peace. I hope Israel will be more accommodating and allow Arafat to perform his historic role.'

Does he share the Palestinian anger? 'I understand their anger. Surely, a Palestinian state can co-exist with Israel.' What should the Arabs do? Wait and watch?

How can I pretend to speak in their name? Yes, boundaries need to be redefined. Jerusalem should remain a common city for all, Jews, Christians and Muslims, and the Arabs must have the right to administer the regions they inhabit. We must make peace with them. Let us not be euphoric and forget either the geographic and demographic realities or the Holocaust. Above all, let's not forget what happened in Yugoslavia. It doesn't take long for the bubble to burst.

The main issue being debated nowadays in the corridors of power is the pullout of Israeli troops from 13 per cent of the West Bank. Nobody talks about the Golan Heights, the status of Palestine, the future of millions of Palestinian refugees living outside their homeland and, above all, the danger Israel may pose to the security of the Arab nations. Surely, a piecemeal solution is no answer to a long-standing problem. The hard-liners, including the far-right lunatics in the cabinet, will not budge an inch. And the Binyamin Netanyahu regime, fighting for survival with his coalition partners, is unlikely to offer tangible concessions to the Arabs. So, we were back so square one.

Peace talks, brokered now or later by the United States, will make sense only if religious nationalists and fundamentalists in Israel mend their ways and pay heed to the warnings of scholars like Wardburg. 'Living', writes David Grossman, 'means not just defending the borders of life, but also doing something about what is going on within those borders. If we don't do this, in the end we will be like those suits of armour that no longer have knights inside them.'

Meanwhile, the land of David and Jesus Christ cries out for peace not blood.

India and Palestine: An Older Covenant

Said Hamlet: 'What a piece of work is a man, how noble in reason, how infinite in faculties, in form and moving, how express and admirable in action, how like an angel in apprehension, how like a god. . . .' This is half the truth. If you wish to know the other half, turn to Palestine where the people's urge for freedom and independence is trampled upon by the Israeli government. Today, Israel's legitimacy as a nation state is not in question, but its military occupation and the denial of basic human rights to the Palestinian people.

Israel, having illegally occupied territories and violated numerous UN resolutions, is eminently qualified to be a 'rogue' state. The stark and painful reality is that the Jewish people, having been brutalized by the Nazi regime in Germany, have not learnt their lessons from history—the virtues of religious tolerance and the futility of fanatical beliefs. Instead of realizing that the continuation of Arab-Israel conflict is disastrous to both, rulers in Tel Aviv have unleashed a reign of terror in the territories they occupy since 1967.

Yet so few are moved by the live images of Palestinian mothers mourning the death of their youthful children, by the destruction of homes, and the dispossession and displacement of thousands of people. Though soldiers and warplanes continue to mow down Palestinian youth with the hope of ultimately reducing the other side to impotence, the international community is quietened by the weight of Israel/Jewish propaganda. Major powers act in unison against Iran and Iraq, but Israel's outrageous conduct is not even mildly censured. Arab governments, having vacated the moral ground they once occupied, have virtually abandoned the beleaguered Palestinians. Strange are the ways of the world we inhabit.

Cynical observers may well argue that India, tied to a global economy and poised for a major economic breakthrough, should eschew involvement in the Israel-Palestinian imbroglio. Such a myopic view needs to be contested.

It is true that, in the realm of foreign policy, India must demonstrate a modicum of flexibility and common sense. At the same time a nation staking its claims in the comity of nations, including a berth in the UN Security Council, needs to take a resolute stand against Zionization, the belligerence of ultra orthodox groups in Israel, and the ill treatment of minorities, notably the Palestinians, by their government. The old shibboleths of the Cold War are shorn of meaning and significance, and yet there is still some space, despite the premature demise of the non-aligned movement, for principled positions in international affairs.

For these reasons Yaseer Arafat's recent letter to the Indian Prime Minister, in which he has urged India to use its weight and influence for resolving tensions in West Asia, is timely. Admittedly, the government of India cannot broker a peace deal in West Asia. Yet, it can take the position that the situation requires a different line of conduct, no longer governed by the motives of the contest for power, but by motives appealing to the common welfare and the common interests of the rival parties. Above all, the foreign minister must join hands with his like-minded counterparts in other countries to ask for a change of mood and a change of aim in Israel's policies towards the legitimate rights of the Palestinian people. After all, it is no longer possible for the Jewish people, or some of them, to desire a world containing no Palestinians.

We will do well to recall our long-standing moral and ideological commitment to the Palestinian cause. Is it now the case that our national interests conflict with that covenant? The Arabs have been our natural allies, a point underlined by Yaseer Arafat, and it will be a mistake to abandon them in preference to a regime that wields the big stick to humble its neighbours. Engagement with Israel may well be a political and economic compulsion even though it is playing such an incredibly dangerous game, and yet we will lose face with the international community if we let down our Arabs friends in their hour of peril.

Jawaharlal Nehru, who had prophesied that Arab nationalism would not be crushed, maintained long ago 'that Palestine is essentially an Arab country, and must remain so, and the Arabs must not be crushed and suppressed in their own homelands'. Gandhi, talked about the plight of the Jews in Nazi Germany but argued that a solution to their problems did not lie in founding a homeland in Palestine: that land, in his view, belonged to the Arabs. 'You see I have come out of my shell and begun to speak to Europe', the Mahatma wrote to C.F. Andrews in October 1938.

Let's not forget that leaders of the Indian national movement were not just concerned with the country's independence but with freedom struggles all over the world. During the inter-War years, in particular, home and international affairs were closely intertwined. The Spanish Civil War—a battle between fascism and democracy in Europe—dominated the attention of the Congress party. The gates of Madrid had become the symbols of human liberty; Nehru organized funds to send food grains from India and an ambulance unit.

Nehru's initial interest in international affairs, kindled as early as 1927, a good twenty years prior to Independence, developed in the 1950s around two vital issues—decolonization and disarmament. To him, both these issues had moral and pragmatic components to them. Thus, he campaigned for the abolition of nuclear weaponry—'these frightful engines of destruction'—because the emergent arms race between the superpowers was to have disastrous consequences not only for the newly decolonized countries in general, but for India in particular. In short, his crusade for decolonization and disarmament and his articulation of an explicit vision for India's foreign policy enhanced the country's stature world-wide.

The world is no longer cast in Nehru's image. Yet the Congress, claiming a part of his heritage, needs to learn a few lessons from his record on international affairs. At the same time, we need to know if the party has, in the light of the post-Cold War developments, prepared a blueprint for guiding the foreign policy of the nation.

If the studious silence on the Palestinian crisis is any indication, the Congress leadership appears to have relegated major foreign affairs into the background. This is bad news for a national political party.

27 December 2000

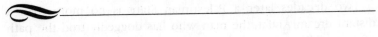

To Arafat, in Anguish

On 23 May 1982, Yasser Arafat visited the Jamia Millia Islamia campus in New Delhi. This was at the height of Israel's invasion of Lebanon. And this is how Anwar Jamal Kidwai, the then Vice-Chancellor, addressed him:

We address you without the ceremonial prefixes of a visiting head of State. We call out to you in the manner in which the early Muslims call out to their prophet and first Caliphs of Islam in the drab little mosque of Medina fourteen hundred years ago. This is because, Ya Abu Amar, in your embattled existence the revolutionary traditions of early Islam live again. In the footsteps of Mohammad, you are in Hijrat from your homeland; you are the Head of a State that is still in the hearts of men and not yet a territory. . . . You are in the vanguard of the struggle that began under Gandhi and Nehru to roll up the vast spread of colonial domination from our part of the world. You are the hope and pride of freedom loving peoples after Ho Chi Minh, and Palestine is the second battlefield of the Third World after Vietnam. Therefore, Ya Abu Ammar, you are more precious to us than all the petrodollars in the world. The Jamia Millia Islamia feels deep affinity with you because we were also born in struggle during the great national movement launched by Gandhi in this country against British rule. . . . The memory of that stirring period in our history still lingers in our mind feel close to liberation struggles in all lands.

Two decades later, a Palestinian State is no more than a distant dream. Arafat, the man who has doggedly trod the path of peace, lives in exile in his own homeland. While he is tormented and isolated from his own people, Israeli tanks roll on even in Bethlehem, the sacred site of the birth of Jesus Christ, killing innocent civilians. The erstwhile victims of the Holocaust are, today, the worst perpetrators of violence and aggression. Travel to Israel to discover the naked face of state-sponsored terrorism.

Indeed, there is no justice in this world for those who demand the right to live in peace in their homeland. There is no concern for the millions of Palestinians who have been living in makeshift camps dotted on West Asia's rugged landscape. The Palestinians mourn their dead, the victims of Israel's military might, and yet the European community sits tight as Israel's military occupation assumes monstrous proportions. The United Nations, acting at the behest of the United States, has lost the moral authority to enforce its own resolutions. Finally, the US endeavors to broker a peace have failed largely because of its axis with the Zionist establishment in Israel. Presumably, the Anglo-Saxon world will wake up only if some tired and angry freedom fighters resort to acts of terrorism.

Ya Abu Ammar, you sent your envoy to New Delhi to elicit the support of our government. Many of us appreciate your gesture, and hope that our bonding with the brave people of Palestine will be strengthened. Hopefully, many of us who have consciously refrained from stepping on the Israeli soil will some day see you in Jerusalem presiding over the destiny of an independent state of Palestine. At the same time you must know that, contrary to our pretensions, my country does not carry much weight in world affairs. All said and done, we, a nation of one billion plus, are weak pretending to be strong. Our weakness is, furthermore, reflected in our subservient attitude towards the United States. In a unipolar world, nothing moves in New Delhi without a nod from Uncle Sam. This has slowly but gradually eroded our standing in the comity of nations.

Ya Abu Ammar, the political landscape in India has changed since your last visit to New Delhi. I can assure you that your customary hug, symbolic of your warm and endearing personality, will now be reciprocated with a cold reception. There was a time when we were barred from visiting South Africa and Israel. Today, those restrictions are gone (South Africa has, of course, dismantled the ugly structures of apartheid and moved towards peace and reconciliation) despite the fact that Israeli government is still wedded to Zionism and to the physical extermination of the Palestinians. We extended diplomatic recognition to Israel, a move that ran contrary to the avowed goals of India's foreign policy, and forged trade, economic and military ties without paying scant attention to its implications on our relations with the Arab countries. It is no exaggeration to say that India is, currently, a part of the Israel and US axis. What have brought these three countries together are not the (exaggerated?) menace of terrorism, but a shared perception of an imaginary green menace.

On your previous visits you would have noticed the liberal and secular ethos in this country and the tremendous enthusiasm for the Palestinian cause. Sadly, the India of today is not the same any more. The votaries of *Hindutva*, a pernicious ideology based on hate and aggression towards the minorities, are steadily undermining the idea of India, exemplified in the leadership of Gandhi and Jawaharlal Nehru, and embodied in the Constitution of the country. The recent pogrom in the western state of Gujarat, organized and conducted by its Chief Minister and his Home Minister, is a reminder of the deep malaise that afflicts some segments of our society. How can we expect such people to respond to your clarion call? No, *Ya Abu Ammar*, they will not. Instead, they will celebrate, as their intellectual mentor Guru Golwalkar did years ago, both the Nazi and Zionist methods.

Jawaharlal Nehru, Mahatma Gandhi and M.N. Roy, who supported the Palestinian cause, were noble men with noble ideals. Today, it is rare to hear these voices except in liberal and left wing circles. None the less, regardless of the ambivalent stand of the Indian government and the brazenly pro-Israel policies of the US, you and your brave men will doubtlessly continue your struggle against military occupation. You have led a purely secular crusade embracing all sections of the Palestinian society, Jews, Christians and Muslims alike, and set an example for all the freedom-loving nations of the world. We pray for your ultimate success.

The Hindu, *9 March 2002*

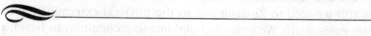

A Bizarre Twist to the
Clash of Civilizations_____

An African proverb says that the proper way to conduct foreign affairs is 'to speak softly and carry a big stick'. The United States is one country that is not only unaccustomed to speaking softly but takes pride in carrying the 'big stick' with impunity. Turn to its record and you will know what we mean. Dropping two lethal atomic bombs on Hiroshima and Nagasaki, killing 1,05,000 persons. The massacre of 1,00,000 North and South Vietnamese civilians as part of the titanic struggle against communism; the support extended to innumerable feudal and military dictatorships in West Asia and elsewhere; the embargo imposed on Cuba, the coup against the popularly-elected Marxist government of Allende in Chile; the invasion of the Caribbean nation of Grenada on 21 October 1983; the seizure of Panama in December 1989, and the conspiracy against the leftist Sandinista regime in Nicaragua.

And, finally, the continuing attacks on Iraq by a President [Bill Clinton] whose own private and public conduct is not above reproach. The UN sanctions after the Gulf war, a decision virtually thrust on the international body by the US that has not even paid its dues for years, has already taken a heavy toll. Some 5,67,000 Iraqis have died due to disease, malnutrition and poor medical care. This is what is called a bizarre 'clash of civilizations'.

I hold no brief for President Saddam Hussain, the archetype of an authoritarian leader. Nobody defends his unwarranted invasion of Kuwait, his persecution of the Kurds, and his ruthless suppression of political dissent. But, then, how is the flawed iron man of Baghdad different from those Arab allies of the US who head conservative and undemocratic regimes? How does Baghdad pose a greater military danger than Tel Aviv does? Is it not true that Israel, the chief US ally in the region, has not ratified the nuclear non-proliferation treaty and the 1972 biological and toxic weapons treaty? Is it not true that Israel has over 200 nuclear warheads? So, where are the Richard

Butlers of the world to monitor the arms build up in that country? They use the big stick to beat the Iraqis or the Palestinians—the other in the Western Hemisphere—but turn a blind eye to Israel's flagrant defiance of UN resolutions.

Emboldened by the collapse of socialism, some industrialized nations, notably the US and the UK, have chosen to impose their diktat on the rest of the world. Their leaders, President Clinton and Prime Minister Tony Blair included, speak the language of nineteenth-century colonialists, and their attitude towards smaller nations is often hostile and belligerent. Living in the shadow of colonialism, their favourite preoccupation has been to break-up larger nations, such as the Soviet Union and Yugoslavia, and redraw geographical boundaries to promote their global economic and political interests. In the process, innocent citizens—Palestinians, Bosnian Muslims, Afghans, Chechens and Kosovo Muslims—have become pawns on the chessboard of Western diplomacy. Likewise, countries like Iraq face reprisals because they dare assert their independence.

Unless public opinion is created world-wide to thwart this neo-colonial project, 'Third World' countries may find it increasingly difficult to maintain their economic and political autonomy. Determined individuals and committed groups need to rally around beleaguered nations like Iraq, find ways of dispersing the pall of fear which at present dims the hopes of 'Third World' societies, and ensure that the self-styled champions of democracy do not spread their creed by force of arms.

This is not the time to sit back and wait for our cities to be targeted by American-British Cruise missiles. The assault on Iraq, coming as it does in the wake of many such belligerent acts in the past, must send tremors across the world and alert the weaker nations to the impending danger to their independence. Whether this will lead to any concerted moves to thwart American excesses is unclear, though one is comforted by the role of Russia, China, France and Italy in recent weeks.

What will perhaps be of great interest in the weeks and months to come is the public mood in Cairo, Damascus and Amman and its possible impact on the Arab governments, many having succumbed to US pressures and made peace with the Western powers. Already, public discontent is mounting about the stalled peace talks over the future of Palestine. The relentless US-British attacks on Iraq, which has alienated the people from their government in the Arab world, may prove to be the last straw.

In the long run, the Arab governments will be expected by their people and the liberal-left forces all around the globe to change their lazy habits and act as a catalyst in reviving the secular and democratic underpinnings of Arab nationalism, pioneered by men like Gemal Abdul Naseer. They must learn a lesson or two from the heroic struggles of the Palestinians who have, in the image of the exemplary martyrs of Karbala (in Iraq), resisted Zionism and colonial manoeuvrings. They must draw strength from the resilience of the Iraqi people, inheritors of the great Mesopotamian civilization, in facing the Anglo-American assault for so many years. This is, to say the least, their only hope of survival in a world dominated by the other. If they fail to satisfy popular aspirations, they will erode whatever little credibility they enjoy at this juncture

Iraq's destruction or Saddam Hussain's removal will serve neither the immediate nor the long-term interests of the Arab rulers. Paradoxically enough, their political survival depends on how best the Iraqi President, a symbol of the Arab people's resolve to resist US aggression, is able to handle the present crisis. If the CIA masterminds his assassination or removal, many heads may roll in Arab capitals, many grand palaces may be laid to siege by angry mobs. The Al-Hamas and other like-minded bodies, the main proponents of an anti-colonial and anti-Zionist ideology, are waiting in the wings to seize such an opportunity. Meanwhile, let us wait and see whether the fantasy of a unipolar world ruled by a single superpower remains a reality or an illusion.

2 January 1999

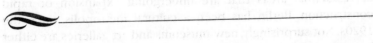

Berlin Reinvents Itself

Once upon a time some of our towns and cities were the envy of travellers from China and the Middle East. Today, those places have been transformed into sprawling urban slums. Sadly, successive governments have turned a blind eye to their continuing decline and decay. Compare our metropolitan cities with Berlin, a city that has either mirrored or determined what has happened in the rest of Europe: heart of the Prussian kingdom, economic and cultural centre of the Weimar Republic and, in the final days of Nazi Germany, the headquarters of Hitler's Third Reich.

It was, of course, the Second World War that defined the shape of today's city. A seventh of all buildings destroyed in Germany were in Berlin, Allied and Soviet bombing razing 92 per cent of all the shops, houses and industry here. At the end of the War, the city was split into French, American, British and Soviet sectors.

Today, there are few signs of that massive destruction. Except for the crumbling tower of the Kaiser-Wilhelm Church, built at the end of the nineteenth-century and destroyed by British bombing in November 1943, most other buildings have been restored to their pre-War condition. This impressive feat is a tribute to the people's determination to rebuild a modern, vibrant city out of the debris of a bloody war.

What is particularly striking is the way the city responded to the collapse of the Berlin Wall in November 1989 and, a year later, to Germany's economic and political unification. A building boom is on both in what was West Berlin and in the eastern districts, where an incredible deficit in construction, redevelopment and planning is still visible today. Spandau, North Karow, South Biesdorf and Rummelsburger Bay are just a few examples of residential areas that are undergoing expansion or rapid construction. Berlin has been a cultural metropolis since the 1920s. Not surprisingly, new museums and art galleries are either being extended or renovated. Public transportation, which already serves 1,863 km of bus lines, 361 km of tramlines and 163 km of underground lines, is being modernized. Our transport authorities in India have much to learn from the scale and efficiency of the operations here.

But all that glitters is not gold. The emotional and material gulf between the 'East' and the 'West' has yet to disappear. In fact, West German-East German divergences are visible in many respects. If you visit Berlin, you can still see and feel where the Wall used to divide the city until 1989. The networks of social communication, including marriage circles, are still structured by this line.

The real problem, one that widens the psychological divide, is economic. The 17 million employees and workers of East Germany face the risk of open unemployment, which, until 1990, was unknown in the GDR and other communist countries. Though rapid progress was achieved in East German restructuring, more than one out of three jobs were lost between 1989 and 1993. More than three million jobs disappeared between 1990 and 1993, unemployment reached unprecedented levels—more than twice as high as in the West. It continues to be much higher today in the East than in the West: 18 per cent compared to 9 per cent in the West.

The pinch is felt by people in the military and Communist Party bureaucracy, and by many skilled and highly educated East Germans who suffer a relative loss of income, influence and status. For them, as indeed for others, both posts and job requirements were redefined. Westerners frequently moved in and took leadership positions. Individual qualifications were re-evaluated in the light of Western standards. Easterners were more likely to be eased out of a shrinking job market.

The shock and trauma of the experience was reflected in a sudden fall in marriage, divorce and birth rates. In effect, the demographic breakdown was connected with the economic and social crisis caused by the abrupt transfer of West Germany's capitalist system to the East.

Public opinion surveys indicate that 55 per cent of East Germans say that they are better off now than before 1990,

20 per cent feel they have suffered a loss, while 25 per cent do not see much of a change. Nowadays, three out of four East Germans regard themselves as second-class citizens. A basic feeling of devaluation, of dependency, of second-rate status, of inequality, has been building up over the years. 'We have begun to feel something of the price which has to be paid for the form of unification we have chosen,' comments historian Jurgen Kocka.

Scholars and generalists talk about the unfinished integration—or rebuilding—of a nation. Some of the issues debated are: are there still two cultures, two societies under one constitutional roof? Has the integration of West and East Germany succeeded or failed? Does present-day Germany differ fundamentally from the Federal Republic of Germany, as it existed until unification in 1990? And what might all this mean for Germany's neighbours?

All said and done, Germany is on the move. The earlier fears about the global repercussions of German unification, voiced by leaders like Margaret Thatcher, have been proven wrong. Recent events point to the momentum towards the evolution of a multipolar economic and political order without a clear-cut leadership position for any individual country or group of countries. Germany poses no threat to anybody.

In the former GDR, the switch to a market economy and parliamentary democracy is opening up new opportunities for the younger generation. Some East Germans may not read *Die Zeit* or *Der Spiegel*. Many others may not bemoan Germany's shocking defeat in the World Cup. But they are nevertheless responding to the winds of change and adjusting to the new political and economic order. A meaningful rapprochement is taking place, while the bitter memories of a divided history are being slowly forgotten. The healing process is well underway. The city of Berlin, a vibrant place for the young and old, takes the lead. It is truly a city of joy.

India has a vital stake in the fortunes of this city, where so many of our leaders and intellectuals developed their strong anti-colonial views. Among them were Zakir Husain, Ram Manohar Lohia and scholars like Mohammad Mujeeb and K.M. Ashraf. These past links need to be strengthened. With investments of a good DM 200 billion between now and 2000, Berlin is the city of the future.

11 July 1998

A Letter from Mauritius

They play soccer and not cricket. The rich send their children to study in Paris and not London or Oxbridge. Most Mauritians read French and not English newspapers. The price tag at the Sir Seewoosagur-Ramgoolam Air Terminal is in French Franc and not Pound Sterling. This is colonization or decolonization for you in Mauritius, a picturesque island that has inherited the dual colonial legacy of France and Great Britain.

Among the countries with an Anglophone-Francophone past are Pondicherry-Madras, Chandernagor, near Calcutta, Yanaon, an eastern coastal settlement surrounded by Andhra Pradesh, and Mahe. Indeed, the long-standing coexistence of a British institutional colonialism with a French cultural one has constituted an important crucible for the postcolonial histories of many other countries. In the case of Mauritius, Britain was the formal colonial power from 1814 to 1968. But the political, economic and cultural imprint of the prior century of French colonization was still quite strong at independence. It still is. Yet, Mauritius has managed what elsewhere has been a much more problematic, if not tendentious, dual colonial inheritance. If anything, this society has developed a dynamic, adaptive approach to sequential colonialism, decolonization and sovereignty.

Mark Twain was moved to exclaim that God modelled heaven on Mauritius. Come to the golden, powder-soft coral beaches and the lagoon waters with the blend of exotic shades of blue, green, turquoise and indigo. Come to this land of beauty and tranquillity and see for yourself how its citizens, Indians, Creoles, Chinese and French included, live in peace and harmony. If you are coming from India, you may be shocked to discover that even the dead, Hindus, Muslims and Christians, are buried or cremated within the same graveyard. The country's multi-religious and multi-cultural social and cultural fabric is intact despite the recent growth of *Hindutva* and Islamist ideologies. Do not be surprised if you notice the relaxed and smiling faces on the streets of Port Louis, the administrative and commercial heart of the country.

After all, the dramatic changes in the country's socio-economic landscape have brought comfort and security to its 1.2 million people. The Free Education for All Scheme, launched in December 1976, was a revolutionary one that has boosted the socio-economic development of the island. With quasi-full employment, an average growth rate of 5.9 per cent per annum and per capita income of US $3,400, Mauritius, once a mono crop agricultural economy has achieved the status of a newly industrialized country and is placed in the category of high Human Development Index countries. Today, the export-processing zone, which aided the rapid economic growth of the 1980s, is dominated by textile industries.

Much of this island's prosperity owes to the massive increase in sugar exports and the phenomenal growth of textile industries which has led the country to import labour from India, China and Sri Lanka. The tourism industry offers direct employment to over 13,000 people (10 per cent of the labour force) and is the country's third largest foreign exchange earner. The Indian tourism industry may learn a lesson or two from their counter-parts in Port Louis. Is it not an astonishing feat to attract over 6,00,000 tourists to enjoy the sun and sand in this tiny island of approximately 1,865 sq. km?

Yet, there are signs of tension and discontent even in this paradise on earth. For one, the linguistic differences have surfaced because the country, having enjoyed the fruits of freedom for 30 years, has failed to reach a consensus on its official language. English is the language of Parliament and the Supreme Court; the TV and print media uses French; Creole, on the other hand, has failed to receive official recognition even though it is widely spoken. People of Indian origin speak Creole, but are now beginning to assert their separate linguistic identity. Recently, the difference between the Tamil and the Hindi-speaking population came to the fore when the government decided to change the order in which these languages were to be printed on the currency.

The protagonists of Hindi and Urdu, patronized by certain organizations in India, are active in their respective domains. Though 405 teachers in 172 out of 280 primary schools teach Urdu, more and more Muslims opt for Arabic. This reminded me of Kerala where Arabic schools and colleges have mushroomed in recent years. However, the most disturbing element, one that upsets the Indian-born Hindi writer Abhimanyu Unnuth, is the growing strain in Hindu-Muslim relations. Hindus and Muslims of Indian origin, long accustomed to sharing each others' cultural and religious symbols, are beginning to invent their own separate and exclusive traditions. Though their links with *Hindutva* and Islamist organizations remain tenuous, they tend to echo the communal debates during the Babri Masjid controversy.

A few years ago much religious passion was generated by Lindsey Collen's second novel *The Rape of Sita*. Some people objected to the title, believing that the Sita in the book title was the Sita of the *Ramayana*. The Prime Minister, speaking the language of our Bal Thackeray, announced his government's decision to ban the novel, an outrage against public and religious morality. The Prime Minister, however, did not carry much authority and his move to ban the novel was eventually stalled by an organized public campaign. How can the Prime Minister of a secular state give himself the power to decide on a subject like religious morality? asked Ram Seegobin, a well-known left-wing intellectual and trade unionist. Perhaps, we should be asking Thackeray the same question following his outburst against the film *Fire*.

The debate triggered by the novel made it clear that most people in Mauritius believed in the importance of literature and were committed to the author's freedom to express their creative talent. Unlike some of our own intellectuals who dither when M.F. Husain [leading painter attacked by the VHP and Bajrang Dal activists for his 'nude' depiction of the goddess, Saraswati, in one of his paintings], Deepa Mehta [prominent filmmaker], Dilip Kumar [repeatedly targeted by the Shiv Sena for having accepted an award from Pakistan], Shabana Azmi [for her role in the film *Fire*, directed by Deepa Mehta] or the liberal-left historians are needlessly condemned and vilified, the intelligentsia in this island were prepared to stand up and be counted in the struggle against obscurantism and fundamentalism of all ilk. This gives hope to people like Ram Seegobin that the Second Dark Ages may not last as long as the first.

19 December 1998